SENTENCE STRUCTURE

COMPOSITION

SPEAKING AND LISTENING

CONTINUED ON BACK END PAPER

English Grammar and Composition

FOURTH COURSE

English Grammar and Composition

FOURTH COURSE

JOHN E. WARRINER

FRANCIS GRIFFITH

SPECIAL CONTRIBUTORS

Allan A. Glatthorn
Harold Fleming
composition

HARCOURT BRACE JOVANOVICH, INC.

New York   Chicago   San Francisco   Atlanta   Dallas

THE SERIES:

English Grammar and Composition: First Course
English Grammar and Composition: Second Course
English Grammar and Composition: Third Course
English Grammar and Composition: Fourth Course
English Grammar and Composition: Fifth Course
English Grammar and Composition: Complete Course

Test booklet and teacher's manual for each title above

CORRELATED BOOKS OF MODELS FOR WRITING:

Composition: Models and Exercises A
Composition: Models and Exercises B
Composition: Models and Exercises C
Composition: Models and Exercises D
Composition: Models and Exercises E
Advanced Composition: A Book of Models for Writing

AUTHORS: John E. Warriner has taught English for 32 years, in junior and senior high schools and in college. He is also a coauthor of the *English Workshop* series. Francis Griffith, who holds a doctor's degree in education from Columbia University, was for many years Chairman of English and Speech in a Brooklyn, New York, high school.

PRINTED IN THE UNITED STATES OF AMERICA
ISBN 0-15-311936-5

Preface

In the *English Grammar and Composition* series, *Fourth Course* comes at that midpoint in the school program that is generally considered the year for catching up loose ends and imposing new and stricter academic disciplines. Teachers of high school classes, while sympathetic toward their students' obvious difficulties in adjusting to adolescence, recognize the importance of firmness in insisting on standards, especially in written work. In a cumulative subject like English, review is invariably necessary at this level. New skills and new understandings about language must be presented as concretely as possible and must be accompanied by plenty of illustrative examples and practice exercises. The wide acceptance of the *English Grammar and Composition* series in its earlier editions indicates that for both review and organized coverage of new material, teachers and students like a clear, direct, businesslike approach accompanied by an abundance of functional exercises to reinforce learning.

From edition to edition, much effort has been made to improve and update the preceding edition without changing the fundamental character of the book. It is a basic text, covering all areas of the English curriculum with the exception of reading and literature: grammar, usage, sentence structure, composition, speaking and listening, mechanics, reference tools, vocabulary development, and the history of the language. By omitting long and discursive discussions *about* writing and by leaving motivation largely to the teacher, the book is able to devote more space to instruction, example, and practice.

Like all books in the series, *Fourth Course* is organized in subject-matter units. All instructional materials on one particular topic are placed together in the same chapter or group of chapters, not distributed piecemeal throughout the book. Teachers like this unit organization because it permits concentration on one skill at a time; students like it because they can easily find what they want when they wish to review a topic on their own. This type of organization also makes the book completely flexible. Just as it imposes no method on the teacher, the book imposes no sequence. With a few necessary exceptions, any chapter may be taught as a separate entity without regard for what immediately precedes or follows. This flexibility assures that the text will fit any course of study, whatever its organizing principle. The clarity and conciseness of the instruction are enhanced by the typography and page layout: the use of a second color for important rules, the open, uncluttered page, and the frequent use of marginal notations and chapter summaries or checklists.

Grammar

The grammar taught and used in the *English Grammar and Composition* series is traditional grammar. This point must be made, now that linguists have presented us with several other ways of describing our language. In the opinion of the authors, the new grammar is not yet clearly enough defined for general use in the schools, and neither are the schools prepared to adopt it completely as a replacement for the traditional. Unless our goal is chaos, we had better bear those ills we have than fly to others that we know not of. Teachers who wish to experiment with the new grammar, however, will find in the *Teacher's Manual* a series of ten grammar lessons based on the structural linguists' description of English. The lessons may be used to introduce important concepts of the new grammar and, if a class is interested and can afford the time, may be followed by further instruction as suggested in the *Manual*.

Usage

The usage chapters reflect a realistic attitude toward current English. The chapter "Levels of Usage," which introduces Part Two, impresses upon the student the fact that language is always changing, and it describes the various usage levels. The succeeding usage chapters take into account, whenever appropriate, recent changes in standard usage. Outmoded distinctions and common misconceptions about what is standard and what is substandard English are either labeled as such or omitted from the text. Chapter 10 is a glossary of usages which the student should know but which, for the most part, are matters of word meaning and language custom rather than matters of grammar.

Sentence Structure

Some parts of the usage chapters also help the student with his sentence structure; for example, the placement of modifiers in Chapter 9. In addition, the chapters on sentence structure in Part Three teach two important sentence-structure skills appropriate to the grade level. Chapter 11, "Writing Complete Sentences," will help those students who are still writing run-on sentences and sentence fragments. Chapter 12, "The Effective Sentence," continues training in the manipulation of sentence parts to produce an effective sentence. Advanced skills—parallelism and shifts in subject and verb, for example—are left to the upper-grade books.

Composition

The major emphasis in the composition program is on serious expository writing, but the chapter on narrative writing and the supplementary chapter, "Creative Writing," give sound advice on storywriting and on the enrichment of style.

The book provides the teacher with enough materials to meet the demands of all three stages in the teaching of composition: instruction, demonstration, and practice. No basic text, however, can afford space for as many models with analyses and as many composition assignments as most teachers would like to have. The teacher who wishes additional models and assignments will find them in abundance in the *Composition: Models and Exercises* series, which has been designed for use with the *English Grammar and Composition* series.

Speaking and Listening

Chapter 18, "Public Speaking," instructs students in the rudiments of public speaking and the techniques of critical listening. Basic concepts of logical thinking are introduced at this point, and faulty argumentation is examined both from the point of view of the student speaker and the student listener. The rest of the chapter is devoted to three speaking situations that make the theoretical material concrete and give the student an opportunity to practice what he has learned by giving a narrative talk, an expository talk, and a persuasive talk. Chapter 19, "Group Discussion," explains the various kinds of group discussion and methods of evaluating such discussions and teaches the rules of parliamentary procedure.

Mechanics

Part Five has the most extensive treatment of capitalization, punctuation, and spelling of any of the six books of the series. In addition, Chapter 25 gives suggestions for manuscript form, including the form in which compositions should be submitted, the rules for writing numbers and for dividing words at the end of a line, and the proper use of abbreviations. Teachers will recognize the importance of this thorough coverage at this level, when students are expected to achieve the mechanics mastery that will free them for study of less pedestrian aspects of written English in the following years.

Aids to Good English

Chapter 27 is a practical guide to the library and the best-known reference tools. Chapter 28 increases the student's familiarity with the arrangement and content of dictionaries. Chapter 29, "Vocabulary," emphasizes the importance of careful word choice in writing and helps the student increase his vocabulary through a knowledge of the meanings of frequently used prefixes and roots. This chapter, which is part of a complete vocabulary program running through the series, includes a word list of three hundred words which constitutes a year's program in vocabulary study.

The History of English

This chapter is a brief history of the English language. The student learns how the language has developed from Old English through Middle English to Modern English and how it has been enriched by borrowings from other languages. The chapter provides a frame of reference for discussions of the nature of language in general and of English in particular—a cultural study not limited to those practical considerations with which the rest of the book is concerned.

A separate booklet of tests, which contains a test for each testable chapter and some end-of-section Mastery Tests, is available at a small cost. *Teaching Tests, Fourth Course*, was written by Mr. Orville Palmer of the Educational Testing Service.

A complete *Teacher's Manual*, including an answer key, is available from the publisher. In addition to a thorough discussion of the teaching of composition and page-by-page suggestions for teaching the text, with suggestions for adapting the teaching to slow classes, the manual contains a suggested course of study, a list of recommended composition assignments for the year, and sample lesson plans.

J. W.

SPECIAL CONTRIBUTORS: Harold Fleming, Assistant Professor of English and Chairman of Freshman Composition at Montgomery County Community College, has taught English for more than 20 years. He is a coauthor of *Composition: Models and Exercises 10* and *11*. His poetry has appeared in *Accent*, *Kenyon Review*, and elsewhere. Allan A. Glatthorn, Principal, Alternate High School, Elkins Park, Pennsylvania, a former John Hay Fellow, has taught English since 1947.

The authors and publishers wish to acknowledge the valuable critical help given by the many teachers who contributed suggestions for this book. Special thanks are due to Mr. Henry Aronson, International School of The Hague, Netherlands; Dr. John R. Arscott, Coordinator, Senior Division, West Essex High School, North Caldwell, New Jersey; Mrs. Margaret R. Bonney, Lexington High School, Lexington, Massachusetts; Miss Jean E. Crabtree, Garden City Senior High School, Garden City, New York; Mr. Raymond E. Kavanagh, Levittown Memorial High School, Levittown, New York; Mrs. Gladys Kronsagen, Glenbard Township High School, Glen Ellyn, Illinois.

Contents

Preface

PART ONE: GRAMMAR

xi

PART EIGHT: DEVELOPMENT OF ENGLISH

SUPPLEMENT

Grammar

CHAPTER 1

The Parts of Speech

Their Identification and Function

Words are classified according to the jobs they perform in sentences. Some name or otherwise identify people and objects; others express action, connect other words, or do still other kinds of work. There are eight main ways that words are used in sentences; the eight kinds of words that perform these jobs are called parts of speech. They are *noun, pronoun, adjective, verb, adverb, preposition, conjunction,* and *interjection.* Even though you may have studied the parts of speech before, you will review them and learn more about them in this chapter.

THE NOUN

1a. A *noun* is a word used to name a person, place, thing, or idea.

A noun names something. Your own name is a noun. The name of your school is a noun. *House* is a noun. The names of things which you cannot see or touch are nouns: for instance, *brotherhood, freedom, length, kindness, justice, equality.* These words do not name tangible things, but they do name qualities or ideas. The name of a quality or an idea is just as truly a noun as the name of anything which has size or shape. A noun names the thing we are talking about.

1a

3

● EXERCISE 1.   There are twenty-four nouns in the following paragraph. List them in order, and place before
each the number of the sentence. If a noun is used more
than once, list it each time it appears.

1. Amber is the petrified resin of ancient forests of evergreens.
2. In ancient times, trading routes wound across Europe northward to the Baltic, where the precious material was mined.
3. The action of the waves sometimes cut deeply into the layers
of blue clay in which the amber had lain for centuries. 4. Floating to the surface, the amber was then carried by the surf to the
shore, where the inhabitants found and collected it. 5. Sometimes, they found preserved in the glassy, yellowish substance
strange insects that had inhabited the forests a million years before.

● EXERCISE 2.   How many nouns can you spot in the following paragraph? List them on your paper. Place before
each noun the number of the sentence in which it appears.
Treat as single nouns all capitalized names of more than
one word.

1. At the beginning of the Age of Exploration, Portuguese
navigators set their course to the south. 2. Their heads were
full of Marco Polo's tales of Cathay, and they bore commissions
from the sovereign to find an eastern waterway to that fabled
place. 3. When they reached the Pillars of Hercules, they did
not sail into the Mediterranean as their ancestors had done.
4. Instead, they sailed on, groping down the huge, dark, and
unknown bulk of Africa. 5. Months passed and the men
dreaded coming to the edge of the earth, where great tides would
suck them over. 6. Therefore, at the end of the day, they would
put ashore on that deserted coast and offer prayers of thanks
for having been preserved from disaster. 7. They also built
towering cairns of rock to show seamen who would follow them
that so far the way was safe. 8. Later, fast ships from all the
busy ports of Europe passed down that coast on their way to
the Cape of Good Hope and wondered at the purpose of these
lonely towers.

The Proper Noun and the Common Noun

Nouns may be divided into two classes: *proper nouns* and *common nouns*. A proper noun names a *particular* person, place, or thing; a common noun names a *class* of things.

PROPER NOUNS	COMMON NOUNS
London, Asia, Lake Michigan	city, continent, lake
Bret Harte, Admiral Nelson	author, admiral
Bronx Zoo, Golden Gate Bridge	zoo, bridge
The Spirit of Seventy-six	painting

◆ NOTE Compound nouns are composed of two or more words put together to form a single noun. Some of them are written solid (*volleyball*), some as two or more words (*high school, Pen and Pencil Club*), and some with hyphens (*brother-in-law*). The compound nouns are in bold-faced type in the following example.

EXAMPLE My **brother-in-law** is a member of the **Rotary Club,** which meets weekly at the **Holiday Inn.**

● EXERCISE 3. For each of the following common nouns, write a proper noun after the corresponding number.

EXAMPLE 1. river
           1. *Mississippi River*

1. novel	6. ship	11. politician
2. mountain	7. school	12. writer
3. car	8. singer	13. building
4. war	9. magazine	14. poem
5. lake	10. state	15. ocean

THE PRONOUN

1b. A *pronoun* is a word used in place of one or more nouns.

EXAMPLE John went to the game with his father and mother. **He** enjoyed **it** more than **they** did. [*He* is used in place of "John," *it* in place of "game," *they* in place of "father and mother."]

1b

PERSONAL PRONOUNS

The pronouns that have appeared in the above example are called *personal* pronouns. In this use, *personal* refers to one of the three possible ways of making statements: The person speaking can talk about himself (first person) or he can talk about the person to whom he is speaking (second person) or he can talk about anyone or anything else (third person). The few pronouns in English that have different forms to show person are called *personal pronouns.*

	Singular	*Plural*
FIRST PERSON	I, my, mine, me	we, our, ours, us
SECOND PERSON	you, your, yours	you, your, yours
THIRD PERSON	he, his, him	they, their, theirs
	she, her, hers	them
	it, its	

Here are some other kinds of pronouns that you will encounter as you study this textbook:

RELATIVE PRONOUNS (used to introduce adjective and noun clauses; see pages 87–88)

who   whom   whose   which   that

INTERROGATIVE PRONOUNS (used in questions)
Who...?   Whose...?   What...?   Whom...?   Which...?

DEMONSTRATIVE PRONOUNS (used to point out a specific person or thing)

this   that   these   those

INDEFINITE PRONOUNS (not referring to a definite person or thing)

all	each	more	one
another	either	most	other
any	everybody	much	several
anybody	everyone	neither	some
anyone	everything	nobody	somebody
anything	few	none	someone
both	many	no one	such

REFLEXIVE PRONOUNS (the *-self, -selves* forms of the personal pronouns)

myself	ourselves
yourself	yourselves
himself, herself, itself	themselves

◆ NOTE   Never write or say *hisself* or *theirselves.*

● EXERCISE 4.   Number your paper 1–6. Referring if necessary to the preceding lists of pronouns, write after each number the pronouns in the correspondingly numbered sentence. You should find twenty-five pronouns.[1]

1. Everybody enjoys going to the amusement park, and some of us really love it. 2. Our group decided to try the roller coaster, although some of the girls raised objections to this.   3. One of the pitchmen called out, "Hurry! Hurry! Step up, all of you, for the most thrilling ride in the park.   4. Many will find it exciting; others will find it the experience of their lives." 5. Some of us were a little scared, but we soon decided to buy our tickets and try it.   6. When we ended the ride, everyone who could still talk agreed this was the ride of his life.

THE ADJECTIVE

1c. An *adjective* is a word used to modify a noun or a pronoun.

Adjectives are words used to make the meaning of a noun or a pronoun more definite. Words used in this way are called *modifiers.*

An adjective may modify a noun or pronoun by telling *what kind* it is:

red hair   **new** ideas   **warm** weather

An adjective may indicate *which one:*

this hat   **those** coats   **that** car

[1] When words in the first list on page 6 immediately precede a noun (*my* friend, *his* brother, etc.), they are considered possessive *pronouns* in this book, rather than *adjectives.*

1c

An adjective may tell *how many:*

seventy-six trombones   two boys   many people

An adjective is not always placed next to the word it modifies. It may be separated from the word it modifies by other words.

The coat was very **expensive.** [expensive coat]

The report sounds **dull.** [dull report]

◆ NOTE   An adjective modifying a pronoun is almost always separated from the pronoun.

She looked **old.**
They seemed **heavy.**

Articles

The most frequently used adjectives are *a*, *an*, and *the*. These little words are usually called *articles*.

A and *an* are indefinite articles; they refer to one of a general group.

EXAMPLES   A woman won the prize.
              An otter slid down the bank.
              We waited **an** hour.

A is used before words beginning with a consonant sound; *an* is used before words beginning with a vowel sound. Notice in the third example above that *an* is used before a noun beginning with the consonant *h*, because the *h* in *hour* is not pronounced. *Hour* is pronounced as if it began with a vowel (like *our*). Remember that the *sound* of the noun, not the spelling, determines which indefinite article will be used.

The is a definite article. It indicates that the noun refers to someone or something in particular.

EXAMPLES   **The** woman won the prize.
              The otter slid down the bank.
              The hour for our departure finally arrived.

● EXERCISE 5. In the following paragraphs the adjectives (except *a, an,* and *the*) are printed in italics. List the adjectives after the appropriate number, and after each one, write the word it modifies.

1. Dad drove us up and down the *busy* street for *twenty* minutes. 2. The day was *hot,* and Dad was *impatient.* 3. From the *back* seat we looked around, trying to spot an *empty* space to park in. 4. We learned the location of *every* hydrant and bus stop.

5. Finally, we saw *two* men climb into a *green* jeep just ahead of us. 6. Our *sudden* yell nearly scared Dad into a *head-on* collision with a *huge* truck.[1] 7. In *anxious* suspense, we waited until, to our *great* relief, the jeep pulled out. 8. Dad summoned his *last* bit of strength to back the *long* car into the *short* space left by the jeep. 9. His task was *difficult* and took *several* minutes. 10. After the *tiresome* hunt in the *stuffy* car, we crawled out into the *hot* sunlight to start our shopping. 11. Then we saw the *dreadful* sign which had been hidden by a *large* station wagon: "Post Office. Five-Minute Parking."

● EXERCISE 6. Copy the following sentences, supplying adjectives in the blank spaces. Try to supply meaningful, interesting adjectives. Read the paragraph through before you start to write.

Horseshoe Lake, one of the —— lakes in our part of the state, is not easily accessible by car. The road is a —— trail, but the —— scenery makes up for this. Once you reach the lake, you obtain a —— view of the —— country. Small —— streams feed the lake, and the water is always —— and ——. Those who stay overnight will be lulled to sleep by the —— waters and the —— sighing of pine trees. The —— riser will witness a —— sunrise as the sun's —— rays gleam across —— mountains. What a —— sight this is to a —— city dweller in search of a —— retreat!

[1] Pronouns used before nouns, like *our* in the sixth sentence, are sometimes called adjectives because they modify a noun. In this book such pronouns are called *possessive pronouns.* Follow your teacher's wishes in referring to such words.

Pronoun or Adjective?

Some words may be used either as adjectives or as pronouns (*this, which, each,* etc.). To tell them apart, you must keep in mind what they do.

Adjectives *modify* nouns, while pronouns *take the place of* nouns. In the first sentence in each pair below, the bold-faced word is used as a pronoun. In the second sentence of each pair, the word is used as an adjective.

PRONOUN   **That** is a stubborn animal.
ADJECTIVE   **That** pony is a stubborn animal.

PRONOUN   **Some** are slender, swift-moving Arabians.
ADJECTIVE   **Some** horses are slender, swift-moving Arabians.

PRONOUN   Do you want **this**?
ADJECTIVE   Do you want **this** colt?

Notice that a noun must follow immediately if the word is used as an adjective.

● EXERCISE 7. List the numbered, italicized words in a column on your paper. After each word, tell whether it is used as a pronoun or an adjective, using the abbreviations *pron.* or *adj.* For each adjective, write the word it modifies.

a. Brown trout, (1) *which* were imported into (2) *this* country in the nineteenth century, are unlike the brook trout (3) *that* we find in the ice-cold streams of Maine.
b. (4) *These* native trout are brilliantly colored.
c. The rainbow trout, (5) *another* native American species, is found in the Far West.
d. (6) *Many* streams are now so impure that the native brook trout cannot live in (7) *them.*
e. Consequently, (8) *many* have been stocked with brown trout, (9) *which* do not seem to mind warm water.
f. (10) *Both* kinds of trout are splendid game fish, and (11) *both* will readily take a dry fly if (12) *it* looks to (13) *them* like a natural insect.
g. (14) *Many* experts tie flies so small that two dozen of (15) *them* may easily be put into a thimble.

h. (16) *Many* tie these tiny flies to the ends of nylon leaders (17) *which* are fifteen feet long.

i. (18) *Some* prefer even longer leaders, (19) *which* are tapered like a bullwhip, from very thick at the butt, or beginning, to very thin at the tippet, or end.

j. (20) *One* fisherman, using (21) *these* flies, may catch dozens of fine trout while (22) *another*, using worms, may simply muddy the water and catch (23) *none*.

k. At (24) *other* times, however, the trout may prefer worms and not be tempted by (25) *any* type of fly.

● **EXERCISE 8.** The following words may be used as either pronouns or adjectives. Write a pair of sentences for each word. In the first sentence of each pair, use the word as a pronoun; in the second, use it as an adjective.

1. more	6. all
2. both	7. neither
3. each	8. many
4. another	9. few
5. these	10. which

Nouns Used as Adjectives

Sometimes nouns are used as adjectives.

coffee urn   **turkey** dinner
book cover   **leather** bag

When you are identifying parts of speech and find a noun used as an adjective, call it an adjective.

THE VERB

1d. A *verb* is a word that expresses action or otherwise helps to make a statement.

All verbs help to make statements. Some do it by expressing action—others by telling something about the subject.

1d

Action Verbs

Words such as *come, tell, go,* and *dance* are action verbs. Some action verbs express an action that cannot be seen; examples are *think, believe, estimate,* and *consider.*

● EXERCISE 9. Make a list of twenty action verbs not including those listed above. Include and underline at least five verbs that express an action that cannot be seen.

There are two general classes of action verbs—*transitive* and *intransitive.* A verb is transitive when the action it expresses is directed toward a person or thing named in the sentence.

EXAMPLES   The boy **waves** the flag. [The action of the verb *waves* is directed toward *flag.* The verb is transitive.]

Natty Bumppo **aimed** the rifle.

In these examples the action passes from the doer—the subject—to the receiver of the action. Words that receive the action of a transitive verb are called *objects.*

A verb is *intransitive* when it expresses action (or helps to make a statement) without reference to an object. The following sentences contain intransitive verbs.

EXAMPLES   The eagle **soars.**

The steamboat **passed.**

The same verb may be transitive in one sentence and intransitive in another. A verb that can take an object is often used intransitively when the emphasis is on the action rather than on the person or thing affected by it.

EXAMPLES   Philo Vance **searched** the room.   [transitive]

Philo Vance **searched** everywhere.   [intransitive]

Mallory **climbs** the mountain.   [transitive]

Mallory **climbs** higher.   [intransitive]

● EXERCISE 10. Some of the action verbs in the following sentences are transitive and some are intransitive. Write the verb of each sentence after the proper number on your paper, and label it as a dictionary would—*v.t.* for transitive, *v.i.* for intransitive.

1. The winter lasted too long.
2. Gradually the snow retreated.
3. The general enjoyed his chats with his old cronies.
4. Sap rose upward in the sugar maples.
5. Sally examined the sulphur-yellow, scimitar-shaped buds of the bitternut hickory.
6. She tasted the blue berries of the hackberry trees.
7. The old berries had a terrible taste.
8. She chewed the twigs of the black birch.
9. The aromatic sap identified the twigs as black birch, not black cherry.
10. On the hilltop stood the grove of chestnut oaks.

Linking Verbs

Some verbs help to make a statement, not by expressing an action, but by serving as a link between two words. These verbs are called *linking verbs.*

The most commonly used linking verbs are forms of the verb *be.* You should become thoroughly familiar with these.

be	shall be	should be
being	will be	would be
am	has been	can be
is	have been	could be
are	had been	should have been
was	shall have been	would have been
were	will have been	could have been

Any verb ending in *be* or *been* is a form of the verb *be.* In addition to *be,* the following verbs are often used as linking verbs.

OTHER COMMON LINKING VERBS

appear	grow	seem	stay
become	look	smell	taste
feel	remain	sound	

Notice in the following sentences how each verb is a link between the words on either side of it. The word that follows the linking verb fills out or completes the meaning of the verb and refers to the subject of the verb.

The hop hornbean and the blue beech are members of the birch family. [hop hornbean and blue beech = members]

The heartwood of the red cedar smells good. [good heartwood]

The leaves of the red maple become scarlet in the fall. [scarlet leaves]

Jack might be a botanist. [Jack = botanist]

◆ NOTE Many of the linking verbs listed above can be used as action (nonlinking) verbs as well.

Jack feels happiest out-of-doors. [linking verb]

Jack feels the rough, deeply creviced bark of the chestnut oak. [action verb]

Black oaks grow tall. [linking verb]

Black oaks grow acorns every two years. [action verb]

Even *be* is not always a linking verb. It may be followed by only an adverb: *She was there.* To be a linking verb, the verb must be followed by a word that refers to (names or describes) the subject.

● EXERCISE 11. For each of the following verbs, write two sentences. In the first sentence, use the verb as a linking verb; in the second sentence, use it as an action verb.

1. appear
2. sound
3. smell
4. grow
5. taste
6. look

The Verb Phrase

A verb frequently has one or more *helping verbs*. The verb and the helping verbs make up a unit that is called the *verb phrase*.

Commonly used helping verbs are *will, shall, have, has, had, can, may, might, do, does, did, must, ought, should, would,* and the forms of the verb *be.*

EXAMPLES A new fuel tank **has been designed.**

Some drivers **have resorted** to strange maneuvers to move fast in heavy traffic.

Ray **will drive** the car.

Did he **clean** the carburetor?

You **should have changed** the oil.

The engine **should have been tuned** last week.

● EXERCISE 12. Study each italicized verb in this paragraph. Tell whether it is an action verb or a linking verb.

1. Situated on the banks of the Nile in Egypt, the ruins at Karnak *are* some of the most impressive sights in the world. 2. The largest ruin *is* the Great Temple of Ammon. 3. Its immense size is astonishing to people who *know* little about the scale of Egyptian architecture. 4. If you *should follow* the avenue of sphinxes which leads to the main entrance, you *would be amazed* at the 142-foot-high gateway. 5. The ceiling of the temple *is* extremely high—more than 76 feet above the floor. 6. The central columns that *support* the stone roof *are* enormous. 7. The surfaces of the columns *are decorated* with low relief carvings, and despite the passage of time, which *has erased* some of the rich coloring, many of the columns still *retain* their bright shades. 8. Even an amateur engineer *can appreciate* the tremendous effort which *must have gone* into the completion of this temple. 9. We now *know* that inclined planes, combined with levers and blocking, *enabled* the ancient Egyptians to raise the large stones. 10. Nevertheless, the temple *seems* an incredible undertaking.

● EXERCISE 13. Write the verbs in the following sentences after the proper numbers on your paper. Be sure to include all the helping verbs, especially when the parts of the verb are separated by other words. The word *not* in a phrase such as *could not go* is not a verb. *Not* is an adverb.

1. Tonight was opening night, and Bob was frantically mumbling his lines as he headed backstage. 2. He clutched a script in his hands, shouted a greeting to some friends, and almost bumped into some scenery from the prop room. 3. The stage crew had finished their jobs yesterday, but Bob noticed that the lighting squad was making a last-minute adjustment to the footlights. 4. Bob knew the saying that a poor dress rehearsal means a good first performance, but nothing as bad as yesterday's fiasco could be reassuring. 5. He had not remembered all his lines, and he had stumbled over a footstool. 6. In addition to that, somebody had put so much brown greasepaint under his eyes that he looked like a raccoon. 7. Well, thought Bob, tonight will be the test. 8. He summoned his courage and walked into the dressing room. 9. "Hi, gang. Is everybody ready for the first round? The crowd is just coming in, and the photographers will be here shortly."

● EXERCISE 14.   After the proper number, list all of the verbs in each of the following sentences. Include all the parts of every verb.

1. Not so very long ago people all over the world marveled when the first man was shot into space and successfully went into orbit around the globe. 2. Do you remember that the original astronaut was a small dog? 3. The first aerial travelers were not men either. 4. If we went back in time to September 10, 1783, we would find excitement running high at Versailles, where the king, the queen, and a large number of spectators were awaiting the flight of a balloon. 5. The balloon, which was painted in oil colors and had a very showy appearance, carried three passengers. 6. A sheep, a duck, and a rooster became the first airborne creatures. 7. These animals had been placed in a cage which was suspended below the balloon, and interest about what would happen to them ran high as the balloon was inflated. 8. The inflation was completed in eleven minutes, and when the balloon was released, it rose to fifteen hundred feet, remained aloft for eight minutes, and then descended about two miles away. 9. Although the rooster suffered an injured wing from a kick he had received from the sheep before the balloon ascended, none of the animals was injured during the flight. 10. All this

happened almost two hundred years ago, but a descendent of one of these animals may be the first living creature that lands on the moon.

THE ADVERB

1e. An *adverb* is a word used to modify a verb, an adjective, or another adverb.

Adverbs qualify the meaning of the words they modify by telling *how*, *when*, *where*, or *to what extent*.

Adverbs Modifying Verbs

Just as there are words (adjectives) that modify nouns and pronouns, there are words that modify verbs. For example, the verb *dance* may be modified by such words as *gracefully*, *awkwardly*, *slowly*, etc. The word *run* may be modified by *quickly*, *fast*, *far*, *rapidly*, etc. A word which modifies a verb is an *adverb*. It qualifies the meaning of the verb.

EXAMPLES   The boy walked **there.**   [*where*]
The boy walked **then.**   [*when*]
The boy walked **slowly.**   [*how*]
The boy walked **far.**   [*to what extent*]

● EXERCISE 15.   Supply two adverb modifiers for each of the following verbs.

1. march	5. finished	8. draw
2. gave	6. talked	9. fell
3. read	7. write	10. learn
4. arrived		

● EXERCISE 16.   There are ten adverbs in the following sentences. List them, and after each, write the verb that it modifies.

1. The Hungarian Crown of Saint Stephen is fascinating because the crown has again and again disappeared and reap-

1e

peared throughout the last nine hundred years. 2. In its turbulent history, it has been secretly hidden in a cushion, carefully disguised as a baby's bowl, and abruptly seized by the Russians before it landed safely in the United States. 3. The crown, which is beautifully decorated with rough-cut stones and enamel inlays, has a tilted cross on the top, but no one knows positively whether this was an accident or part of the original design. 4. What we do know definitely is that, in order to become king of Hungary, one had to gain possession of the crown. 5. This fact readily accounts for the many intrigues connected with the crown.

Adverbs Modifying Adjectives

Sometimes an adverb modifies an adjective.

EXAMPLES   It was a **bitterly** cold day. [The adverb *bitterly*, telling *how cold*, modifies the adjective *cold*.]

The teacher was a **deeply** thoughtful man. [The adverb *deeply* modifies the adjective *thoughtful*.]

◆ NOTE Probably the most frequently used adverb is *very*. It is so overworked that you should avoid it whenever you can find a more exact word to take its place.

● EXERCISE 17. In each of the following sentences, there is an adverb modifying an adjective. List these adverbs on your paper, and after each one, write the adjective which it modifies.

1. A wagon train that was very long started out from Denver.
2. Both oxen and mules were used to pull unusually large wagons.
3. The trail through the mountains was fairly hazardous.
4. A moderately hard rain could turn the trail into a swamp.
5. When the trail was too muddy, the heavier wagons became mired.
6. Wagons that were extremely heavy then had to be unloaded before they could be moved.
7. Stopping for the night along the trail was a very welcome experience.
8. It offered relief to thoroughly tired bones and muscles.

9. Nights in the mountains could be extremely cold.
10. On terribly cold nights, the men would roll themselves in blankets and sleep close to their campfires.

Adverbs Modifying Other Adverbs

You have learned that an adverb may modify a verb or an adjective. An adverb may also modify another adverb.

EXAMPLE The scientist worked **somewhat** cautiously.

You can recognize *cautiously* as an adverb modifying the verb *worked*. It tells *how* the scientist worked. You can also see that *somewhat* modifies the adverb *cautiously*. It tells *how* cautiously.

◆ NOTE Many adverbs end in *–ly*. Do not make the mistake, however, of thinking that all words ending in *–ly* are adverbs. For instance, the following words are adjectives: *costly, lovely, friendly, deadly*. Moreover, some common adverbs do not have the *–ly* ending: *always, never, very, soon*, etc.

● EXERCISE 18. Use each of the following adverbs in a sentence. Draw an arrow from the adverb to the word it modifies.

1. politely
2. too
3. utterly
4. often
5. rapidly
6. more
7. back
8. yesterday
9. soon
10. even

● EXERCISE 19. There are twenty-five adverbs in the following paragraphs. List them after the appropriate number on your paper. After each, write the word that the adverb modifies, and tell whether this word is a verb, an adjective, or another adverb.

1. Although people often say that bread is the staff of life, few know much about bread, except that it can be easily purchased in the grocery store. 2. Nobody knows exactly when the

first seeds of grasses were ground, mixed with water, and baked into bread; but remains of the Swiss Lake Dwellers positively prove that man already was baking bread in prehistoric times. 3. Egyptian art clearly depicts the planting, harvesting, and baking of grain. 4. Somehow the Egyptians discovered that allowing wheat dough to ferment produced an unusually light loaf, and they soon learned to build ovens in which they could cook the bread properly.

5. Flat breads, usually made from barley, oats, or rye, were the fare of the common people in the European world until the seventeenth century. 6. White bread was extremely expensive and was rarely eaten, except by the nobility. 7. Although acorn cakes are still eaten in primitive areas of the world, we do not ordinarily consider crushed acorns as the ideal ingredient for bread.

8. Until improvements in the methods of milling flour were made, it was almost impossible to obtain the fine grade of flour mainly used in the white bread we now eat. 9. The early baker diligently ground his grain by hand, but the resulting flour was fairly coarse and produced an extremely dark and rough loaf. 10. Early stone mills, which were powered by donkeys or water, seldom produced anything but a gritty flour; finely ground wheat became a reality only recently when steel rollers made a fine grinding possible.

● EXERCISE 20. The following words may be used as either adjectives or adverbs. Write a pair of sentences for each word. In the first sentence, use the word as an *adjective;* in the second, as an *adverb.*

EXAMPLE   1. kindly
           1. *John had a kindly manner.* [adjective]
              John spoke kindly. [adverb]

1. daily   4. more
2. high   5. far
3. late

● REVIEW EXERCISE. List on your paper the italicized words in the following paragraph. After each word, tell what part of speech it is. In a third column, write the word modified by each italicized adjective and adverb.

In the nineteenth century large sections of (1) *our* (2) *western* (3) *plains* were (4) *black* with the herds of American buffalo. (5) *They* fed on the (6) *lush* grass of the prairies and roamed (7) *far* and wide over the land. (8) *These* animals were (9) *generally* (10) *placid* and would not attack unless sufficiently provoked. Great numbers of buffalo were killed by the Indians, (11) *who* (12) *highly* (13) *prized* their juicy and savory flesh, which (14) *closely* (15) *resembles* beef. The (16) *mature* buffalo often weighed as much as two thousand pounds and stood six feet high at the shoulder. The animals were swift and had (17) *so* keen a sense of (18) *smell* that hunters (19) *often* (20) *had* (21) *difficulty* in approaching them. The Indians often set fire to the prairie grass to drive (22) *them* in a (23) *particular* (24) *direction*. Frequently the herd was driven over a cliff. The chase of the buffalo was attended with (25) *some* (26) *danger* because (27) *occasionally* the animals (28) *trampled* the hunters under their hooves. Pemmican, a favorite food, was made from the flesh and fat, and the skins were used for blankets and clothing. The great (29) *herds* of the plains have disappeared, but (30) *small* (31) *numbers* of buffalo (32) *still* (33) *exist*.

THE PREPOSITION

1f. A *preposition* is a word that shows the relationship of a noun or a pronoun to some other word in the sentence.

Prepositions are important because they point out different relationships. Notice in the examples below how the prepositions in bold-faced type show three different relationships between *hill* and *strolled* and between *corner* and *car*.

He strolled **over** the hill.	He owns the car **at** the corner.
He strolled **down** the hill.	He owns the car **near** the corner.
He strolled **up** the hill.	He owns the car **around** the corner.

1f

A preposition always introduces a phrase (see page 60). The noun or pronoun that ends a prepositional phrase is the *object* of the preposition which introduces the phrase. In the preceding examples the objects of the prepositions are *hill* and *corner*.

COMMONLY USED PREPOSITIONS

aboard	below	for	past
about	beneath	from	since
above	beside	in	through
across	besides	inside	to
after	between	into	toward
against	beyond	like	under
along	but (meaning	near	underneath
amid	*except*)	of	until
among	by	off	up
around	concerning	on	upon
at	down	onto	with
before	during	outside	within
behind	except	over	without

Compound prepositions consist of more than one word.

according to	in addition to	instead of
because of	in front of	on account of
by means of	in spite of	prior to

◆ NOTE   The same word may be either an adverb or a preposition depending on its use in a sentence.

EXAMPLES   The soldiers marched **past**. [adverb]
The soldiers marched **past** the stand. [preposition]

● EXERCISE 21.   Use the following words as prepositions in sentences. Underline the phrase which each preposition introduces. Be able to tell between which words the preposition shows relationship.

1. during	3. through	5. beyond	7. into	9. aboard
2. beneath	4. with	6. between	8. toward	10. among

● EXERCISE 22. Use the following words as adverbs in sentences.

1. up	5. down	8. around
2. near	6. past	9. by
3. on	7. along	10. over
4. across		

THE CONJUNCTION

1g. **A *conjunction* joins words or groups of words.**

Conjunctions are used to join parts of a sentence that function in the same way or in a closely related way. The parts joined may be words, phrases, or clauses. In the following examples the conjunctions are in bold-faced type, and the words they join are underscored.

EXAMPLES   He had three <u>hamburgers</u> **and** a <u>quart</u> of milk for lunch.

You may <u>buy your lunch here</u> **or** <u>bring it from home.</u>

<u>I saw George,</u> **but** <u>he didn't see me.</u>

There are three kinds of conjunctions: *coordinating, correlative,* and *subordinating.*

Coordinating conjunctions. Conjunctions that join equal parts of a sentence are called coordinating conjunctions. They are *and, but, or, nor, for,* and *yet.*[1]

Correlative conjunctions. Some conjunctions are used in pairs. Examples of these are *either . . . or; neither . . . nor; both . . . and; not only . . . but also.* Study the pairs of conjunctions in the following sentences. Conjunctions of this kind, which are used in pairs, are *correlative conjunctions.*

---

[1] The conjunctions *and, but, or,* and *nor* can join words, phrases, or clauses. However, *for* and *yet* can join only clauses, and for this reason some grammarians consider these two words subordinating conjunctions, not true coordinating conjunctions. Follow your teacher's wishes in classifying these two conjunctions.

1g

Either the editor of the yearbook **or** his assistant will contact the photographer.

Neither the business manager **nor** his staff will attend the conference.

Both the seniors **and** the faculty had their pictures taken for the yearbook.

The yearbook is sold **not only** to students **but also** to teachers, parents, and alumni.

Subordinating conjunctions will be discussed later in connection with subordinate clauses (pages 90–91).

● EXERCISE 23.   List the coordinating and correlative conjunctions in the following paragraphs.

1. Once Nantucket and New Bedford were home ports of great whaling fleets.   2. Nantucket was the first whaling port in New England, but New Bedford soon became larger and more important.   3. Whaling channeled tremendous profits into these ports, but the golden days of whaling ended about the time of the Civil War.   4. The men on a whaling ship could not count on receiving regular wages or a pay check.   5. Both the captain and the crew worked on a profit-sharing basis.   6. Each man received a share in the profits of a trip, and the size of the share depended upon the importance of his job.   7. Naturally the captain's portion was the largest and was usually about one tenth of the total.

8. A whaling trip was no pleasure cruise for either the captain or his crew, for they worked long hours during a run of good luck.   9. Discipline was severe or lenient depending upon the captain.   10. Maintaining order was no easy task on a long voyage because the food and living conditions gave rise to discontent.

11. Inevitably the men had time on their hands, for they didn't encounter a whale every day.   12. To break the dullness and boredom on long voyages, whaling ships often would exchange visits.   13. Not only the captain but also the whole crew looked forward to such visits.   14. All enjoyed the chance for a chat and an exchange of news.

15. The decline of whaling and of the whaling ports began about 1860. 16. Our country no longer needed large quantities of whale oil; for kerosene, a cheaper and better fuel, had replaced it.

THE INTERJECTION

1h. **An** *interjection* **is a word that expresses emotion and has no grammatical relation to other words in the sentence.**

There are a few words which are used to show sudden or strong feeling, such as fright, anger, excitement, joy, etc.

EXAMPLES **Horrors! Help! Wow! Whew! Gosh! Good grief!**

These words are usually followed by an exclamation mark. An interjection that shows only mild emotion is followed by a comma:

Oh, he will win the race.

● EXERCISE 24. Make a list of ten interjections other than those given above. Be sure to include an exclamation point after each interjection.

DETERMINING PARTS OF SPEECH

1i. **What part of speech a word is depends on how the word is used.**

In the following sentences you will see that one word is used as three different parts of speech.

What part of speech is *iron* in each sentence?

Margie plugged in the electric **iron.**
An **iron** deer adorned her lawn.
The girls **iron** their skirts daily.

1
h-i

● EXERCISE 25.   Number your paper 1–20. Study the use of each of the italicized words in the following sentences. On your paper, write the part of speech of the word after the proper number. Be prepared to explain to the class why the word is that part of speech.

1. We went to the greenhouse for *cut* flowers and plants.
2. The florist and his assistants *cut* five hundred roses each day.
3. One of them has a *cut* on his thumb.
4. Many customers *long* for red roses.
5. Roses with *long* stems are very expensive.
6. How *long* do you think roses last?
7. Each day the *plants* are thoroughly watered.
8. The gardener *plants* many new seedlings each day.
9. On a large *stand* in the greenhouse are pots of geraniums.
10. They *stand* in a bright corner of the room.
11. The manager told the salesman, "*Back* your car up."
12. The truck was at the *back* door.
13. The driver went *back* to see the manager.
14. The florist *bills* his customers at the end of the month.
15. Some of the *bills* are paid by check.
16. We were blinded by the *light*.
17. Please *light* the fire.
18. The box looked heavy, but it was really very *light*.
19. This year we are studying *plane* geometry.
20. One of the boys will *plane* these boards for you.

● REVIEW EXERCISE A.   Write three sentences for each of the following words, using the word as a different part of speech in each sentence. At the end of the sentence, write the part of speech.

1. right	4. light
2. out	5. wrong
3. trim	

● REVIEW EXERCISE B.   Now that you have reviewed the eight parts of speech, you should be able to classify each italicized word in the following paragraph. List the words on your paper, and after each, write what part of speech it is.

When summer comes, (1) *it* brings vacation time to millions (2) *of* (3) *very* (4) *weary* (5) *people.* A (6) *restful* few weeks (7) *at* home with chances for (8) *leisurely* (9) *naps* (10) *seem* like paradise after a year of hard work. (11) *Sooner* (12) *or* (13) *later*, however, the urge to sit and relax (14) *vanishes*, and a nice (15) *quiet* (16) *day* at home begins to seem (17) *terribly* (18) *dull*. Soon the members of the family (19) *pack* their luggage, and (20) *they* (21) *depart* for a (22) *large* (23) *resort* or for a little cabin in the woods. Almost everyone forgets (24) *either* a toothbrush (25) *or* a comb, (26) *but* there is one thing that (27) *nobody* should (28) *ever* forget. (29) *That* one (30) *thing* is money.

● REVIEW EXERCISE C. List the thirty-three italicized words and expressions on your paper. After each word or expression, write what part of speech it is.

In early colonial days the (1) *most* (2) *reliable* means of transportation was the (3) *saddle horse*, since the condition of the roads prevented any (4) *very* (5) *extensive* use of wheeled vehicles. (6) *Some* well-to-do families in the towns did keep family carriages. Usually (7) *these* were heavy, lumbering vehicles (8) *that* were drawn by two (9) *or* more horses. The carriages were satisfactory for short trips within the town, (10) *but* they were not very (11) *practical* for long journeys.

Stagecoaches (12) *were introduced* in (13) *America* about 1750. By this (14) *time* there were roads running between such major cities as New York (15) *and* Boston. Although the roads (16) *were* little more than rough, (17) *muddy* tracks, (18) *they* were wide enough for a four-wheeled coach. (19) *Three* or four (20) *pairs* of horses were harnessed to a coach. The coaches were so heavy, however, that the horses (21) *tired* (22) *rapidly* and had to be changed frequently at post houses (23) *along* the route.

In the (24) *western* parts of the colonies, where there were no roads at all, the (25) *Conestoga wagon* was developed for use on long trips. It (26) *had* huge wheels that were (27) *sometimes* six feet in diameter, and (28) *its* body was built like a barge, (29) *with* raised sides and a curved bottom. When a Conestoga wagon (30) *came* (31) *to* a river that was (32) *too* deep to be forded, the wagon was floated (33) *across*.

Summary of Parts of Speech

RULE	PART OF SPEECH	USE	EXAMPLES
1a	noun	names	**Jim** raises **dogs.**
1b	pronoun	takes the place of a noun	**She** and **I** go. Speak to **nobody.**
1c	adjective	modifies a noun or a pronoun	It's a **fine** day. The sun is **warm.**
1d	verb	shows action or helps to make a statement	He **runs** and **leaps.** He **could be** the winner.
1e	adverb	modifies a verb, an adjective, or another adverb	He runs **fast.** He is **very** good. He runs **quite** fast.
1f	preposition	relates a noun or a pronoun to another word	The birds are **in** the tree **in** the yard **behind** the house.
1g	conjunction	joins words	Sue **or** Mary won.
1h	interjection	expresses strong emotion	**Good grief!** **Oh,** no you don't!

CHAPTER 2

The Sentence

Subjects, Predicates, and Complements

In speech, we often leave out parts of our sentences. For example, we often answer a certain kind of question in a few words, not bothering to speak in sentences.

"Why was Jack late?"
"Car trouble."
"Really?"
"Yes."

When we write, however, our words have to convey the whole message. Our reader cannot hear us, and if he does not understand, he cannot ask for a repetition. Therefore, when we put our thoughts on paper, we are expected to express them in complete sentences. Before we discuss all that can go into a complete sentence, we must review the definition of a sentence.

2a. A *sentence* is a group of words containing a subject and verb and expressing a complete thought.

The two parts of this definition are closely related. To express a complete thought, a sentence must refer to someone or something (the subject), and it must tell us something about that person or thing. This job of telling about something is done by the predicate, which always contains a verb.

2a

29

SUBJECT AND PREDICATE

2b. A sentence consists of two parts: the *subject* and the *predicate*. The *subject* of the sentence is that part about which something is being said. The *predicate* is that part which says something about the subject.

subject   *predicate*
The most dangerous saltwater fish | is probably the great barracuda.

    predicate   *subject*
Sleek and sharp-eyed are | the members of this species.

   subject   *predicate*
All West Indian divers | fear the attack of the barracuda.

● EXERCISE 1.   Find the subject and predicate of each of the following sentences. If your teacher directs you to copy the sentences onto your paper, draw *one* line under the complete subject and *two* lines under the complete predicate. Keep in mind that the subject may come after the predicate.

1. The fabric known as batik has an interesting history.
2. The dyeing of batik became an art in Java more than a thousand years ago.
3. The sarong of a Javanese girl frequently represents many hours of labor.
4. A native can read in its intricate design volumes of information about the wearer.
5. One design might tell him of her family, her village, and her tribe.
6. He might learn from another her family connections and the respect due her.
7. The finest batiks have a soft, creamy tone unknown in Western fabrics.
8. The design is painted on the cloth with wax.
9. The waxed part of the fabric resists the dye in the vat.
10. Boiling removes the wax and leaves the design.

The Simple Predicate and the Complete Predicate

The predicate of a sentence is that part which says something about the subject. This part is properly called the *complete predicate*. Within the complete predicate, there is always a word (or words) that is the "heart" of the predicate. It is essential because it is the key word in completing the statement about the subject. This word (or words) is called the *simple predicate*, or *verb*.

2c. The principal word or group of words in the complete predicate is called the *simple predicate*, or the *verb*.

EXAMPLES   Dolphins **communicate** with each other by high-pitched whistles and grunts. [complete predicate: *communicate with each other by high-pitched whistles and grunts;* verb: *communicate*]

A couple of flashlights **blinked** in the distance. [complete predicate: *blinked in the distance;* verb: *blinked*]

The Verb Phrase

Often the simple predicate, or verb, will consist of more than one word. It will be a verb phrase like the following: *are walking, will walk, has walked, might have walked*, etc. When this is so, do not forget to include all parts of a verb phrase when you are asked to pick out the simple predicate of any sentence.

EXAMPLES   Has Jane arrived yet? [simple predicate: *has arrived*]

The new stadium will certainly accommodate many more fans. [simple predicate: *will accommodate*]

In the following sentences, the verb is underscored; the complete predicate is in bold-faced type. Study the sentences carefully so that you will be able to pick out the verb in the sentences in the next exercise.

2
b-c

The coach <u>posted</u> the names of the basketball players on the bulletin board.

He <u>had chosen</u> the members very carefully.

Everybody <u>rushed</u> to read the notice.

I <u>was biting</u> my nails from nervousness.

Some of the boys <u>were disappointed</u> by the news.

Throughout the rest of this book, the simple predicate is referred to as the verb.

● EXERCISE 2.   Number from 1–10 in a column on your paper. Find the verb in each of the following sentences, and write it after the proper number on your paper. If you find a verb phrase, be sure to include all the helping verbs.

1. In 1608 a Dutch maker of spectacles held two ordinary lenses in his fingers.
2. Idly, he stared through one of them at a nearby church steeple.
3. The steeple, of course, appeared smaller.
4. Lippershey sighed with boredom.
5. The long hot summer afternoon was drowsy with sun and quiet.
6. Listlessly, he lifted both lenses to the steeple.
7. Despite himself, he gasped with astonishment.
8. In the nearer lens of the telescope, the steeple had miraculously grown in size.
9. This little scene may never have occurred.
10. Nevertheless, legend gives this account of the discovery of the telescope.

The Simple Subject and the Complete Subject

The subject of a sentence is that part about which something is being said. This part is properly called the *complete subject*. Within the complete subject there is always a word (or group of words) which is the "heart" of the subject, and this principal word within the complete subject is called the *simple subject*.

2d. The *simple subject* is the main word or group of words in the complete subject.

EXAMPLE   The **speed** of light is 186,000 miles a second.   [complete subject: *the speed of light;* simple subject: *speed*]

In naming the simple subject, consider compound nouns as one word.

EXAMPLE   The **Taj Mahal** in India is one of the most beautiful buildings in the world.   [complete subject: *the Taj Mahal in India;* simple subject: *Taj Mahal*]

Throughout the rest of this book unless otherwise indicated, the word *subject* will mean "the simple subject."

Caution: Remember that *noun* and *subject* do not mean the same thing. A *noun* is the name of a person, place, thing, or an idea. A *subject* is the name of a part of a sentence; it is usually a noun or pronoun.

How to Find the Subject of a Sentence

Because the subject may appear at almost any point in the sentence, you will find it easier to locate the subject if you pick out the verb first. For instance:

The leaders of the troops were carefully chosen.

The verb is *were chosen.* Now ask yourself, "Who or what were chosen?" Your answer is *leaders;* hence *leaders* is the subject. In the sentence *Into the house rushed the dog* the verb is *rushed.* Ask yourself, "Who or what rushed?" Your answer is *dog;* hence *dog* is the subject.

● EXERCISE 3.   Number your paper 1–10. Find the subject and verb of each sentence, and write them down, subject first, then verb, after the proper number on your paper. Underline the subject once and the verb twice.

1. A year later in Venice, Galileo heard of the curious story of the Dutchman's experience with the lenses.
2. On fire with eagerness, Galileo hurried home to Padua.

2d

3. He set a convex lens in one end of a lead tube and a con-
   cave lens in the other end.
4. The primitive telescope focused clearly only on objects a
   certain distance away.
5. Those nearer or farther away would blur.
6. The distance between the lenses must be changed for different distances.
7. Galileo quickly taught himself the art of lens-grinding.
8. He soon scanned the skies with an efficient telescope.
9. With Padua beneath him, he turned the telescope on Jupiter.
10. For the first time, the four large moons around the planet
    appeared to human eyes.

● EXERCISE 4.   Follow the directions for Exercise 3.

1. Military men first made extensive use of camouflage during
   World War I.
2. The use of camouflage has become a science in modern war-
   fare.
3. Aerial photography makes the concealment of equipment,
   installations, and troops extremely difficult.
4. Camouflage can fool the eye but not the camera.
5. In a black-and-white photograph, a shiny green roof no
   longer blends in with the green trees and grass.
6. Decoys played an important role in World War II.
7. During World War II, decoy airfields in England drew
   enemy bombers away from the real airfields.
8. The art of military deception, however, has been practiced
   throughout the ages.
9. A classic example of such deception was the use of the
   Trojan Horse by the Greeks during the siege of Troy.
10. George Washington once tricked the Hessians by means of
    "dummy" campfires.

● EXERCISE 5.   Add predicates to the subjects listed below.
After you have done so, underline the simple subject once
and the verb twice.

1. These days	3 My best friend
2. A single pink dogwood	4. Most athletes with ability

5. The members of the team
6. The ocean
7. Life on the ranch
8. The strange beast
9. The snow in the mountains
10. The best possible time

The Subject in an Unusual Position

There are two kinds of sentences which may at first confuse you when you wish to find the verb and its subject. These are (1) sentences that begin with the words *there* or *here*, and (2) sentences that ask a question.

Sentences Beginning with There or Here

When the word *there* or *here* comes at the beginning of a sentence, it may appear to be the subject, but it is not. Use the "*who* or *what*" formula to find the subject. This will prevent you from mistaking *here* and *there* for the subject.

EXAMPLE There are many trees in his yard. [What are? *Trees.*]

Sentences That Ask Questions

Questions usually begin with a verb or a verb helper. Also they frequently begin with words like *what, when, where, how, why,* etc. Either way, the subject usually follows the verb or verb helper.

EXAMPLES Why are **you** leaving?
Will she come again?

In questions that begin with a helping verb, the subject always comes between the helping verb and the main verb. Another way to find the subject is to turn the question into a statement, find the verb, and ask "Who?" or "What?" in front of it.

EXAMPLES Were the boys late?
becomes
The boys were late. [Who were late? *Boys.*]

Has the dog been fed?
becomes
The dog has been fed. [What has been fed? *Dog.*]

● EXERCISE 6. Number 1–10 in a column. Select the verb and the simple subject in each of the following sentences, and write them after the proper number on your paper. Select the verb first. Be sure to write down all parts of a verb phrase.

1. There were two candidates for the office.
2. Here are my reasons in favor of the voting machines.
3. Where do you go for voter registration?
4. Will many people cast their ballots in this election?
5. There will be a gigantic rally this evening.
6. Where will we place the posters?
7. There were too many campaign speeches last year.
8. Are there enough seats in the hall?
9. Where shall we hold the next meeting?
10. Did you vote in the last election?

Sentences in Which the Subject Is Understood

In requests and commands the subject is usually left out of the sentence. The subject of a command or request is *you* (understood but not expressed).

EXAMPLES Close the door.
Take this to the office.

In these sentences the verbs are *close* and *take.* In both sentences the subject is the same. Who must *close* and *take?* The subject is *you,* even though the word does not appear in either of the sentences. A subject of this kind is said to be *understood.*

Compound Subjects and Verbs

2e. Two or more subjects connected by *and* or *or* and having the same verb are called a *compound subject.*

EXAMPLE **Mr. Holmes** and his **friends** went on a fishing trip. [verb: *went;* compound subject: *Mr. Holmes* (and) *friends*]

2f. Two or more verbs joined by a connecting word and having the same subject are called a *compound verb.*

EXAMPLES On our last trip to Europe, we **sailed** on a freighter and **saved** a great deal of money. [compound verb: *sailed* (and) *saved;* subject: *we*]

I **have cut** the grass and **clipped** the hedges. [The subject is *I;* the compound verb is *have cut* (and) *have clipped.* Notice that the helping verb *have* goes with both *cut* and *clipped.*]

2g. The subject is never in a prepositional phrase.

A prepositional phrase is a group of words which begins with a preposition and ends with a noun or pronoun: *around the house, of us.* Finding the subject when it is followed by a phrase may be difficult.

EXAMPLE One of my Dalmatians has won many blue ribbons.

You see at once that the verb is *has won.* When you ask, "Who has won?" you may be tempted to answer *Dalmatians.* However, that is not what the sentence says. The sentence says, *"One of* my Dalmatians has won many blue ribbons." The subject is *One.* Notice that *Dalmatians* is part of the phrase *of my Dalmatians.* In many sentences you can easily isolate the subject and verb simply by crossing out all prepositional phrases.

EXAMPLE The bus ~~with the skiers~~ will leave ~~for the lodge in three minutes.~~ [verb: *will leave;* subject: *bus*]

EXERCISE 7. Write two sentences containing an understood subject, two containing a compound subject, two containing a compound verb, two in which the subject follows the verb, and two in which the subject is followed by a prepositional phrase.

2
e-g

● EXERCISE 8. Number your paper 1–10. Write the subject and the verb of each sentence. If the subject of the sentence is understood, write *you* as the subject, placing parentheses around it.

EXAMPLES
1. Fortunately, there are two gallons of ice cream in the freezer.
1. *gallons   are*
2. My niece and nephew will arrive early in August and stay for three weeks.
2. *niece, nephew   will arrive, will stay*
3. Lend me your notebook.
3. *(you)   lend*

1. Confusion and misery were written on the faces of the lost boys.
2. Are there enough steaks for dinner?
3. There are many new cottages at the lake this year.
4. Save now for a home at Horseshoe Lake.
5. Frank either pitches or plays shortstop.
6. Where are you and Liz going for your vacation?
7. Both of your answers were wrong.
8. Use your brakes!
9. There is too much confusion at my house on Saturdays.
10. Will one of you boys take the dog for a walk?

FRAGMENTS

You have learned that a sentence contains a verb and its subject. However, not all groups of words containing a subject and verb are sentences. Some do not express a complete thought. For example, *When he was sixteen* contains a verb and its subject—the verb is *was;* the subject is *he.* Yet the group of words is not a sentence because it does not express a complete thought. It suggests that more is to be said. It is a fragment, a part of a longer sentence.

He passed his driving test when he was sixteen.

Now you have a sentence. The thought has been completed.

● EXERCISE 9.   Number your paper 1–20. If a word group is a sentence, put an *S* beside the proper number on your paper. If it is not a sentence, write an *F* for fragment. Ask yourself whether the group of words has a verb and a subject and whether it expresses a complete thought.

1. My big brother is leaving for college next week
2. Having won a scholarship
3. His success in school puzzles me
4. Because I have always considered my brother a little incompetent
5. After packing and repacking his luggage dozens of times
6. And after discarding as unsuitable dozens of fine shirts
7. He is still intensely dissatisfied with his wardrobe
8. He complains that his shoes are really not dirty enough
9. He offered me his varsity sweater
10. Which a year ago he would have defended with his life
11. "If you have any use for this thing"
12. "Take it and be welcome to it"
13. In his room, from which issue clouds of smoke
14. He sits and sighs and makes entries in his diary
15. He is also "breaking in" two new pipes
16. In order to keep these pipes lit
17. He employs unbelievable quantities of matches
18. An occasional wisp of pale smoke and a soft and dismal gurgling like the sound of ancient plumbing
19. These are the only results so far of my brother's pipe-smoking
20. This spectacle makes my mother's eyes bright with tears and brings a pained expression to my father's face

THE SENTENCE BASE

Every sentence has a base. The base may be compared to the foundation of a building. It is the part upon which all other parts rest. The sentence base is composed usually of two parts: the subject and the verb.

EXAMPLES   A cloud of smoke appeared.   [base: *cloud appeared*]
Our plans for the trip were discussed.   [base: *plans were discussed*]

In these examples, the sentence base consists of only a subject and verb. In many sentences, however, something else is required in the predicate to complete the meaning of the subject and verb. This third element is a *complement* (a completer).

COMPLEMENTS

2h. **A *complement* is a word or group of words which completes the meaning begun by the subject and verb.**

The following example will show you how the complement does this.

```
          s      v       c
The drought ruined the crops.
```

"The drought ruined" would not be a complete statement by itself, even though it contains a subject and a verb. "The drought ruined *what?*" a reader would ask. The word *crops* completes the meaning of the sentence by telling *what* the drought ruined. Study the following sentences, in which subjects, verbs, and complements are labeled. Name the part of speech of each complement.

```
      s   v       c
Mr. Hill is our new senator.
```

```
s  v    c
He is very tall.
```

```
      s        v      c
The drill sergeant gave an order.
```

```
     s     v   c
The moon is a satellite of the earth.
```

```
    s      v   c
The ground feels dry.
```

```
   s         s     v       c
Both Jim and George appeared quite confident.
```

● EXERCISE 10. Construct sentences from the following
sentence bases. Do not be satisfied with adding only one or
two words. Make interesting sentences.

SUBJECT	VERB	COMPLEMENT
1. boy	left	room
2. remarks	were	clever
3. hunter	shot	deer
4. chemical	was discovered	
5. child	looked	unhappy
6. report	was	short
7. shirts	were	warm
8. bells	rang	
9. teacher	helped	student
10. library	furnishes	information

◆ NOTE Like the subject of a sentence, a complement is never
in a prepositional phrase.

The police caught **one** of the robbers. [The complement is
one, not *robbers*, which is in a prepositional phrase.]

An adverb is never a complement. Complements may be
nouns, pronouns, or adjectives, but not adverbs.

That noise is **mysterious**. [*Mysterious*, an adjective, is a
complement.]

Frank studies hard. [*Hard*, an adverb, is not a complement.]

● EXERCISE 11. Number your paper 1–20 in a column.
For each of the following sentences, list the subject and
verb. If there is a complement, list it after the verb.

1. Every year the Arctic Ocean contains more open water.
2. Melting ice will raise the level of the oceans.
3. The sea could invade coastlands and could submerge islands.
4. Millions of people in the Temperate Zone would fear the
   approach of winter.
5. Outside, the wind would moan ceaselessly throughout the
   short days.
6. Great quantities of moisture would evaporate from the ice-
   free waters of the Arctic Ocean.

2 h

7. This moisture would condense and would fall on the continents as snow.
8. The warmth of the short, cool summers would not melt the huge drifts of winter.
9. Autumn would bring new and more terrible blizzards.
10. A thousand years of storms would create mountains of ice.
11. Their own weight would set the glaciers in motion southward.
12. These masses of ice would create vast lakes.
13. Along the forefront of these glaciers, blizzards would rage continually.
14. Farther southward, heavy rains would change the deserts.
15. The Sahara and Gobi deserts would become vast, rich grasslands.
16. Enormous herds of antelope would darken the grasslands.
17. Sheets of ice might cover most of North America.
18. The refreezing of the Arctic Ocean would probably bring the cycle to a halt.
19. Once again, the seas would grow warmer.
20. At last the great storms would slacken and would then stop altogether.

The Subject Complement

2i. A *subject complement* is a noun, pronoun, or adjective that follows a linking verb. It identifies, describes, or explains the subject.

EXAMPLES Michael is an eagle **scout.**
Susan grew **weary.**

In the first example, *scout* identifies the subject *Michael*. In the second, *weary* describes the subject *Susan*.

There are two kinds of subject complements. If the subject complement is a noun or a pronoun, it is a *predicate nominative*. If the subject complement is an adjective, it is a *predicate adjective*.

Predicate nominatives (nouns and pronouns) explain the subject or give another name for the subject. Predicate adjectives describe the subject. Both predicate nominatives and predicate adjectives are linked to the subject by linking verbs. The common linking verbs are *be, become, feel, smell, taste, look, grow, seem, appear, remain, sound, stay.*[1]

EXAMPLES The acorn becomes an **oak**. [predicate nominative]
The flower appears **red** but is actually **purple**. [predicate adjectives]

● EXERCISE 12. Number your paper 1–10. Select the subject complement from each of the following sentences, and write it after the corresponding number on your paper. (First find the verb and its subject, then the complement.) After each complement, write what kind it is: predicate nominative or predicate adjective.

1. The music in the opera *Aïda* is very melodic.
2. The small plants were zinnias.
3. The trumpet sounded loud.
4. This apple tastes sour to me.
5. The patient grew worse each hour.
6. Steve's story about camp life is a good one.
7. The time of the novel is the period of the Trojan War.
8. Your statements are incorrect.
9. The men were weak from the heat.
10. The room certainly looks attractive.

Distinguishing Between Subject and Complement

When the subject is not in the normal position before the verb, it is sometimes hard to tell which is the subject and which is the complement. When the word order is normal, there is no problem—the subject comes before the verb and the subject complement comes after:

$$\overset{\text{s}}{\text{Sir Edmund Hillary}} \quad \overset{\text{v}}{\text{is}} \quad \overset{\text{c}}{\text{a famous explorer.}}$$

[1] The forms of *be* are *am, is, are, was, were,* and verb phrases ending in *be* or *been: can be, has been,* etc.

2i

When the word order is reversed, as in questions, the subject still comes before the subject complement in most cases:

v   s   c
Was he the leader of the expedition?

Sometimes, however, a writer or speaker may put the subject complement first for emphasis:

c   v   s
How sweet is freedom!

c   s   v
What a fine athlete Charles is!

When this happens you must consider which word is more likely to be the subject of the sentence. In most cases the subject will be the word that specifically identifies the person or thing that the sentence is about. The first example above presents little difficulty because *sweet* is an adjective and cannot be the subject. In the second example, however, both the subject complement (*athlete*) and the subject (*Charlie*) are nouns. In this case you must ask yourself which noun more specifically identifies the subject. *Charlie* has a more specific meaning than *athlete*, and consequently it is a more likely subject for the sentence.

● EXERCISE 13.   Copy the following sentences, and pick out the subject, the verb, and the subject complement. Label the subject of the sentence *S*, the verb *V*, and the subject complement *C*.

1. Were my directions clear?
2. How soft the night air seems.
3. Tenzing Norgay is a man of magnificent courage.
4. "Tiger of the Snows" is a wonderful story.
5. Does he appear sad?
6. What a pretty girl Sally is!
7. What a giant Joe has become!
8. How happy he looks!
9. When does a boy become a man?
10. Sleep is a gentle thing.

Direct Objects and Indirect Objects

There is another kind of complement that does not refer to the subject. Instead, it receives the action of the verb or shows the result of the action.

EXAMPLE   The secretary typed the **report**. [base: *secretary typed report*]

In sentences of this kind, the complement is called the *direct object*.

2j. The *direct object* is a word or group of words that directly receives the action expressed by the verb or shows the result of the action. It answers the question "What?" or "Whom?" after an action verb.

EXAMPLES   The dentist cleaned my teeth.
$$\overset{\text{S}}{}\quad\overset{\text{V}}{}\quad\quad\overset{\text{DO}}{}$$

He filled a small cavity.
$$\overset{\text{S}}{}\quad\overset{\text{V}}{}\quad\quad\overset{\text{DO}}{}$$

In the first sentence, *teeth* is the direct object. It directly receives the action expressed by the verb. It answers the question "What?" after the verb. Cleaned what? Cleaned *teeth*. In the second sentence, *cavity* is the direct object, telling *what* he filled.

Objects are used after action verbs only. Verbs like *think, believe, imagine*, which express mental action, are action verbs just as truly as verbs like *jump, hit*, or *knock*, which express physical action.

● EXERCISE 14.   List the direct objects on your paper. Be able to name the verb whose action the object receives. *Caution:* Like all complements, the object of a verb is never part of a prepositional phrase.

1. The preparations for my trip to Europe exhausted me.
2. I needed a passport.

2j

3. The airlines allowed forty pounds of luggage to a passenger on the economy flight.
4. I packed my suitcase about ten times.
5. I finally carried my raincoat over my arm.
6. My family and I reached the airport an hour early.
7. I took a sleeping pill on the plane.
8. The representative of the tourist bureau met me in Amsterdam.
9. We had rented a car for the journey through Europe.
10. The car, a Volkswagen, pleased all of us immediately.

2k. **An *indirect object* is a noun or pronoun in the predicate that precedes the direct object. It tells "to whom" or "for whom" the action of the verb is done.**

EXAMPLES   The instructor gave some lessons.
            The instructor gave **me** some lessons.

You recognize *lessons* as the direct object in both sentences. It tells what the instructor gave. In the second sentence you have another word which also receives the action of the verb. That word is *me*. *Me*, which comes before the direct object, tells *to whom* the lessons were given. It is an *indirect object.*

What is the indirect object in this sentence?

Experience taught the campers many things.

Things is the direct object. *Campers* is the indirect object. It is the campers to whom things were taught.

If the words *to* and *for* are used, the word following them is part of a prepositional phrase and not an indirect object. Compare the following pairs.

Barbara baked me a cake.   [*Me* is the indirect object.]

Barbara baked a cake for me.   [no indirect object]

The teacher told the class a story.   [*Class* is the indirect object.]

The teacher told a story to the class.   [no indirect object]

Caution: When identifying complements, do not be confused by adverbs in the predicate.

We went **home.** [noun used as adverb telling *where*]
We built a new **home.** [direct object]

● EXERCISE 15. Number your paper 1–10. After the proper number, write the objects in each sentence. Write *i.o.* after an indirect object and *d.o.* after a direct object. Not all sentences contain both kinds of objects.

1. Last fall George told us his plans for the summer.
2. He wanted a job at a camp.
3. We gave him the name of a camp near Tupper Lake.
4. We also gave him all kinds of advice.
5. George wrote the manager a letter.
6. The letter of application cost him a great deal of effort.
7. Usually camps need many counselors for the summer.
8. Most camps do not pay their counselors much money.
9. A job as counselor does provide free room and board for two months.
10. The manager offered George a position.

Compound Complements

Complements may be compound.

EXAMPLES The names of the dogs are **Gypsy and Boots.** [compound predicate nominative]

He is **tall** and **slim.** [compound predicate adjective]

The next group includes the **collies** and the **terriers.** [compound direct object]

The noise had given my **brother** and **me** a scare. [compound indirect object]

● EXERCISE 16. Write two sentences containing a compound subject, two containing a compound verb, two containing a compound predicate nominative, two containing a compound predicate adjective, two containing a compound direct object, and two containing a compound indirect object.

2k

SENTENCES CLASSIFIED BY PURPOSE

21. Sentences may be classified according to their purpose.

There are four kinds of sentences: (1) declarative, (2) imperative, (3) interrogative, and (4) exclamatory.

(1) A sentence which makes a statement is a *declarative* sentence.

Its purpose is to declare something. Most of the sentences you use are declarative.

EXAMPLES   As far as I'm concerned, a house can't be built with too many closets.

In the summer I am constantly fighting crabgrass and Japanese beetles.

(2) A sentence which gives a command or makes a request is an *imperative* sentence.

EXAMPLES   Tell the truth.
Please, keep off the grass.

(3) A sentence which asks a question is an *interrogative* sentence.

An interrogative sentence is followed by a question mark.

EXAMPLES   Can you keep a secret?
Where are you going?

(4) A sentence which expresses strong feeling is an *exclamatory* sentence.

It exclaims. An exclamatory sentence is followed by an exclamation mark.

EXAMPLES   What a beautiful boat this is!
How he loved a fast sloop!

Caution: A declarative, an imperative, or an interrogative sentence may be spoken in such a way that it will be exclamatory. Then it should be followed by an exclamation mark.

EXAMPLES That noise must stop! [Declarative becomes exclamatory.]

Use the brakes! [Imperative becomes exclamatory.]

What do you want! [Interrogative becomes exclamatory.]

● EXERCISE 17.   Classify the sentences in Exercise 8 (page 38) according to whether they are *declarative, imperative, interrogative,* or *exclamatory.*

DIAGRAMING SENTENCES

Many students find that they can understand sentence structure better when they draw a diagram. A diagram is a way of arranging a sentence in picture form. The picture shows clearly how the various parts of the sentence fit together and how they are related.

The first thing to do in making a diagram is to draw a horizontal line on your paper. On this horizontal line you will write the sentence base. In approximately the center of the line you will draw a short vertical line cutting the horizontal one. This vertical line is the dividing point between the complete subject and the complete predicate. The subject and all words relating to it (complete subject) go to the *left* of this vertical line; the verb and all words relating to it (the complete predicate) go to the *right*.

Diagraming the Subject and Verb

The subject of the sentence is written first on the horizontal line. The verb is written on the second half of this line.

| subject | verb |

21

For an understood subject, use the word *you* in parentheses as the subject in your diagram.

EXAMPLE   Ring the bell.

| (you) | Ring |

Diagraming Modifiers

Modifiers of the subject and verb (adjectives and adverbs) are written on slanting lines beneath the subject or the verb.

EXAMPLE   **The angry** customer walked **suddenly away.**

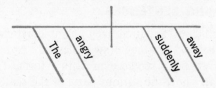

Diagraming Compound Subjects and Compound Verbs

If the subject is compound, diagram it as in the following example. Notice the position of the coordinating conjunction on the dotted line.

EXAMPLE   **Theresa** and **Marlene** are swimming.

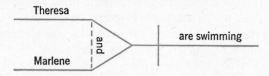

If the verb is compound, diagram it in this way:

EXAMPLE   Bill **runs** and **hides.**

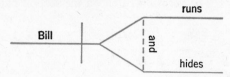

If the sentence has both a compound subject and a compound predicate, diagram it in this way:

EXAMPLE **He and I live and learn.**

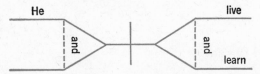

Notice how a compound verb is diagramed when the helping verb is not repeated:

EXAMPLE Sue **was washing** and **ironing.**

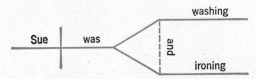

Since *was* is the helping verb for both *washing* and *ironing*, it is placed on the horizontal line, and the conjunction *and* joins the main verbs *washing* and *ironing*.

When the parts of a compound subject or a compound predicate are joined by correlative conjunctions, diagram the sentence in this way:

EXAMPLE **Either** Mary **or** Sue will **not only** wash **but also** dry.

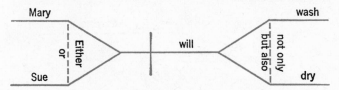

Diagraming Here, There, and Where as Modifiers

When the words *here*, *there*, and *where* are modifiers of the verb, diagram them as in the following illustrations on page 52.

Where are you going?

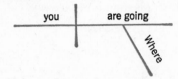

There they are.

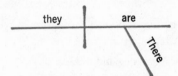

Here come the boys!

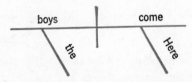

Diagraming <u>There</u> When It Does Not Modify Anything

When *there* begins a sentence but does not modify either the verb or the subject, it is diagramed on a line by itself, as in the following example. When used in this way, *there* is called an expletive.

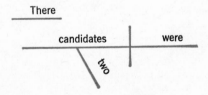

Diagraming a Modifier of a Modifier

A word which modifies another modifier is diagramed like *very* in the following example on page 53.

They played **very** well.

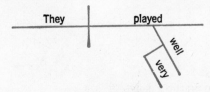

EXERCISE 18. Diagram the following sentences. Diagrams of the first five are provided for you to copy and fill in.

1. Sound travels very rapidly.

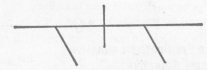

2. A plane circled low.

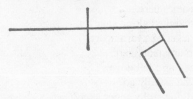

3. The plane rose quickly and flew silently away.

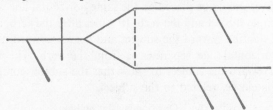

4. There was a loud scream.

5. Never eat too fast.

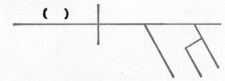

6. The team practices daily.
7. Our new members play quite professionally.
8. The small white dog ran away yesterday.
9. Where is my new hat?
10. An unusually heavy rain fell today.
11. Alan often comes here.
12. The cadets marched along smartly.
13. The heavy jacket was torn apart.
14. There are no amateurs here.
15. I stepped back and fell down.
16. Where does he usually go?
17. Does the old dog still wander away?
18. Forward march!
19. Margaret sings very well and dances beautifully.
20. The old man and his son were born and raised here.

Diagraming the Predicate Nominative and the Predicate Adjective

A subject complement (predicate nominative or predicate adjective) should be placed on the same horizontal line with the simple subject and the verb. It comes after the verb, and a line slanting toward the subject and drawn upward from the horizontal line separates it from the verb. The line slants toward the subject to show that the subject complement is closely related to the subject.

PREDICATE NOMINATIVE　Our dog is a fat **bulldog.**

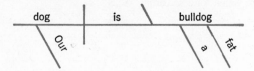

PREDICATE ADJECTIVE   Our dog is **fat.**

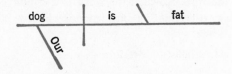

● EXERCISE 19.   Diagram the following sentences.

1. Some old houses are very large.
2. Does the report seem dull?
3. That might have been his latest record.
4. Tennis is my favorite game.
5. Some people are always cheerful.
6. Are you the director?
7. Beginners should be more careful.
8. Charles has become lazy recently.
9. The price was too high.
10. The young boxer is a good fighter.

Diagraming the Direct and Indirect Object

The direct object is diagramed in almost the same way as the predicate nominative. The only difference is that the line separating the object from the verb is vertical (not slanting) as in the following examples:

Frank joined the **team.**

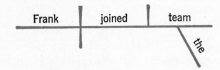

We heard **grunts** and **groans.**

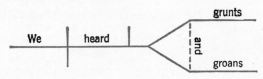

The indirect object is diagramed on a horizontal line beneath the verb of which the word is the indirect object. Notice how the slanting line extends slightly below the horizontal line.

Everybody promised **her** a surprise.

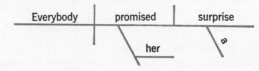

● EXERCISE 20.   Diagram the following sentences.

1. The nights were long and cold.
2. The stars looked exceptionally bright.
3. The cold weather froze the pond.
4. My friends and I usually enjoy winter sports.
5. My parents recently gave me some figure skates.

● REVIEW EXERCISE A.   Before you continue your study of the parts of a sentence, you should review what you have learned so far. Be sure that you understand everything you have covered because you will be building constantly upon what you have just learned. Can you give in your own words a definition of each of the following and make up an example to illustrate it?

1. A sentence
2. A complete subject
3. A complete predicate
4. A subject (simple)
5. A subject complement
6. A verb (simple predicate)
7. A verb phrase
8. A direct object
9. An understood subject
10. An indirect object

● REVIEW EXERCISE B.   Number 1–15 in a column on your paper. Select from each of the following sentences the subject and the verb, and write them after the proper number on your paper. Be especially careful to include all parts of a verb phrase.

1. How would you like a trip to a dog show?
2. There will be a number of fine dogs there.

3. All of the dogs have been washed and brushed by their owners.
4. Are there many of these shows each year?
5. There must have been hundreds of champion dogs at Madison Square Garden.
6. A young handler in a blue apron stopped his work and answered a few of our questions.
7. All training and teaching should be done by word and by the tone of your voice.
8. Never smack a dog with your hand.
9. The tone of your voice will convey your feelings.
10. A few hours of training may well be worthwhile.
11. Where will Larry and I find the collies?
12. Do you see them over there?
13. Look at these short little dogs.
14. What do you call them?
15. Tell me the Chinese legend about the origin of the Pekinese.

● REVIEW EXERCISE C. Copy the numbered underlined words in a column on your paper. After each, write the correct one of the following identifications, using these abbreviations: subject, *s.;* verb, *v.;* predicate adjective, *p.a.;* predicate nominative, *p.n.;* direct object, *d.o.;* indirect object, *i.o.;* object of a preposition, *o.p.*

Did you ever wonder about the (1) pyramids of Egypt? How could an ancient (2) race, even with 100,000 slaves, build such enormous (3) monuments? Almost every visitor (4) makes a trip out into the desert to see the massive tombs. They appear (5) majestic from a distance. The Great Pyramid of Khufu was (6) one of the wonders of the ancient world. (7) It was once encased with blocks of polished (8) limestone. However, weather and man (9) have combined to destroy its original casing. The pyramids (10) look (11) weather-beaten. Still, they are impressive (12) sights.

Invading Arabs about A.D. 650 needed (13) stone for the palaces and mosques in Cairo. Naturally it was (14) easier for them to obtain blocks of stone from the pyramids than to cut new ones from the (15) quarries. They removed the outer limestone blocks, but the two-ton (16) <u>blocks</u> at the bases of the pyramids were too (17) <u>heavy</u>. The task became (18) <u>impossible</u>. There was no (19) <u>way</u> of leveling the pyramids to the ground.

One Arab ruler decided to rob the tomb of Khufu. This ruler was (20) <u>one</u> of many people who believed there were vast treasures hidden in the Great Pyramid. With hundreds of workers at his disposal, he gave the (21) <u>men</u> his (22) <u>instructions</u>. The workers (23) <u>hacked</u> through the solid blocks of granite. The stone was (24) <u>hard</u>; their chisels were (25) <u>poor</u>. By accident, they suddenly (26) <u>broke</u> into a tunnel. Imagine the (27) <u>excitement</u>! All too soon they (28) <u>discovered</u> an enormous (29) <u>plug</u> of granite blocking their way. They cut a passage around the plug and soon reached the inner (30) <u>chamber</u>.

Strangely enough, there was no (31) <u>gold</u>. No vast treasures (32) <u>sparkled</u> under the light of the torches. Probably the tomb had been robbed many centuries earlier by (33) <u>Egyptians</u> familiar with its secret entrance-ways.

CHAPTER 3

The Phrase

Prepositional, Verbal, and Appositive Phrases

You already know that a group of words used as a verb is a verb phrase. Two or more words may serve together as "one" verb. *Have been sleeping, is sleeping,* and *will be sleeping* are examples of verb phrases. Similarly, other groups of words sometimes serve together to perform the function of a single part of speech. Some word groups, or *phrases,* may serve as adjectives or adverbs or nouns.

3a. A *phrase* is a group of related words that is used as a single part of speech and does not contain a verb and its subject.

In the first of each of the following pairs of examples, a single word is bold-faced. In the second part of each pair, a group of words which performs exactly the same function in the sentence appears in bold-faced type. These word groups are *phrases.*

Air is a **colorless** substance. [adjective]
Air is a substance **without color.** [adjective phrase]

The **morning** is the best time to study. [noun]
In the morning is the best time to study. [noun phrase]

He parked his car **there.** [adverb]
He parked his car **in the driveway.** [adverb phrase]

3a

Phrases can be classified in two ways: according to the job they do in sentences (adjective, adverb, noun, verb) or according to the way in which they are formed. We use the latter method in distinguishing prepositional, participial, gerund, and infinitive phrases.

PREPOSITIONAL PHRASES

3b. A *prepositional phrase* is a group of words beginning with a preposition and usually ending with a noun or pronoun.

The prepositional phrases are bold-faced in the following examples:

We waited **at the corner.**
The girl **with red hair** is Polly.
The letter was addressed **to me.**

The preposition in the last example is *to*. Do not confuse this common preposition with the *to* that is the sign of the infinitive form of a verb: *to play, to see, to run.*

3c. The noun or pronoun that ends the prepositional phrase is the *object* of the preposition that begins the phrase.

PHRASE	PREPOSITION	OBJECT
during the long winter	during	winter
in the last inning	in	inning
beyond the forest	beyond	forest
after his next birthday	after	birthday
before him	before	him

A preposition may, of course, have a compound object:

in schools and colleges
by bus, train, or plane

Prepositional phrases usually do the work of adjectives and adverbs in sentences.

Adjective Phrases

Prepositional phrases may be used to modify nouns or pronouns in much the same way as single-word adjectives:

EXAMPLES   a **heroic** act   an act **of heroism**
           the **blue** one   the one **in blue**

3d.

The rooms **of the house** smelled damp and musty.

Few **of the villagers** had ever been there before.

Several adjective phrases often modify the same noun:

The boy **with the trumpet in the next house** keeps us awake.

An adjective phrase may also modify the object of another prepositional phrase:

The book on the table **in the hallway** is mine.   [*In the hallway* modifies *table*, the object of the preposition *on*.]

● EXERCISE 1.   Each of the following sentences contains two adjective phrases. List them in order on your paper. After each phrase, write the noun it modifies.

EXAMPLE   1. The veterans of the war in Gaul remained loyal.
          1. *of the war—veterans*
            in Gaul—war

1. The roads of ancient Rome linked the far corners of the empire.
2. Large blocks of the hardest stone paved the surface of the Appian Way.
3. Close communication between provinces strengthened the position of the Roman rulers.

**3
b-d**

4. Caesar's comments about his engineers reflected his interest in military roads.
5. The Roman engineers were one reason for the success of Caesar's campaigns.

Adverb Phrases

3e. A prepositional phrase that modifies a verb, an adjective, or another adverb is an *adverb phrase*.

EXAMPLES   The fox escaped **into his hole.** [The phrase modifies the verb *escaped*.]

Mr. Williams was always careful **with his money.** [The phrase modifies the adjective *careful*.]

The sun rises earlier **in the morning** now. [The phrase modifies the adverb *earlier*.]

Adverb phrases tell *when, where, why, how,* or *to what extent.*

EXAMPLES   The wind came up **during the night.** [when]
We spent the day **at the beach.** [where]
The children combed the shore **for shells.** [why]
I usually travel **by bus.** [how]
He missed the train **by a few seconds.** [to what extent]

Unlike adjective phrases, which always follow the words they modify, adverb phrases can appear at various places in the sentence. More than one adverb phrase can modify the same word.

EXAMPLE   **In the first few innings** Fireball pitched **with admirable control.** [The adverb phrases *In the first few innings* and *with admirable control* both modify the verb *pitched*. The first tells *when* and the second tells *how*.]

● EXERCISE 2.   Number 1–10, and list the adverb phrases in the following sentences. After each phrase, list the word it modifies and the part of speech of that word. Be prepared to explain your answer.

1. The boys searched the ground for beechnuts.
2. The black ash grows in swampy places.
3. The white oak is famous for its strength.
4. In colonial days country wives made brooms from hickory saplings.
5. Many young boys carry buckeye nuts in their pockets for good luck.
6. Very early in our history, New England was covered by a white pine forest.
7. A squirrel might travel for a hundred miles through pine tops and never descend to earth.
8. For its weight, white pine is very strong.
9. The early settlers were often careless of our forests.
10. In this century conservationists preserve the forests.

Diagraming Prepositional Phrases

Prepositional phrases are diagramed in much the same way as adjectives and adverbs. The preposition that begins the phrase is placed on a slanting line leading down from the word the phrase modifies. The object of the preposition is placed on a horizontal line drawn from the slanting line. As with the indirect object, the slanting line extends slightly below the horizontal line.

EXAMPLE   The steep slopes **of the mountains** are covered **with forests.**

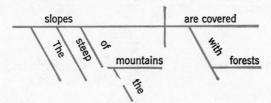

3e

EXAMPLE   They sailed late **in the fall.**   [adverb phrase modifying an adverb]

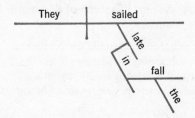

EXAMPLE   They were imprisoned **without food and water.**

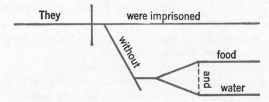

EXAMPLE   **Down the valley** and **over the plain** wanders the river.

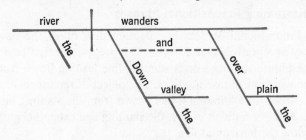

EXAMPLE   The princess lived in a castle **on the mountain.**

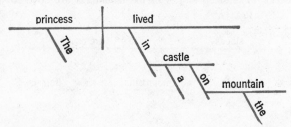

● EXERCISE 3.   Diagram the following sentences.

1. Jan buys tickets at the box office.
2. The tourist wandered across the street and into the store.
3. They gave help to every person in need.
4. In Texas in the early spring the bluebells cover the fields.

● EXERCISE 4.   Complete each sentence by inserting an appropriate prepositional phrase in each blank. Be able to tell whether it is an adjective or an adverb phrase.

EXAMPLE   1. —— Mr. Wagner cut the grass.
     1. *After lunch Mr. Wagner cut the grass.*

1. —— the boys watched the sun rise.
2. I heard the noise ——.
3. My friend suggested a hike ——.
4. Their mascot ran ——.
5. The hikers climbed slowly ——.
6. Thousands —— appeared.
7. The steep path wound ——.
8. —— they reached the top.
9. There —— stood a tall pine.
10. The class lasts ——.

● EXERCISE 5.   Complete the following four sentences, adding adverb phrases according to the directions.

1. The seaman repaired the sail ——. (Tell how.)
2. The sail was needed ——. (Tell why.)
3. The job was finally done ——. (Tell when.)
4. The new sail was raised ——. (Tell where.)

VERBALS AND VERBAL PHRASES [1]

Verbals are forms of a verb that are used not as verbs but as other parts of speech. Verbals act very much like verbs: they may be modified by adverbs and may have complements. Their chief function, however, is to act as other parts of speech: adjective, noun, adverb.

---

[1] For work on verbal phrases as sentence fragments, see page 220. For verbals as dangling modifiers, see page 190.

There are three kinds of verbals: *participles*, *gerunds*, and *infinitives*.

The Participle

3f. A *participle* is a verb form used as an adjective.

Since the participle is part verb and part adjective, it might be called a "verbal adjective."

EXAMPLES The **burning** leaves smelled good.
A **cracked** record can ruin a needle.

In the first example, *burning* is part verb because it carries the action of the verb *burn*. It is also part adjective because it modifies the noun *leaves*—*burning leaves*. In the second example, *cracked*, formed from the verb *crack*, modifies the noun *record*. Because they are formed from verbs and used as adjectives, *burning* and *cracked* are participles.

There are two kinds of participles: *present participles* and *past participles*.

(1) Present participles consist of the plain form of the verb plus −ing.

EXAMPLES The **sleeping** dog groaned.
Glancing at the clouds, the farmer shook his head.

In the first example, *sleeping* (formed by adding −ing to the verb *sleep*) is a present participle modifying the noun *dog*. In the second, the present participle *glancing* (consisting of the plain form of the verb *glance* plus −ing) modifies the noun *farmer*—*glancing farmer*. Verb forms used as adjectives, like *sleeping* and *glancing* in these sentences, are participles.

In addition to its use as a verbal, the present participle can be part of a verb phrase:

EXAMPLES The dog **was sleeping**.
The farmer **is glancing** at the clouds.

A present participle alone cannot be a verb. It can, however, be part of a verb phrase if it is preceded by a helping verb: *was sleeping*. A participle in a verb phrase is part of the verb; it is not considered as a separate adjective.

(2) *Past participles* consist of the plain form of the verb plus *-d* or *-ed*. A few are irregularly formed.[1]

EXAMPLES   **Bruised** by the fall, the **defeated** runner limped to the sidelines. [The past participles *bruised* and *defeated* modify the noun *runner*.]

Discouraged by the mishap, the boy hung his head. [The past participle *discouraged* modifies the noun *boy—discouraged boy*.]

Like a present participle, a past participle can also be part of a verb phrase.

EXAMPLES   I **was** not **surprised.**

I **had been informed** that Mr. Jones would not be there.

● **EXERCISE 6.** Number your paper 1–10. List the participles used as adjectives in the following sentences. After each participle, write the noun or pronoun modified.

1. Thrashing into the air, the first helicopter attained a height of forty feet.
2. Overjoyed at its performance, the designers slapped each other on the back.
3. We cut down the infested elm tree and burned it.
4. In Japan, blossoming cherry trees are one of the chief signs of spring.
5. The red maple, marked by its fiery red twigs and buds, is easy to identify.
6. Passenger pigeons, migrating in vast numbers every spring and fall, were considered a nuisance by many farmers in the last century.
7. The roosting birds would often so overburden the trees that all but the largest branches would break off and fall.

[1] See the discussion of irregular verbs, on pages 157–58.

3f

8. John Audubon, wandering through such a roosting site after the birds had left, likened the damage to the effects of a hurricane.
9. Once numbered in the billions, passenger pigeons have now become extinct.
10. A severe hailstorm, killing many of the birds and destroying their eggs, wiped out one enormous flock of birds at a single stroke.

● EXERCISE 7.   Combine each of the following pairs of sentences into one sentence by using a participle. You may change a present participle to a past participle or a past participle to a present participle if you need to. Underline the participle in each of your sentences. Punctuate the sentences correctly. (See pages 441–56.)

EXAMPLES   1. The radio was blaring. It irritated me.
　　　　　　 1. *The blaring radio irritated me.*
　　　　　　 2. Bob held tight to his books. He sprang over the ditch.
　　　　　　 2. *Holding tight to his books, Bob sprang over the ditch.*   or   *Springing over the ditch, Bob held tight to his books.*

1. Laurie walked through the woods. She gathered a bouquet of mountain laurel.
2. They saw him in the parade. He was riding a pinto pony.
3. Bert got off the train at Grand Central. He took a taxi to Fifty-first Street.
4. The stream overflowed its banks. It covered the road and halted traffic.
5. The heavy, wet snow fell continuously. It meant the beginning of the skiing season.
6. Washington's army wintered at Valley Forge. They were only twenty-two miles from British-held Philadelphia.
7. The hermit thrush often escapes our notice. He sings only in the early morning and at nightfall.
8. American naval vessels visited Japan in the 1800's. Their visit brought an end to the centuries-long isolation of that island nation.

9. Janet prepared the potatoes. She peeled them and cut out the eyes.
10. Jim held out his hand. He welcomed us cordially.

● EXERCISE 8.   Pick out from the following sentences all the participles, both present and past. List them on your paper, and after each one, write the word which the participle modifies. Be careful not to confuse participles with the main verbs of the sentences.

EXAMPLE   1. The discarded rifle, its bore choked with dirt and its stock broken, lay in the trench.

     1. *discarded—rifle*
      choked—bore
      broken—stock

1. The coat, worn and frayed, looked very shabby.
2. The silverware bought in Denmark arrived yesterday in time for the dinner party.
3. Wrapped in a coat of foil, the potatoes were put into the oven.
4. Sensing the danger, the fox avoided the trap.
5. Harried by the noises from the airport, many town residents moved to new locations.
6. Hugging close to the warmth of the fire, the frozen hunters began to thaw out.
7. Food kept in a freezer lasts indefinitely.
8. Examining the necklaces and exclaiming over their prices, the buyers crowded around the loaded counter.
9. The executive officer of the submarine, worried by the sound of droning planes, gave the order to submerge.
10. Yelling at the top of his voice, the annoyed fan protested the umpire's decision.

The Participial Phrase

A participle may be modified by an adverb or by a prepositional phrase used as an adverb, and it may have a complement. These related words combine with the participle to make a participial phrase.

3g. A *participial phrase* consists of a participle
and its related words, such as modifiers and
complements, all of which act together as an
adjective.

The participial phrase in each of the following sentences
is in bold-faced type. An arrow points to the noun or pronoun which the phrase modifies.

♦ NOTE   Some participial phrases contain one or more prepositional phrases.

EXAMPLES   **Approaching the curve,** the truck slowed down.

I could see Frank **sitting three seats away.**

I heard him **practicing his trumpet.**

Acquitted by the jury, the defendant shook hands with
his lawyer.

The ship, **buffeted by the storm,** struggled to safety.

● EXERCISE 9.   Each of the following sentences contains
one or more participial phrases. Copy each participial
phrase, and write after it the noun or pronoun it modifies.

1. Drowsing in the crow's-nest, the lookout suddenly
   awoke, sang out, and, pointing off the starboard
   quarter, drew the captain's attention to a distant
   sail.

1. *Drowsing in the crow's nest—lookout*
   pointing off the starboard quarter—lookout

1. Known for his exploits in the Caribbean, Drake was one of
   Queen Elizabeth's favorite captains.
2. Annoyed by the Spanish successes in the New World, Elizabeth
   summoned Drake to the palace.
3. The Queen wanted a share of the gold going to the Spanish
   treasury from America.
4. In 1577, Queen Elizabeth, seeking new sources of gold, spon-
   sored Drake's exploratory venture to America.

5. Spain's Atlantic treasure fleets, well armed and convoyed, Drake ignored for obvious reasons.
6. The Spaniards had no warships stationed in the Pacific and few transport vessels armed with guns.
7. Ranging the Pacific, Drake seized loot without much struggle, treated his prisoners graciously, and sent them on their way.
8. At the end of three years, Drake's ship sailed into home port loaded with fantastic treasures.
9. On a sunny day in 1581, the voice of Queen Elizabeth, ringing loudly across the crowded deck, announced the knighthood of Sir Francis Drake.

● EXERCISE 10.   Participles can add variety to your writing. Use the following participial phrases in sentences of your own.

1. torn from its mooring
2. taken by surprise
3. chained to a stake
4. viewed from the bridge
5. recorded last week
6. sitting very still
7. clutched in her hand
8. winning the prize
9. adding sugar
10. blocking the path

The Gerund

Gerunds and present participles are formed exactly alike. Both are formed by adding *-ing* to the plain form of the verb. The difference between them is in their use. Present participles are used as adjectives; *gerunds are used as nouns.*

3h. A *gerund* is a verb form ending in *-ing* that is used as a noun.

Study the bold-faced words in the following sentences. They are gerunds. Prove that each word is part verb and part noun. For instance, *walking* in the first sentence is formed from the verb *walk;* yet it names an action. It is the name of something; therefore it is used as a noun. Further proof that *walking* is used as a noun is its use as the subject of a sentence.

3
g-h

EXAMPLES   **Walking** is good exercise.
            Pointing is impolite.
            I enjoy **playing** the flute.
            Watering the grass produced good results.
            We avoided the rush by **mailing** the cards early.

You can see that each of the bold-faced words is used as a noun. In some sentences it is used as the subject; in one it is used as the object of the verb; in the last sentence it is used as the object of a preposition. Note that gerunds always end in *ing*.

● EXERCISE 11.   Number your paper 1–10. In each of the following ten sentences, you will find verbals ending in *–ing*. Some will be gerunds and some will be present participles. Copy them, and label them—*G* for gerund and *P* for participle. If the verbal is a gerund, tell how it is used (subject, object, predicate nominative, object of a preposition). If the verbal is a participle, tell what word it modifies.

EXAMPLES   1. Thinking clearly is essential.
            1. *thinking—G—subject*
            2. A thinking man will avoid excess.
            2. *thinking—P—man*

1. Her whispering caught the attention of the teacher.
2. Shirley enjoys hiking.
3. Besides eating, what else do you like to do?
4. A discriminating viewer occasionally shuts off the TV and reads a good book.
5. Telling the difference between the twins is hard even for their mother.
6. An unforgettable experience was visiting the zoo for the first time.
7. Climbing to the top of the mountain, Carl could see for miles.
8. Jenny occupied herself by reading a novel.
9. My sister Maureen does not like staying by herself in an empty house.
10. Feeling the silence oppressive, he began to whistle.

● EXERCISE 12. From the following verbs, make gerunds, and use each one in a sentence. Tell how each is used. It may be one of the following in the sentence: subject of verb, object of verb, predicate nominative, object of a preposition.

1. leave	6. dream
2. grow	7. go
3. work	8. row
4. plant	9. hike
5. talk	10. draw

The Gerund Phrase

3i. A *gerund phrase* consists of a gerund together with its complements and modifiers, all of which act together as a noun.

EXAMPLES   **Looking at the clock** is a bad habit. [The gerund phrase is used as the subject of the sentence. The gerund *looking* is modified by the prepositional phrase *at the clock*.]

Constant nibbling of after-dinner snacks is certain to cause overweight. [The gerund *nibbling* is modified by the adjective *constant* and by the prepositional phrase *of after-dinner snacks*. The whole phrase is used as the subject of the sentence.]

She fears **their malicious gossiping.** [The gerund phrase is used as the direct object of the verb. The phrase consists of the gerund itself and the adjectives that modify it.]

Our spirits were dampened by **Amy's being unable to come.** [The gerund phrase is used as the object of the preposition *by*.]

● EXERCISE 13. Write five sentences, each containing one or more gerund phrases. Underline each phrase, and write above it how it is used. Use the following abbreviations—*subj.*, subject; *obj.*, object; *p.n.*, predicate nominative; *o.p.*, object of a preposition. Include an example of each use.

3i

The Infinitive

3j. An *infinitive* is a verb form, usually preceded by *to*, that is used as a noun, adjective, or adverb.

An infinitive consists of the plain form of the verb, usually preceded by *to*. It can be used as a noun, an adjective, or an adverb. Study the following examples carefully.

Infinitives used as nouns

To forgive is sometimes difficult.   [The infinitive *to forgive* is the subject.]

Lorna attempted **to flee.**   [The infinitive *to flee* is the direct object of the verb *attempted.*]

Infinitives used as adjectives

He is a candidate **to watch.**   [The infinitive *to watch* modifies the noun *candidate.*]

The doctor **to call** is Enright.   [The infinitive *to call* modifies the noun *doctor.*]

Infinitives used as adverbs

The plane was ready **to go.**   [The infinitive *to go* modifies the adjective *ready.*]

The tiger tensed his muscles **to spring.**   [*To spring* modifies the verb *tensed.*]

◆ NOTE   *To* plus a noun or pronoun (*to the store, to school, to him*) constitutes a prepositional phrase. *To* is only the sign of the infinitive when it is followed by the plain form of a verb (*to be, to discuss, to see*).

● EXERCISE 14.   List on your paper the infinitives in the following sentences. After each infinitive, tell how it is used —as subject, object, predicate nominative, adjective, or adverb. You may use abbreviations.

1. Don't you want to come to the game?
2. One must not be afraid to try.

3. One restful way to swim is to float.
4. That's good to hear.
5. He got up to leave.
6. It is much too early to go.
7. To learn, you must listen.
8. He hopes to win the tournament.
9. To stroll down a country lane is a great pleasure.
10. To know him is to like him.

The Infinitive Phrase

3k. An *infinitive phrase* consists of an infinitive together with its complements and modifiers.[1]

Like infinitives alone, infinitive phrases can be used as adjectives, adverbs, and nouns.

EXAMPLES **To lay down a good bunt** is very difficult. [The infinitive phrase is used as a noun, as the subject of the sentence. The infinitive has an object, *bunt*, and is modified by the adverb, *down*.]

This kind of book is hard **to read rapidly.** [The infinitive *to read* is used as an adverb to modify the adjective *hard*. The infinitive is itself modified by the adverb *rapidly*.]

He wants **to be the captain.** [The infinitive *to be* is the direct object of the verb *wants* and is followed by the predicate nominative *captain*.]

The Infinitive with "to" Omitted

Occasionally, the *to* that is usually the sign of the infinitive will be omitted in a sentence. This happens frequently

---

[1] Unlike the other verbals, an infinitive may have a subject: *I asked him to come to my party.* (*Him* is the subject of the infinitive *to come*.) An infinitive phrase that includes a subject may sometimes be called an *infinitive clause.*

3
j-k

after such verbs as *see, hear, feel, watch, help, know, dare. need, make, let,* and *please*.

EXAMPLES Did you watch him [to] **run the race?**
She doesn't dare [to] **tell the teacher.**
He would not let the dog [to] **go.**

● EXERCISE 15. List on your paper the infinitive phrases in the following sentences. After each phrase, tell how it is used—as subject, object, predicate nominative, adjective. or adverb.

1. Stephen Decatur's orders were to destroy the frigate *Philadelphia*.
2. Commanding the schooner *Enterprise*, he tried to slip into the harbor of Tripoli.
3. To set fire to the *Philadelphia* was his aim.
4. He expected to surprise the Barbary pirates.
5. To board the ship might mean hand-to-hand combat.
6. There was no other sure way to destroy the *Philadelphia*.
7. To set fire to the frigate proved fairly easy.
8. To escape from the harbor, however, was not so easy.
9. Many gunboats attempted to prevent the escape of the *Enterprise*.
10. Decatur and his men were able to escape and reported that their mission was accomplished.

Diagraming Verbals and Verbal Phrases

Participles and participial phrases are diagramed as follows:

EXAMPLE **Walking to school,** Ted saw the first spring robin.

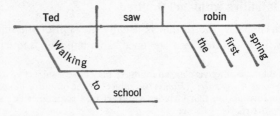

EXAMPLE **Waving his hat,** Dave flagged the train **speeding down the track.**

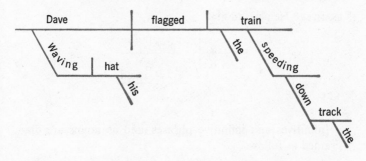

Gerunds and gerund phrases are diagramed somewhat differently.

EXAMPLE **Waiting patiently for hours** is usually a sure means of **observing wild animals.** [The gerund phrase *waiting patiently for hours* is used as the subject of the verb *is;* the gerund phrase *observing wild animals* is used as the object of the preposition *of.* The first gerund phrase is modified by the adverb *patiently* and the prepositional phrase *for hours.* The second gerund phrase has a direct object, *animals.*]

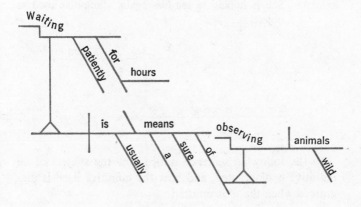

Infinitives and infinitive phrases used as modifiers are diagramed like prepositional phrases.

EXAMPLE   He plays **to win.**

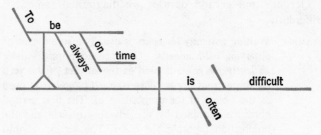

Infinitives and infinitive phrases used as nouns are diagramed as follows.

EXAMPLE   **To be always on time** is often difficult.   [infinitive used as subject]

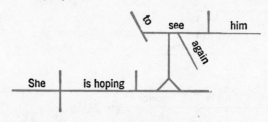

EXAMPLE   She is hoping **to see him again.**   [infinitive used as object]

In the following sentence notice how the subject of an infinitive is diagramed, and how the infinitive itself is diagramed when the *to* is omitted.

EXAMPLE My brother watched me climb the tree.

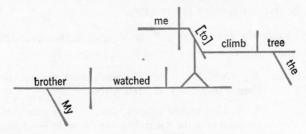

● EXERCISE 16. Diagram the following sentences.

1. Speeding up, Betty passed the truck.
2. I have never liked waiting in line.
3. Carol gets good marks by concentrating on her work.
4. To pay cash is surely the best way to buy.
5. Ed saw me run away.

APPOSITIVES AND APPOSITIVE PHRASES

Nouns and pronouns, as you know, are modified by adjectives and adjective phrases. Occasionally a noun or pronoun will be followed immediately by another noun or pronoun that identifies or explains it.

EXAMPLE My older brother **Thomas** is twenty-one.

In this sentence the noun *Thomas* tells which brother. The noun *Thomas* is said to be in apposition with the noun *brother*. *Thomas* in this sentence is called an *appositive*.

31. An *appositive* is a noun or pronoun that follows another noun or pronoun to identify or explain it.

Like any noun or pronoun, an appositive may have adjective or adjective phrase modifiers. If it does, it is called an *appositive phrase*.

31

3m. An *appositive phrase* is made up of an appositive and its modifiers.

Examine the appositives and the appositive phrases in the examples below. They are in bold-faced type.

EXAMPLES My uncle, **Mr. James Giovanni,** owns a store, **the Empire Shoe Shop on Main Street.**

A good all-around athlete, this boy is a promising candidate for the decathlon, **the Olympic event that tests ten different skills.**

◆ NOTE Occasionally (as in the first appositive in the last example above) an appositive phrase precedes the noun or pronoun explained.

Appositives and appositive phrases are set off by commas, unless the appositive is a single word closely related to the preceding word. The comma is always used when the word to which the appositive refers is a proper noun.

EXAMPLES Dr. A. Blumenthal, our family doctor, is a fine man.

His son Bill is my best friend.

Natalie, his daughter, is another good friend.

In diagraming, place the appositive in parentheses after the word with which it is in apposition.

EXAMPLE Ed Robbins, **our newest classmate,** comes from Goshen, **a town near Middletown.**

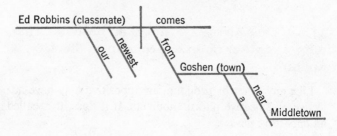

● Exercise 17.   List on your paper the appositive phrases in each of the following sentences. Underline the appositive in each phrase, and be sure you know the word to which each appositive refers.

1. My hobby, amateur botany, is lots of fun.
2. My laboratory, the patch of meadow and woods along the river, contains dozens of interesting species.
3. Mr. Jeffers, an old friend of the President's, will be our new ambassador to India.
4. Hausa, a language of the Sudan, is widely used as a trade language throughout western Africa.
5. The new sponsor, the Acme Razor Company, objected to the parts of the series in which the hero always seemed to need a shave.

● Review exercise A.   Number your paper 1–10. Identify the following words and phrases in italics by writing *p.* for participle, *g.* for gerund, *i.* for infinitive, *prep.* for prepositional phrase, and *ap.* for appositive.

1. She soon learned *to play the clarinet*.
2. *Handing the music to me* took only an instant.
3. *After the concert*, the musicians took a bow.
4. After *finishing his performance*, he took a rest.
5. *Practicing daily*, he improved his tone.
6. *Practicing his music* eliminated minor flaws.
7. He walked to the nearest town, *a village with only twenty-five houses*.
8. Phil had *to make a speech*.
9. The flowers, *purple asters*, were picked in the meadow.
10. A *rolling* stone gathers no moss.

● Review exercise B.   The following sentences contain verbal and appositive phrases. List the phrases on your paper; there are fifteen of them. After each, tell what kind it is: participle, gerund, infinitive, or appositive. Modifiers and complements of a verbal are considered part of the phrase. You may use abbreviations.

EXAMPLE   1. To perform well, any musician devoted to his art must study the playing of experts.

   1. *to perform well—i.*
      devoted to his art—p.
      the playing of experts—g.

1. The United States Marine Band, a group of one hundred men, has participated in our nation's history by playing at official functions for one hundred and sixty-one years.
2. Dressed in their scarlet uniforms, the bandsmen seem to add a special touch to any program.
3. Marching in parades or playing at the White House, the band strives to uphold its tradition of faultless performance.
4. Arriving for tea with the President, guests may find the band ready to entertain them by playing popular tunes.
5. The members of the band, all expert musicians, rehearse daily during the concert season.
6. Listening to the concerts is a good way to relax.
7. In the early days of the Marines, the band spent much time playing in the streets to encourage enlistments.

● REVIEW EXERCISE C.   Copy the verbal phrases from the following sentences in order. After each, tell what kind it is: participial, gerund, or infinitive.

Driving a car is a skill learned only by much experience. Some beginners think they have learned to drive when they can start a car, steer it around the block, and stop it. Anyone above the age of five can start a car by turning a key and by pressing the accelerator. Steering a car through deserted streets is child's play. Handling an automobile, however, requires quick judgment and automatic responses based on experience. Taking the car out, you face a series of emergency situations demanding quick action. You may run into a traffic jam; you will almost certainly have to make a left turn when you are facing traffic. A driver must always anticipate the actions of other drivers. Perhaps most difficult of all is estimating distance and speed when you are passing a car going in the same direction.

CHAPTER 4

The Clause

Independent and Subordinate Clauses

A clause, like a phrase, is a group of related words used together as part of a sentence. Clauses, however, contain a subject and verb, whereas phrases do not.

PHRASE   We went home **after work.** [The prepositional phrase *after work* contains neither a subject nor a verb.]

CLAUSE   We went home **after our work was finished.** [*Work* is the subject of the clause and *was finished* is the verb.]

4a. A *clause* is a group of words that contains a verb and its subject and is used as part of a sentence.

KINDS OF CLAUSES

All clauses have a subject and verb, but not all of them express a complete thought. Those that do are called *independent clauses*. Such clauses could be written as separate sentences. We think of them as clauses when they are joined with one or more additional clauses in a single larger sentence. Clauses that do not make complete sense by themselves are called *subordinate clauses*. Subordinate clauses function as nouns, adjectives, or adverbs just as phrases do. In this chapter you will study both types of clauses.

4 a

83

Independent Clauses

4b. An *independent* (or *main*) *clause* expresses a complete thought and can stand by itself.

Each of the following sentences is the same as an independent clause:

The people grumbled more every day.
The army threatened to revolt.

To show the relationship between these two ideas, we can combine them as independent clauses into a single sentence:

The people grumbled more every day, and the army threatened to revolt.

Independent clauses may also be joined by the conjunctions *but, or, nor, for,* and *yet.*

He forgot about it, or else he never intended to come.
The general was not cowardly but his men were.

Subordinate Clauses

4c. A *subordinate* (or *dependent*) *clause* does not express a complete thought and cannot stand by itself.

Subordinate means "lesser in rank or importance." Subordinate clauses are so called because they need an independent clause to complete their meaning.

SUBORDINATE CLAUSES
who was the hero of a famous novel
that he would find honor and glory
because it is so funny

Notice that each of these subordinate clauses has an incomplete sound when read by itself. Each one leaves you expecting more to be said. Words like *if, when, although, since,* and *because* always make the clause they introduce sound unfinished. These words signal that what follows is only part of a sentence. The subordinate clauses given as examples above fit into sentences as follows:

Don Quixote, **who was the hero of a famous novel,** roamed Spain in search of adventure.

He hoped **that he would find honor and glory.**

Because it is so funny, the novel has been popular reading since the seventeenth century.

● EXERCISE 1.   Number your paper 1–10. After the corresponding number, identify each italicized clause as *independent* or *subordinate*.

1. Joan, *who was an experienced baby-sitter*, was never short of cash.
2. *The King did not express his suspicions about his brother;* instead, he sent him to almost certain death in battle.
3. Mrs. Dillon likes to have plenty of room *when she parks her car.*
4. *As soon as the program is over*, refreshments will be served.
5. *The children behaved perfectly* while we were watching them.
6. The people *that live there* own a riding stable.
7. If the burglars had realized that the door was open, *they would not have broken in through the window.*
8. *Fred had made two bad mistakes*, but that was not many.
9. We guessed *that we were not very welcome.*
10. People *who really value privacy* won't care for this neighborhood.

Complements and Modifiers in Subordinate Clauses

A subordinate clause, like an independent clause or a simple sentence, may contain complements and modifiers.

EXAMPLES   This is the book **which** the critics attacked. [*Which* is the direct object of *attacked*.]

I did not know **who** he was. [*Who* is a predicate nominative: He was *who*.]

**4
b-c**

Because she gave me the letter . . . [*Me* is the indirect object of *gave; letter* is the direct object of *gave.*]

If you are so sure . . . [*Sure* is a predicate adjective.]

While she was dancing with me . . . [*With me* is an adverb phrase modifying *was dancing.*]

● EXERCISE 2. Copy on your paper the italicized subordinate clauses in the following sentences. In each clause, underline the subject once and the verb twice, and identify any complements, using the abbreviations listed below.

d.o.—direct object   *p.n.*—predicate nominative
i.o.—indirect object   *p.a.*—predicate adjective

If the verb has more than one word, underline each word.

EXAMPLE   1. *When she has finally given us her permission,* I will thank her.

                              i.o.   *d.o.*
      1. *When she has finally given us her permission*

1. I'd like to know *who did this.*
2. I know *who the captain was,* but I don't know *which team won the game.*
3. He is the player *whom you were watching.*
4. Is this the suit *that you wore to church?*
5. We saw a man *who was very tall.*
6. *When you see Gary,* please give him my message.
7. He left *before I could give him the message.*
8. *Although he had waited for me,* I missed him.
9. Do you know *when he sent us the order?*
10. *If you can possibly spare a dollar,* give it to him.

● EXERCISE 3. Write ten sentences containing subordinate clauses. Underline the clauses and, using the abbreviations in Exercise 2, name the complements in each.

THE USES OF SUBORDINATE CLAUSES

Subordinate clauses fulfill the same function in sentences as adjectives, adverbs, and nouns. Subordinate clauses are named according to the job they do in sentences.

The Adjective Clause

4d. An *adjective clause* is a subordinate clause used as an adjective to modify a noun or pronoun.

EXAMPLES   The school **that Ken attended last year** is not anxious to have him back.

The old high school, **which had long been abandoned,** was destroyed by fire.

An adjective clause always follows the noun or pronoun it modifies. It is sometimes set off by commas and sometimes not. If the clause is needed to identify the word modified, no commas are used. Thus in the first example, the adjective clause is not set off because it tells *which* school the sentence is about. If the clause merely adds information that is not essential, as in the second example, commas are used. (See pages 447–49.)

Relative Pronouns

Adjective clauses are usually introduced by the pronouns *who, whom, whose, which,* and *that.* These pronouns are called *relative pronouns* because they relate the adjective clause to the word the clause modifies (the antecedent of the relative pronoun). In addition to referring to the word the clause modifies, the relative pronoun has a job to do within the adjective clause.

EXAMPLES   Edison was the man **who invented the phonograph.** [The relative pronoun *who* relates the adjective clause to *man.* It also functions as the subject of the adjective clause.]

Ellen is one of the people **whom I invited.** [*Whom* relates the adjective clause to *people;* it also functions as the direct object of the clause: *I invited whom.*]

The answer for **which you have been searching** is obvious. [*Which* relates the clause to *answer;* it

4d

functions as the object of the preposition *for* within the adjective clause.]

The boys apologized to the man **whose window they had broken.** [*Whose* relates the clause to *man*. Within the adjective clause it functions as a modifier of *window*.]

In some cases the relative pronoun is omitted. The pronoun is understood and still is thought of as having a function in the clause.

EXAMPLE   He is the boy [**that**] **I meant.** [The relative pronoun— *that* or *whom*—is understood. The pronoun relates the adjective clause to *boy* and functions as the direct object of the adjective clause.]

Is this the coat [**that**] **you talked about?** [The relative pronoun *that* or *which* is understood.]

In addition to relative pronouns, adverbs are sometimes used to introduce adjective clauses.

EXAMPLES   There are times **when Mr. Willard loses his temper.**

This is the place **where I found it.**

● EXERCISE 4. Number your paper 1–10. After the proper number, copy the adjective clause from the corresponding sentence, circling the relative pronoun that introduces the clause. Underline the subject once and the verb twice. Then list the antecedent of the relative pronoun after the clause.

EXAMPLE   1. Admiral Nelson was a man whose bearing and action identified him as a leader.

    1. (*whose*) *bearing and action identified him as a leader —man*

1. Nelson, who had begun his naval career in 1770, retired from the sea in 1800.
2. But he was quickly called from retirement when the war with France, which had halted for a time, was resumed.
3. Nelson became the leading figure in the dramatic naval campaign that was waged from 1803 to 1805.

4. Nelson, whom the French considered a formidable enemy, meant to annihilate Bonaparte's ships.
5. Contact with an enemy fleet, which numbered thirty-three French and Spanish warships, was made near Cape Trafalgar.
6. Roar after roar echoed from the *Victory's* guns, which poured destruction into the French flagship at point-blank range.
7. The raking broadsides demolished the French ship, which was soon a floating wreck.
8. The *Victory* crashed into a warship that carried seventy-four guns.
9. Riflemen on the French ship fired down from the rigging at the British marines, who returned the fire with great accuracy.
10. The British won a decisive victory, but Nelson, who had been fatally wounded, died aboard the *Victory*.

Diagraming Adjective Clauses

An adjective clause beginning with a relative pronoun is joined to the noun it modifies by a dotted line. The line runs from the modified word to the relative pronoun.

EXAMPLE   The coat **that I wanted** was too expensive.

EXAMPLE   The box **that contained the treasure** was missing.

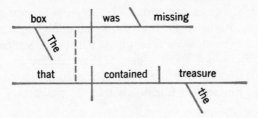

EXAMPLE   He is the man **from whom we bought the used car.**

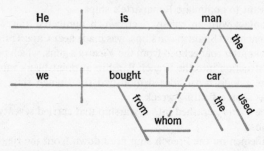

The Adverb Clause

4e. An *adverb clause* is a subordinate clause that modifies a verb, an adjective, or an adverb.

Like adverbs, adverbial clauses qualify the meaning of the words they modify by telling *how, when, where,* or *under what conditions.*

EXAMPLES   He looks **as if he had heard the good news.** [*As if he had heard the good news* tells *how* he looks.]

When we went on vacation, we left our dog in a kennel. [*When we went on vacation* tells *when* we left the dog.]

Wherever you go, you will find other tourists. [*Wherever you go* tells *where* you will find other tourists.]

If we win the game, we will be in first place. [*If we win the game* tells *under what condition* we will be in first place.]

The Subordinating Conjunction

Adverb clauses are introduced by subordinating conjunctions. As its name suggests, a subordinating conjunction makes its clause a subordinate part of the sentence—a part that cannot stand alone. Unlike relative pronouns, which introduce adjective clauses, subordinating conjunctions do not serve a function within the clause they introduce.

COMMON SUBORDINATING CONJUNCTIONS

after	before	unless
although	if	until
as	in order that	when
as if	since	whenever
as long as	so that	where
as soon as	than	wherever
because	though	while

◆ NOTE   Many of the words in this list can be used as other parts of speech. For instance *after, as, before, since,* and *until* can also be used as prepositions.

Diagraming Adverb Clauses

An adverb clause is written on a horizontal line below the independent clause and is joined to it by a dotted line connecting the verb of the adverb clause to that word in the independent clause (usually the verb) which the clause modifies. On the dotted line, write the subordinating conjunction which introduces the subordinate clause.

EXAMPLE   **Before a hurricane strikes,** ample warning is given.

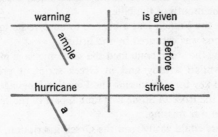

● EXERCISE 5.   Copy the adverb clause from each of the following sentences. Circle the subordinating conjunction in each clause.

1. Harry worked on the car while I painted the garage.
2. The car looked as if it really needed polish.
3. Wherever you looked, you saw rust on the chrome.
4. Harry brought some rags so that he could wash the windows.

4e

5. He put the polish down where he could reach it easily.
6. When you want to do a good job, you should take your time.
7. After he had polished the car, it sparkled in the sun.
8. He vacuumed the upholstery because it was dusty.
9. As soon as the job was finished, Dad gave him some money.
10. Harry acted as though he were reluctant to accept it.

● EXERCISE 6.   Write ten sentences, using in each a different one of the subordinating conjunctions in the list already given on page 91. After each sentence, state whether the clause tells *how*, *when*, *where*, *why*, or *under what conditions*.

● REVIEW EXERCISE A.   List on your paper the subordinate clauses in the following sentences. After each clause, state whether it is an adjective clause or an adverb clause.

1. Egyptology is the branch of learning which is concerned with the language and culture of ancient Egypt.
2. Until the Rosetta Stone was discovered in 1799, the ancient Egyptian language was an enigma to scholars.
3. Boussard, who was a captain in the engineers under Napoleon, found the stone in the trenches near Rosetta, a city near the mouth of the Nile.
4. Before the French had a chance to analyze its inscriptions, the stone was captured by the British.
5. Because the stone contained the same message in two kinds of Egyptian writing and in Greek script, it provided the needed key for deciphering the Egyptian language.
6. When the Rosetta Stone was found, part of the hieroglyphic portion was missing.
7. Scholars could easily read the Greek inscription, which was nearly complete.
8. In 1818 Thomas Young succeeded in isolating a number of hieroglyphics that he took to represent names.
9. The message that was written on the stone was not very exciting in itself.
10. Since the priests of Egypt were grateful for benefits from the king, they were formally thanking the king for his generosity.

The Noun Clause

4f. A *noun clause* is a subordinate clause used as a noun.

Compare the two sentences in each pair below. Notice that in the second sentence in each pair, a *subordinate clause takes the place of a noun in the first sentence.*

Tell whether the clause in each of the following pairs of sentences is used as the subject, object, or predicate nominative.

He believes **the adage.**
He believes **that hard work means success.**

His illness was Todd's excuse.
That he was ill was Todd's excuse.

Books have been written about **Edison's inventions.**
Books have been written about **what Edison invented.**

I do not remember **the assignment.**
I do not remember **what the assignment was.**

We knew **the author** of the book.
We knew **who the author was.**

Noun clauses are usually introduced by such connectives as *that, whether, what, who, whoever, whose, where, why,* etc. Sometimes the introductory word does not have any function in the clause.

S   V   D.O.
EXAMPLE I know **that he will find them.**   [The connecting word *that* plays no part in the clause.]

At other times, the introductory word does function in the clause.

D.O. S V
EXAMPLE I know **what they want.**

Like adjective clauses, noun clauses are sometimes used without the usual introductory word. Compare the noun clauses in the paired sentences on page 94.

4f

The teacher said **that the class could leave.**

The teacher said **the class could leave.** [The conjunction *that* is understood.]

● EXERCISE 7.   There are ten noun clauses in the following sentences. Copy them on your paper. Label the subject and the verb of each noun clause. After each clause, tell whether it is the subject of the sentence, the direct object, the indirect object, the predicate nominative, or the object of a preposition. You may abbreviate.

1. Give the book to whoever wants it.
2. How the fire started is still a mystery.
3. He never told us he had traveled in Spain.
4. We will bring whatever you need.
5. Whoever leaves last should put the lights out.
6. This is what I want.
7. The candidate will give whoever asks him a full statement of his program.
8. Bob knows who broke the window.
9. The reason is that you are too slow.
10. What his report will say is anybody's guess.

Diagraming Noun Clauses

A clause used as subject, object, predicate nominative, or object of a preposition is supported by an upright line resting on the line of the subject, object, predicate nominative, or object of a preposition.

NOUN CLAUSE AS SUBJECT   **What he said** convinced me.

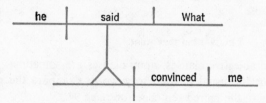

NOUN CLAUSE AS OBJECT   We know **that you won the prize.**
[*That* introduces the clause but plays no part in it.]

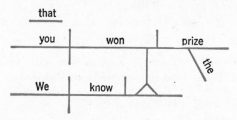

● EXERCISE 8.   Diagram the sentences in Exercise 7.

● REVIEW EXERCISE B.   Here are ten sentences containing all three kinds of subordinate clauses: adjective, adverb, and noun. Copy each clause on your paper. Label the verb and the subject in the clause, and name the kind of clause.

1. When the West was young, travelers often had difficulty finding accommodations for the night.
2. Experienced travelers, who realized they would frequently have to camp out, brought tents along on their journeys.
3. After stagecoach routes were opened, crude inns were built along the trails.
4. These early inns were what we would call a combination store, tavern, and farmhouse.
5. Spending the night in a sod-house inn was a strange experience for those who were accustomed to more luxurious surroundings.
6. When the wind blew, the dirt from the sod would fall on the sleepers.
7. Another complaint about the inns was that the food was poor.
8. The presence of fleas, mice, and other vermin was another thing that annoyed the early travelers.
9. Because the partition walls of some early Western hotels were made of calico, fire was a great danger.
10. The ground floors of many railroad hotels were given over to dance palaces that resounded with the noisy revelry of cowboys.

SENTENCES CLASSIFIED BY STRUCTURE

4g. Classified according to structure, there are four kinds of sentences—*simple, compound, complex, compound-complex.*

(1) A *simple sentence* is a sentence with one independent clause and no subordinate clause.

EXAMPLE   Cats are independent animals.

Although we often think of simple sentences as short, this is not necessarily the case.

EXAMPLE   On his way home from the game, Jake stopped for a
$\overset{\text{S}}{}$ $\overset{\text{V}}{}$
hamburger at the diner with the rest of the gang.
[Notice that there are plenty of phrases but only one
subject and one verb.]

(2) A *compound sentence* is a sentence composed of two or more independent clauses but no subordinate clauses.

EXAMPLES   I bought the shirt, but the tie was given to me.   [two
independent clauses]

The plants are not large, but they are healthy, and
they bloom regularly.   [three independent clauses]

Other words used to join the clauses of a compound sentence are *consequently, therefore, nevertheless, however, moreover, otherwise,* etc. These are called conjunctive adverbs. When a word of this kind is used between two independent clauses, it is preceded by a semicolon.

Each independent clause in a compound sentence is diagramed like a separate sentence. A dotted line joins the clauses. The line is drawn between the verbs of the two clauses, and the conjunction is written on a solid horizontal line connecting the two parts of the dotted line.

EXAMPLE I bought the shirt, but the tie was given to me.

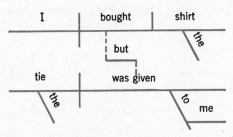

Caution: Do not confuse the compound predicate of a simple sentence with the two subjects and two predicates of a compound sentence.

EXAMPLES

$$\overset{\text{S}}{\text{He}} \overset{\text{V}}{\text{turned}} \text{ on the television and } \overset{\text{V}}{\text{watched}} \text{ a baseball}$$
game. [simple sentence with a compound predicate]

$$\overset{\text{S}}{\text{He}} \overset{\text{V}}{\text{turned}} \text{ on the television, and } \overset{\text{S}}{\text{he}} \overset{\text{V}}{\text{watched}} \text{ a base-}$$
ball game. [compound sentence with two independent clauses]

(3) A *complex sentence* is a sentence containing one independent clause and one or more subordinate clauses.

EXAMPLE When we reached the pier, the boat had docked.

Since you have already learned how to diagram a sentence containing a subordinate clause (adjective, adverb, and noun clause), you know how to diagram a complex sentence.

(4) A *compound-complex sentence* contains two or more independent clauses and one or more subordinate clauses.

EXAMPLE The house that Phil painted had been white, but he changed the color. [two independent clauses and one subordinate clause]

4g

In diagraming a compound-complex sentence, first diagram the independent clauses. Then attach the subordinate clauses to the words they modify. Give yourself plenty of room.

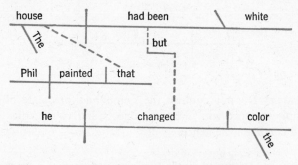

● EXERCISE 9.   Write and label two simple sentences, two compound sentences, and two complex sentences.

● EXERCISE 10.   Number your paper 1–10. After the proper number, write what kind of sentence each of the following is: simple, compound, complex, compound-complex.

1. While your manners are faultless, your attitude leaves something to be desired.
2. Mrs. Bauer played the piano, and Mr. Henry played the drums.
3. If it takes as long to explore the moon as it did to explore America, none of us will be around when the job is finished.
4. Finally, after the war, statesmen sat down together and settled their differences.
5. With the admission of so many new nations, the balance of power in the United Nations shifted in favor of the world's small countries.
6. When you can see both sides of an issue equally well, you find it difficult to take a stand, but everyone insists you must stand on one side or the other.
7. Although new media of communication bring nations closer together, new ideologies tend to keep them apart.
8. Pride is a powerful factor in an individual's behavior; it is also the cause of much disharmony among nations.

9. Prosperity is dependent on a nation's ability to produce salable goods, but security depends on a nation's military strength.
10. Competition, which is an important factor in trade, is also the cause of much of the tension that exists between nations.

● EXERCISE 11. What kind of sentence is each of the following? Be prepared to explain your answer.

1. After the supplies are delivered, we will decorate the gym.
2. We know that the art department has worked very hard, and we appreciate their efforts.
3. Place the chairs wherever you wish.
4. If we start early, we can finish before noon.
5. Arrange the flowers artistically.
6. Have you made the arrangements for the tickets?
7. Somebody must stand at the door and collect the tickets.
8. This dance should be a success, because we have already sold several hundred tickets.
9. We have elected a king and queen for the dance, and they will lead the Grand March.
10. The clean-up committee will report tomorrow at noon.

● EXERCISE 12. Diagram the sentences in Exercise 11.

● REVIEW EXERCISE C. Number your paper 1–33. After the proper number, identify each of the italicized word groups by means of the following abbreviations: *prep. ph.* (prepositional phrase); *part. ph.* (participial phrase); *inf. ph.* (infinitive phrase); *adj. cl.* (adjective clause); *adv. cl.* (adverb clause); *n. cl.* (noun clause).

Today no one doubts (1) *that Marco Polo's fame was justly earned.* (2) *Recognized as the foremost medieval traveler,* he was the first man to describe the wealth of China and (3) *to tell about Tibet, Japan, and Ceylon.* (4) *Hearing his colorful tales,* his listeners must have doubted Marco Polo's accuracy.

(5) *When he was a young man,* he began the long journey (6) *to Cathay.* (7) *Traveling three years across Asia,* Marco Polo arrived (8) *at the western end* of the Great Wall. Here young Marco and his companions were met by representatives of the

Great Khan, (9) *who escorted them to the summer capital in Mongolia.* (10) *Having been shown great favor by Kublai Khan,* Marco Polo became a trusted member of the court. He was ordered (11) *to go on missions to India* where he saw cities (12) *whose advanced civilization astonished him.*

(13) *As the Khan grew older,* Marco Polo and his companions feared (14) *what might follow his death.* They decided (15) *to leave Mongolia,* but the Khan heard their request (16) *with great displeasure.* In 1292 they seized an opportunity (17) *that came unexpectedly.* A Persian kinsman of the Khan, (18) *desiring a wife,* requested (19) *that a bride be sent to him.* The envoys of the kinsman, (20) *who decided to return by sea,* requested Marco Polo's company. (21) *When the Khan granted this request,* a fleet of fourteen ships, (22) *bearing Marco Polo, the bride, and valuable gifts,* departed for Persia.

After an absence (23) *of twenty-four years,* Marco Polo returned (24) *to Venice.* The Venice (25) *that he saw* could not compare with (26) *what he had seen in China.* The cold reception by relatives (27) *who had long considered him dead* changed (28) *when they saw the fabulous gems* (29) *which he brought with him.* Three years later, in a war (30) *between Venice and Genoa,* Marco Polo was captured. (31) *While he was in prison,* he described his adventures (32) *to a fellow prisoner* (33) *who wrote them down.*

PART TWO

Usage

CHAPTER 5

Levels of Usage

What Is Good English?

English books like this one make two kinds of statements about language. The first describes a fact about language—how words may be classified or how they are put together to form phrases, clauses, and sentences. The second kind of statement describes a choice between ways of saying something; in addition to describing the choice, this kind of statement usually says that one way is better than the other. The next five chapters contain many statements of this second kind. Before studying them, you should know what is involved in such choices and in what way one choice is better than another.

To be clear about the kind of choice this part of the book is concerned with, let's consider the following pair of sentences:

George don't know the answer.
George doesn't know the answer.

Is one of these sentences clearer or more meaningful than the other? It's hard to see how. The speaker of sentence 1 and the speaker of sentence 2 both convey the same message about George and his lack of knowledge. If language only conveyed information about the people and events that a speaker is discussing, we would have to say that one sentence is just as good as the other. However, language often carries messages the speaker does not intend. The words he uses to tell us about events often tell us something about the speaker himself. The extra, unintended message conveyed by "George don't know the answer" is that the speaker does not know or does not use one verb form that is universally preferred by educated users of English. If the speaker makes other choices that differ in the same way from those of educated people, he runs the risk of having his listeners assume that he is not educated.

It is important to be educated—not just to spend a certain number of years inside schoolhouses, but to know the things that educated people know. The people who run our government and businesses, doctors, lawyers, teachers, ministers, and others who play an important role in our society may differ in other respects, but they usually have in common a certain level of education. They also share a common language that is characterized by such choices as *doesn't* over *don't* after a subject like *George*. To be taken for an educated person, it is usually necessary to make the language choices that educated people make.

Perhaps it is not fair to judge people by how they say things rather than by what they say, but to some extent everyone does it. It's hard to know what is in a person's head, but the language he uses is always open to inspection, and people draw conclusions from it. The people who give marks and recommendations, who hire employees or judge college applications, these and others who may be important in your life are speakers of educated English. You may not be able to impress them merely by speaking their language, but you are likely to impress them unfavorably if you don't. The language you use tells a lot about you. It is worth the trouble to make sure that it tells the story you want people to hear.

● EXERCISE 1. Some of the following statements give facts about grammar—the way in which words are classified and put together in sentences. Others state choices between ways of saying things. If the statement is of the first kind, mark it *G* for grammar. If it is of the second kind, mark it *U* for usage.

1. A noun is the name of a person, place, thing, or idea.
2. The correct form of the verb *go* to use after *have* is *gone*, not *went*.
3. A verb that connects the subject with a word in the predicate that means the same thing is a linking verb.
4. Pronouns that follow a form of the verb *be* should be ones like *he* and *she*, not *him* and *her*.
5. The pronoun *everybody* as a subject calls for a singular verb.

● EXERCISE 2. *He doesn't* is regarded by educated people as being preferable to *he don't*. List five different situations in which it might be important for you to use *he doesn't* rather than *he don't*.

STANDARD AND SUBSTANDARD ENGLISH

The choice between *George don't* and *George doesn't* illustrates one difference between the two kinds of English spoken in the United States. The English of the educated—those who choose *George doesn't*—is called standard English. The English of those who do not make the same choices as most educated speakers is called substandard. Choosing *George don't* is one example of substandard usage; choosing *brung* instead of *brought* and choosing *have went* instead of *have gone* are others.

The word "standard" implies a measure or model against which things are judged. In this case, the standard is the speech and writing of educated people. Substandard English is characterized by usages that most educated people would reject. The rules and exercises in this chapter are concerned with teaching standard English usage. Except incidentally, little more will be said about substandard English. However, it is well to remember that substandard English is the language of millions of Americans and that you can master the conventions of standard English without having to lord it over people who don't use it. If a friend or member of your family uses substandard forms, it is not your job to tell him he is wrong. You will probably do more by example than by making corrections. In any case, there is more to being educated than using standard English—good manners, for example.

Two Kinds of Standard English

We often speak of English as though it were always the same, but of course it isn't. The English of 1100 was very different from the English of the 1970's. The language spoken in the British Isles is different from the English spoken in your community. Just as time and geography make for differences in language, so does the situation in which language is used. We use one kind of language on the athletic field and another in church, one kind in a friendly letter, another in a formal report.

There are many other situations, each of which calls for an appropriate kind of language. We can't name all of the different kinds, but we can distinguish two general types of standard English: *formal* and *informal*. Formal English is the language of serious and solemn occasions. A President's inaugural address, a court decision, a scholarly book or article, and the kind of formal report that has footnotes and a bibliography are situations in which formal English is likely to be used. Like formal dress, formal English is used for special occasions.

Informal English, on the other hand, is the everyday language of educated people. Because it is used in a wide variety of situations, informal English has many gradations. When it appears in books and magazines, it is often close to formal English; when it appears in friendly conversations and letters, it may contain some slang. The examples below will give you a better idea of the differences between formal and informal English and between different levels of informal English.

Here is an example of formal writing:

> The greatest difficulty which stands in the way of a meeting of the minds of the scientist and the nonscientist is the difficulty of communication, a difficulty which stems from some of the defects of education to which I have alluded. The mature scientist, if he has any taste in these directions, can listen with pleasure to the philosopher, the historian, the literary man, or even to the art critic. There is little difficulty from that side because the scientist has been educated in our general culture and lives in it on a day-to-day basis. He reads newspapers, magazines, books, listens to music, debates politics, and participates in the general activities of an educated citizen.
>
> Unfortunately, this channel of communication is often a one-way street. The nonscientist cannot listen to the scientist with pleasure and understanding. Despite its universal outlook and its unifying principle, its splendid tradition, science seems to be no longer communicable to the great majority of educated laymen. They simply do not possess the background of the science of today and the intellectual tools necessary for them to understand what effects science will have on them and on the world. Instead of understanding, they have only a naive awe mixed with fear and scorn. To his colleagues in the university, the scientist tends to seem more and more like a man from another planet, a creature scattering antibiotics with one hand and atomic bombs with the other.[1]

If you read part of this passage aloud, you will notice that the sentences have a formal sound that is quite different from ordinary conversation. More than anything else, it is the structure of the sentences that gives us this impres-

[1] From "Scientist and Humanist" by I. I. Rabi, *The Atlantic Monthly*, January 1956. Reprinted by permission of the author.

sion. Such carefully organized sentences as the first one in the passage are usually born on paper, even though they may be spoken later from a platform or pulpit. Formal English is chiefly written English. Its sentences are likely to be longer than those of informal English, and one idea is often balanced against another. The vocabulary is formal, too; words like *alluded, communicable,* and *naive* may appear in speech, but they appear much more often in writing. Formal English rarely admits slang and makes little use of contractions. Like the structure of the sentences, all these features suggest a calm and unhurried comment on a subject.

The following is an example of informal writing:

All advertisements show automobiles in unusual circumstances. The ads depict smiling, handsome people in evening clothes arriving in glittering hardtops beneath the porte cocheres of tropical restaurants. A polished convertible, top down, filled with laughing young people in yachting costumes, whispers along an idealized shoreline. A ruggedly healthy Mom, Pop, Sis, and Buzz smile the miles away as their strangely dustless station wagon whisks over the Rockies. Sometimes automobiles are mysteriously perched atop revolving pedestals; sometimes they slip through astral voids like comets. None of the advertisements show you and me in the automobile as most of us know it—that is, wedged in a fuming line of commuter traffic at 8:30 A.M., or locked in an even worse outbound line at 6 P.M.

A manufacturer, of course, would commit economic harakiri if he were to try to sell us a car on truthful grounds, for how could he ask anyone to pay $4,500 for a three-hundred-horsepower contraption on grounds that it would be used only two hours a day for 240 working days a year, and would at all other times—except briefly, on vacations—be parked in an expensive parking lot or sit depreciating at a curb? Would you buy such a car if it were truthfully put to you that the thing would cost you more than $9 an hour to use? No manufacturer in his right mind would plead with you to buy a luggage compartment only slightly smaller than Delaware in order that you could use part of this space just twice a year.[1]

Although there are some words and expressions in this piece of writing that suggest the formal vocabulary (*depict, astral voids, depreciating*), at least two of these are used for humorous effect. Moreover, they are balanced off against words like *hardtops, Mom, Pop, whisks,* and *contraption,* which have a distinctly informal flavor. In addition, there is a reference to "you and me" that suggests that the author is chatting with us. The sentences are carefully constructed— perhaps more care went into the writing of them than those in the previous passage—yet they have a sound that is much closer to the sound of good conversation.

Good formal writing always sounds as though it has been written and carefully edited; good informal prose usu- ally has been carefully written and edited, but it tries not to sound like it. It sticks much closer to the vocabulary and rhythms of speech, making use of contractions, slang, and everyday expressions.

● EXERCISE 3. Decide whether each of the following passages is standard or substandard English, and label it accordingly after the proper number on your paper. If the passage is standard, indicate whether it is formal or in- formal standard English. If it is substandard English, be able to show what words or expressions make it so.

1. It come to me that morning in the cornfield that this was the time to go. Before I'd hoed to the end of my first row, I knowed I couldn't put it off no longer. I had to go to the mountain.[2]

---

[1] From "The Call of the Open Road" from *The Insolent Chariots* by John Keats. Copyright © 1958 by John Keats. Reprinted by permission of J. B. Lippincott Company.

[2] From "High Lonesome Place" by Fred Gipson from *Rocky Mountain Empire*, edited by Elvon L. Howe. Copyright 1948 by Post Printing and Publishing Co. (Doubleday and Company, Inc.).

2. It is interesting to speculate what an orthodox Marxist historian would have prophesied for Mankind had he lived a few thousand years before Christ and had he seen Egypt in its static power, Crete crumbling, the Sumerians a memory, and Babylon at its zenith. Which empire would he have chosen as a source of future power and influence? [1]

3. A big, burly, choleric dog, he always acted as if he thought I wasn't one of the family. There was a slight advantage in being one of the family, for he didn't bite the family as often as he bit strangers. Still, in the years that we had him, he bit everybody but mother, and he made a pass at her once, but missed. [2]

4. Matt don't get very good grades in English, but he always done real good in math.

5. I stroked my chin thoughtfully: It so happened that I knew where to get my hands on a raccoon coat. My father had had one in his undergraduate days; it lay now in a trunk in the attic back home. It also happened that Petey had something I wanted. He didn't *have* it exactly, but he had first rights on it. I refer to his girl, Polly Espy. [3]

Despite the differences within standard English, in most cases formal and informal English make certain choices that distinguish them from substandard English. These choices are the ones that are discussed in the next five chapters. Occasionally, in an exercise, you will be asked to make a choice between forms that are different in formal and informal English. In this case, you are to select the formal way. This is done to give you needed practice in using formal English, not because you are expected always to be solemn.

[1] From *Policy for the West* by Barbara Ward, W. W. Norton & Company, Inc., 1951. Reprinted by permission.

[2] From "The Dog That Bit People" from *My Life and Hard Times* by James Thurber. Copyright 1933 by James Thurber. Published by Harper & Row, Publishers, Inc. Reprinted by permission.

[3] From *The Many Loves of Dobie Gillis* by Max Shulman. Copyright 1951 by Max Shulman. Published by Doubleday and Company, Inc. Reprinted by permission.

CHAPTER 6

Correct Agreement

Subject and Verb, Pronoun and Antecedent

Agreement, as it is used here, refers to the fact that certain closely related words in sentences have matching forms. Subjects are closely related to their verbs, and a careful speaker makes them agree with each other by matching verb forms to subject forms. In the same way pronouns and their antecedents are closely related and must be made to agree with each other by matching forms. When such words are correctly matched, we say that they agree. When they fail to match, we say there is an error in *agreement*.

SINGULAR AND PLURAL NUMBER

6a. When a word refers to one person or thing, it is *singular* in number. When a word refers to more than one, it is *plural* in number.

The bold-faced words below agree in number.

EXAMPLES   **One** of the members **has** not cast **his** vote.   [singular]

            Many of the members **have** not cast **their** votes. [plural]

Nouns and pronouns have number. The following nouns and pronoun are singular because they name only one person or thing: *building, woman, it, poem.* The following are plural because they name more than one person or thing: *buildings, women, they, poems.*[1]

EXERCISE 1.   List the following words on your paper. After each plural word, write *P* for plural; after each singular word, write *S* for singular.

1. alumni	6. anybody	11. diabetes
2. one	7. many	12. neither
3. several	8. aeronautics	13. both
4. few	9. either	14. measles
5. somebody	10. each	15. woman

AGREEMENT OF SUBJECT AND VERB

Verbs, too, have number; certain forms are used when a verb's subject is singular and others when the subject is plural. An educated person makes his verbs agree with their subjects.

6b. A verb agrees with its subject in number.

(1) Singular subjects take singular verbs.

EXAMPLE   Grace **dyes** her hair, but Wendy **does** not.   [The singular verb *dyes* agrees with the singular subject *Grace;* the singular verb *does* agrees with the singular subject *Wendy.*]

(2) Plural subjects take plural verbs.

EXAMPLE   Grace and Wendy **dye** their hair, but the other girls **do** not.   [The plural verb *dye* agrees with the plural subject *Grace and Wendy,* and the plural verb *do* agrees with the plural subject *girls.*]

[1] For rules regarding the formation of plurals of nouns, see pages 512–14.

6
a-b

In general, nouns ending in *s* are plural (*boys, girls, friends, stores*) but verbs ending in *s* are singular (*plays, eats, is, was, has*). Singular *I* and *you*, however, generally take verbs which do not end in *s* (*I go, you go, I am, you are*).

◆ NOTE The form *were* is normally plural except when used with singular *you* and in sentences like the following:

If I were king, I would make some changes around here.
Were Johnny here now, he would protest.

● EXERCISE 2. Decide which one of the words in parentheses should be used to agree with the subject given.

1. soldier (walks, walk)
2. one (is, are)
3. several (runs, run)
4. few (works, work)
5. somebody (breaks, break)
6. everybody (sings, sing)
7. many (looks, look)
8. two (was, were)
9. either (plays, play)
10. each (works, work)

11. dogs (barks, bark)
12. neither (appeals, appeal)
13. both (believes, believe)
14. Englishmen (sails, sail)
15. women (seems, seem)
16. anyone (thinks, think)
17. oxen (drags, drag)
18. Fran and Tom (goes, go)
19. the books (lies, lie)
20. each boy (buys, buy)

6c. The number of the subject is not changed by a phrase following the subject.

Do not be confused when a phrase comes between the subject and the verb. Since the subject is never a part of a phrase, a word in a phrase cannot influence the verb.

EXAMPLES **One** of the girls **is** going. [The phrase *of the girls* does not affect the number of the subject *one: one is*, not *girls are*.]

Both girls in the family **are** in the chorus. [The phrase *in the family* does not affect the number of the subject *girls: girls are*, not *family is*.]

As the diagrams show, if you drop the phrase, the subject becomes clearer.

EXAMPLES One ~~of the girls~~ is going.
Both girls ~~in the family~~ are in the chorus.

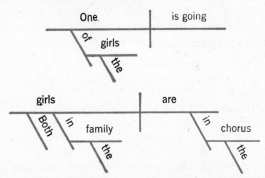

Even prepositional phrases beginning with expressions like *with, together with, in addition to, as well as,* and *along with* do not affect the number of the verb.

EXAMPLES Miss Walsh, with her two sisters, **has** gone to visit friends. [Miss Walsh . . . has]

The star, as well as the producer and the director, **was** a little nervous on opening night. [The star . . . was]

Your conduct, in addition to your poor marks, **makes** you ineligible for the Honor Society. [Your conduct . . . makes]

The logic of this will be clearer to you if you rearrange the first sentence about Miss Walsh:

EXAMPLE Miss Walsh **has** gone with her two sisters to visit friends.

Another source of trouble is the negative construction. When such a construction comes between the subject and its verb, it is often mistakenly allowed to affect the number of the verb and so to throw it out of agreement with its proper subject. Treat negative constructions exactly like phrases following the subject.

EXAMPLE Jim, not Roger and his friend, **is** coming with me.

6c

● EXERCISE 3. In each of the following sentences, you have a choice of verbs. Write the subject of each verb on your paper. Remembering that the verb and subject must agree in number, select the one of the two verbs in parentheses which agrees in number with the subject.

1. One of these boys (is, are) going to win.
2. A large pile of broken bricks and stones (was, were) left outside of town.
3. Carelessness in the use of simple tools (causes, cause) many household accidents.
4. An exhibit of student drawings and photographs (is, are) on display in the main hall.
5. The buildings along the waterfront (seems, seem) to be unoccupied.
6. Judy, along with Iris, Barbara, and Natalie, (has, have) decided to become a teacher.
7. The sound of the violins (was, were) pleasing.
8. The fancy basket of apples (was, were) a gift.
9. The plans of the troop (was, were) kept secret.
10. Deputies from the sheriff's office (was, were) trying to calm the mob.
11. A letter from Ned's relatives (explains, explain) the easiest route to take.
12. The coach's remarks concerning Gene (was, were) most flattering.
13. The price of the albums (was, were) too high.
14. This picture of my grandparents (was, were) taken many years ago.
15. The opinions of the critics, not the acclaim of the audience, often (determines, determine) the success of a play.
16. The players on our team (looks, look) tired.
17. The fire lit by the shipwrecked sailors (was, were) seen by one of the search vessels.
18. The loss of the last two track meets (puts, put) us in last place.
19. In bobsledding, perfect rhythm on the turns, in addition to a certain disregard of danger, (is, are) necessary to win.
20. One of the movie projectors (has, have) been sent to the shop for repairs.

6d. **The following pronouns are singular:** *each, either, neither, one, everyone, everybody, no one, nobody, anyone, anybody, someone, somebody.*

These words are called indefinite pronouns because they refer only generally, indefinitely, to some thing or person. Very often they are followed by a prepositional phrase containing a plural word. In this case be sure to make the verb agree with the indefinite pronoun, not with a word in the prepositional phrase.

WRONG One of the uniforms were green. [The verb *were* does not agree with the singular subject, *one*.]

RIGHT **One** of the uniforms **was** green. [The verb agrees with the subject.]

Read the following pairs of sentences aloud, stressing the subjects and verbs in bold-faced type.

EXAMPLES **Neither is** going.

Neither of the boys **is** going.

Each was working on a project.

Each of the students **was** working on a project.

One was silver.

One of the rings **was** silver.

Everybody takes English.

Everybody in both classes **takes** English.

Everyone plans to attend the game.

Every one of the girls **plans** to attend the game.

6e. **The following pronouns are plural:** *several, few, both, many.*

EXAMPLES **Several** of the boys **are** discouraged.

Few in the audience **were** aware of the danger.

Both have given up.

Many of the workers **draw** their pay and **leave.**

6
d-e

6f. The pronouns *some, all, any, most,* and *none,* may be either singular or plural.

A writer may use either a singular or a plural verb to agree with the words *some, any, none,* or *all,* depending upon the meaning he has in mind. These words are plural if they refer to a number of persons or things; they are singular if they refer to an amount, or quantity, of something.

SINGULAR   **Some** of the cargo **was** lost. [a quantity]

PLURAL   **Some** of the books **were** damaged. [a number of books]

SINGULAR   **Has any** of the paint been delivered? [a quantity]

PLURAL   **Have any** of the guests arrived? [a number]

SINGULAR   **All** of the cake **has** been eaten. [the whole amount]

PLURAL   **All** of the bicycles **have** been rented. [the whole number]

In each of the examples above, the prepositional phrase following the subject provides a clue to the number of the subject. When the object of the preposition is singular, the pronoun subject is singular, but when it is plural, the pronoun subject is also plural. These pronouns can also be used without a prepositional phrase after them:

EXAMPLES   **Some was** lost. [an amount of money, time, cargo, etc.]

Some were damaged. [a number of books, cars, houses, etc.]

● EXERCISE 4.   *Oral Drill.* Repeat each of the following sentences aloud three times, stressing the italicized words.

1. *One* of these pens *is* mine.
2. Every *one* of them *writes* well.
3. *Neither* of the girls *has* a new hat.
4. *Some* of the apples *are* green.
5. Not *one* of the stories *appeals* to me.
6. *One* of us *is* sure to win.

7. *Neither* of the plays *was* interesting.
8. *Either* of the books *is* acceptable.
9. *Several* of the trees *were* affected by a blight.
10. *Every* player on the team *trains* diligently.

● EXERCISE 5. Rewrite each of the following twenty sentences according to the directions in parentheses. If necessary, change the number of the verb to agree with the new subject or to accord with the altered sense of the sentences.

1. Each of the flowers is beautiful. (Change *each* to *some*.)
2. Some of the grain was shipped. (Change *grain* to *tractors*.)
3. Both of the girls were fifteen. (Change *both* to *neither*.)
4. All of the money was marked. (Change *money* to *dollar bills*.)
5. Have any of the cookies been eaten? (Change *cookies* to *bread*.)
6. Somebody was here before. (Change *somebody* to *few*.)
7. Everyone is going to be there. (Change *everyone* to *most of us*.)
8. Each of the baskets needs repair. (Change *each* to *several*.)
9. The size of the insects was astonishing. (Change *insects* to *insect*.)
10. Have all of the tickets been punched? (Change *all* to *each*.)
11. None of the glasses were imported. (Change *glasses* to *iron ore*.)
12. Everyone eats in the cafeteria. (Change *everyone* to *nobody*.)
13. Is there enough paper to go around? (Change *paper* to *books*.)
14. Few of the elms are healthy. (Change *few* to *not one*.)
15. Both of the movies were good. (Change *both* to *one*.)
16. One of your answers is incorrect. (Change *one* to *neither*.)
17. Most of the days were sunny. (Change *days* to *day*.)
18. Either of them is able to play first base. (Change *either* to *both*.)
19. Have any of the girls arrived? (Change *any* to *either*.)
20. A wagon loaded with corn was blocking the lane. (Change *corn* to *pine logs*.)

● EXERCISE 6. Number 1–20 in a column on your paper. Read each of the sentences carefully. If the verb and sub-

6f

ject agree, write a + after the proper number on your paper.
If the verb and subject do not agree, write a 0 after the
proper number.

1. Every one of the screens needs paint.
2. One of the submarines was powered by atomic energy.
3. Neither of my two brothers have been elected to the Student Council.
4. Some of the dogs in this neighborhood are poorly trained.
5. Every one of them have to report to the principal.
6. Both of the tables is lopsided.
7. Neither of them is capable of repairing the faucet.
8. Each of the cheerleaders practice after school every day.
9. One of us has to be on time.
10. Several of the missing works of art has been found in Italy.
11. All of the chairs were near the barbecue pit.
12. Neither of my friends bowl very well.
13. Are one of the boxes large enough?
14. Either of the boys goes for the mail.
15. Each of the boxers is well known.
16. Some of the machines were in good condition.
17. Some of the play was rather boring.
18. Many of the termites were destroyed.
19. Not one of us were going to tell you.
20. One of Helen's letters was delivered to Henry by mistake.

The Compound Subject

6g. **Most compound subjects joined by** *and*
take a plural verb.

EXAMPLES   Oscar and he **do** the gardening.

His right arm and his left leg **were** broken.

A few compound subjects joined by *and* name a single
person or thing and therefore take a singular verb.

EXAMPLES   Ham and eggs **is** my favorite dish. [one dish]

Law and order **was** maintained by the police. [one
civil responsibility]

6h. Singular subjects joined by *or* or *nor* take a singular verb.

EXAMPLES   Neither rain nor snow **stops** the delivery of mail.

Has either Grandmother or Grandfather arrived yet?

Neither the record player nor the tape recorder **works** very well.

Note that the word *either* may be omitted, but the number of the subject is not changed so long as the parts are joined by *or*.

EXAMPLE   Mary or her sister **was** going to do the cooking for the family.

Note also that this use of *either . . . or, neither . . . nor* should not be confused with that of the correlative conjunction *both . . . and*, which takes a plural verb.

EXAMPLES   Both the American Legion and the Kiwanis Club **are** planning a parade.

Neither the American Legion nor the Kiwanis Club **is** planning a parade.

6i. When a singular subject and a plural subject are joined by *or* or *nor*, the verb agrees with the nearer subject.

EXAMPLES   Neither their brother nor the girls **want** to go to the pool. [girls want]

Either his assistants or the cook himself **is** at fault. [cook . . . is]

In the first sentence *girls* is nearer to the verb *want* than *brother*, the other part of the compound subject. The verb must be plural to agree with the nearer subject, *girls*. Likewise, in the second sentence the verb *is* must agree with *cook*, since this singular part of the compound subject is nearer to it. This kind of construction is often awkward, however, and it is usually best to avoid it.

6
g-i

EXAMPLES   The girls **don't** want to go to the pool, and neither **does** their brother.

Either the cook himself **is** at fault, or his assistants **are.**

● EXERCISE 7.   *Oral Drill*. Repeat each of the following sentences aloud three times, stressing the italicized words.

1. *Each* of the boys *has* gone.
2. *Neither* Joe *nor* Bill *is* interested.
3. A *few* of our plans *were* made.
4. *Either* Julia *or* Helen *has* your pen.
5. *One* of the books *was* lost.
6. Every *one* of his teeth *was* extracted.
7. *Both* Florence *and* Joan *are* hockey players.
8. *Several* of them *were* here yesterday.
9. *Each was* welcome.
10. Not *one* of the trucks *was* working.

● EXERCISE 8.   From the parentheses in the following sentences, choose the correct verb. Write the verbs in a column on your paper.

1. Neither Bob nor they (believes, believe) that story.
2. Both Bob and he (hopes, hope) to attend the game.¹
3. Neither the geranium nor the begonias (was, were) blooming.
4. Either the principal or the class adviser (is, are) going with us.
5. Neither the carnations nor the dahlias (has, have) been weeded.
6. Either the captains or the umpire (calls, call) time out.
7. Larry and he (was, were) editors of the yearbook.
8. My parents and yours (pays, pay) state and local taxes.
9. My fraternity or yours (is, are) going to build a float for the parade.
10. Either her voice or the microphone (needs, need) drastic improvement.
11. Both New York and San Francisco (has, have) world-famous bridges.
12. Cake or pie (is, are) a good dessert.
13. The director and the producer of the play (is, are) awaiting the verdict of the critics.

14. Either my horse or his almost always (wins, win).
15. The news story and the feature article (differs, differ) from the editorial.
16. Neither the refrigerator nor the stove (has, have) been installed.
17. Both the mayor and the people (was, were) opposed to the village ordinance.
18. The worst feature of such storms (was, were) the blowing sand.
19. Marie or Eileen (has, have) been elected to the Student Council.
20. Neither fishing nor hunting (appeals, appeal) to his wife.

Other Problems in Agreement

6j. Collective nouns may be either singular or plural.

You may be in doubt at times about the number of a word which names a group of persons or objects. This kind of word is known as a *collective noun*.

A collective noun is singular and takes a singular verb when the group is thought of *as a unit or whole*.

A collective noun is plural and takes a plural verb when members of the group are thought of *as individuals acting separately*. Study the following pairs of sentences.

The faculty **has** a meeting this afternoon. [*Faculty* is thought of as a unit.]

The faculty **were** giving **their** ideas on the new marking procedure. [*Faculty* is thought of as a number of individuals.]

Jo's family **has** gone to Myrtle Beach for the summer. [*Family* is a unit.]

Jo's family **have** been dividing the chores among **themselves.** [Family members are acting as individuals.]

The class **is** a very large one. [one unit]

The class **are** writing **their** compositions. [The class is thought of as individuals.]

6j

The following is a list of some collective nouns:

jury	crowd	flock	team
herd	class	choir	committee
club	troop	group	audience
army	fleet	swarm	faculty

● EXERCISE 9. Select five collective nouns, and write five pairs of sentences like those given above, showing clearly how the words you choose may be either singular or plural.

● EXERCISE 10. Rewrite the following ten sentences according to the instructions in parentheses, changing the number of the verb if necessary.

1. Either Jill or her brothers were expected momentarily. (Reverse the order of the subjects.)
2. The committee is making a joint report. (Change *joint report* to *individual reports.*)
3. Neither of the girls has left. (Change *neither* to *both.*)
4. Both Kay and Sylvia do good needlework. (Change *both . . . and* to *neither . . . nor.*)
5. None of the teachers were available. (Change *teachers* to *money.*)
6. Bill and Orville expect to be chosen. (Change *and* to *or.*)
7. The troop of scouts was observed marching in good order. (Change *marching in good order* to *going their separate ways.*)
8. All of his poems are here. (Change *all* to *both.*)
9. Each sophomore girl has been asked to serve on a committee. (Change *each* to *every.*)
10. Ham and eggs is a good midnight snack. (Change *and* to *or.*)

6k. A verb agrees with its subject, not with its predicate nominative.

In the examples below the subject is marked S and the predicate nominative PN.

EXAMPLES
 S   PN
The biggest **problem** in gardening **is** the **weeds.**
 S   PN
Weeds are the biggest **problem** in gardening.

S   PN
A requirement for safe driving **is** good **tires.**
S   PN
Good **tires are** a **requirement** for safe driving.

Often this kind of agreement problem can be avoided by changing the sentence so as to avoid using a predicate nominative:

EXAMPLE   Safe **driving requires** good **tires.**

61. When the subject follows the verb, as in sentences beginning with *there* and *here*, be careful to anticipate the subject and make sure that the verb agrees with it.

WRONG   There is fourteen thousand people in my town. [not *people . . . is*]

RIGHT   There **are** fourteen thousand people in my town. [*people . . . are*]

● EXERCISE 11.   Number 1–20 in a column on your paper. Read each sentence aloud. If the verb agrees with the subject, put a + on your paper after the proper number. If the verb does not agree with the subject, write a 0. Be ready to explain the reasons for your choice.

1. Pork and beans is a favorite food for campers.
2. Here's the items you ordered, Mrs. Jones.
3. Neither the station wagon nor the jeep are in the garage.
4. Where was the fullback and the halfbacks at that moment?
5. Both my grandfather and my uncle live in Colorado.
6. Either my dog or yours are going to be picked as the winner.
7. Macaroni and cheese are my favorite dish.
8. There's several cars in the driveway.
9. Every one of these socks have a hole in the toe.
10. There's some strawberries in the freezer.
11. Each of the neighbors has a new car.
12. There's more than enough jobs to go around.
13. Here is several widely varying interpretations of the same poem.

6
k-l

14. Edward, as well as Agnes and Frank, were at home.
15. Neither of the policemen uses strong-arm methods.
16. Do every one of your relatives live in Seattle?
17. Both Mary Ann and Jean are officers in the Press Club.
18. The dog and cat, together with the white mice and the hamsters, are creating difficulties in the family.
19. Have any of the boys turned in their compositions?
20. Mr. Hofman, not his two sons, are painting the house and garage.

6m. Words stating amount are usually singular.

EXAMPLES   Fifteen dollars **was** too much to pay for the hat.

Three weeks **is** the usual incubation period.

Six percent of the working force **is** unemployed.

When the sense of the sentence indicates that the subject designates a collection of individual parts rather than a single unit or quantity, the verb must be plural in number.

EXAMPLES   Two nickels **are** on the table.

Three long weeks **pass** before the eggs hatch.

Six percent of the compositions **were** failures.

Two such amount-stating expressions deserve special mention—*the number of* and *a number of*. They should not be confused. *The number of* takes a singular verb, and *a number of* takes a plural verb.

EXAMPLES   **The number of** women in the professions **is** increasing.

A number of women **are** attracted to the professions.

6n. *Every* or *many a* before a word or a series of words is followed by a singular verb.

EXAMPLES   **Every** man, woman, and child **is** proud of the city's record.

Many a philosopher **has** wondered about that question.

6 o. The title of a work of art, literature, or music, even when plural in form, takes a singular verb.

EXAMPLES   Brahms' *Variations on a Theme by Haydn* is a lovely work.

Millet's *The Gleaners* is a famous nineteenth-century French painting.

John Dos Passos' *Three Soldiers* condemns the stupidity of war.

6p. *Don't* and *doesn't* must agree with their subjects.

With the subjects *I* and *you*, use *don't* (*do not*); with other singular subjects use *doesn't* (*does not*); with plural subjects use *don't* (*do not*).

EXAMPLES   I **don't** want to go.
You **don't** know the answer.
It (he, she) **doesn't** answer the question.
They **don't** want to sing.

Do not use *don't* after *he*, *she*, or *it*.

WRONG   It don't seem possible.
RIGHT   It **doesn't** seem possible.

WRONG   He don't want the ticket.
RIGHT   He **doesn't** want the ticket.

● EXERCISE 12.   Write in a column on your paper the correct form (*don't* or *doesn't*) for the following sentences.

1. Your answer —— sound right.
2. It —— seem possible.
3. He —— want to attend the rally.
4. She —— believe that she won the prize.
5. It —— happen very often.
6. You —— have to appear in the play.
7. —— he ever get tired?
8. —— it make sense?

6
m-p

9. Harry —— like to dance.
10. Some of the girls —— like the color.

● EXERCISE 13.   Choose the correct one of the two verbs given in parentheses in the sentences below, and list them in a column on your paper.

1. The President, as well as two aides, (was, were) in the reviewing stand.
2. Phil, and not Joyce or Sally, (is, are) making the decorations for the party.
3. They (wasn't, weren't) interested in helping us.
4. Christmas, of all the holidays, (appeals, appeal) most to me.
5. Some of us (learns, learn) faster than others.
6. *Popular Sport Stories* (has, have) been read by every member of the class.
7. The boat to the islands (leaves, leave) the dock at noon.
8. Rex, one of the best fox terriers in his class, (is, are) sure to win first prize.
9. Several of the older boys, including my brother John, (is, are) taking the college entrance examination.
10. (Doesn't, Don't) Bryan want to do the weeding?
11. Todd, as well as several other boys, (was, were) called on to read his report.
12. I am sure that nobody in the resort business (welcomes, welcome) rainy days during the busy season.
13. A new box of artist's crayons (was, were) left on the table by mistake.
14. My father, like many baseball fans, (plans, plan) to attend the opening game of the series.
15. Neither of his parents (wants, want) him to take up scuba diving.
16. There (is, are) too many books in my bookcase now.
17. It (doesn't, don't) matter how you go, as long as you get there.
18. The museum, which has a large collection of Rembrandt's paintings, (has, have) made plans to acquire one more.
19. (Doesn't, Don't) all of you remember the difficulty we had with agreement?
20. Both of the swimmers (is, are) hoping to become members of the Olympic team.

● REVIEW EXERCISE A. In some of the following sentences, the verbs agree with their subjects; in others, the verbs do not agree. Number 1–33 in a column. If the verb and subject agree in a sentence, write *C* after the proper number. If the verb does not agree with its subject, supply the correct form of the verb after the proper number.

1. The jury has returned its verdict.
2. Apple pie and cheese is his favorite dessert.
3. Either Judy or Joan are supposed to be there.
4. Neither of the men leaves until five o'clock.
5. Several of the girls in the chorus are absent today.
6. He don't do very well in the track meets.
7. Neither Lois nor her sisters was going to the dance.
8. There's one pair of candlesticks on the table.
9. Do every one of the committee members think that Russ will win the election?
10. Several of the boys appear to have colds.
11. Trudy, as well as her two sisters, seems to have a knack for cooking.
12. Neither of us care to go.
13. Each of the basketball fans were excited by the game.
14. A few other things, in addition to his speaking voice, has contributed to the candidate's success.
15. There is few that can equal his ability.
16. Not one of those horses is dangerous.
17. *The Three Musketeers* deals with the period in French history from 1625 to 1665.
18. Neither Dave nor Helen have any intention of going to the dance.
19. Where was the jewels hidden?
20. Some of these lobsters are rather small.
21. Only a few of my friends like to play cards.
22. One of the players ignore training rules.
23. In the trunk there's some nails and a hammer.
24. The audience was divided in their opinions about the school play.
25. Each of us has a long way to go.
26. Every one of the new automatic washers come with a free box of detergent.

27. A swarm of bees was buzzing about the hive.
28. Three quarters of the supplies were piled in the warehouse.
29. The men's clubs in this community perform many charitable deeds.
30. Where have the club decided to hold its rally?
31. It don't really matter to me.
32. There, in a pile of old clothes, was both of the missing kittens.
33. Doesn't these questions bother you?

AGREEMENT OF PRONOUN AND ANTECEDENT

Personal pronouns (*I*, *you*, *he*, etc.) have matching forms that must agree with their antecedents. The antecedent is the word to which a pronoun refers.

6q. **A pronoun agrees with its antecedent in gender and number.**

A small number of nouns in English name persons or things that are clearly masculine: *boy*, *actor*, *rooster*. About the same number name persons or things that are feminine: *girl*, *actress*, *hen*. Most nouns name things that may be either masculine or feminine (*student*, *child*) or to which the idea of sex does not apply (*house*, *streetcar*). Nouns which apply to both masculine and feminine, or which do not carry any idea of either masculine or feminine, are said to be *neuter* or to have *common gender*.

Personal pronouns usually match the gender of their antecedents.

EXAMPLES   Has **Alice** forgotten **her** appointment again?   [The pronoun *her* is feminine to agree with *Alice*.]

If you find my **book,** please bring **it** with you.   [The pronoun *it* agrees with *book* in gender.]

Personal pronouns also have forms that reflect the number of their antecedents.

EXAMPLES The **soldiers** wanted **their** pay. [The pronoun is plural to agree with *soldiers*.]

The **soldier** left **his** post. [This time the antecedent is singular and the singular pronoun is used.]

(1) The words *each, either, neither, one, everyone, everybody, no one, nobody, anyone, anybody, someone, somebody* are referred to by a singular pronoun — *he, him, his, she, her, hers, it, its.*

The use of a phrase after the antecedent does not change the number of the antecedent.

EXAMPLES **Each** of the planes kept **its** place in the formation.

Everyone in the club cast **his** [not *their*] vote against the motion.

Look, **somebody** left **his** [not *their*] notebook here.

When the antecedent may be either masculine or feminine, as in the last two examples above, it is customary to use only the masculine pronoun.

◆ USAGE NOTE   On certain occasions when the *idea* of the sentence (the meaning of the antecedent) is clearly plural, one must use the plural pronoun even though the singular form of the pronoun is called for grammatically. For example, to use a singular pronoun in the following sentence would be absurd:

If **everyone** comes to the party, it will be impossible to accommodate **them** [not *him*].

It is usually possible to avoid such constructions.

BETTER   If **all** of the guests come to the party, it will be impossible to accommodate **them**.

(2) Two or more singular antecedents joined by *or* or *nor* should be referred to by a singular pronoun.

EXAMPLE   Neither the sergeant nor the captain had brought **his** compass with **him**.

(3) Two or more antecedents joined by *and* should be referred to by a plural pronoun.

6q

EXAMPLE   The captain and the sergeant have **their** wits about them.

(4) **The number of a relative pronoun (*who, which, that*) is determined by the number of the word to which it refers — its antecedent.**

EXAMPLES   Stan is one of those **boys who are** continually amazed by **their** own misfortunes. [*Who* is plural because it refers to *boys*. Therefore the plural forms *are* and *their* are used to agree with *who*.]

Let **anyone who has** no wish to risk **his** life quit the field. [*Who* is singular because *anyone* is singular. Therefore the singular forms *has* and *his* are used to agree with *who* in this sentence.]

● EXERCISE 14.   Number 1–15 in a column on your paper. For each blank in the following sentences, select a pronoun which will agree with its antecedent, and write it after the proper number on your paper.

1. After the march, all of the soldiers complained that —— feet hurt.
2. Either John or Steve will give —— speech first.
3. Everybody in the band is responsible for having —— own uniform cleaned and pressed.
4. Every policeman did —— duty.
5. Each of the girls in the troop has to make —— own bed.
6. Several of the boys brought —— Scout handbooks.
7. Every chef has —— favorite recipe.
8. Nobody in the class has turned in —— book report yet.
9. Sam and his brother were so thirsty —— tongues were hanging out.
10. Both applicants brought —— credentials with them.
11. If anyone calls, get —— name and telephone number.
12. Everyone has —— own opinion about the coach.
13. Few of the campers put —— tents in good locations.
14. Neither girl did —— best.
15. Charles and his brother received —— tetanus shots at the clinic.

● EXERCISE 15. List on your paper the singular or the plural form of the verb *be* for the sentences that require verbs. List a singular or plural pronoun for the sentences that require pronouns.

1. Both of the bats —— cracked.
2. Neither of them —— usable.
3. One of the boys sprained —— ankle.
4. Each sailor did —— own laundry.
5. Where —— your books?
6. If one of the boys —— still there, ask him to wait.
7. Neither Dad nor Mother —— likely to agree with you.
8. Each of the students has received —— report card.
9. One of them did not sign —— name.
10. If anyone asks, tell —— your name.

● REVIEW EXERCISE B. In some of the following sentences, either a verb does not agree with its subject or a pronoun does not agree with its antecedent. Number your paper 1–20. If a sentence is correct, place a + after the corresponding number; if it is incorrect, place a 0.

1. Neither of the tractors were in good condition.
2. One of the men is always boasting that he can make more sales than anyone else.
3. Ralph, along with several other seniors, have won many awards.
4. Neither Ted nor Herb has finished their test.
5. Both of the boys clean up their rooms in the morning.
6. There was three members absent from the last meeting.
7. A few of the club members handed in their resignations.
8. Either Frank or Jim will bring his microphone.
9. Each of the boys was supposed to bring their own flashlight.
10. Neither of the dogs want to eat their food.
11. Every one of the trees is diseased.
12. Either of them could get an A if he worked at it.
13. Is there any volunteers for the job?
14. Another rule everyone learns is to leave the camping area neater than they found it.
15. Some of the campers had their first-aid kits with them.

16. Each choir member had their own robe.
17. If anyone doesn't like my cooking, they can starve.
18. One soon learns to keep his mouth closed.
19. Where's the six dollars you owe me?
20. Both Leo and Harry make their own trout flies.

● REVIEW EXERCISE C. Number your paper 1–20. In each sentence, select the correct one of the two forms given in parentheses, and write it after the corresponding number on your paper.

1. Everyone insisted on having (his, their) own way.
2. Neither Muriel nor her two brothers (was, were) ever seen again in our town.
3. If anybody wants to buy a ticket, (he, they) had better hurry.
4. Neither of the tires (needs, need) air.
5. Each of the candidates (seems, seem) well qualified.
6. Either Paul or his brother (is, are) in charge of refreshments.
7. Mr. Faston, as well as his two partners, (attends, attend) every town meeting.
8. There (is, are) not enough pencils to go around.
9. A few of our men (was, were) wounded.
10. Where (is, are) the groceries we ordered?
11. If anyone wishes to see the principal, (he, they) must make an appointment.
12. Nobody likes to find (himself, themselves) left out of school activities.
13. Muriel, as well as her two brothers, (was, were) missed by everyone.
14. Several of the buses (was, were) late.
15. Neither of the sick dogs could raise (its, their) head.
16. Where (is, are) the girls?
17. *The Reivers* (is, are) a book by William Faulkner.
18. Every one of the clarinet players (was, were) on time for the rehearsal.
19. Anyone who plays on the football team should take (his, their) bruises like a man.
20. Occasionally someone is smart enough to find (himself, themselves) a seat in the front row.

● REVIEW EXERCISE D. Rewrite each of the following sentences, (1) following the directions in parentheses, (2) changing the number of the verb to agree with the subject if necessary, and (3) changing the number of the pronoun to agree with its new antecedent.

EXAMPLE 1. The girls have finished their biology assignments. (Change *the girls* to *each of the girls.*)

        1. *Each of the girls has finished her biology assignment.*

1. All club members have until next Friday to pay their dues. (Change *all club members* to *each club member.*)
2. Elizabeth, together with her sister, has not arrived yet. (Change *her sister* to *her sisters.*)
3. Neither Tim nor his two sisters have ever been out of Alabama. (Change *neither Tim nor his two sisters* to *neither his two sisters nor Tim.*)
4. The swarm of hornets has abandoned its nest. (Change *the swarm of* to *many of the.*)
5. Have William and Nan ever been to Salt Lake City? (Change *and* to *or.*)
6. Some of the girls have brought their own lunch. (Change *some* to *not one.*)
7. The number of failures has been announced. (Change *the number of* to *a number of.*)
8. Three books were ordered. (Change *three* to *a set of three.*)
9. Nobody in the group has brought his money. (Change *nobody* to *many.*)
10. Few of my friends get along very well with their parents. (Change *few* to *neither.*)

CHAPTER **7**

Using Pronouns Correctly

Nominative and Objective Case

A small number of pronouns have three forms: a *nominative* form that is used when the pronoun is a subject or predicate nominative; an *objective* form that is used when it is a direct or indirect object or the object of a preposition; and a *possessive* form that is used to show possession. These three forms, called *cases*, are illustrated below.

NOMINATIVE CASE **I** voted for Betty.
She voted for someone else.

OBJECTIVE CASE I voted for **her**.
Betty voted for **him**.

POSSESSIVE CASE It was **my** vote.
She wasted **her** vote.

CASE FORMS OF PERSONAL PRONOUNS

Personal pronouns are those pronouns which change form in the different persons.

First person is the person speaking: *I* (*We*) go.

Second person is the person spoken to: *You* are going.

Third person is a person or thing other than the speaker or the one spoken to: *He* (*She, It, They*) will go.

Study the following list of personal pronouns, noticing the changes in person and case form.

PERSONAL PRONOUNS

Singular

	NOMINATIVE CASE	OBJECTIVE CASE	POSSESSIVE CASE
FIRST PERSON	I	me	my, mine
SECOND PERSON	you	you	your, yours
THIRD PERSON	he, she, it	him, her, it	his, her hers, its

Plural

	NOMINATIVE CASE	OBJECTIVE CASE	POSSESSIVE CASE
FIRST PERSON	we	us	our, ours
SECOND PERSON	you	you	your, yours
THIRD PERSON	they	them	their, theirs

Two of the pronouns in the list above—*you* and *it*—have the same form in the nominative and objective case; therefore they present no special problems. Ignore these two and concentrate on the following forms:

NOMINATIVE CASE	OBJECTIVE CASE
I	me
he	him
she	her
we	us
they	them

● EXERCISE 1. On your paper, write the case of each pronoun below. If you find that you need to consult the list of pronouns above, you should review the nominative and objective forms until you know them thoroughly.

1. me   2. him   3. she   4. I   5. them
6. her   7. we   8. they   9. he   10. us

● EXERCISE 2. Write from memory the following personal pronouns.

1. First person plural, objective case
2. Third person singular, nominative case, feminine

3. Third person plural, nominative case
4. First person plural, nominative case
5. Third person singular, possessive case, masculine
6. First person singular, objective case
7. Third person singular, objective case, feminine
8. Third person plural, objective case
9. First person singular, nominative case
10. Third person singular, possessive case, neuter

THE NOMINATIVE CASE

7a. The subject of a verb is in the nominative case.

EXAMPLES   Both **he** and **I** noticed the mistake. [*He* and *I* are subjects of the verb *noticed*.]

My parents and **she** arrived on time. [*She* is the subject of *arrived*.]

We expected that **he** would drive. [*We* is the subject of *expected*, and *he* is the subject of *would drive*.]

Most errors involving pronouns as subjects arise when the subject is compound. People who would never say, "Me went to the movies," often do make the mistake of saying, "George and me went to the movies." The best way of avoiding this error is to try each subject separately with the verb, adapting the verb form as necessary. Your ear will tell you which form is correct.

WRONG   Him and me are cocaptains. [*Him* is a cocaptain? *Me* is a cocaptain?]

RIGHT   He and I are cocaptains. [*He* is a cocaptain. *I* am a cocaptain.]

The pronouns *we* and *they* frequently sound awkward as part of a compound subject. In such cases, it is usually easy enough to revise the sentence.

AWKWARD   We and they plan to go to camp together.
BETTER   We plan to go to camp with them.

Pronouns are sometimes used with a noun appositive:

We sophomores have a hard time of it.

To determine the right case form to use in such a situation, try reading the sentence without the appositive.

We have a hard time of it.

● EXERCISE 3. *Oral Drill.* Read each of the following sentences aloud several times, stressing the italicized words.

1. *She* and *I* are good friends.
2. Irving and *he* plan to buy the boat.
3. Either Nancy or *she* will record the minutes.
4. *We* judges have made up our minds.
5. Neither *we* nor *they* are at fault.
6. When are *you* and *he* coming to see me?
7. The team and *we* cheerleaders have to leave early.
8. At the end of the movie, *he* and *she* get married.
9. Are *she* and *I* partners again?
10. Our family and *they* have known each other for years.

● EXERCISE 4. Number your paper 1–15. Choose correct pronouns for the blanks in the following sentences. Vary your pronouns. Do not use *you* and *it*.

1. The others and —— saw the movie.
2. Ted and —— went to the game last week.
3. My friend Walt and —— proved our answer.
4. Finally —— fellows found the subway.
5. —— and —— didn't have the right change.
6. The usher said that —— and —— were in the wrong seats.
7. Neither Betsy nor —— has ever been to Seattle.
8. Yesterday —— and —— mailed our applications for the job.
9. Mother explained why —— and —— would not be able to attend.
10. —— girls are having a hockey game this afternoon.
11. Mrs. Hanifan suggested that —— and —— serve the refreshments.
12. —— and —— were the proofreaders for the yearbook.
13. Rick and —— delivered the newspapers.

7a

14. —— boys had been given some tough assignments.
15. Mary and —— sauntered down the hall.

● EXERCISE 5. Use the following subjects in sentences of your own.

1. My best friend and I
2. We experts
3. They and their parents
4. Betty, Alice, and she
5. He and I

● EXERCISE 6. Number 1–20 in a column on your paper. Read each of the following sentences *aloud*. Decide whether the italicized pronouns are in the correct case. If all of them in a sentence are correct, put a + after the proper number on your paper; if any of them is not, put a 0 and write the correct form of any incorrect pronoun.

1. Frank and *he* are taller than Bob and *I* are.
2. You know that Bob and *me* are short for our age.
3. You and *I* were selected to represent our school in the finals.
4. *Him* and *me* went to see the guidance counselor.
5. Louise and *her* decided to join the Glee Club.
6. *He* and the principal have been talking for a long time.
7. *We* sophomores are going to play the juniors next week.
8. Everybody believed that you and *him* were good friends.
9. You and *her* should take the five o'clock train.
10. What did *he* and your friend want?
11. You and *him* must have known each other a long time.
12. Can Tom and *she* borrow the record player?
13. My kid brother and *him* always embarrassed Helen.
14. Abe and *him* will be pleased with the results.
15. Did you know that Ann and *me* were planning a victory party?
16. Your mother and *he* look very happy.
17. Will you and *she* collect the tickets?
18. *Us* band members got new uniforms.
19. I hope that Fred and *me* don't get lost.
20. Sara and *I* will supply the cake for the party.

7b. A predicate nominative is in the nominative case.

A predicate nominative is a noun or pronoun in the predicate that refers to the same thing as the subject of the sentence. It follows a linking verb. The exercises and examples in this chapter concentrate on pronouns as predicate nominatives, since nouns in this position present no problem.

COMMON FORMS OF <u>BE</u>		PREDICATE NOMINATIVE
am		I
is, are		he
was, were	*are*	she
may be, can be, will be, etc.	*followed*	we
may have been, etc.	*by*	you
want to be, like to be, etc.		they

EXAMPLES   It was **they** who suggested the picnic.
Are you sure it was **she**?
It might have been **he**.

◆ USAGE NOTE   It is now perfectly acceptable to use *me* as a predicate nominative in informal usage: *It's me*. (The construction rarely comes up in formal situations.) The plural form (*It's us*) is also generally accepted. However, using the objective case for the third person form of the pronoun (*It's him*, *It's them*) is still often regarded as unacceptable. When you encounter any of these expressions in the exercises in this book or in the various tests you take, you will be wise to take a conservative attitude and use the nominative forms in all instances.

● EXERCISE 7.   Remembering that a predicate nominative is in the nominative case, supply the pronouns specified for the following:

1. It might have been ——. (Third person singular, feminine)
2. It could be ——. (Third person plural)
3. That was ——. (Third person singular, masculine)
4. It certainly wasn't ——. (Third person plural)

7b

● REVIEW EXERCISE A.   Number your paper 1–20. After the proper number, write a pronoun that will correctly fill each space in the following sentences. Try to use as many different pronouns as you can. Do not use *you* or *it*. Be ready to explain the reasons for your choice.

1. Dad and —— put the screens up.
2. I didn't know it was ——.
3. I hope that Tom and —— will attend the reception.
4. —— clarinet players were told to report to the band room.
5. Everyone watched when Pat and —— did the rumba.
6. What do John and —— think?
7. Did you know that —— and —— were there?
8. The best writers for the paper are —— and ——.
9. Sally and —— were going to typing class.
10. It was —— who delivered the message.
11. Mike and —— will arrange the posters in the display case.
12. Was it —— or Jean who wanted a special meeting of the Student Council?
13. Jerry believed that it was Lester and —— who had made the arrangements.
14. They said that —— girls should go to the end of the line.
15. Neither Richard nor —— can attend practice today.
16. My aunt and —— come from Richmond, Virginia.
17. —— girls can't make up our minds.
18. —— and —— are never satisfied with their work.
19. I am sure that the winner could not have been ——.
20. Did —— and —— object to your leaving so early?

THE OBJECTIVE CASE

The pronouns *me*, *him*, *her*, *us*, and *them* are in the objective case. These pronouns are used as direct and indirect objects and as objects of prepositions.

7c. The object of a verb is in the objective case.

EXAMPLES   The deer suddenly sighted **us**. [direct object]
I handed **him** the rifle. [indirect object]

As with the nominative forms, the objective forms are mainly troublesome in compound constructions. It is unnatural to say, "The explosion frightened *I*," but you might carelessly say, "The explosion frightened Jim and I." Once again, the solution is to try the parts of the compound object separately.

Pronouns in the objective case may also have noun appositives. Whenever a pronoun is used with a noun in this way, you can always determine the case by omitting the noun.

Everyone blames **us** delinquents.   [They blame *us*, not *we*.]

● EXERCISE 8.   Remembering that the pronoun objects are always in the objective case, supply appropriate pronouns for the blanks in the following sentences. Avoid using the same pronoun throughout. Do not use *you* or *it*.

1. The City Council invited —— to their next meeting.
2. The jury acquitted —— after a long trial.
3. The private saluted —— in an odd way.
4. Did you see Muriel and ——?
5. I thanked —— for his help.
6. The neighbors left —— their dog.
7. Where did you meet ——?
8. We asked his brother and —— about their trip.
9. He accused Roger and —— of not helping with the cooking.
10. Do you really dislike Peggy and ——?
11. She helped Joan and —— with our assignment.
12. I invited Agnes and —— to the barbecue.
13. The new rule affects neither —— nor ——.
14. Did you choose Ray and —— for your committee?
15. The coach criticized Paul and —— for sloppy blocking.
16. Has the artist sketched either Mabel or —— yet?
17. He told —— boys what we wanted to know.
18. The mayor decided to force the governor and —— into declaring their views on the new taxes.
19. The hot sun affected Linda and —— more than it affected me.
20. Father sent —— girls several gifts from Sweden.

7c

● EXERCISE 9. Write ten sentences using personal pronouns (except *you* and *it*). Divide the ten in the following way.

three using pronouns as subjects of verbs
three using pronouns as predicate nominatives
four using pronouns as objects of verbs or as objects of prepositions

● EXERCISE 10. Write ten sentences, each of which uses one of the verbs below. After each verb use a pronoun in a compound direct or indirect object. Do not use *you* and *it*.

1. tell	4. baffle	7. select	10. convince
2. met	5. ask	8. recommend	11. leave
3. encourage	6. grasp	9. expect	12. guarantee

● REVIEW EXERCISE B. Number your paper 1–10. After the proper number, write the personal pronoun that can be substituted for each italicized expression. In those sentences calling for [1st person pron.], use the appropriate one of the following pronouns: *I, we, me, us*.

EXAMPLES 1. Did you call Rose and *Sheila?*
1. *her*
2. Only [1st person pron.] was to blame.
2. *I*

1. The boys were Andy and *Larry*.
2. Mr. Pence showed *Julia* and her mother his new house.
3. She knitted Pete and [1st person pron.] some socks.
4. The lieutenant and *the sergeant* were in a dangerous position.
5. Did my father give you and *Janet* his usual greeting?
6. Please tell Dan and [1st person pron.] what you want us to do.
7. Was it *Charlie* that you were discussing?
8. The best swimmers in camp are Robert and *Eric*.
9. When were you expecting Jane and [1st person pron.]?
10. Everyone was astonished to learn that the culprits were *Jeff and Stanley*.

● REVIEW EXERCISE C. Number your paper 1–15. Select the correct one of the two pronouns in parentheses, and write it after the corresponding number on your paper. Be ready to explain your answers.

1. Bob called Harry and (I, me) last week.
2. Several others and (he, him) were planning a fishing trip.
3. (We, Us) boys would charter a boat.
4. The only inexperienced fishermen would be two other boys and (I, me).
5. Bob gave the teacher and (I, me) directions on how to get to the dock in Freeport.
6. When we arrived at the dock, the captain told Harry and (we, us) where to park our cars.
7. After I had parked the car, the others and (I, me) climbed aboard the boat.
8. I looked for Bob and noticed that (he, him) and the captain were discussing something.
9. The captain warned (we, us) novices that the ocean was rough.
10. (He, Him) and the crew thought it would be perfectly safe.
11. It must have been the experienced fishermen and (he, him) who finally convinced the rest of us.
12. It soon became clear to the others and (I, me) that the captain had meant what he told Harry and (I, me).
13. The boat tossed about on the waves, and Bob and (I, me) clutched at the railing.
14. Neither (he, him) nor (I, me) did any fishing that day.
15. Harry, Bob, and (I, me) could hardly wait to get back on dry land.

● REVIEW EXERCISE D. Using the pronouns below, write ten correct sentences of your own. Include sentences with pronouns used as subjects, predicate nominatives, and objects of verbs. After each sentence, tell how the pronouns are used.

1. he and Al
2. he and I
3. you and me
4. my aunt and them
5. us girls
6. she and I
7. Vera and they
8. Fred and him
9. you and he
10. we students

7d. The object of a preposition is in the objective case.

A prepositional phrase begins with a preposition and ends with a noun or pronoun that is the *object of the preposition*. When the object of a preposition is a pronoun, it must be in the objective case. The bold-faced words below are objects of the prepositions that begin the phrases.

EXAMPLES for **us**   between **you** and **me**   to **him**

Errors in usage occur most often when the object of a preposition is compound. You can usually tell the correct pronoun by trying the parts of the compound object separately.

EXAMPLE I wrote to Martha and (she, her).
            I wrote to she. [wrong]
            I wrote to her. [right]
            I wrote to Martha and her.

Try this test on the following correct examples:

Jobs were available for my *brother* and *me.*

My mother gave the jewelry to *Gail* and *me.*

Did a letter come from *Bess* and *her*?

● EXERCISE 11. In the following sentences, pick out the prepositions which take pronoun objects and list them on your paper. After each, write the correct one of the two pronouns given in parentheses.

1. The coach gave instructions to Chuck and (I, me).
2. The costumes were exactly right for Abby and (she, her).
3. He yelled at Beth and (I, me).
4. All of us can drive except Cindy and (she, her).
5. The feelings against Don and (he, him) became worse.
6. Everybody except Paula and (I, me) had taken the test.
7. The performance was directed by Todd and (he, him).
8. The dog ran after Elmer and (she, her).
9. Will you go with Ann and (I, me)?
10. The editor assigned the story to Greg and (I, me).

● EXERCISE 12.   Select the correct one of the two pronouns in parentheses, and write it on your paper.

1. The complaints were presented to the Student Council by (he, him) and (I, me).
2. When Father said that they had shown good sense, he paid a high compliment to Madge and (he, him).
3. The President had to choose between the colonel and (he, him).
4. They were talking about you and (she, her) for a long time.
5. The distribution of the posters was assigned to (they, them) and (we, us).
6. We took a bus tour yesterday with Terry and (he, him).
7. The guide stood behind Marc and (I, me).
8. The mayor lives near you and (she, her).
9. Mr. Lindsay had nothing to say to Ken and (I, me).
10. The dog growled at (they, them) and (we, us) all during the visit.

● EXERCISE 13.   Write sentences of your own, using each of the following prepositions with a compound object, at least one part of which is a pronoun.

EXAMPLE   1. to
              1. *We are grateful to John and him for their assistance.*

1. into
2. toward
3. from
4. against
5. without

6. beyond
7. for
8. by
9. over
10. except

● EXERCISE 14.   *Oral Drill.* Read *aloud* five times each of the following sentences, stressing the italicized words.

1. The boy finished *after* Ken and *me.*
2. They sent gifts *to* *him* and *me.*
3. Nothing was done *by* either Mr. Arnold or *him.*
4. I left *before* Jan and *her.*
5. Divide the papers *between* Howard and *him.*
6. The man was walking *toward* Doug and *me.*
7. I went to the movies *with* Don and *them.*

7d

8. The pictures look exactly *like* Sue and *her*.
9. Get the tickets *for* Steve and *us*.
10. The joke was *on* Linda and *me*.

SPECIAL PROBLEMS IN PRONOUN USAGE

Who and Whom

The use of *who* and *whom* in questions can no longer be reduced to a strict law. In modern spoken English the distinction between *who* and *whom* is gradually disappearing, and *whom* is going out of use. Among educated people, one often hears *Who do you mean? Who do you know?* According to the rule you have learned about the case of the object of a verb, the speaker should say *whom* in these sentences. However, the rule is applied strictly only in formal writing.

Using *who* and *whom* in subordinate clauses, however, is a different matter. In subordinate clauses the distinction between *who* and *whom* is generally observed in both formal and informal writing.

7e. The use of *who* and *whom* in a subordinate clause is determined by the pronoun's function in the clause.

EXAMPLE   Ed was the reporter **who wrote the stories.** [*Who* is in the nominative case because it is the subject of the verb *wrote* in the subordinate clause.]

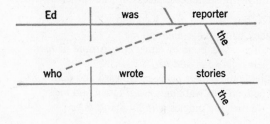

EXAMPLE Ed was the reporter **whom the critics praised.** [*Whom* is in the objective case because it is the object of the verb *praised*, the verb in the subordinate clause.]

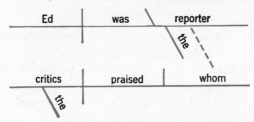

EXAMPLES He is the one **about whom we were talking.**
or
He is the one **whom we were talking about.** [*Whom* is in the objective case because it is the object of the preposition *about* in the subordinate clause.]

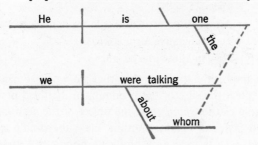

Follow these steps in deciding whether to use *who* or *whom* in a subordinate clause:

1. Pick out the subordinate clause.
2. Decide how the pronoun is used in that clause.
3. Determine the case of the pronoun according to the usual rules.
4. Select the correct form of the pronoun.

PROBLEM Peter is the boy (who, whom) discovered the fire.

Step 1 The subordinate clause is (*who, whom*) *discovered the fire.*

Step 2 The pronoun is the subject of the clause.

7e

Step 3   Since it functions as a subject, the pronoun must be in the nominative case.

Step 4   The nominative form is *who.*

SOLUTION   Peter is the boy **who** discovered the fire.

PROBLEM   That is my friend Carol, (who, whom) I met at camp.

Step 1   The subordinate clause is (*who, whom*) *I met at camp.*

Step 2   The pronoun is the object of the verb *met: I met (who, whom).*

Step 3   The object of a verb is in the objective case.

Step 4   The objective form of *who* is *whom.*

SOLUTION   That is my friend Carol, **whom** I met at camp.

PROBLEM   Do you know (who, whom) he is?

Step 1   The subordinate clause is (*who, whom*) *he is.*

Step 2   The pronoun is the predicate nominative: *he is (who, whom).*

Step 3   A predicate nominative is in the nominative case.

Step 4   The nominative form is *who.*

SOLUTION   Do you know **who** he is?

It is important to remember that no words outside the clause affect the case of the pronoun. In the third problem, the whole clause *who he is* is the object of the verb *know* in the independent clause. Within the subordinate clause, however, *who* is used as a predicate nominative and takes the nominative case.

◆ USAGE NOTE   *Whom* is often omitted (understood) in subordinate clauses.

EXAMPLE   The girl [whom] I marry must be a good cook.

● EXERCISE 15.   Copy on your paper each subordinate clause in the sentences below. Then tell how the pronoun (*who* or *whom*) is used in its own clause—as subject, predicate nominative, object of a verb, or object of a preposition.

EXAMPLE   1. He is someone whom we all admire.
              1. *whom we all admire, object of verb*

1. Henry Ford, who was a young machinist in Detroit in 1890, began experimenting with engines.
2. He was one of those men whom we all can admire for their diligence and persistence.
3. In 1896 he surprised those who scoffed at the idea of a horse-less carriage by building his first automobile.
4. Whomever young Henry spoke to soon realized the ambition of the young machinist.
5. At first there were many who found the cost of the cars prohibitive.
6. Henry Ford, whom we acknowledge as a pioneer in mass production, was one of the first to use assembly-line methods.
7. He was also one of the first who introduced a profit-sharing plan into business.
8. Before you read this, did you know who it was that put America on wheels?

● EXERCISE 16. Number your paper 1–10. After the proper number, give the use of the pronoun in parentheses. After the use, write the correct form of the pronoun.

EXAMPLE 1. James Boswell, (who, whom) wrote *The Life of Johnson,* is also known for the famous journal that he kept.

    1. *subject of subordinate clause, who*

1. Dr. Samuel Johnson, (who, whom) James Boswell idolized, was considered one of the most influential men of the eighteenth century.
2. He was a man (who, whom) helped to mold the literary standards of his age.
3. The literary men of his time, with (who, whom) he was always talking or arguing, considered him a genius.
4. We know (who, whom) many of Samuel Johnson's friends were.
5. David Garrick, Oliver Goldsmith, and Sir Joshua Reyɔlds were some (who, whom) he numbered among his friend:.
6. This famous man supported many unfortunate people (who, whom) happened to need help.
7. Gruff and stern as he often seemed, there were few (ѵ ɩo, whom) could resist his conversation.

8. James Boswell, (who, whom) was regarded by many as a foolish idler, talked with Dr. Johnson on many different occasions.
9. Fortunately the young biographer (who, whom) recorded Dr. Johnson's conversations was also a gifted writer.
10. Through his great book, the young man (who, whom) few took seriously became as famous as Dr. Johnson himself.

● REVIEW EXERCISE E. Number your paper 1–20. After the proper number, write how the pronoun in parentheses is used—subject, predicate nominative, object of a verb, object of a preposition. Use the usual abbreviations for these terms.

On the basis of its use, select the correct pronoun and write it on your paper.

1. The instructions were given to Steve and (I, me).
2. Everyone knew (who, whom) the astronauts were.
3. The teacher wants to see you and (I, me) after school.
4. Are Marie and (she, her) in charge of the dance?
5. Have the packages arrived for Doris and (I, me)?
6. You may ask (whoever, whomever) you want.
7. My mother was seated near Dad and (I, me).
8. (He, Him) and (I, me) run the school store.
9. The boys selected as ushers were Hank and (he, him).
10. Was it you or (he, him) who bought the tennis racket?
11. The director interviewed (whoever, whomever) was interested in the part.
12. I believe you know (who, whom) we are referring to.
13. Is there anyone (who, whom) she likes?
14. There are some letters for Don and (he, him) on the table.
15. My aunt and (she, her) always shop at that store.
16. They introduced Jay and (I, me) to the new girls.
17. After the dance we took Eve and (she, her) to Hamburger Heaven.
18. He sounds like somebody (who, whom) knows what he is talking about.
19. Do you suppose it might have been (they, them)?
20. My sister and (I, me) argue constantly.

● REVIEW EXERCISE F. Number your paper 1–20. Write the correct pronoun next to the proper number.

1. This book appeals to Joe and (he, him).
2. I just told you (who, whom) they are.
3. We don't know (who, whom) we should send.
4. Kevin will meet (whoever, whomever) arrives by train.
5. Between you and (I, me), he won't play in the first game.
6. Were you and (he, him) here when they arrived?
7. (We, Us) boys used the car last night.
8. Give the book to (whoever, whomever) asks for it.
9. Judy passed the note to Sally and (I, me).
10. Think of all the people (who, whom) she has helped.
11. The boss fired Ellen and (I, me).
12. Lou and (we, us) rented tuxedos for the dance.
13. Don't you know (who, whom) he likes?
14. The officer gave a warning to him and (I, me).
15. They thanked Paul and (I, me) for our help.
16. (Whoever, Whomever) sits in the last seat will distribute the dictionaries.
17. Tell Helen and (I, me) all the details.
18. (We, Us) girls enjoyed talking to you.
19. We sat so far away that we could not tell (who, whom) the player was.
20. Consider how Frank and (he, him) must be sweltering under the hot sun.

● REVIEW EXERCISE G. Number your paper 1–20. For each correct sentence in which the pronouns are all in the proper case, place a + after the corresponding number on your paper; for each incorrect sentence, place a 0.

1. May Max and I bring our guitars?
2. Tell Dad and me what you need.
3. I do not know who you mean.
4. The client selected the broker who Mr. Calhoun recommended.
5. Your statements are incorrect according to Jean and she.
6. He explained the procedure to Tim and I.
7. The usher showed Ben and me to our seats.
8. We laughed at Irene and her.

9. They handed Carl and him the banners.
10. Under the tree were sitting Louise and he.
11. The announcer introduced we girls to the audience.
12. Peggy and me had practiced for days.
13. Everybody but Ken and him crossed the finish line.
14. You and I know the value of good marks.
15. The book was written for people like Neil and he.
16. Faye and me fixed the broken latch.
17. We saw your brother and them at the bus station.
18. Harriet showed Gwen and me her new dress.
19. The rains came before he and I had a chance to close the windows.
20. It was us girls who were caught in the storm.

The Pronoun in Incomplete Constructions

7f. After *than* and *as* in an incomplete construction, use the form of the pronoun you would use if the construction were completed.

The following are examples of incomplete constructions. In each one, part of the sentence is omitted and is included in the brackets.

My brother is older than **I.**   [than I am old]
They like him more than **me.**   [than they like me]

From these two examples of an incomplete construction, you will notice that you should use the form of the pronoun which you would use if you completed the sentence. Thus in the first sentence, *I* is correct because it is the subject of the clause *I am old.* In the second sentence, *me* is correct because it is the object of the verb *like* in the clause *they like me.*

Now examine this pair of sentences:

I know Jerry better than **he.**   [than *he* knows Jerry]
I know Jerry better than **him.**   [than I know *him*]

As you can see, the case of the pronoun depends on how the sentence is completed. Both the sentences above are correct, but the sentences are quite different in meaning; they are completed in different ways.

● EXERCISE 17. Write out each of the following sentences, supplying the omitted part and using the correct form of the pronoun. After the sentence, write the use of the pronoun in its clause. Some of the sentences may be completed in two different ways.

1. Few get better grades than (he, him).
2. We ate more than (they, them).
3. Hazel left just as early as (I, me).
4. I am a little shorter than (he, him).
5. Mrs. Jones likes Melinda more than (she, her).
6. Owen complained that he needed more practice than (we, us).
7. Did you do as well in the test as (I, me)?
8. Isabel started later than (we, us).
9. She did more for Marge than (I, me).
10. I'm sure I can't run as fast as (he, him).

● REVIEW EXERCISE H. Number your paper 1–20. Select the correct one of the two pronouns given in parentheses, and write it after the proper number on your paper. Be prepared to give reasons for your answer.

1. Betty and (he, him) sang a duet.
2. The coach gave the equipment to (whoever, whomever) needed it.
3. Can you speak French as well as (he, him)?
4. The majorettes were Linda, Janet, and (she, her).
5. I met Kathy and (she, her) at the corner.
6. He planned to sit across from Ted and (I, me).
7. Somebody must know (who, whom) caused the delay.
8. I would rather ask you than (he, him).
9. No one else can draw as well as (she, her).
10. You and (I, me) should get together soon.
11. The check was cashed by either Perry or (he, him).
12. Marie saw both Sandy and (I, me) at the game.
13. Dad taught Ronnie and (I, me) how to drive.
14. The man praised (he, him) and (I, me).

7f

15. It is necessary for (he, him) and (I, me) to reduce our expenses.
16. Did they arrive earlier than (we, us)?
17. Did you receive a card from Al and (he, him)?
18. We are just as excited as (they, them).
19. The soldier (who, whom) the general had decorated stood at attention.
20. The dog frisked around Kevin and (I, me).

● REVIEW EXERCISE I. Number your paper 1–25. If a sentence contains an incorrect pronoun, write the correct form after the proper number on your paper. For each correct sentence, write *C* after the corresponding number on your paper.

1. I don't know whom it was.
2. You should do better than her.
3. Don and him play in the backfield.
4. Can you tell the difference between his brother and him?
5. No one knew to whom the article referred.
6. Mr. Keene gave Bill and I a ride home.
7. Ask Sam and he when they are leaving.
8. Jessie and me will take turns.
9. Gary is better prepared than I.
10. I will take whomever wants to come.
11. I do not know who I should believe.
12. Karen and her can make up their work.
13. If it was them, you will soon know it.
14. The boat was built by Sid and he.
15. There are some students whom no teacher can interest.
16. Kurt and I decided not to bother you and them.
17. Ned and he discovered whom the thief was.
18. Is there any mail for Dorothy or I?
19. I am sure that us students will be criticized.
20. He is a man whom everyone likes.
21. I met Fred and she at the bus station.
22. Jim and he are not so successful as them.
23. Is Phil expecting you or I?
24. Please tell Keith and I what she said.
25. If you expect we boys to help you, you must help us.

CHAPTER 8

Using Verbs Correctly

Principal Parts, Tense, Voice

The choice of an incorrect verb is one of the most common and noticeable of usage errors. The writer who wants to suggest that a character is poorly educated has only to make him say, "I should have went" or "He brung it" to create the impression he is after. Of course, the notion that all such errors are signs of lack of education is silly; many errors in verb usage are simply the result of carelessness. In any case, mistakes in verb usage are noticeable, and it is well worth your while to find which ones you make regularly and to correct them.

KINDS OF VERBS

All verbs help to make a statement about their subjects. *Action* verbs do so by expressing an action performed by the subject:

ACTION VERBS   Ruth **swims** like a fish.

Macbeth **remembered** the witches' prediction.

As the second example indicates, the action expressed may be mental as well as physical: *dream, think,* and *ignore* are action verbs, just as *run, jump,* and *strike* are.

155

Some verbs help to make a statement by linking with the subject a word in the predicate that explains, describes, or in some other way makes the subject more definite. Such verbs are called *linking* verbs.

LINKING VERBS   Our opponents **were** jubilant. [The adjective *jubilant* describes the subject *opponents*.]

At least we **are** good losers. [The noun *losers* gives information about the subject *we*.]

Some verbs can be either action or linking verbs depending upon the way they are used:

ACTION VERB   The detective **looked** for clues.
LINKING VERB   The detective **looked** puzzled.

There are not many linking verbs in English; you will find a list of the commonly used ones on page 13. The main reason for knowing the difference between linking and action verbs is to be able to choose the appropriate form of a pronoun that follows the verb.

PRINCIPAL PARTS

Verbs have four basic forms from which all other forms are made. These are called the principal parts of the verb.

8a. The principal parts of a verb are the *infinitive*, the *present participle*, the *past*, and the *past participle*.

INFINITIVE	PRESENT PARTICIPLE	PAST	PAST PARTICIPLE
play	(is) playing	played	(have) played
go	(is) going	went	(have) gone

The words *is* and *have* are included to remind you that the present participle is used with some form of the helping verb *be* and the past participle mainly with a form of the helping verb *have*.

Regular Verbs

8b. A *regular verb* is one that forms its past and past participle by adding *–ed* or *–d* to the infinitive form.[1]

INFINITIVE	PAST	PAST PARTICIPLE
work	work**ed**	(have) work**ed**
receive	received	(have) received
saddle	saddle**d**	(have) saddle**d**

Irregular Verbs

8c. An *irregular verb* is one that forms its past and past participle in some other way than a regular verb.

Some irregular verbs form the past and past participle forms by changing the vowels, some by changing the consonants, and others by making no change at all.

INFINITIVE	PAST	PAST PARTICIPLE
bring	brought	(have) bro**ught**
begin	began	(have) beg**un**
fly	flew	(have) flown
bu:st	burst	(have) burst
sit	sat	(have) sat
tear	tore	(have) tor**n**

Since irregular verbs form their past and past participles in unpredictable ways, there is nothing to do but memorize the forms of at least the most common ones. You doubtless already know most of the irregular verbs listed below. Nevertheless, you should study the list carefully, concentrating on the ones that give you trouble.

[1] A few regular verbs have an alternative past form ending in *–t*; for example, he *burns* (present), he *burned* or *burnt* (past), and he has *burned* or *burnt* (past participle).

8
a-c

COMMON IRREGULAR VERBS

INFINITIVE	PRESENT PARTICIPLE	PAST	PAST PARTICIPLE
begin	beginning	began	(have) begun
blow	blowing	blew	(have) blown
break	breaking	broke	(have) broken
bring	bringing	brought	(have) brought
burst	bursting	burst	(have) burst
choose	choosing	chose	(have) chosen
come	coming	came	(have) come
do	doing	did	(have) done
drink	drinking	drank	(have) drunk
drive	driving	drove	(have) driven
fall	falling	fell	(have) fallen
freeze	freezing	froze	(have) frozen
give	giving	gave	(have) given
go	going	went	(have) gone
ride	riding	rode	(have) ridden
ring	ringing	rang	(have) rung
run	running	ran	(have) run
see	seeing	saw	(have) seen
shrink	shrinking	shrank	(have) shrunk
speak	speaking	spoke	(have) spoken
steal	stealing	stole	(have) stolen
swim	swimming	swam	(have) swum
take	taking	took	(have) taken
throw	throwing	threw	(have) thrown
write	writing	wrote	(have) written

● EXERCISE 1. Your teacher will dictate to you the first principal part of the twenty-five irregular verbs listed above. Write from memory the past and the past participle. Placing *have* before the past participle will help you to learn that this is the form used with *have*, *has*, and *had*.

● EXERCISE 2. After the appropriate number on your paper, write the correct form (past or past participle) of the verb given at the beginning of the sentence. If necessary, refer to the list above.

1. *do*   Yesterday the girls —— their assignments in the study hall.

2. *come*   Nobody —— to take away our rubbish last week.

3. *begin*   Lucy had already —— to get seasick.

4. *run*   Because Adam had —— the projector before, we didn't need any help.

5. *see*   In the newspaper last Saturday, Barry —— an advertisement for transistor radios.

6. *write*   She has —— to them for information.

7. *ring*   The late bell has not —— yet.

8. *go*   The family has —— to Glacier Park for their vacation.

9. *give*   Clyde has —— the garage two coats of paint.

10. *drink*   He —— a whole quart of milk with his lunch.

11. *break*   She has —— her watch again.

12. *speak*   The guidance counselor had —— to the seniors about the new college requirements.

13. *swim*   Last week he —— the entire length of Long Lake.

14. *throw*   My mother has —— all the old shoes out.

15. *take*   They had —— ten dollars with them.

16. *ride*   We have —— on this bus once too often.

17. *blow*   The fence had been —— down by the storm.

18. *burst*   The small child —— into the room and began looking for the presents.

19. *choose*   The candidates have been —— by the student body.

20. *bring*   Had anybody —— the can opener?

21. *fall*   A few shingles had —— off the roof the year before.

22. *drive*   Haven't you ever —— a car before?

23. *shrink*   My shirt has —— in the wash.

24. *steal*   Somebody has —— his gym shoes.

25. *freeze*   The pond has —— over twice this year.

● EXERCISE 3. Choose the correct one of the two verbs in parentheses, and write it after the proper number on your paper. When your paper has been corrected, read each sentence to yourself several times, using the correct word.

1. The teacher sat down behind the desk and (began, begun) to take the attendance.

2. He had (wrote, written) to his grandmother.

3. The coach really (threw, throwed) a fit because you missed practice.
4. He (did, done) the best he could.
5. Who has (drank, drunk) all the soda?
6. The principal (came, come) into the room and asked to speak with Mike.
7. I've (saw, seen) that movie twice already.
8. The puppy has (tore, torn) the slippers to bits.
9. Who's (took, taken) the newspaper?
10. My car had (broke, broken) down in Maryland.
11. What (give, gave) you the idea that he was going?
12. He has (ran, run) the press several times before.
13. I wish you had (spoke, spoken) to me last week.
14. I dived into the pool and (swam, swum) to the opposite side.
15. Millie (rang, rung) the bell, but nobody answered.
16. They just (came, come) from Virginia yesterday.
17. We should have (went, gone) long before this.
18. The King had never (ate, eaten) pizza before.
19. The rain (blowed, blew) in through the window.
20. We would have (froze, frozen) if we had waited for the bus.
21. The balloon (burst, bursted) when he stuck a pin into it.
22. Dean was not (chose, chosen) to be on the team.
23. He (brought, brung) his library books back.
24. He was (drove, driven) to distraction by all the noise.
25. The lion had (fell, fallen) into the trap again.

● EXERCISE 4. Number your paper 1–20. If the first principal part is given, change it to the past form. If the past form is given, change it to the past participle. Write *have* before the past participle form.

    EXAMPLES 1. see
                1. *saw*
                2. ran
                2. *have run*

1. break	6. rode	11. drank	16. throw
2. climbed	7. steal	12. fall	17. write
3. swam	8. rang	13. shrink	18. brought
4. drive	9. blew	14. do	19. go
5. chose	10. froze	15. spoke	20. took

TENSE

Verbs change form to show the time of the action or the idea they express. The time indicated by the form of a verb is called its *tense*. There are six tenses, each of which is formed in one way or another from the principal parts of the verb. A systematic listing of all the verb forms used in the six tenses is called a *conjugation*.

The conjugations that follow for the verbs *walk* and *grow* illustrate the tense forms of two common verbs, one regular and the other irregular.

8d. Learn the names of the six tenses and how the tenses are formed.

CONJUGATION OF THE VERB <u>WALK</u>

Present infinitive: *to walk*   Perfect infinitive: *to have walked*

PRINCIPAL PARTS

INFINITIVE	PRESENT PARTICIPLE	PAST	PAST PARTICIPLE
walk	walking	walked	walked

PRESENT TENSE

Singular	*Plural*
I walk	we walk
you walk	you walk
he, she, it walks	they walk

Present progressive: *I am walking*, etc.[1]

PAST TENSE

Singular	*Plural*
I walked	we walked
you walked	you walked
he, she, it walked	they walked

Past progressive: *I was walking*, etc.

[1] The present progressive is not a separate tense but a form of the present tense since it shows present time. There is a progressive form for each of the six tenses.

8d

FUTURE TENSE

(*will* or *shall* + the infinitive[1])

Singular	*Plural*
I will (shall) walk	we will (shall) walk
you will walk	you will walk
he, she, it will walk	they will walk

Future progressive: *I will be walking*, etc.

PRESENT PERFECT TENSE

(*have* or *has* + the past participle)

Singular	*Plural*
I have walked	we have walked
you have walked	you have walked
he, she, it has walked	they have walked

Present perfect progressive: *I have been walking*, etc.

PAST PERFECT TENSE

(*had* + the past participle)

Singular	*Plural*
I had walked	we had walked
you had walked	you had walked
he, she, it had walked	they had walked

Past perfect progressive: *I had been walking*, etc.

FUTURE PERFECT TENSE

(*will have* or *shall have* + the past participle)

Singular	*Plural*
I will (shall) have walked	we will (shall) have walked
you will have walked	you will have walked
he, she, it will have walked	they will have walked

Future perfect progressive: *I will have been walking*, etc.

CONJUGATION OF THE VERB <u>GROW</u>

Present infinitive: *to grow*   Perfect infinitive: *to have grown*

PRINCIPAL PARTS

INFINITIVE	PRESENT PARTICIPLE	PAST	PAST PARTICIPLE
grow	growing	grew	grown

[1] For a discussion of the use of *shall* and *will*, see pages 207–08.

PRESENT TENSE

Singular	*Plural*
I grow	we grow
you grow	you grow
he, she, it grows	they grow

Present progressive: *I am growing*, etc.

PAST TENSE

Singular	*Plural*
I grew	we grew
you grew	you grew
he, she, it grew	they grew

Past progressive: *I was growing*, etc.

FUTURE TENSE

(*will* or *shall* + the infinitive)

Singular	*Plural*
I will (shall) grow	we will (shall) grow
you will grow	you will grow
he, she, it will grow	they will grow

Future progressive: *I will be growing*, etc.

PRESENT PERFECT TENSE

(*has* or *have* + the past participle)

Singular	*Plural*
I have grown	we have grown
you have grown	you have grown
he, she, it has grown	they have grown

Present perfect progressive: *I have been growing*, etc.

PAST PERFECT TENSE

(*had* + the past participle)

Singular	*Plural*
I had grown	we had grown
you had grown	you had grown
he, she, it had grown	they had grown

Past perfect progressive: *I had been growing*, etc.

FUTURE PERFECT TENSE

(*will have* or *shall have* + the past participle)

Singular	Plural
I will (shall) have grown	we will (shall) have grown
you will have grown	you will have grown
he, she, it will have grown	they will have grown

Future perfect progressive: *I will have been growing*, etc.

8e. Learn the uses of the six tenses.

Each of the six tenses has its own uses. Sometimes the tense of a verb expresses time only; at other times tense may tell whether or not the action is still going on. Study the following explanations and examples carefully, and then refer to these pages frequently as you work the exercises.

(1) The *present tense* is used to express action (or help to make a statement about something) occurring now, at the present time.

EXAMPLES   Sonja **drives** a tractor.
Elmer **is** our new president.
He **is planning** a party.

◆ NOTE   The third example illustrates the present progressive tense. Each tense has a progressive form, which is used to indicate that the action expressed by the verb is continuing.

In addition to indicating present time, the present tense has some special uses. It is used to indicate habitual action:

He **practices** the piano an hour every day.

The present tense is also used to express a general truth—something that is true at all times.

Gus found it hard to believe that the earth **is** [not *was*] round.

(2) The *past tense* is used to express action (or help to make a statement about something) that occurred in the past but did not continue into the present. The past is regularly formed by adding *-d* or *-ed*.

EXAMPLES   The pitcher **scowled** at the catcher.
            The pitcher **was scowling** at the catcher.
            I **used to baby-sit** for the neighbors.

(3) The *future tense* is used to express action (or help to make a statement about something) at some time in the future. The future tense is formed with *will* or *shall*.

EXAMPLES   I **will study** harder from now on.
            I **will be studying** harder from now on.

There are several other ways of indicating future time.

EXAMPLES   I **am going to study** harder from now on.
            I **start tomorrow.** [present with another word clearly indicating future time]

(4) The *present perfect tense* is used to express action (or help to make a statement about something) occurring at no definite time in the past. It is formed with *have* or *has*.

EXAMPLE   She **has spoken** often before.

The present perfect tense is also used to express action (or help to make a statement about something) occurring in the past and continuing into the present.

EXAMPLES   She **has stayed** here for two weeks. [She is still staying here.]
            I **have been doing** my homework for hours. [I am still doing it.]

(5) The *past perfect tense* is used to express action (or help to make a statement about something) completed in the past before some other past action or event. It is formed with *had*.

EXAMPLES   After she **had stayed** for two weeks, she grew homesick. [The action of staying preceded the action of growing homesick.]
            When he **had worked** for an hour, he suddenly quit.

8e

(6) The *future perfect tense* is used to express action (or help to make a statement about something) which will be completed in the future before some other future action or event. It is formed with *shall have* or *will have*.

EXAMPLES By the time I finish, I **shall have used** up all my paper. [The using up will precede the finishing.]

By the time I finish, I **shall have been working** steadily for three hours.

● EXERCISE 5. Explain the difference in meaning between the sentences in the following pairs. Both sentences in each pair are correct. Name the tense used in each sentence.

1. She took ballet lessons for two years.
   She has taken ballet lessons for two years.
2. How long have you been here?
   How long were you here?
3. When I am nineteen, I shall join the Marines.
   When I am nineteen, I shall have joined the Marines.
4. What went on at the dance?
   What has been going on at the dance?
5. Have you waited long?
   Had you waited long?
6. Nina was told that her mother was impatient.
   Nina was told that her mother had been impatient.
7. When you come back, I shall finish.
   When you come back, I shall have finished.
8. I believed the car was running well.
   I had believed the car was running well.
9. The coach said Hal had poison ivy.
   The coach said Hal had had poison ivy.
10. Georgette was a cheerleader for two years.
    Georgette has been a cheerleader for two years.

● EXERCISE 6. Copy the following sentences on your paper, changing the tenses of the verbs as indicated in parentheses.

1. When the bell rings, I shall finish. (Change *shall finish* to future perfect.)
2. Ivan worked there for a year. (Change to past perfect.)
3. Is she waiting? (Change to present perfect progressive.)
4. Were you sick? (Change to past perfect.)
5. When I leave, will you wash the dishes? (Change *will wash* to future perfect.)
6. Olivia enjoys bowling. (Change to future tense.)
7. The dog barks. (Change to present perfect.)
8. The truck had broken down. (Change to past.)
9. At four, Joel will have finished. (Change to future.)
10. I was in Paris for two weeks. (Change to present perfect.)

Young writers, especially when writing informal essays or narratives, sometimes begin their compositions in one tense and then lapse into another tense. Such lapses are due largely to carelessness, for students usually understand the error when it is pointed out to them. The exercises on the next few pages are intended to make you aware of this kind of error in written English.

Consistency of Tense

8f. Do not change needlessly from one tense to another.

WRONG   Luke *(past)* lunged at the basketball and *(present)* grabs it before the Meadville player *(past)* could reach him. [mixture of past and present tenses]

RIGHT   Luke *(past)* lunged at the basketball and *(past)* grabbed it before the Meadville player *(past)* could reach him. [past tense throughout]

RIGHT   Luke *(present)* lunges at the basketball and *(present)* grabs it before the Meadville player *(present)* can reach him. [present tense throughout]

8f

● EXERCISE 7. Before doing this exercise, review the rules on the use of tenses (pages 164–67). Number your paper 1–20. After each number, list the verbs that are in the wrong tense. After each, write the appropriate tense form. If there are no incorrectly used verbs in a particular sentence, write *C* after the proper number on your paper.

1. In 480 B.C. the vast army of Xerxes came down through Thessaly, laying waste to the land. 2. Below them, protected only by the narrow pass at Thermopylae, lie the Greek city states, unprepared and ripe for plunder. 3. As the Persian host paused at the foot of the mountain and prepares to pass through, scouts filter back from the van. 4. They bring the report that the pass is occupied by a little band of Spartans, led by young Leonidas. 5. Leonidas sends his defiance and swore never to budge from the pass. 6. Xerxes laughs when he hears this report and beckons forward his veteran legions of Medes and Cissians. 7. He bids them to bring him the head of this madman to hang on his chariot.

8. The next day goes badly for Xerxes. 9. He chafed all day in the hot sun while, high above him in the windy pass, the haughty Persians throw themselves on the lances of the Greeks. 10. That night 20,000 campfires sparkled around him on the vast plain like fireflies. 11. In his tent Xerxes stalks up and down like a caged tiger. 12. In the morning he summons his "Immortals," heroes who would have fought with gods, and sent them into the "hot gates," as the pass was called. 13. That night when the red sun had at last sunk into the west, a few last survivors stumble into camp, sobbing with pain and weariness. 14. In his tent Xerxes hid his face in his hands.

15. On the third day, Ephialtes, a Greek traitor, showed the Persians a way to come upon the Greeks from the rear. 16. High among the crags, Leonidas was brought word that the Persians have cut off his retreat. 17. With his three hundred men, he decides to hold the pass as long as possible. 18. In spite of the hopelessness of his cause, Leonidas doesn't lose heart. 19. A messenger told him that the sky was darkened by Persian arrows. 20. "Good," says Leonidas, "then we will fight in the shade."

ACTIVE AND PASSIVE VOICE

In most English sentences, the subject performs the action of the verb. If there is a receiver of the action, it is expressed by the object of the verb, as in this example:

EXAMPLE The raging flood waters **destroyed** the bridge. [The subject, *waters*, performs the action; the object, *bridge*, tells what was destroyed.]

A verb that expresses action performed by the subject is said to be in the *active voice*.

For reasons of emphasis, however, such sentences are often switched around so that the object becomes the subject:

EXAMPLE The bridge **was destroyed** by the raging flood waters.

Notice that the object has been moved forward to the subject position and that the original subject is now expressed in a prepositional phrase. In addition, the verb has been changed from *destroyed* to *was destroyed*. Verbs that express action performed *upon* their subjects are said to be in the *passive voice*. The passive verb is always a verb phrase consisting of some form of *be* (*is*, *was*, etc.) plus the past participle.

ACTIVE The manager **closes** the theater every Wednesday.
PASSIVE The theater **is closed** every Wednesday.

ACTIVE It **will reopen** on Thursday.
PASSIVE It **will be reopened** on Thursday.

ACTIVE No one **had reported** the fire.
PASSIVE The fire **had** not **been reported.**

Notice that the passive sentences above do not give the performer of the action. When it is important to know who or what performed the action in a passive sentence, the performer is named in a prepositional phrase.

Although the passive construction is useful in situations in which the performer of the action is unknown or unimportant, it can easily be overused. A succession of passive sentences has a weak and awkward sound and should be avoided.

WEAK PASSIVE	The party was enjoyed by all of the guests.
BETTER	All of the guests enjoyed the party.
AWKWARD PASSIVE	When he needed new shoes, another pair of sneakers was bought by him.
BETTER	When he needed new shoes, he bought another pair of sneakers.

● EXERCISE 8. After the appropriate number, indicate whether each of the following sentences is active or passive.

1. Stony Beach is used only by tourists.
2. Until then, everything was going along nicely.
3. Gunpowder was invented by the Chinese.
4. The umpire ejected the manager and several of his players.
5. Jeff was hoping for a better grade.
6. The prize was won by an unknown architect.
7. The jury quickly acquitted the defendant.
8. Because of the heavy fog, all the planes were grounded by the control tower.
9. The homecoming game has been postponed indefinitely by the principal.
10. Some people on a clambake discovered the treasure.

● EXERCISE 9. There are five passive sentences in Exercise 8. Rewrite each one as an active sentence.

SIX TROUBLESOME VERBS

There are three pairs of verbs in English that account for many usage errors: *lie, lay*; *sit, set*; and *rise, raise*. Because the meanings of each pair are related and their forms are similar, it is easy to get them mixed up. The exercises in this section will help you to keep these common verbs straight.

Lie and Lay

The verb *lie* means "to recline" and does not take an object. Its principal parts are *lie, lying, lay, (have) lain.*

The verb *lay* means "to put or place" and takes an object. The principal parts of lay are *lay, laying, laid, (have) laid.*

INFINITIVE	PRESENT PARTICIPLE	PAST	PAST PARTICIPLE
lie (to recline)	lying	lay	(have) lain
lay (to put or place)	laying	laid	(have) laid

EXAMPLES The rug **lies** on the floor.
The tree **lay** across the path.
It **has lain** there for months.

Lay the book on the table.
Workmen **laid** the foundation.
He **has laid** the package on the desk.

● EXERCISE 10. *Oral Drill.* Read each of the following sentences aloud three times, stressing the italicized verbs. Be able to explain, in the light of the information above, why each verb is correct.

1. Let the leaves *lie* around the plants this winter.
2. The smoke *lay* in front of us like a curtain yesterday.
3. She *laid* the letter down unopened.
4. The letter was *lying* there a long time.
5. The mayor *laid* the cornerstone yesterday.
6. *Lay* the hammer over there.
7. Please *lie* still.
8. The patient had just *lain* down.
9. The plane *laid* a smoke screen over the troops.
10. The package is *lying* around somewhere.

● EXERCISE 11. Number your paper 1–10, and write the correct form of *lie* or *lay* for each of the following blanks.

1. The glasses —— on your bureau all day yesterday.
2. Who —— them there?

3. The rake has —— outside for at least a week.
4. Yesterday we —— our plans before the Student Council.
5. —— there helplessly, the old dog seemed to be pleading for help.
6. I —— the packages on the hall table.
7. I was so tired I had to —— down and rest.
8. You must have been —— in the sun for hours.
9. Do you want to —— those books down?
10. You must —— some straw around those plants.

● EXERCISE 12.   Select from each sentence the correct one of the two words in parentheses, and write the word after the proper number on your paper.

1. The town (lies, lays) in the heart of the mountains.
2. A mist (lay, laid) over the valley.
3. He (lay, laid) the letter on the table.
4. Don't (lie, lay) those records there.
5. The snow has (lain, laid) on the ground for six weeks without melting.
6. Your hat is (lying, laying) on the chair.
7. Ben (lay, laid) the tape recorder on the bench.
8. The fishermen were (lying, laying) their hand-woven nets in the sun to dry.
9. That material must have (lain, laid) in the stockroom for years.
10. Mitch was (lying, laying) under the tree.
11. How long has he (lain, laid) there?
12. I hadn't (lain, laid) the package there.
13. (Lie, Lay) the plants around the borders of the garden.
14. You must (lie, lay) awake nights dreaming up those schemes.
15. Tupper Lake (lies, lays) between Saranac Lake and Long Lake.
16. (Lying, Laying) the jewelry on the counter, the salesgirl began to show us the rings.
17. Our furniture has (lain, laid) in storage since we sold our old house.
18. He (lay, laid) most of the flagstones for the path.
19. Were you (lying, laying) down?
20. The gambler (lay, laid) his cards on the table.

● EXERCISE 13. Number 1–20 in a column on your paper. Read each of the following sentences, and determine whether the verb is correctly used. If it is correct, place a + after the corresponding number on your paper; if it is incorrect, place a 0. Think of the *meaning* of the verb.

1. Don't lay too long in the sun and get sunburned.
2. He must have lain in the sun for hours.
3. The clothes lying in the basket have just been washed.
4. When the doctor arrived, the patient lay in a coma.
5. After lunch he decided to lay down and take a nap.
6. Was he lying there long?
7. Look at all the papers laying on the floor.
8. The painter laid the brushes on the ladder.
9. During a storm, you can find the dog lying under the bed.
10. Lay the dishes in the sink, and we'll do them later.
11. He lay his book down and looked out the window.
12. All you can do in the summer is lay around and try to keep cool.
13. The soldier was laying in wait for the enemy.
14. Looking all over the room, he found the pen laying just where he had been working.
15. It was lying under some papers.
16. Last week he lay the tarpaulin over the unfinished boat.
17. Don't you think you have laid around long enough?
18. The principal glanced up and lay the phone down.
19. The child was lying peacefully in his crib.
20. When I went out, the book laid on the table.

Sit and Set

The verb *sit* means "to be in a sitting position." The principal parts of *sit* are *sit, sitting, sat, (have) sat.*

The verb *set* means "to put," "to place (something)." The principal parts of *set* are *set, setting, set, (have) set.*

INFINITIVE	PRESENT PARTICIPLE	PAST	PAST PARTICIPLE
sit (to rest)	sitting	sat	(have) sat
set (to put)	setting	set	(have) set

Study the following examples:

Please **sit** here.	Books **sit** on the shelves.
Set the case down.	He **sets** them on the shelf.

You will have little difficulty using these verbs correctly if you will remember two facts about them: (1) Like *lie*, the verb *sit* means "to be in a certain position." It almost never has an object. (2) Like *lay*, the verb *set* means "to put (something)." It may take an object. *Set* does not change form in the past or the past participle. Whenever you mean "to place" or "to put," use *set*.[1]

● EXERCISE 14. *Oral Drill.* Read each of the following sentences aloud three times, stressing the italicized verb.

1. *Sit* down and rest for a few minutes.
2. *Set* the plates on the table.
3. Last night we *set* out the plants in the garden.
4. I have *sat* here long enough.
5. How long have you been *sitting* there?
6. Steve *set* the time of the crash at 5 P.M.
7. She spoke and then *sat* down.
8. Do you intend to *sit* there all day?
9. Did you *set* a good example for him?
10. We *sat* under the trees.

● EXERCISE 15. Select from each sentence the correct one of the two words in parentheses, and write the words in a column on your paper.

1. He (sat, set) back and pretended to be asleep.
2. Several of them were (sitting, setting) around the campfire.
3. Mary (sat, set) the flowers on the mantel.
4. Where did he (sit, set) the bag of groceries?
5. Let's (sit, set) out under the trees.
6. He likes to (sit, set) on the porch and rock.
7. She (sat, set) the plant on the table.
8. I often (sit, set) here in the sun.

[1] Several uses of the verb *set* do not mean "to put" or "to place"; for example: "the sun sets," "setting hens," "set your watch," "set a record," "set out to accomplish something."

9. Mike (sat, set) the glass on the floor.
10. (Sitting, Setting) by the window, Nick can see the activities on the athletic field.

● REVIEW EXERCISE A. Number your paper 1–20. Choose the correct verb in parentheses, and write it after the proper number on your paper.

1. (Sitting, Setting) on the mantel was a Swiss clock.
2. (Sit, Set) the hamper in the corner, please.
3. She (lay, laid) awake for hours.
4. (Sit, Set) back in your chair, and be comfortable.
5. Having (lain, laid) in the rain for hours, the knife was rusty.
6. He (lay, laid) the book down and left.
7. I always (sit, set) in the leather chair.
8. He might have (lain, laid) his cards down earlier and won more points.
9. (Sitting, Setting) in the car were two highway patrolmen.
10. They say that a treasure chest has (lain, laid) in that peat bog for centuries.
11. Have you ever (sat, set) in a movie house all afternoon?
12. (Sitting, Setting) down to watch TV, my girl paid no further attention to me.
13. On the coffee table (sat, set) a large black cat.
14. Yesterday he (lay, laid) under an apple tree and slept.
15. She (sat, set) near the window and watched the rain.
16. Having (sat, set) down as directed, Julie began her testimony.
17. Penny (lay, laid) the packages on the bed.
18. (Lying, Laying) scattered on the rug were the fragments of the vase.
19. Roy was (sitting, setting) on the step.
20. Having (lay, laid) down his pack, Joe felt much lighter.

Rise and Raise

The verb *rise* means "to go in an upward direction." Its principal parts are *rise, rising, rose, (have) risen.*

The verb *raise* means "to move something in an upward direction." Its principal parts are *raise, raising, raised, (have) raised.*

Study the following:

PRESENT	PRESENT PARTICIPLE	PAST	PAST PARTICIPLE
rise (go up)	rising	rose	(have) risen
raise (force upward)	raising	raised	(have) raised

Just like *lie*, *rise* never has an object. Like *lay* and *set*, *raise* may have an object.

● EXERCISE 16. Fill in the blanks in the following sentences with a correct form of *rise* or *raise*, whichever is required by the meaning.

1. Prices have —— in the last few years.
2. The curtain always —— a few minutes late on opening night.
3. —— the windows, and let some fresh air in.
4. Higher and higher —— the eagle.
5. Jerry —— his grade in math this term.
6. Slowly the old woman —— out of her chair.
7. Whenever you know the answer, —— your hand.
8. They said that the sun would —— in an hour.
9. Your question —— a new problem for us to solve.
10. The farmer —— at dawn to do his chores.

● EXERCISE 17. Number 1–10 in a column on your paper. Select from each sentence the correct one of the two words in parentheses, and write it after the corresponding number on your paper.

1. As our plane (rose, raised) from the runway, I held my breath.
2. We couldn't take off until the fog had (risen, raised).
3. If the price has (risen, raised), you can't afford it.
4. A column of smoke was (rising, raising) over Bear Lake.
5. The tide (rises, raises) at 4 P.M. today.
6. How high will the balloon (rise, raise)?
7. Stock prices (rose, raised) during the afternoon.
8. The flood waters have (risen, raised) to new heights.
9. The sun had just (risen, raised) when we started on the fishing trip.
10. Heated air (rises, raises).

● Review exercise B. Number 1–40 in a column on your paper. Read each of the following sentences, and determine whether it is correct. If it is correct, place a + after the corresponding number; if it is incorrect, place a 0.

1. The detective lay the file on his desk and examined it closely.
2. Set the candlesticks down.
3. Your clothes are laying in a heap on the floor.
4. The dog has been sitting by the gate waiting for the children to return.
5. Why don't you lay back and relax?
6. What makes a plane rise?
7. Stewart set the dial for his favorite program.
8. Instead of laying down, you should be cutting the grass.
9. Interest has risen in our new project.
10. Set your chair in the shade.
11. The dishes have laid in the sink since breakfast.
12. Shall we sit in the orchestra or the balcony?
13. Gasping for air, the diver raised to the surface.
14. The sophomores rose when the seniors entered the auditorium.
15. We laid out the maps and began to plot our route.
16. Everybody raised from his seat when the President finished his speech.
17. Out at sea the submarine raised from the depths.
18. Isn't it too cold to lie on the beach today?
19. Just set anywhere you want, Mrs. Wright.
20. As the runner reached the finish line, the excitement of the crowd rose higher and higher.
21. Haven't you laid the boundary lines yet?
22. The boy was thrilled when he set in the Governor's chair.
23. The tulip bulbs lay dormant during the cold weather.
24. We were sitting in the station waiting for the train to come in.
25. A howl of despair raised from the throats of the fans.
26. Set up straight in your chair.
27. There the dog laid with his head on his paws.
28. Engineers expect the river to rise another foot.
29. The humidity hasn't risen in three days.

30. The ambassador lay his protest before the committee.
31. You may have one of the pictures laying on the table.
32. Everyone was fascinated by the little puffs of steam that were raising from the pool.
33. The pipe was so hot it must have lain out in the sun for hours.
34. Setting there in his office, I grew nervous.
35. We set the boxes in the trunk.
36. He set there smiling at me.
37. There the boat laid in only a few feet of water.
38. He skillfully lay the mortar on.
39. Because the bank stock raised in value, he felt elated.
40. The dog always lies on my favorite chair.

● REVIEW EXERCISE C. Number your paper 1–40. After the corresponding number on your paper, write the correct one of the two words in parentheses.

1. Have you (wrote, written) the directions down?
2. The enemy was (lying, laying) in wait for us behind the trees.
3. You might have (thrown, throwed) your arm out of joint.
4. We had (took, taken) our visitors to the Empire State Building.
5. He was instructed to (lie, lay) the nets in the sun.
6. I haven't (swam, swum) in the pool this year.
7. Who has (stole, stolen) my stapler?
8. The frightened animal (shrank, shrunk) back into the corner.
9. The child (burst, bursted) the balloon.
10. Nobody enjoys (sitting, setting) in a cold room.
11. There it (lay, laid), covered with mold.
12. They certainly have (ran, run) a successful dance.
13. He (rose, raised) to his feet and protested the umpire's decision.
14. After I (saw, seen) it, I couldn't believe it.
15. She has (rode, ridden) this horse in all the local parades.
16. I (brought, brung) you a sample of my writing.
17. What could have (went, gone) wrong with the engine?
18. The dog has (broke, broken) his leash.
19. It was so cold I was almost (froze, frozen).

20. The bad weather has (began, begun) to clear up.
21. When the bell (rang, rung), the wrestlers came out of their corners.
22. The tree was (lying, laying) across the road.
23. The thief had (fell, fallen) into the detective's trap.
24. They (did, done) all the math problems in class.
25. We (sat, set) for an hour in the waiting room.
26. He (drank, drunk) the medicine without any protests.
27. The wind has (blown, blowed) the leaves all over the yard.
28. He hasn't (gave, given) us any trouble so far.
29. I looked out of the plane and saw the mountains (lying, laying) below.
30. Have you ever (drove, driven) a foreign car?
31. When you (come, came) back, was the door locked?
32. She (lay, laid) the clothes in the cedar chest.
33. The cheers (rose, raised) from all parts of the room.
34. Tony had (chose, chosen) the wrong number.
35. Why don't you (sit, set) in a more comfortable chair?
36. I could have (ran, run) the machine better.
37. That tape recorder hasn't (gave, given) us any trouble.
38. Janet (lay, laid) the record down carefully.
39. Last night the boys (came, come) in at one o'clock.
40. Nobody could have (run, ran) the mile as fast as Vic.

CHAPTER 9

Using Modifiers Correctly

Comparison, Placement of Modifiers

Knowing when to use an adverb and when to use an adjective is not just a matter of form, but of meaning. Notice the difference in meaning in the following two sentences:

Sam made **careful** plans.   [adjective]
Sam made the plans **carefully.**   [adverb]

A modifier is a word or a group of words that makes more definite the meaning of another word. Two parts of speech are used as modifiers: the adjective, which modifies a noun or pronoun; and the adverb, which modifies a verb, an adjective, or another adverb.

ADJECTIVE AND ADVERB FORMS

You will have little difficulty using most adjectives and adverbs correctly. Almost the only common problem in distinguishing an adverb from an adjective concerns the following three pairs: *bad–badly, good–well, slow–slowly.* Your problem is to learn when to use the adverb form and when to use the adjective form.

Apply the following rule to the three troublesome pairs.

9a. If a word in the predicate modifies the subject of the verb, choose the adjective form. If it modifies the verb, choose the adverb form.[1]

EXAMPLES The driver is **cautious.** [The adjective *cautious* modifies the noun *driver—cautious driver.*]

He drives **cautiously.** [The adverb *cautiously* modifies the verb *drives—drives cautiously.*]

Linking verbs are usually followed by a predicate adjective. The following are the most commonly used linking verbs: *be, become, seem, grow, appear, look, feel, smell, taste, remain, stay, sound.*

In general, a verb is a linking verb if you can substitute for it some form of the verb *seem.*

She **looked** tired. [She seemed tired.]

The crowd **remained** calm. [The crowd seemed calm.]

Because many verbs may be used as either linking verbs or action verbs, you must be able to tell which way a verb is used in a particular sentence.

LINKING The corn **grew** tall. [verb followed by an adjective modifying the subject: The corn *seemed* tall.]

ACTION The corn **grew** slowly. [verb modified by an adverb]

LINKING The actor **appeared** nervous. [verb followed by an adjective modifying the subject: The actor *seemed* nervous.]

ACTION The actor **appeared** briefly in the skit. [verb modified by an adverb]

LINKING The teacher **looked** calm. [verb followed by an adjective modifying the subject: The teacher *seemed* calm.]

ACTION The teacher **looked** calmly around the room. [verb modified by an adverb]

[1] Most adjectives become adverbs by adding *–ly: nice–nicely, vague–vaguely, incidental–incidentally.* A few adjectives, however, also end in *–ly* (*lively, lonely, sickly*), so you cannot always be sure that an *–ly* word is an adverb.

9a

Bad and Badly

Bad is an adjective; in most uses *badly* is an adverb.

EXAMPLES   The play was **bad.** [bad play]

The play was written **badly.** [adverb modifying the verb *was written*]

The weather looked **bad.** [After the linking verb *looked*, the adjective *bad* modifies the subject *weather.*]

The boat performed **badly.** [The adverb *badly* modifies the verb *performed.*]

With linking verbs the adjective form is used.

WRONG   The fish smell badly.

RIGHT   The fish smell **bad.** [The adjective *bad* modifies the subject *fish.*]

WRONG   These look badly.

RIGHT   These look **bad.** [The verb *look* is a linking verb. *Bad* modifies the subject *these.*]

◆ USAGE NOTE   One prominent exception to this rule is the use of *badly* after the sense verb *feel.* In informal English either *bad* or *badly* is acceptable after *feel.*

He feels **bad** about his remarks.
He feels **badly** about his remarks.   [informal]

However, formal English calls for *bad* after *feel.*

He feels **bad** [not *badly*] about his remarks.

Follow the rules for formal written English in doing the exercises in this book.

Well and Good

Well may be used as either an adjective or an adverb. As an adjective, *well* has three meanings:

1. To be in good health

Alice is well.
He feels well.

2. To appear well-dressed or well-groomed

   She looks well in her gray suit.

3. To be satisfactory

   It is well.
   All is well.

   As an adverb, *well* means *capably*.

   The work was done well.

Good is always an adjective. It should not be used to modify a verb.

WRONG   He skates **good.**
RIGHT   He skates **well.**

WRONG   The band played good.
RIGHT   The band played **well.**

RIGHT   That suit looks **good** on you. [adjective following linking verb]

♦ USAGE NOTE   *Well* is also acceptable in sentences like the last example above: That suit looks *well* on you.

Slow and Slowly

Slow is used as both an adjective and an adverb. *Slowly* is always an adverb.

EXAMPLES   Drive **slow.** [*Slow* is an adverb modifying *drive*.]

Drive **slowly.** [*Slowly* is an adverb modifying *drive*.]

In most adverb uses (other than *Go slow* or *Drive slow*), it is better to use the form *slowly* as an adverb instead of *slow*.

EXAMPLES   He mounted the ladder **slowly.**

Very **slowly** the tiger crept forward.

♦ USAGE NOTE   Certain words like *loud, hard, deep, fast* may be used as adverbs without changing their forms.

EXAMPLES   The horse ran **fast.**

He dived **deep** into the lake.

Wes hit the nail **hard.**

● EXERCISE 1. Number your paper 1-20. Select the correct one of the two words in parentheses, and write it after the corresponding number on your paper.

1. The dog obeys his trainer's signals (well, good).
2. The lines on the basketball court are marked (well, good).
3. The shrubs look (bad, badly).
4. He certainly moves (slow, slowly) for a halfback.
5. He plays the clarinet very (well, good).
6. You certainly dance (well, good) to that music.
7. It doesn't fit (bad, badly) at all.
8. The director said that we must play the music (slow, slowly).
9. How (well, good) did you do on the exam?
10. She cut the material (bad, badly).
11. The uniform fits you (well, good).
12. The plane taxied very (slow, slowly) down the field.
13. That meat smells (bad, badly).
14. How (well, good) can you draw?
15. The peaches look too (bad, badly) to use.
16. We felt (bad, badly) that you didn't win.
17. He can't sing as (well, good) as I can.
18. The line moved so (slow, slowly) that we thought we would never get the tickets.
19. The car performed (bad, badly) on the trip.
20. To stress his remarks, the man spoke (slow, slowly).

● EXERCISE 2. Number your paper 1-20. If the sentence is correct, place a + after the corresponding number; if it is incorrect, place a 0. Be able to explain your answers.

1. All went well at the dance.
2. He talks too slow to suit me.
3. We walked back to camp slow.
4. If you can't see good, get glasses.
5. Bart felt bad about losing the match.
6. I didn't think that he played so bad.
7. Chris writes very slow.
8. That color looks well on you.
9. By turning the lens very slow, you can focus the projector.
10. She arranged the flowers good.

11. That horse may look slow, but he isn't.
12. Because he did so bad in math, Mickey was invited to attend the review classes.
13. I didn't do as well as I had hoped.
14. I did as good on the test as Shirley.
15. You certainly play the piano good.
16. Don't feel bad about not being able to take typing this year.
17. The job he did was done good.
18. The train went very slow before it came to the underpass.
19. The car ran good all winter.
20. Speak slow, so we can take notes.

COMPARISON OF MODIFIERS

Adjectives state qualities of nouns or pronouns:

a **bright** light   **happy** people   **rough** cloth

You can show the degree or extent to which one noun has a quality by comparing it with another noun which has the same quality. For instance:

This light is **brighter** than that one.

Similarly, you can show degree or extent by using adverbs to make comparisons:

We play well, but they play even **better.**

9b. The forms of modifiers change as they are used in comparison.

There are three degrees of comparison: *positive, comparative,* and *superlative.* Notice below how the forms of modifiers change to show comparison.

POSITIVE	COMPARATIVE	SUPERLATIVE
low	lower	lowest
fearful	more fearful	most fearful
promptly	more promptly	most promptly
bad	worse	worst
good	better	best

9b

Regular Comparison

(1) A modifier of one syllable regularly forms its comparative and superlative by adding _-er_ and _-est_.

POSITIVE	COMPARATIVE	SUPERLATIVE
cold	colder	coldest
late	later	latest

(2) Some modifiers of two syllables form their comparative and superlative degrees by adding _-er_ and _-est;_ other modifiers of two syllables form their comparative and superlative degrees by means of _more_ and _most_.

In general, the _-er_ and _-est_ forms are used with two-syllable modifiers unless they make the word sound awkward. The _more, most_ forms are used with adverbs ending in _-ly_.

POSITIVE	COMPARATIVE	SUPERLATIVE
humble	humbler	humblest
pretty	prettier	prettiest
famous	more famous	most famous
slowly	more slowly	most slowly

◆ USAGE NOTE   Some two-syllable modifiers may use either _-er_, _-est_, or _more, most_ correctly: _handsome, handsomer, handsomest_ or _handsome, more handsome, most handsome._

(3) Modifiers having more than two syllables form their comparative and superlative degrees by means of _more_ and _most_.

POSITIVE	COMPARATIVE	SUPERLATIVE
industrious	more industrious	most industrious
favorably	more favorably	most favorably
fortunate	more fortunate	most fortunate

(4) Comparison to indicate less or least of a quality is accomplished by using the words _less_ and _least_ before the modifier.

POSITIVE	COMPARATIVE	SUPERLATIVE
useful	less useful	least useful
often	less often	least often

Irregular Comparison

Adjectives and adverbs that do not follow the regular methods of forming their comparative and superlative degrees are said to be compared irregularly.

POSITIVE	COMPARATIVE	SUPERLATIVE
bad	worse	worst
good well	better	best
little	less	least
many much	more	most

Caution: Do not add *-er, -est* or *more, most* to irregular forms: *worse,* not *worser* or *more worse.*

● EXERCISE 3. Write the comparative and superlative forms of the following modifiers.

1. beautiful
2. curious
3. old
4. cloudy
5. rich
6. agreeable
7. simple
8. well
9. stern
10. substantial
11. cruel
12. little
13. smoky
14. wily
15. good

Use of Comparative and Superlative Forms

9c. Use the comparative degree when comparing two things; use the superlative degree when comparing more than two.

The comparative form of a modifier is used for comparing two things, as these examples indicate.

EXAMPLES One twin seems **brighter** than the other.
Texas is **larger** than Rhode Island.
Greg can pass **better** than Charlie.

9c

The superlative form of a modifier is used for comparing three or more things.

EXAMPLES   Alaska is the **largest** state in the Union.
Greg is the **best** passer on the team.
Which of the three did you like **best**?

In informal speech it is common to use the superlative for emphasis, even though only two things are being compared.

May the **best** man [of two] win.
Put your **best** foot forward.

In writing, however, you will do well to observe the distinction stated in 9c.

● EXERCISE 4.   Write five sentences correctly using adjectives or adverbs to compare two things, and five sentences using the same adjectives and adverbs to compare three or more things.

9d. Do not omit the word *other* or *else* when comparing one thing with a group of which it is a part.

It is absurd to say "Stan is taller than anyone in his class." Stan must obviously be a member of the class himself, and he can hardly be taller than himself. The word *else* should be supplied: "Stan is taller than anyone else in his class."

WRONG   Our cabin was smaller than any in the camp. [This would mean that the cabin was smaller than itself.]

RIGHT   Our cabin was smaller than any **other** in the camp.

WRONG   Ellen is smarter than anybody in her class. [This means that Ellen, a member of her class, is smarter than herself.]

RIGHT   Ellen is smarter than anybody **else** in her class.

WRONG   New York is larger than any city in America.

RIGHT   New York is larger than any **other** city in America.

9e. Avoid double comparisons.

A double comparison is one in which the comparative or superlative is incorrectly formed by adding *-er* and *-est* in addition to using *more* or *most*.

WRONG   Today is even more colder than yesterday.
RIGHT   Today is even colder than yesterday.

WRONG   She is the most liveliest person I know.
RIGHT   She is the most lively [or *liveliest*] person I know.

9f. Be sure your comparisons are clear.

In making comparisons, you should always state clearly what things are being compared. For example, in the sentence "The population of New York is greater than Chicago," the comparison is not clear. *The population of New York* is not being compared to Chicago, but rather to the *population* of Chicago. The sentence should read: "The population of New York is greater than the population of Chicago."

WRONG   The Biggs family prefers camping in the wilderness to big hotels.

RIGHT   The Biggs family prefers camping in the wilderness to staying at big hotels.

Often an incomplete clause is used in making comparisons. Both parts of the comparison should be fully stated if there is danger of misunderstanding.

NOT CLEAR   I like her better than Tina.
BETTER   I like her better than I like Tina.
    I like her better than Tina does.

● EXERCISE 5. If the sentence is correct, write a + after the corresponding number on your paper; if it is incorrect, write a 0. Be prepared to explain your answers.

1. He peered out of the nearer of the two windows.
2. Your story is good, but mine is even more better.

9
d-f

3. Doris is the most happiest girl I've ever seen.
4. Which is the better of the two books?
5. Who is the youngest, Harvey or Tim?
6. Of the two scientists, Einstein is perhaps the best known.
7. This is the shortest route I know to Spirit Lake.
8. Of all the mountain lakes, this is the most beautiful.
9. Which of the two jackets do you like best?
10. The flowers look more lovelier than ever this year.
11. Traveling in airplanes is supposed to be safer than automobiles.
12. Our dog is more friendlier than yours.
13. New York City has a larger population than any city in the United States.
14. It is difficult to say which problem was the most hardest.
15. The weather couldn't have been worser.
16. He was considered the most reliable boy in school.
17. Our room sold more subscriptions in the magazine drive than any room in the building.
18. He says that if he could train every day he could run more faster than you.
19. Which is biggest, Lake Superior or Lake Huron?
20. The earth is closer to the sun than Mars is.

DANGLING MODIFIERS

9g. A phrase or clause that does not clearly and sensibly modify a word in the sentence is a *dangling modifier*.

A modifier consisting of a phrase or a clause may be momentarily confusing to a reader if it appears to modify a word that it cannot sensibly modify. Verbal phrases are particularly likely to dangle, since they have only a loose grammatical relationship with the rest of the sentence.

WRONG   Sitting in the back row of the theater, the actors could hardly be heard. [The participial phrase seems illogically to modify *actors*.]

Convinced of my sincerity, I was given one more chance.   [The participial phrase seems to modify *I*.]

In both examples the participial phrase appears to modify a word that it cannot logically modify. The word that each phrase is supposed to modify has been omitted from the sentence. Compare the following correct examples.

RIGHT   Sitting in the back row of the theater, we could hardly hear the actors.

Convinced of my sincerity, the principal gave me another chance.

Dangling modifiers can be corrected by rearranging the words in the faulty sentence or by adding words that make the meaning clear and logical.

WRONG   Watching the auto races, an accident occurred.

RIGHT   Watching the auto races, I saw an accident occur.

WRONG   Stirring the batter well, the spices were put in next.

RIGHT   Stirring the batter well, Vicky put the spices in next.

RIGHT   After she had stirred the batter well, the spices were put in.

WRONG   After rehearsing for weeks, the play was a success.

RIGHT   After rehearsing for weeks, we had a successful play.

RIGHT   After we had rehearsed for weeks, the play was a success.

● EXERCISE 6.   Study the following sentences containing dangling modifiers. Rewrite each sentence so that the modifier *clearly* and *sensibly* modifies a word in the sentence. You may have to supply some words to fill out the sentence properly.

1. After reading the assignment again, it still was not clear.
2. Finishing her performance, the audience applauded the singer.
3. To learn to dance, a few lessons should be taken.
4. We noticed several caves walking down the highway.

9g

5. While typing my report, the keys jammed.
6. By saving part of his allowance, the transistor radio was soon his.
7. At the age of seven, my grandfather took me to visit some relatives in Ohio.
8. Peering over the cliffs, the canyon seemed gigantic.
9. While shaving, his lip started to bleed.
10. Hanging in the closet, he found the jacket.

● EXERCISE 7.   Follow the instructions for Exercise 6

1. After finishing our dinner, coffee and cake were served.
2. Ringing the bell at Jud's house, a voice shouted that I should go in.
3. While playing the violin, my dog started to howl.
4. While eating lunch, the phone rang.
5. After correcting a few mistakes, the editorial was ready for the printer.
6. To start the engine, the switch must be turned on.
7. To learn the rules of the game, a book was bought.
8. Cleaning up the cabin, pine needles were found in the corner.
9. To put a good shine on the floors, a little elbow grease must be used.
10. While sick in bed, your get-well card caused chuckles.
11. After launching the boat, a celebration was suggested.
12. When on vacation, the dog is sent to Dr. Stevenson's kennel.
13. Upon entering the museum, your camera must be left with the attendant.
14. Having walked a few blocks, my new shoes started to hurt.
15. Drinking soda in gulps, the glass was soon emptied.

MISPLACED MODIFIERS

9h. Modifying words, phrases, and clauses should be placed as near as possible to the words they modify.

Most of the errors in modification in the preceding examples resulted from the omission of the word that was supposed to be modified. Unclear sentences can also result from placing modifiers too far away from the words they modify.

Misplaced Phrase Modifiers

(1) Modifying phrases should be placed as near as possible to the words they modify.

The sentences below will indicate the importance of observing this rule.

WRONG   Did you see a boy in the bus with a brown cap?

RIGHT   Did you see a boy with a brown cap in the bus? [The phrase *with a brown cap* obviously modifies *boy*. It should be placed next to *boy*. Otherwise it appears to modify *bus* and gives the impression that it was a bus with a brown cap.]

WRONG   I read your editorial about juvenile delinquents with enthusiasm.

RIGHT   I read with enthusiasm your editorial about juvenile delinquents.

WRONG   We borrowed an extension ladder from a neighbor thirty-five feet long.

RIGHT   We borrowed an extension ladder thirty-five feet long from a neighbor.

BETTER   From a neighbor we borrowed an extension ladder thirty-five feet long.

● EXERCISE 8.   Read each of the following sentences. Pick out the misplaced phrase, decide what word the phrase should modify, and rewrite the sentence, placing the phrase near this word.

1. Bob slammed the door in a bad frame of mind.
2. We found the dog walking home from school.
3. He spoke of the need for building new tennis courts in the strongest possible terms.

9h

4. She bought the dress at Macy's with the brown collar.
5. Mrs. Stevens went to Florida after her husband had joined the army to live with relatives.
6. Perry was stung by a bee hoeing weeds in his garden.
7. I came upon an interesting old bookshop wandering about the narrow streets.
8. Mr. Beatty saw many Japanese beetles looking over his garden.
9. We saw a lady talking to a policeman in a green dress and a white coat.
10. A package was delivered by a messenger boy wrapped in red paper.
11. Marty served him a soda dressed in a white jacket.
12. We saw a great deal of farming country riding along in our car.
13. The children were offered a piece of chocolate layer cake by a strange lady with white frosting.
14. A collision occurred in the middle of the block between a delivery car and a fire truck.
15. I had been talking to a lady on the train with three children.
16. Careening down the street out of control, fortunately no pedestrians stood in the path of the runaway car.
17. A strange-looking dog was led onto the stage by one of the actors with shaggy hair and a stubby tail.
18. We watched plane after plane land and take off sitting in the observation tower at the airport.
19. I saw them leave before the sun came up in a long red car.
20. He described the part of the story about killing the lion in English class.

Misplaced Clause Modifiers

In using modifying clauses, you should follow the rule which applies to phrases.

(2) Place the clause as near as possible to the word it modifies.

The following sentences will show you how a misplaced clause may make a sentence ridiculous.

WRONG A ship sailed into the harbor that carried a cargo of wheat.

RIGHT A ship that carried a cargo of wheat sailed into the harbor.

The modifying clause *that carried a cargo of wheat* modifies *ship*, not *harbor*. In the second sentence the clause has been put next to the word it modifies.

WRONG There are books on the counter that must be distributed.

RIGHT On the counter there are books that must be distributed.

WRONG Sue mailed a letter from one of the cities she visited that lacked sufficient postage.

RIGHT From one of the cities she visited, Sue mailed a letter that lacked sufficient postage.

● EXERCISE 9. Read each of the following sentences. Take out the misplaced clause, decide what word the clause should modify, and rewrite the sentence, placing the clause near this word. If you find a misplaced phrase, correct it.

1. They drove to the lake in their new car where they always spent their vacations.
2. A large automobile drew up to the curb which was profusely draped with flags.
3. I liked the picture of you on the diving board that you sent me.
4. The new bicycle was standing on the porch which we had ordered from Chicago.
5. I took the test after school that I had missed.
6. He gave the letter to the mailman that he just typed.
7. We cleaned the attic on Saturday that had not been touched in years.
8. We found the book in the attic that had been missing.
9. We caught a dozen fish with the new bait which we fried for supper.
10. Norman showed the pictures to his friends that he had taken in Hawaii.

● REVIEW EXERCISE.   Most of the following sentences contain errors in the use of modifiers (words, phrases, clauses). Rewrite such sentences, correcting the faulty modifiers. If a sentence is correct, write *C* after its number on your paper.

1. While doing my homework, the telephone interrupted me five times.
2. Two bodies were discovered by firemen that could not be identified.
3. Replying to reporters, the coach said that this year's team was better than any other team he had coached.
4. Wilma plans to work after she gets married for a little while.
5. While Percy's essay was the most funniest, it was not written so good as Ralph's or Bob's.
6. Listen very careful to the two recordings and tell me which one you prefer.
7. By working slowly, the job lasted all day.
8. Students are excused from last-period study halls that have a B+ average.
9. An award was presented to Gus Dugan for a job well done by the principal.
10. During the two-week examination period, all extracurricular activities are canceled.
11. Marion can't sing as good as Yvonne because, of the two, Yvonne has the truest voice.
12. Because Jimmy obviously felt bad about his grades, his father did not scold him severely.
13. Approaching the Capitol from the south, a long flight of stone steps confronts the visitor.
14. Although the captain is faster than any player on the team, he didn't play so good in last night's game.
15. One of the men was picked up by a policeman who had been acting suspiciously.

CHAPTER 10

Glossary of Usage

This chapter contains a short glossary of English usage to supplement the material in Chapters 5–9. You may wish to work right through the chapter, using the exercises to test your ability to use these expressions correctly. However, the glossary is intended mainly for reference. Get in the habit of referring to it whenever you are uncertain about a point of usage.

Several kinds of usage problems are treated here. In some, a choice is described between standard and substandard ways of saying things. In such cases, you will be advised to follow the standard practice. Other choices are between formal and informal usages. Here you should follow the formal practice in doing the exercises. Problems arising from the confusion of similarly spelled words are treated in Chapter 26.

accept, except   *Accept* is a verb; it means "to receive."
Except may be either a verb or a preposition. As a verb it means "to leave out"; as a preposition it means "excluding."

EXAMPLES   Toby will **accept** the trophy from the principal.
No one will be **excepted** from this assignment.
All may go **except** Anita.

affect, effect   *Affect* is usually a verb; it means "to influence." *Effect* used as a verb means "to accomplish," or "to bring about." Used as a noun, *effect* means "the result of some action."

EXAMPLES   The bad news seemed not to **affect** him at all.

The new drug **effected** a cure immediately.

The **effect** of the coach's pep talk was remarkable.

all the farther, all the faster   These expressions are used informally in some parts of the country to mean "as far as" and "as fast as." In formal English, *as far as* and *as fast as* are the correct expressions.

DIALECT   That is all the farther the bus goes.

STANDARD   That is **as far as** the bus goes.

allusion, illusion   An *allusion* is a reference to something. An *illusion* is a "false, misleading, or overly optimistic idea."

EXAMPLES   The teacher made many **allusions** to a book she had read.

After the first game, our basketball team had no **illusions** about its chances of winning the championship.

and etc.   Since *etc.* is an abbreviation of the Latin "et cetera," which means "and other things," you are using *and* twice when you write "and etc." The *etc.* is sufficient.

anywheres, everywheres, nowheres   Use these words and others like them without the *s*.

Anywhere you go in the United States, travelers' checks are accepted.

at   Do not use *at* after *where*.

WRONG   Where were you sitting at?

RIGHT   Where were you **sitting**?

being as, being that   Use *since* or *because.*

SUBSTANDARD   Being that he was in a hurry, he took a plane to Los Angeles.

STANDARD   Since he was in a hurry, he took a plane to Los Angeles.

SUBSTANDARD   Being as she's a star, we treat her like royalty.

STANDARD   Because she's a star, we treat her like royalty.

beside, besides   *Beside* means "by the side of"; *besides* means "in addition to."

EXAMPLES   Nobody sat **beside** him in the auditorium.
Did anybody **besides** you sell candy at the game?

between, among   *Between* implies two people or things; *among* implies more than two. This distinction in meaning is usually observed in formal English; however, use *between* when you are thinking of two items at a time, regardless of whether they are part of a group of more than two. (See the third example below.)

EXAMPLES   The two friends had only twenty-five cents **between** them.

The five committee members shared the work **among** them.

What is the difference in meaning **between** *timid, cautious,* and *circumspect?* [*Between* is correct because the speaker is thinking of one word and another word — *two* at a time.]

The rivalry **between** the students at Central and those at North has always been intense. [Although more than two students are involved, the rivalry exists between two groups.]

bring, take   *Bring* means "to come carrying something." *Take* means "to go away carrying something." The situation is complicated by the fact that a speaker sometimes adopts the point of view of the person he is speaking to out of politeness: "Shall I bring my bathing suit when I come to your party?" In most cases it is helpful to think of *bring* as related to *come* and *take* as related to *go*.

EXAMPLES **Bring** your literature books to class tomorrow.
Please **take** this slip when you go to the principal's office.

bust, busted Avoid using these words as verbs. Use a form of either *burst* or *break*.

SUBSTANDARD I busted my arm last week.
STANDARD I **broke** my arm last week.

SUBSTANDARD The dress busted at the seams.
STANDARD The dress **burst** at the seams.

● EXERCISE 1. Number your paper 1–30. Choose the correct one of the two words in parentheses, and write it after the proper number on your paper.

1. When you visited Louisville, where did you (stay, stay at)?
2. The lawyer (accepted, excepted) our congratulations on his winning the case.
3. (Being that, Since) the puppy was only a few weeks old, it needed much care.
4. The speaker made several (allusions, illusions) to the current international situation.
5. The trouble was caused by a water pipe that had (busted, burst).
6. Everyone passed the test (accept, except) Dan.
7. The proceeds from the Community Chest drive will be divided (between, among) several dozen charities.
8. (Bring, Take) your books home with you when you go.
9. This is (all the faster, as fast as) I can go.
10. Tell Ginny to (bring, take) me her excuse.
11. Steady practice has (affected, effected) a marked improvement in his playing.
12. No one (accept, except) Art will be admitted.
13. His sudden rise to fame did not (affect, effect) his fundamental modesty.

14. The outdoor chores are shared (between, among) the four boys in the family.
15. (Being that, Because) he was in a hurry, he was careless.
16. We could not find you (anywheres, anywhere).
17. When you go shopping, (bring, take) money with you.
18. The "ghost" proved to be a simple (allusion, illusion) caused by the reflection of a distant light.
19. Who (busted, broke) the light bulb?
20. The seniors soon felt the (affects, effects) of the principal's ruling.
21. Has anyone (beside, besides) Brenda finished the assignment?
22. (Everywheres, Everywhere) in Polk County, the dogwoods are flowering.
23. The new coach (affected, effected) a great change in the team's morale.
24. (Bring, Take) your swim suit with you when you come to my house.
25. This is (all the farther, as far as) I can climb.
26. Tony was (accepted, excepted) from the requirement after he explained his situation to the principal.
27. The rope (busted, broke) and the mountaineer fell.
28. The strain of waiting (affected, effected) Maureen's nerves badly.
29. Who else (beside, besides) you and Dan bought tickets to the game?
30. The expression "sour grapes" is an (allusion, illusion) to Aesop's fable "The Fox and the Grapes."

can't hardly, can't scarcely See **The Double Negative** (page 213).

could of *Could have* sounds like *could of* when spoken. Do not erroneously write *of* with the helping verb *could.* Use *could have.* Also avoid *ought to of, should of, would of, might of,* and *must of.*

EXAMPLE Anne could **have** [not *of*] called us earlier.

discover, invent   *To discover* means "to find something that already exists." *To invent* is "to be the first to make something not known before."

EXAMPLES   Edison **invented** the incandescent lamp.

Leif Ericson is said to have **discovered** North America about A.D. 1000.

don't   A contraction of *do not*, *don't* should not be used with a singular noun or a third person singular pronoun (*he, she, it*). Use *doesn't*. See page 125.

SUBSTANDARD   He don't want to go to the movies.
STANDARD   He **doesn't** want to go to the movies.
SUBSTANDARD   It don't matter to me.
STANDARD   It **doesn't** matter to me.

effect   See **affect, effect.**

emigrate, immigrate   *Emigrate* means "to go from a country to settle elsewhere." *Immigrate* means "to come into a country to settle there."

EXAMPLES   His ancestors **emigrated** from Scotland many years ago.

Canadians welcome the many people who **immigrate** to their country every year.

everywheres   See **anywheres.**

except   See **accept, except.**

fewer, less   *Fewer* is used in referring to things that can be counted. It is used with plural words. *Less* is used to refer to quantities that cannot be counted. It is used with singular words.

EXAMPLES   There are **fewer** detours on this route.

Geometry will give you **less** trouble if you learn the theorems.

good, well　*Good* is an adjective. Do not use it to modify a verb.

SUBSTANDARD　You sing good.
STANDARD　　 You sing well.

Well is an adverb except in three uses: (1) when used to mean "healthy," (2) when used to mean "neatly groomed" or "attractively dressed," (3) when used to mean "satisfactory." In all of these instances, *well* is an adjective.

EXAMPLES　The band played well. [adverb]
　　　　　You don't look well. [adjective]
　　　　　Blondes look well in black. [adjective]
　　　　　All is well. [adjective]

had of　See **of.**

had ought　See **ought.**

hardly　See **The Double Negative** (page 213).

he, she, they　Do not use unnecessary pronouns. This error is sometimes called the *double subject.*

SUBSTANDARD　My older brother he goes to college.
STANDARD　　 My older brother goes to college.

illusion　See **allusion, illusion.**

immigrate　See **emigrate, immigrate.**

imply, infer　*Imply* means "to suggest something." *Infer* means "to interpret" or "to derive a certain meaning from a remark or an action."

EXAMPLES　In his composition he **implied** that he was given too much homework.

　　　　　From other remarks that he has made, I **infer** that he feels overworked.

● EXERCISE 2. Number your paper 1–20. Choose the correct form in parentheses, and write it after the proper number on your paper.

1. Was it Elias Howe or Isaac Singer who (discovered, invented) the sewing machine?
2. Dad's remark (implied, inferred) that we soon might get a new car.
3. If you check your answers carefully, you will make (fewer, less) mistakes.
4. If you do (good, well) on this test, you will have a better understanding of usage.
5. Archimedes (discovered, invented) the principle of specific gravity.
6. During the entire season, the team played exceptionally (good, well).
7. Many Huguenots (emigrated, immigrated) from France to escape religious persecution.
8. Because of the stormy weather, there were (fewer, less) shoppers in the store than usual.
9. By using the newly invented telescope, Galileo (discovered, invented) the four moons of Jupiter.
10. (Emigration, Immigration) into the United States reached its peak soon after 1900.
11. In his estimation, nobody does anything as (good, well) as he.
12. (My father, My father he) bowls in the 200's.
13. His band uniform didn't fit very (good, well).
14. He (don't, doesn't) mean to be rude.
15. From what the author said, I (implied, inferred) that he was against capital punishment.
16. If she (don't, doesn't) come, we shall be sorry.
17. Could you (of, have) forgotten our appointment?
18. Because of a drop in the market, the factory ordered (fewer, less) shipments of grain.
19. People who (emigrate, immigrate) into this country today are just as likely to arrive by plane as by ship.
20. Celia might (have, of) done much better than she did.

invent See **discover, invent.**

kind of, sort of These expressions are often used in informal English to mean "rather" or "somewhat." Avoid them in formal written English.

INFORMAL He was kind of tired.
FORMAL He was **rather** tired.

INFORMAL It grew sort of chilly.
FORMAL It grew **somewhat** [or *rather*] chilly.

kind of a, sort of a The *a* is unnecessary. Leave it out.

EXAMPLE What **kind of** hat did you buy?

learn, teach *Learn* means "to acquire information." *Teach* means "to instruct" or "to give out knowledge."

EXAMPLES He wanted to **learn** how to read music.
The music director **taught** him after school.

leave, let *Leave* means "to go away." *Let* means "to allow" or "to permit."

EXAMPLES **Let** (not *leave*) me show you my new skis.
You should have **let** (not *left*) him go.

lie, lay See Chapter 8, page 171.

like, as *Like* is usually a preposition. *As* is usually a conjunction.

EXAMPLES She cried **like** a baby. [prepositional phrase]
She responds to criticism **as** a baby would. [subordinate clause introduced by a conjunction. In this construction *like* is often used informally, but *as* is preferred in formal written English.]

like, as if Phrases such as *as if*, *as though* are used as conjunctions to introduce a subordinate clause. In writing, avoid using *like* in place of these conjunctions.

INFORMAL The room looked **like** a tornado had struck it.
FORMAL The room looked **as if** [or *as though*] a tornado had struck it.

might of, must of See **could of.**

nowheres See **anywheres.**

of Do not use *of* with prepositions such as *inside*, *off*, *outside*, etc.

> EXAMPLES **Outside** [not *outside of*] the house it was cool.
> The robber leaped **off** [not *off of*] the roof.

Of is also unnecessary with *had.*

> EXAMPLE If he **had** [not *had of*] remembered to come, I would not have had to walk.

off of See **of.**

ought The verb *ought* should never be used with *had.*

> SUBSTANDARD Pam had ought to be finished by now.
> STANDARD Pam **ought** to be finished by now.
>
> SUBSTANDARD You hadn't ought to tease your sister so much.
> STANDARD You **ought** not to tease your sister so much.

respectfully, respectively *Respectfully* means "with respect or full of respect." *Respectively* means "each in the order given."

> EXAMPLES The visiting dignitaries were greeted **respectfully** by the President.
>
> Milt, Bruce, and Rodney won blue, red, and white ribbons **respectively.**

● EXERCISE 3. Number your paper 1–20. Choose the correct form in parentheses, and write it after the proper number on your paper.

1. (Leave, Let) me have your answer by tomorrow.
2. My sister (learned, taught) me how to dance.
3. The petition was (respectfully, respectively) presented.
4. (Leave, Let) me finish my work.

5. He always drives (like, as if) he were alone on the road.
6. Don't do (like, as) I do; do (like, as) I say.
7. What (sort of, sort of a) movie did you see last night?
8. Simon was hurt when he fell (off, off of) the barn roof.
9. Although we didn't agree with the speaker, we listened to him (respectfully, respectively).
10. When the meeting is over, (let, leave) Peter lock the room.
11. You can actually (learn, teach) an old dog new tricks.
12. Gentlemen, I regret to say that Secretary Reeves will not appear owing to the fact that he feels (kind of, rather) ill.
13. (Leave, Let) sleeping dogs lie.
14. Willy (ought, had ought) to be here by this time.
15. She acted (like, as if) she had seen a ghost.
16. "(Leave, Let) me have some more of that," he said.
17. For two years now, Mr. Bruni has been trying in vain to (learn, teach) me Latin.
18. If you (had of, had) brought your glove, we could have had a game of catch.
19. Vince dived (off, off of) the bridge into the river.
20. (Inside, Inside of) the library, all was quiet.

rise, raise   See pages 175–76.

same   *Same* is used as an adjective (the *same* day, the *same* person) and as a pronoun (more of the *same*). In the latter use, *same* should always be used with *the*. Such uses as the following should be avoided:

> Four witnesses saw the crime and reported same to the police. [In this sentence, *it* is preferable.]

hall, will   Some careful users of English consistently use *shall* in the first person in forming the future and future perfect and *will* in second and third persons. Those who observe this distinction usually reverse this procedure in emphatic statements.

EXAMPLES   I **shall** go. [simple future]   I **will** go. [emphatic]
He **will** go. [simple future]   He **shall** go. [emphatic]

However, only a few educated speakers of American English observe this distinction. Other educated speakers use *will* to form the simple future in the first person as well as in the second and third persons.

STANDARD **I will go.**

sit, set See pages 173–74.

so In writing avoid using this overworked word as a conjunction meaning "therefore."

POOR The undertow grew very strong, so Kate came out of the surf.

BETTER Because the undertow grew very strong, Kate came out of the surf.

In writing do not use *so* in the place of *so that*.

POOR She put on sandals so the sand wouldn't burn her feet.

BETTER She put on sandals **so that** the sand wouldn't burn her feet.

some In writing do not use *some* for *somewhat* as an adverb.

SUBSTANDARD When the tide turned, the swimming was some easier.

STANDARD When the tide turned, the swimming was **somewhat** easier.

sort of See **kind of, sort of.**

take, bring See **bring, take.**

than, then Do not use *then* in the place of *than*. *Than* is a conjunction used in comparisons.

EXAMPLE He is smarter **than I.**

Then is an adverb telling when.

EXAMPLE Rose added eggs; **then** she stirred the batter.

them *Them* is not an adjective. Use *these* or *those*.

SUBSTANDARD He ordered one of them power lawn mowers.
STANDARD He ordered one of those power lawn mowers.

this here, that there *Here* and *there* are unnecessary.

SUBSTANDARD This here chair is an antique.
STANDARD This chair is an antique.

try and In writing and in formal speaking, the correct form is *try to*.

INFORMAL If you try and relax, you won't be so nervous.
FORMAL If you try to relax, you won't be so nervous.

way, ways Use *way*, not *ways*, in referring to distance.

EXAMPLE He stopped a little way [not *ways*] down the path.

what Do not use *what* to mean *that*.

EXAMPLE The supplies that [not *what*] we carried with us lasted four days.

when, where Do not use *when* or *where* incorrectly in writing a definition.

WRONG A double-header is when the same two teams play each other twice on the same day.
RIGHT A double-header is a pair of games played by the same two opposing teams on the same day.

where Do not use *where* for *that*.

EXAMPLE I read that [not *where*] the new addition to the school was turned down by the voters.

where . . . at See at.

which, that, who *Which* is used to refer only to *things*. *That* is used to refer either to *people* or *things*. *Who* is used to refer only to *people*.

EXAMPLES   He sat in a chair **which** was broken.

He is the boy **who** [not *which*] is the editor of the school paper.

Here comes the boy **that** is the editor of the school paper.

who, whom   See pages 146–48.

● EXERCISE 4.   The following sentences contain examples of the errors listed after Exercise 3. Rewrite each sentence correctly, and then practice saying aloud the corrected form.

1. A peninsula is when a land area is surrounded on three sides by water.
2. I read where they have developed a new kind of engine what uses solar energy, or "sun power."
3. The students which ride this here bus make too much noise in the morning.
4. Them math problems look harder then they really are.
5. I ordered a box of stationery from you two weeks ago, but I have not yet received same.
6. A noun is where a word names a person, place, or thing.
7. Them girls always wear slacks.
8. Sandy read in the paper where it might snow tomorrow.
9. Aline packed her bag early so she would be on time.
10. They were the very ones which complained about the lack of service.
11. Them boys from Boyton live a little ways down this road.
12. After the nurse's visit, Jody felt some better.
13. I'm afraid my brother is much smarter then I am.
14. Them girls which are wearing corsages are to be ushers for today's assembly.
15. The band members were told to arrive early so they could rehearse.
16. The new mayor said that he would try and find a solution to the parking problem.
17. Put three egg whites into the bowl; then whip same into a fine froth.

18. I see in the paper where the mayor wants to hold a special referendum.
19. Myopia is when you can't see distant objects clearly.
20. This here automatic shift makes driving too easy.

● REVIEW EXERCISE A. Number your paper 1–10. Choose the correct form in parentheses, and write it after the proper number on your paper.

1. The Bar-H Ranch is (somewheres, somewhere) near Cheyenne.
2. Nora is much taller (than, then) Pauline.
3. Wally read (where, that) the governor had vetoed the bill.
4. Unless you cooperate, it will be impossible to (learn, teach) you how to speak French.
5. Every spring we see (fewer, less) bluebirds.
6. You (had ought, ought) to congratulate yourself on your good luck.
7. It was Thomas Edison who (discovered, invented) the electric light bulb.
8. One of us must (of, have) made a mistake, for our answers disagree.
9. It (don't, doesn't) matter to me.
10. The treasurer's responsibilities consist of collecting dues, paying bills, keeping a running account of expenditures, (and etc., etc.).

● REVIEW EXERCISE B. Write twenty original sentences correctly using the following words or phrases.

1. the effect
2. as if
3. not accepting
4. not excepting
5. brought
6. taken
7. beside Dotty
8. besides Dotty
9. they emigrated
10. they immigrated
11. among the three boys
12. between the two boys
13. as though
14. leave him
15. let him
16. Ted, Edith, and I respectfully
17. Ted, Edith, and I respectively
18. it affected
19. it effected
20. like

● REVIEW EXERCISE C.   Number your paper 1–30. Choose
the correct form in parentheses, and write it after the proper
number on your paper.

1. When Lincoln was first elected President, many people did
   not know what (kind of, kind of an) attitude he would take
   toward slavery.
2. If I could sing as (good, well) as you, I would (of, have)
   joined the Glee Club.
3. Tony must (have, of) walked a long (ways, way) in the wrong
   direction.
4. Margie (don't, doesn't) know how to balance equations.
5. He should (of, have) finished his homework by now.
6. She (doesn't, don't) usually like (them, those, that) kind
   of fish.
7. You shouldn't (of, have) taken advanced algebra when you
   could (of, have) taken business math.
8. The speakers took their (respectful, respective) places on the
   stage.
9. (Beside, Besides) being on the track team, Paul is editor of
   the school paper.
10. She refuses to be (learned, taught) how to operate the switch-
    board.
11. Did he really see a ghost, or was it just an (allusion, illusion)?
12. The (affects, effects) of the drought were disastrous.
13. When you have tea with Aunt Ellen, please act (as if, like)
    you were enjoying yourself.
14. Please (bring, take) your schedule card with you when you
    go to your next class.
15. If you (leave, let) me do it, I will finish the posters tonight.
16. Do you think that the poor corn harvest will (affect, effect)
    the price of beef?
17. None of the wrestlers did very (good, well) in the tourna-
    ment.
18. She addressed her teacher (respectfully, respectively).
19. "Smoking," said the coach, "will seriously (affect, effect)
    your performance in a game."
20. I cannot find my books (anywhere, anywheres).
21. (Being that, Because) a strike was called, no trucks went
    out that day.

22. Now that I have bought a ring, I hope that you will (accept, except) it.
23. Rainy days don't seem to have any (affect, effect) on student attendance.
24. Because my grandfather was weary of the bleak Midlands, he (emigrated, immigrated) from England in 1908.
25. Does his escape (imply, infer) that he is guilty?
26. Virginia refused to (accept, except) the nomination.
27. We divided the duties (between, among) the five of us.
28. The inspector's face was drained of blood; he looked (like, as if) he had seen a ghost.
29. (Inside of, Inside) the cabin were two porcupines.
30. Every year there are (fewer, less) trout in our streams.

THE DOUBLE NEGATIVE

A *double negative* is a construction in which two negative words are used when one is sufficient. Before the eighteenth century, two or more negatives were often used in the same sentence to make the meaning more emphatic. Standard modern English no longer uses this method of gaining emphasis, and a double negative is generally considered to be substandard.

can't hardly, can't scarcely The words *hardly* and *scarcely* should not be used with *not* (or the contraction of *not*, *n't*).

> EXAMPLES I **can** [not *can't*] **hardly** hear you when you speak so softly.
>
> We **had** [not *hadn't*] **scarcely** enough money to get home on.

haven't but, haven't only In certain uses, *but* and *only* convey a negative meaning and should not be used with *not*.

> EXAMPLES We **have** [not *haven't*] **but** three more tickets to sell.
>
> We **have** [not *haven't*] **only** one more chance.

no, nothing, none Do not use these negative words with another negative.

SUBSTANDARD	There isn't no need to be afraid of the dog.
STANDARD	There **is no** need to be afraid of the dog.
SUBSTANDARD	At first we couldn't see nothing.
STANDARD	At first we **could see nothing.**
STANDARD	At first we **couldn't see anything.**
SUBSTANDARD	We looked for a drugstore, but there weren't none open.
STANDARD	We looked for a drugstore, but there **weren't any** open.
STANDARD	We looked for a drugstore, but there **were none** open.

● EXERCISE 5. The following sentences contain many of the usage errors covered in this chapter. Rewrite each sentence correctly. Practice saying *aloud* the correct sentences.

1. He might of drowned if it hadn't been for Dave's clear thinking.
2. He don't know if he should ask Hope to the dance because she hasn't hardly spoken to him in three days.
3. My grandfather he said that we hadn't ought to use the boat in such bad weather.
4. My grandfather has always been kind of timid.
5. I can't hardly help thinking she don't listen to what I say.
6. My cousins didn't hardly know how to ski, but they wouldn't of missed going to the ski lodge.
7. If you had of been at the meeting, we wouldn't of had no arguments.
8. He don't have nothing to do tonight.
9. The suit didn't hardly fit me no more.
10. The little kitten what we found in the vacant lot didn't hardly seem alive.
11. Hadn't you ought to come to the meeting?
12. Try and remember where you hid them keys at.

13. That there heap of junk is not the kind of a secondhand car that I want.
14. Them apples what you brought were wormy.
15. The boys which are in charge of checking the coats don't have no more hangers.
16. The symbol x in algebra stands for when a quantity is not given a specific value.
17. I read in the paper where the Dodgers bought them new players from the Giants.
18. These kind of books are the most popular in Mr. Wardner's class.
19. It don't look right to me, but then I don't know nothing about art.
20. She said that she was feeling some better now.
21. When the sun set, the woods suddenly became sort of gloomy.
22. The police department requested additional funds so it could purchase a new squad car.
23. Sarah don't have but three more pages to do.
24. So I could swim faster, I bought a pair of swim fins.
25. By the end of the year, Bob was taller than any boy in his class.

● REVIEW EXERCISE D. The following sentences contain many of the common errors you have been studying. Rewrite the sentences correctly.

1. That there book isn't no good.
2. She lives a long ways from here.
3. He don't hardly know what he's talking about.
4. I couldn't hardly remember having made them mistakes; my mind must of been a blank.
5. There goes a man what has never done nobody any harm.
6. Being that my brother left for college, I can't wear his clothes no more.
7. There isn't no state in this here country that he hasn't visited.
8. My mother she can't hardly help bragging about my brother's winning the four-year scholarship.
9. He fell off of a ladder and busted his leg.
10. You hadn't ought to of walked home in that there rain.

11. You can't hardly smell the smoke from here; the wind must of changed.

12. Because there was so much to do before Christmas, I hadn't hardly no time at all to buy the present what I saw in the catalogue.

13. A haze settled over the town, and you couldn't hardly see where you were going.

14. Lisa is some taller than Fran.

15. The scientist applied for a grant so he could continue his research.

16. If you hadn't only enough books for half the students, you should of gone to the bookroom for more.

17. Our water pipes they bursted during the cold snap, and when my father he received the repair bill, he almost busted.

18. Being that my mother won't let me use the phone after eight o'clock, my friends they think she is strict.

19. A *tsunami* is when there is a tidal wave caused by an earthquake.

20. In this here paper I read where the mayor has appointed a new chairman of the park board.

21. You should of received your notice in the mail, since Inez don't never forget to send out the cards.

22. It don't seem right that Mr. Hodson should always pick on Gloria, being that she can't hardly help it if the bus is always late.

23. Here is a boy which should try and do better.

24. Hadn't you ought to clean out this here locker?

25. My brother he says he can't hardly carry all them packages by himself.

PART THREE

Sentence Structure

CHAPTER 11

Writing Complete Sentences

Sentence Fragments and Run-on Sentences

Two of the most common errors in student writing result from carelessness in marking the end of one sentence and the beginning of the next. The first kind of error, the *sentence fragment*, occurs when a part of a sentence—a phrase or subordinate clause, for example—is written as a complete sentence. The second, the run-on sentence, occurs when two or more sentences are run together with only a comma, or no punctuation at all, between them.

SENTENCE FRAGMENTS

11a. A *sentence fragment* is a group of words that does not express a complete thought. Since it is only a part of a sentence, it should not be allowed to stand by itself but should be kept in the sentence of which it is a part.

A group of words is not a sentence unless it has both a subject and a verb and expresses a complete thought. The following examples are fragments because they fail to meet one or both of these conditions.

FRAGMENT   The quarterback having a poor memory for numbers. [The *-ing* form of a verb cannot function as the verb in a sentence unless it has a helping verb with it.]

FRAGMENT   Since the quarterback had a poor memory for numbers. [The subordinating conjunction *since* signals that what follows is only part of a larger sentence. Taken by itself, the fragment does not express a complete thought.]

Both of the fragments illustrated above are really parts of a longer sentence:

EXAMPLES   All the plays were identified by girls' names, the quarterback having a poor memory for numbers.

All the plays were identified by girls' names since the quarterback had a poor memory for numbers.

Good writers sometimes punctuate fragments as sentences for stylistic reasons. For example, you may sometimes notice a fragment like this in a story:

FRAGMENT   Murchison finally managed to get out of the third grade. *On his third try.*

The second part is not a complete sentence. It is only a prepositional phrase. The writer used a capital letter at the beginning and a period at the end of the phrase for humorous effect, thinking the point would be lost otherwise:

Murchison finally managed to get out of the third grade on his third try.

A better solution would have been to use a dash, thus gaining the desired emphasis while remaining within the limits of conventional punctuation:

Murchison finally managed to get out of the third grade—on his third try.

Although the use of fragments can be justified, the practice requires experience and judgment, and the beginning writer will do well to avoid it.

11a

The Phrase Fragment

A phrase is a group of words acting as a single part of speech and not containing a verb and its subject.

You will recall from your study of verbals (pages 65–76) that present participles and gerunds are words ending in *–ing*. Words ending in *–ing* cannot be used as verbs unless they follow a helping verb. With a helping verb like *am*, *are*, *has been*, *will be*, etc., they become complete verbs. It is the same with infinitive phrases. Like participial and gerund phrases, infinitive phrases can never stand alone. In order to make sense, they must be attached to a preceding or following sentence or be completed by being developed into a proper sentence.

A participial phrase must not be written as a sentence.

FRAGMENT   The dog barking at a stranger. [a phrase; no verb]

CORRECTED   The dog **was barking** at a stranger. [The present participle has been made into a complete verb by the addition of the helping verb *was*.]

FRAGMENT   We examined the building. Burned and partially destroyed by fire. [The participial phrase modifies the word *building*. It must be included in the sentence with the word it modifies.]

CORRECTED   We examined the building, **burned and partially destroyed by fire.** [The fragment is corrected by including the participial phrase in the sentence with the word it modifies.]

A gerund phrase must not be written as a sentence.

FRAGMENT   Sue dislikes working in the kitchen. Cleaning and scrubbing objects which in a few hours will be dirty again. [Here a gerund phrase functioning as an appositive of *working* is cut off from it by the period. It must be reconnected.]

CORRECTED   Sue dislikes working in the kitchen, **cleaning and scrubbing objects which in a few hours will be dirty again.** [The gerund phrase fragment is corrected by including it in the sentence.]

An infinitive phrase must not be written as a sentence.

FRAGMENT   You must first learn to float. To swim properly and with confidence. [The phrase cannot stand alone. It should be attached to the preceding sentence.]

CORRECTED   You must first learn to float **to swim properly and with confidence.**

A prepositional phrase or a succession of prepositional phrases must not be written as a sentence.

FRAGMENT   The swimming hole is on Kelly Brook. On the far side of the west pasture of the Johnson farm. [Here three successive prepositional phrases are isolated. They make sense only when included in the sentence of which they are a part.]

CORRECTED   The swimming hole is on Kelly Brook **on the far side of the west pasture of the Johnson farm.**

In each of the examples above, the sentence fragments were cut off from the sentences they were part of by improper punctuation. This kind of mistake is easily corrected: simply attach the isolated phrase to the parent sentence.

● EXERCISE 1.   Below are ten phrase fragments. Convert each one into a complete sentence by using one of two methods: (1) attach it to an independent clause, or (2) develop the phrase into a complete sentence.

EXAMPLE   1. pulling on her gloves
          1. *Pulling on her gloves, Cindy left the theater.* [attached]
             or
          1. *Cindy pulled on her gloves.* [developed]

1. standing on the deck beside the captain
2. to make set shots consistently from outside the pivot position
3. on lower Main Street under the Lexington Bridge
4. captured by the Hurons
5. to stay alert
6. after finishing his assignment

7. murmuring something about a meeting
8. burned and blistered by the sun
9. playing tennis in the hot sun
10. performing the chemistry experiments

The Appositive Fragment

An appositive is a noun or pronoun that follows another noun or pronoun to identify or explain it. An appositive phrase is made up of an appositive and its modifiers; it should not be written as a separate sentence.

EXAMPLES   Mike, **the best mechanic in the garage,** worked on my car. [*The best mechanic in the garage* is an appositive. It is in apposition with *Mike.*]

In two years I will graduate from Madison High School, **a red brick building with a golden cupola.** [*A red brick building with a golden cupola* is in apposition with *Madison High School.*]

Sometimes a hasty writer will treat an appositive phrase as a complete sentence and leave it standing alone, even though it lacks a verb and subject and does not express a complete thought.

FRAGMENT   The amateur boat-builder was constructing a simple model. A small outboard cruiser of conventional design.

CORRECTED   The amateur boat-builder was constructing a simple model, **a small outboard cruiser of conventional design.** [The appositive phrase has been attached to the sentence in which it belongs.]

● EXERCISE 2.   The examples below contain appositives written as sentence fragments. Repair the fragments by making them parts of complete sentences.

1. Our word *tobacco* comes from the Spanish word *tabaco*. A word which means "cigar" in the Arawak Indian language.
2. Columbus' crew was astonished to find the natives puffing on huge cigars in Hispaniola. The island which is now divided between Haiti and the Dominican Republic.

3. The cigars were made from *Nicotiana tabacum.* A hybrid of two wild plants first grown in Peru and Bolivia.
4. This tobacco from Hispaniola was not the kind smoked by the other Indians of North America. Habitual users of tobacco, also.
5. This second and much more widely used kind of tobacco was *Nicotiana rustica.* A hybrid that is native only to the western slopes of the Andes.
6. From there its cultivation and use spread into North America at about the same time as the cultivation of maize. A staple grain crop.
7. Archeologists find the first pipes among Indian artifacts at the level that they find the first evidence of maize cultivation. A fact which suggests that the Indians learned to smoke and to grow corn at the same time.
8. This tobacco was so strong that the Algonkians mixed it with sumac leaves and the inner bark of the dogwood and called it *kinnikinnik.* A word meaning "that which is mixed."
9. Most Indians favored pipes, some ate tobacco leaves, some drank tobacco, and still others preferred cigarettes. Shredded tobacco wrapped in corn husks.
10. "Drinking tobacco" became popular in Elizabethan England after 1565. The year the leaf was first imported from the West Indies.

The Subordinate Clause Fragment

Although the subordinate clause does have a verb and a subject, it depends upon the independent clause of a sentence to complete its meaning. Standing alone, a subordinate clause suggests a question which it does not answer.

EXAMPLES   Because the machine is dangerous. [Well . . .? What will happen?]

If you do not know how to operate it. [Well . . .? What will happen?]

An isolated subordinate clause must be attached to an independent clause in order to complete its meaning. It should not be written as a sentence.

FRAGMENT   Television makeup differs from stage makeup. Because it must withstand the intense heat from the studio lamps.

CORRECTED   Television makeup differs from stage makeup **because it must withstand the intense heat from the studio lamps.**

FRAGMENT   Lamps that burned fat or olive oil served as the only source of artificial light until 1600. When petroleum was discovered.

CORRECTED   Lamps that burned fat or olive oil served as the only source of artificial light until 1600, **when petroleum was discovered.**

◆ NOTE   In combining an adverb clause with an independent clause, the adverb clause may either precede or follow the independent clause.

EXAMPLES   **If you bring your guitar to the picnic,** we can have some music. [adverb clause first]

          We can have some music **if you bring your guitar to the picnic.** [adverb clause last]

● EXERCISE 3.   The following paragraph contains several sentence fragments. They are all subordinate clauses that should be attached to an independent clause. Copy the paragraph, changing the punctuation to eliminate the subordinate clause fragments.

Xenophon, who was the author of the *Anabasis*, was a pupil of Socrates. Who was unwilling to follow his master's call to a life of contemplation, seeking instead a life of action. Athens provided little scope for the young man's ambition. Because at that time the city was divided against itself. Accordingly, when the report went round that Cyrus the Younger was recruiting a Greek army to help him invade Persia and overthrow Artaxerxes, the tyrant of that country. Xenophon joined the expedition as a junior officer. "The 10,000," as the Greek mercenary army was called, marched 1,300 miles into Asia Minor. Where at Cunaxa in the fall of the year it met the Persian army in battle. Cyrus was killed, his Asiatic forces were scattered, and the Greeks were left 1,300 miles from safety in the heart of a hostile country. Even worse, the army was without leaders. Because Artaxerxes had invited the Greek commanders to a peace parley and then had treacherously murdered them. Xenophon was put in command and in the ensuing five months accomplished a great feat. That will live in the annals of military history. In the dead of winter he brought his army through deserts and mountains, through pitched battles and constant harassment by wild mountain tribes, to the sea and safety. The first sight of the sea was deeply moving to the Greeks. Who had grown up always within sight, sound, and smell of the Aegean. Hearing a great tumult and shouting at the head of the dusty column, Xenophon rushed forward to direct the defense against what he assumed to be another attack. Soon, however, his heart lifted in joy. Because the men of the vanguard were shouting, "Thalassa! Thalassa!" ("The sea! The sea!") Soon the whole army crowded up to the ridge. Where the comrades embraced each other and wept for joy.

● Exercise 4. Add an independent clause either at the beginning or at the end of each of the following subordinate clauses to make ten complete sentences. When an adverb clause comes at the beginning of a sentence, it should be followed by a comma.

1. if we break the equipment
2. when they send the message
3. who drop out of high school
4. which I have never read
5. as we shut off the motor
6. what you forgot to say
7. before you do anything impulsive
8. that he was your brother
9. until he can cut the grass
10. while I was in the dentist's office

● Exercise 5. Some of the following groups of words are complete sentences. Others are fragments. On your paper, mark the complete sentences with an *S*, and correct the fragments by making them parts of complete sentences.

1. Furnished with beautifully finished cottages, the resort was one of the finest in the area.
2. Running and dodging are features of lacrosse. Whose original object among the Indians seems to have been the development of endurance and agility.
3. If you decide to go.
4. The women shopped all day at the huge department store.
5. Elected by an overwhelming number of the students.
6. As he opened the door and peered out.
7. Because it was foggy and the visibility was poor.
8. Located in the middle of a swamp. The cabin was four miles from the highway.
9. Driving at night can be dangerous. Blinded by the lights of an approaching car. We almost hit a tree.
10. Because they wanted to escape the heat. They left for the mountains. Setting out in the early part of August.
11. To climb up the steep cliff with a heavy pack and rifle slung on his back was difficult.
12. He was plagued with difficulties. Losing his way, running out of water, and falling over vines and creepers.
13. How he envied the hawk. Gliding effortlessly high over the tangle of the swamp and thickets.
14. To break through the last thicket of brambles and dwarf cedar into the clearing. This was the hope that drove him on.
15. This was the Maine wilderness. Through which Arnold and his men had dragged cannon and other heavy equipment on their way to Quebec.

THE RUN-ON SENTENCE

11b. Avoid the run-on sentence. Do not use a comma between sentences. Do not omit punctuation at the end of a sentence.

There are two main ways in which independent clauses can be combined in a single sentence: (1) by means of a comma plus a word like *and* or *but;* (2) by means of a semicolon. The following examples illustrate these two methods.

Skiing is a matter of balance, and a skier must use his poles as counterweights and his knees as shock absorbers. [A comma plus *and* is used to join the two independent clauses.]

Skiing is a matter of balance; a skier must use his poles as counterweights and his knees as shock absorbers. [A semi-colon is used to join the clauses.]

Other devices, such as the colon and the dash, are sometimes used, but a comma alone is never enough between independent clauses. Using a comma or no punctuation at all in this situation results in a run-on sentence:

Skiing is a matter of balance, a skier must use his poles as counterweights and his knees as shock absorbers.

Like the sentence fragment, the run-on sentence is sometimes used effectively by experienced writers, especially when its parts are very short. A famous example is the translation of Julius Caesar's boast "I came, I saw, I conquered," which is sometimes written with commas and sometimes with semicolons.

An easy test for spotting run-on sentences consists of simply reading your compositions aloud. The rise or fall of your voice and the pause you make at the end of a sentence sound quite different from the intonation and pause that a comma usually signals.

● EXERCISE 6. The following passages contain a number of run-on sentences. Determine where each sentence properly begins and ends, and write the last word in the sentence with the proper end mark after it. Then write the first word of the following sentence with a capital letter.

1. Having been excused early, we hurried to the locker room and changed to our baseball suits, when the coach called us, we were ready to go the big bus drew up in the drive, and just as we had done a dozen other times, we piled in and took our usual seats this trip was different, however, every boy knew how different it was we would return either as champions of the state or as just another second-rate ball team.

11b

2. It was the hottest day we could remember, coming down the street, we were sure we could see heat waves rising from the sidewalk, we felt as though we'd never get home we ambled up the street in a daze, hoping we'd last just one more block, we knew if we could make it there would be large bottles of ice-cold soda awaiting us.

3. Working on a lake steamer all summer was monotonous, it was also better than any other job I could have obtained, I loved the water and the ships and the rough and ready men with whom I worked, the food was good the work was not too strenuous, if it hadn't been for the sameness of the routine day after day, I should probably never have left.

● REVIEW EXERCISE. Read the following paragraphs carefully. They contain sentence fragments and run-on sentences. Copy the passage, removing all fragments and run-ons by changing the punctuation and capital letters whenever necessary.

Our national bird is the great bald eagle. As most Americans know. Similar to the bald eagle is the golden eagle. Which has a wingspread up to seven and a half feet. The national bird is protected by law, but the golden eagle is not, the result is that hunters are rapidly diminishing the number of these great birds. If the golden eagles are not also given the protection of the law, they may become extinct. In a few years.

The National Audubon Society says that the annual slaughter of golden eagles is a national disgrace. Some hunters bagging hundreds of eagles a year. Texas and Oklahoma are the principal hunting territories, the birds are often shot from airplanes by gunners. Who are paid both by sheep ranchers and by manufacturers. Who want the feathers. Sheep ranchers claim the eagles menace sheep, tourists buy the feathers. Protecting the golden eagle will also provide further protection for the bald eagle. Because hunters often mistakenly kill bald eagles. Which, at a certain stage in growth, resemble golden eagles.

The golden eagle migrates to Texas and Oklahoma from northern regions. Such as Canada, Alaska, and our other Northwestern states. Golden eagles will be protected. If Congress amends the Bald Eagle Act. To include golden eagles.

CHAPTER 12

The Effective Sentence

Emphasis and Variety in Sentences

While a knowledge of grammar and punctuation is of obvious help in learning to write correct sentences, there is a good deal more to effective writing than avoiding errors in sentence structure. The main difference between good writing and bad writing is not a matter of correctness, but a matter of *style*.

Style is a hard word to define exactly, but its essential meaning is "a way of doing something." The idea of style has many other applications in addition to its application to writing. For example, a tennis champion and an ordinary player perform essentially the same operations in serving the ball, yet even a spectator who knows little about the game can usually see a difference. In tennis, and in most other things, there is a difference between doing things well and doing them any old way.

Of course, there are many more ways of writing a sentence than there are ways of serving a tennis ball. Still, from the point of view of style, it is quite easy to tell a good sentence from a bad one. It is considerably harder to write good sentences all of the time. Nevertheless, there are some simple principles that should help.

VARYING SENTENCE BEGINNINGS

12a. Vary the beginnings of your sentences.

The normal way to form an English sentence is to begin with the subject and end with the predicate. Any piece of writing in which most of the sentences depart from this natural order is certain to strike a reader as artificial. However, an unbroken sequence of subject-predicate sentences may result in another stylistic fault—monotony. Such a sequence is monotonous because it lacks the logical connections and special emphasis that variation in sentence structure can provide.

Compare the following versions of the same paragraph. In the first, each sentence begins in the same way. In the second, an attempt has been made to achieve emphasis and clarity by varying sentence beginnings.

NOT VARIED

The trial had been scheduled for two o'clock. The audience was noisily settling itself in the courtroom for the coming show. The lawyers were quietly talking and shuffling piles of papers at the polished tables in the front of the room. The bell in the courthouse tower struck two in resounding tones. Judge Walker, dignified in his long black gown, walked slowly to his bench. The clerk rasped out, "Everyone rise." The room seemed suddenly to lift for a moment; then it settled back into an ominous silence. The judge opened the case of the People vs. John Strong in a bored manner which seemed to imply that murder trials happened every day of his life.

VARIED

The trial had been scheduled for two o'clock. In the courtroom the audience was noisily settling itself for the coming show. At the polished tables in the front of the room, the lawyers were quietly talking and shuffling piles of papers. When the bell in the courthouse tower struck two in resounding tones, Judge Walker, dignified in his long black gown, walked slowly to his bench. "Everyone rise," rasped the clerk. Suddenly the room seemed to lift for a moment; then it settled back into an ominous silence. In a bored manner which seemed to imply that murder trials happened every day of his life, the judge opened the case of the People vs. John Strong.

The normal order of sentences need not be avoided merely for the sake of variety. It is often possible to increase the force and clarity of a statement by beginning with an important modifier.

The exercises that follow are intended to give you practice in using different kinds of sentence openers. Used sparingly, such devices will improve your writing.

(1) You may begin a sentence with a single-word modifier—an adverb, an adjective, or a participle.

EXAMPLES **Instantly** I felt better. [adverb]

Thick and slimy, the mud oozed from under the wheels. [adjectives]

Grinning, Myra turned on her favorite program. [present participle]

Dejected, the coach sat on the bench and brooded over his team. [past participle]

● EXERCISE 1. The following sentences, all of which begin with a simple subject, contain single-word modifiers which can be placed at the beginning of the sentence. Find this modifier and rewrite the sentence, placing the modifier first. The sentences in this and the following exercises are good sentences. You are asked to rewrite them so that you will learn a variety of ways of expressing the same idea.

EXAMPLE 1. The curtain opened suddenly.
1. *Suddenly the curtain opened.*

1. The detective began slowly and carefully to examine the evidence.
2. The scout crept forward silently.

12a

3. The rope, old and frayed, broke under the boy's weight.
4. The puffing and grunting wrestler pinned his opponent.
5. We laughed at ourselves later for having been afraid.
6. The jacket, cleaned and pressed, looked almost new.
7. The car, old and battered, chugged up the steep hill.
8. The doctor skillfully performed the dangerous operation.
9. The director stormed angrily out of the studio.
10. The dog, surprised, gave a yelp and scrambled under the bed.

● EXERCISE 2.   Write five sentences of your own beginning with single-word modifiers. Include at least one adjective, one adverb, and one participial modifier.

**(2) You may begin a sentence with a phrase: a prepo-
sitional phrase, a participial phrase, an appositive
phrase, or an infinitive phrase.**

EXAMPLES   **At the sound of the bell,** the teacher collected the
papers.   [prepositional phrase]

Having examined the records, the lawyer prepared a
new deed.   [participial phrase]

An excellent example of modern architecture, the
new city hall is a favorite tourist site.   [appositive
phrase]

To learn to swim better, we took lessons at the pool.
[infinitive phrase]

● EXERCISE 3.   The following sentences, all of which begin with the subject, contain phrase modifiers which can be
placed at the beginning of the sentence. Rephrase the sentences by placing the modifying phrases at the beginning.
Place a comma after each introductory phrase.

1. Pompeii was a well-to-do commercial city at the foot of Mt.
Vesuvius.
2. Its population at the time of its destruction was about
30,000.
3. Archeologists have discovered many facts about the life and
times of ancient Pompeii to add to our knowledge of bygone
days.
4. Wealthy Romans, attracted by the beauty of the location
and the healthfulness of the climate, built many villas there.

5. The streets, paved with blocks of lava, were usually wide and straight.
6. The Forum was a rectangular square, completely surrounded by temples and public buildings, near the western edge of the city.
7. Mt. Vesuvius had never given any indication of its volcanic character up to the year A.D. 63.
8. The inhabitants, still rebuilding their city from the ravages of earthquakes, were overwhelmed by the sudden eruption of August 24, A.D. 79.
9. The people fled the city to save their lives.
10. The existence of Pompeii was forgotten during the Middle Ages, and it was not until 1763 that excavations of the city began.

● EXERCISE 4. Rewrite the following sentences so that each begins with either a word or a phrase modifier. In rearranging the sentences, you may wish to drop some of the words or add others; you may do so provided you keep the original meaning. Hints are given for the first five.

EXAMPLE   1. We were tired and decided to leave the party early.

1. *Tired, we decided to leave the party early.*

1. Tommy flopped into the nearest chair and kicked off his shoes. [Begin with *kicking.*]
2. He looked through *TV Guide* to find what time the program started. [Begin with *to find.*]
3. He switched on his favorite program at seven o'clock sharp. [Begin with *at.*]
4. We scraped the old bureau down to the natural wood and discovered that it was real mahogany. [Begin with *scraping.*]
5. Our boat, trim and fast, won the race. [Begin with *trim.*]
6. My car was greased last week, and now it runs perfectly.
7. The stage crew, working evenings after school for weeks, completed the sets on schedule.
8. The band marched around the field and entertained the spectators during the half.

9. Garden City High School has good school spirit and always has a large attendance at the football games.
10. The light bulb, flickering on and off for several seconds, finally went out.

(3) You may begin a sentence with a subordinate clause.

EXAMPLES   I was unable to attend the Junior Prom because I had the flu.

Because I had the flu, I was unable to attend the Junior Prom.

Steve was interested in joining the Masquers Club and the Film Group, but he did not have time to attend the meetings.

Although Steve was interested in joining the Masquers Club and the Film Group, he did not have time to attend the meetings.

● EXERCISE 5.   Rephrase each sentence so that it begins with a subordinate clause instead of the subject. Place a comma after an adverb clause coming first in the sentence.

1. The praying mantis is a welcome guest in any garden because it destroys many harmful pests. [Because . . .]
2. The insects are not large in this country, but their South American relatives are big enough to devour small birds. [Although . . .]
3. The Hottentots regarded the mantis highly, and the alighting of the local species on any person was considered a token of saintliness and an omen of good fortune.   [Since . . .]
4. They watch patiently for their prey, and these creatures assume a sort of kneeling position.   [When . . .]
5. Superstitious people believed these insects to be engaged in prayer, and so mantises were often called soothsayers or prophets.   [Because . . .]
6. This insect can fly, but it prefers to wait on shrubs for its unsuspecting dinner to come by.
7. The mantis moves quietly and carefully, and seldom does its prey get away.

8. The forelegs shoot out like lightning, and the victim is caught in the mantis' trap.
9. The female lays small groups of eggs, and she attaches these to boards or twigs.
10. The eggs hatch in May or June, and the small mantises look almost exactly like their parents.
11. The baby mantises develop wings as they mature.
12. The female mantis harbors no love for her mate, and a male mantis may find himself his wife's dinner if he is not fast on his feet.
13. These voracious eaters of destructive pests are protected by law in many areas, and a person may be fined for harming them.

● EXERCISE 6. Change the following sentences in the manner suggested.

1. The steak was thick and juicy, and it just seemed to melt in my mouth. [Begin with single-word modifiers.]
2. The batter swung wildly at the ball. [Begin with a single-word modifier.]
3. The Student Council elected a parliamentarian to settle all disputes about conducting a meeting. [Begin with an infinitive phrase.]
4. Bob forgot his lines in the middle of the second act. [Begin with prepositional phrases.]
5. The house was appraised at $20,000 last year and sold for $22,000 this week. [Begin with a past participial phrase.]
6. The bookstore in our town gives special discounts at Christmas time. [Begin with a prepositional phrase.]
7. The coach was annoyed at Joe's failure to show up for practice and benched him for two games. [Begin with a past participial phrase.]
8. Mrs. Wentworth came into the room and told us to report to the auditorium for our seventh-period class. [Begin with a subordinate clause.]
9. We rowed across the lake and camped at Paradise Point. [Begin with a participial phrase.]
10. I liked *A Separate Peace* very much and have recommended it to all my friends. [Begin with a subordinate clause.]

VARYING SENTENCE STRUCTURE

12b. Vary the kinds of sentences.

You learned in Chapter 4 that, when classified according to their structure, there are four kinds of sentences: *simple, compound, complex,* and *compound-complex.* If you are not sure of the characteristics of each of these, you should turn back to pages 96–97 and refresh your memory before going further.

Just as it is possible to achieve variety in your writing by varying the beginnings of your sentences, it is also possible to achieve variety by varying the kinds of sentences you use. Using simple or compound sentences all the time tends to make your style monotonous. For example, read the following paragraph composed almost entirely of simple and compound sentences.

1. My dad always gets a yearning for a family reunion just before Thanksgiving. 2. At this time, the magazines show smiling families sitting around tables laden with the most massive turkeys outside a zoo. 3. Mom smiles bravely at his resolution and resigns herself. 4. I sit there and glower. 5. The magazines never really show the "before and after" of sitting down to consume the traditional fare. 6. Mom has a mania for cleanliness. 7. With company coming, we will turn the house upside down to create a good impression. 8. We will rearrange the house thoroughly and clean the silverware and do other odd jobs. 9. These tasks finally completed, we will stagger to the door to greet our guests. 10. Then we will put a sizable dent in the turkey; then we will have endless varieties of leftover food. 11. We will have hot and cold turkey sandwiches, creamed turkey, turkey hash, turkey surprise, and finally turkey soup. 12. Eventually we will throw the skeletal remains out and feel the strangest urge to gobble. 13. I must not forget one thing. 14. Cinderella, that's me, will have a gala time with the pots and pans. 15. I would like to change the routine. 16. I hate drudgery.

Now read the next paragraph, which tells the same tale but contains many complex sentences (the new subordinate clauses are italicized). You will see the superiority of this version over the first one.

1. My dad always gets a yearning for a family reunion just prior to Thanksgiving *when the magazines show smiling families sitting around tables laden with the most massive turkeys outside a zoo.* 2. Mom smiles bravely at his announcement and says, "Yes, dear." 3. I sit there and glower. 4. The magazines never really show *what goes on before and after the merry throng sits down to consume the traditional fare.* 5. *Because Mom has a mania for cleanliness,* we will turn the house upside down to create a good impression for the expected company. 6. We will rearrange the house thoroughly and clean silverware and do other odd jobs. 7. These tasks finally completed, we will stagger to the door to greet our guests. 8. *After we have put a sizable dent in the turkey,* we will have endless varieties of leftover food. 9. We will have hot and cold turkey sandwiches, creamed turkey, turkey hash, turkey surprise, and finally turkey soup. 10. *Before the skeletal remains are thrown out,* we will feel the strangest urge to gobble. 11. I must not forget to mention *that Cinderella, that's me, will have a gala time with the pots and pans.* 12. Do you think for one instant *that I would change the family routine in spite of the drudgery?* 13. You bet your life *I would!*

Actually, all that had to be done to break the monotony of the first version was to change some of the less important ideas from independent clauses to subordinate clauses. A subordinate clause in a sentence makes the sentence complex.

Using subordinate clauses not only gives variety to your writing but also helps you to show how the ideas in a sentence are related. One idea may be the cause or the result of another idea in the sentence, or it may give the time of the other. Study the following pairs of sentences. The first sentence in each pair is compound; the second is complex.

12b

Notice that in the second sentence the relationship between ideas is clearer than in the first sentence.

EXAMPLES   Our school is very crowded this year, and most of the study halls are in the auditorium.

Because our school is very crowded this year, most of the study halls are in the auditorium. [The first idea expresses the *cause* of the second.]

The Cabinet met in emergency session, and the President consulted his staff.

Before the Cabinet met in emergency session, the President consulted his staff. [One idea gives the *time* of the other.]

The band members rehearse every day after school, and then they can give a good performance at their concert.

The band members rehearse every day after school **so that they can give a good performance at their concert.** [The idea in the subordinate clause states the reason for the idea in the main clause.]

The following words, when used at the beginning of a subordinate clause, help to make clear the relationship between the sentence ideas:

CAUSE because, since, as
RESULT OR REASON so that, in order that
TIME when, while, as, since, until, after, before, whenever

Whenever you are combining ideas, make sure that your connectives are appropriate.

● EXERCISE 7. Change each of the following compound sentences into a complex sentence by expressing one of the ideas in a subordinate clause. Begin each subordinate clause with a word which will show how the ideas in the sentence are related: cause, result or reason, time.

1. I have two study halls tomorrow, and so I plan to go to the library then to work on my research paper.
2. Marie took careful notes in social studies, and then she was prepared for the big test today.

3. Mr. Stein had taken the attendance, and he began to distribute the uniforms.

4. Our team scored a touchdown, and the fans in the stands roared their approval.

5. Write your answers in two columns, and then your paper will be easier to correct.

6. The time to give my speech neared, and I grew more nervous with each passing second.

7. My dad likes the Adirondack Mountains, and we spend our summers there at Horseshoe Lake.

8. I went to the box office to buy tickets, and it was closed for the day.

9. Hollywood makes many movies, and it is the film capital of the United States.

10. He was shaving, and he cut his lip.

● EXERCISE 8. The following paragraphs consist chiefly of simple and compound sentences. Rewrite them, varying the style by changing or combining some of the sentences into complex sentences. Do not try to make all your sentences complex, for your purpose is to get variety.

1. My first day in high school was one of the most hectic days of my life. It all seems ridiculous now, but it was no joke then. With my heart in my mouth, I boarded the school bus that morning. Many of my old friends from junior high days were seated there, but for some strange reason they did not want to talk very much. Everybody was abnormally quiet, and the air was electric with the tension. Gus, the bus driver, must have enjoyed the ride. Usually he has to tell us about twenty times to pipe down.

2. The silent bus soon arrived at the high school, and we filed quickly into the courtyard. For the tenth time in five minutes, I looked at my instructions for the first day. These instructions had come in the mail the week before, and by now I had practically memorized them. Still, I did not want to lose them. "Proceed to the student lobby and check your name on the lists posted there," stated the valuable paper. To make a long story short, I did just that and soon located my name on the bulletin board. The next step was to find Room 134, my official homeroom according to the list on the wall.

3. I wandered all over the school looking for Room 134. I should have asked for directions and saved myself a lot of trouble, but I was too stupid. At least, that's my excuse today. I bumped into Ray and Mike, my best friends last year. They were looking for Room 147. They didn't know the location of 134, but Ray did have a map of the school. I looked at it closely and found that Room 134 was right next to the student lobby.

4. I entered Room 134 slowly and glanced around. There wasn't a familiar face in sight. Where could all these strange people have come from? A short, red-haired man strode toward me and told me to take a seat. Sitting in the front makes me feel very conspicuous, so I selected a choice spot in the back of the room. I just can't stand a million eyes bouncing off the back of my head. The red-haired man was our homeroom teacher, and he explained about fire drills, cafeteria procedure, absentee notes, and countless other school rules. He was wasting his time. It sounded like mumbo jumbo to me, and it went in one ear and right out the other. Soon he distributed the program cards and a map of the school and told us to report to the first class at the ringing of the bell. The bell cut the silence of the room, and off I went on my big adventure.

5. The rest of the day was a real nightmare. I got lost many times, I got pushed around in the halls, and I felt like a rat prowling around in a gigantic maze. Some upperclassmen, chuckling to themselves, tried to sell me a ticket to the swimming pool on the third floor. I didn't fall for that, however. There isn't any swimming pool, and there isn't any third floor. I met all my new teachers, and each one kindly presented me with a book weighing about three pounds. I could hardly walk around. The books kept slipping out of my arms. And so I came to the end of that first day and boarded the bus with my head swimming with *do*'s and *don't*'s. The ride home was just like old times. It wasn't quiet, and sure enough, Gus had to exercise his lungs and tell us to pipe down.

● EXERCISE 9. Write a one-page account of one of your own experiences working with a class committee or preparing for a special event—a school picnic, a family reunion, Christmas, an assembly program, etc. The purpose of your writing is to show that you can avoid a monotonous style by varying the form of your sentences. Before writing, review the three ways of beginning a sentence. Include some complex sentences in your composition.

VARYING SENTENCE LENGTH

12c. Vary the length of your sentences.

A composition consisting entirely of short sentences gives the effect of being chopped up. A series of short sentences may sometimes be used to describe exciting action because short sentences give the effect of speed. In general, however, avoid such style as that in which the following paragraph is written.

> The largest desert in the world is in North Africa. The Sahara extends for more than 3,000 miles in length. It is seldom less than 1,000 miles wide. The boundaries range from the Atlantic Ocean to the Nile Valley. The surface of the Sahara is not one level stretch of sand dunes. Sharp contrasts may be noted. The average elevation is about 1,000 feet. There are also areas 50 to 60 feet below sea level. One may also encounter peaks 11,000 feet high. The sandy desert is called the *erg*. The largest *erg* is the Libyan Erg. This area contains over 200,000 square miles. These vast areas of sand dunes are avoided by the desert people. They prefer to dwell in the rocky desert or in the gravelly desert. Water is more easily found in those areas.

● EXERCISE 10. Combine each group of short sentences below into one long sentence. Take special pains to make the long sentences read smoothly. Appositives, introductory expressions, subordinate clauses, and compound subjects are suggested means.

1. My dog is black and white. Her name is Gypsy. She is ten years old. She hates the mailman. He must have startled her one time.

12c

2. Every Tuesday my parents play bridge. I have the house to myself. I make lots of fudge. I also listen to my favorite records.

3. Art said goodnight at the door. The moon put a spotlight on Jean's face. Art thought she was beautiful. Suddenly her mother opened the door.

4. Our cabin is located in the Sierra Nevada Mountains. It is near Lake Tahoe. It is very small. It also needs a new roof.

5. "O-oh, never," said the announcer. "You must never use ordinary soap on your hair. Ordinary soap dulls it. It makes your hair hard to manage."

6. My aunt and uncle drove to California last summer. They visited Betsy Croan. Betsy is their niece. She lives in San Francisco.

7. Frank is the editor of the *Echo*. He is a senior. The *Echo* is our school newspaper. It is published every week.

8. The Anglo-Saxons migrated to the British Isles. They came in the fifth century. They found dense woods. These woods covered the land.

9. Nat has never been on a horse in his life. He doesn't know a horse from a mule or a donkey. He wants to go riding. He wants to go tomorrow.

10. The math teacher was disgusted with our class. His name is Mr. Allen. He kept us after school for one hour. He explained the problems again. They were all easy with the right formula.

11. Arthur Conan Doyle wrote many detective stories. Most of them were very exciting. Sherlock Holmes was his famous detective. He always solved the crimes.

12. Helen took her first driving lesson yesterday. It lasted half an hour on a deserted highway. She was a nervous wreck after it.

● REVIEW EXERCISE. Using any means you wish—compound verbs, appositives, modifying phrases, subordinate clauses, etc.—combine the sentences in the paragraph on page 241 into sentences of greater length. Vary the beginnings of your sentences and the kinds of sentences. Work to avoid monotony. Make the passage read smoothly.

PART FOUR

Composition

CHAPTER 13

The Paragraph

Unity and Coherence
in Paragraphs

A paragraph is a physical division of a composition which marks a stage in the writer's thought. It is possible for a reader to make his way through a long, unbroken piece of writing, just as it is for a motorist to find his way over unmarked roads to his destination. But like the motorist, the reader expects to find an occasional signpost to show him the way.

The indention, or spacing, that marks the beginning of a paragraph signals a change in the direction of the writer's thought—a new idea, a change in place, time, or situation, a slightly different point of view. One paragraph is different from another in length, content, and organization, but it is possible to form an idea of the kind of average paragraph that is likely to appear in a student composition. It is likely to be from 100 to 150 words in length, to consist of a general statement supported by specific statements, and to have a single unifying idea. It is not always easy to organize what you have to say into good paragraphs with these characteristics. This chapter provides you with instructions, examples, and practice to help you master the writing of effective paragraphs.

THE STRUCTURE OF A PARAGRAPH

13a. A *paragraph* is a series of sentences developing a single topic.

The writer of the following paragraph wanted to compare the social life of young people today with that of young people of a generation ago. He begins with a general statement about dances then and now and goes on to show exactly what he means by giving specific details.

> The dances have perhaps changed most visibly of all the social institutions. While the system of going steady has become more formalized, dances have tended to become more informal. (Why dress up for someone you see so often and know so well?) They have tended to become shorter. (When you dance with only one partner, two hours or so is enough.) There is a good deal of sitting around and listening to music or entertainment instead of dancing. In fact, an effort is made to secure bands worth listening to rather than those whose music is especially suitable for dancing. The dances are a little heavy and somber because the excitement and shifting around of cutting in has disappeared and because neither the boys nor the girls feel under any special obligation to be gay or entertaining. The big dance of the prom type is slowly fading away. Since a couple is going to dance together anyhow, they may as well do it in an informal fashion to phonograph records, or at a night spot, without going to the trouble and expense of attending a big formal affair.[1]

In this paragraph, the writer states his main idea in the first sentence. The rest of the sentences in the paragraph support this statement by showing five ways in which the dances attended by young people today differ from those attended by their parents. Most of the paragraphs you will read in this chapter are organized in essentially the same way.

[1] From "American Youth Goes Monogamous" by Charles W. Cole, *Harper's Magazine*, March 1957. Reprinted by permission of the publishers.

13a

The Topic Sentence

13b. The sentence stating the topic of a paragraph is called the *topic sentence.*

Most paragraphs, like the one about dances, have a general statement, or topic sentence, giving the main idea. (Paragraphs in stories often do not have a topic sentence, but they are a special case.) The topic sentence usually comes at the beginning where it can tell the reader at once exactly what the paragraph is about. Putting the topic sentence at the beginning can be a help to the writer, too, by compelling him to make a clear statement of his idea at the outset and thus preventing him from wandering from his subject.

Occasionally the topic sentence appears in the middle of the paragraph, and sometimes it comes at the end. Coming at the end, the topic sentence often serves as the climax to the series of details that led up to it. It is a conclusion based on the evidence presented in the paragraph.

Read the following paragraphs, noting the topic sentences in bold-faced type.

TOPIC SENTENCE IN THE MIDDLE

Recently, while fishing in a clear stream, I picked a rough twig out of the water. Growing out of the twig were the tightly furled petals of some strange yellow bud. In seconds this "bud" had blossomed into a pale, golden fly with a long, gracefully tapered body and upright wings like sails. As I watched, the wings dried, became taut and fit, and the insect took flight, mounting high over the stream until it disappeared. **Surely there are few stranger creatures in nature than this little mayfly of the order *ephemeroptera*.** The Greeks named him "flower of the river," and the names given to him by trout fishermen are no less poetic—"golden drake" and "pale evening sun." The insect spends all but the last few days of his life on the stream bottom where as a nymph he undergoes as many as twenty metamorphoses. Then, in response to some mysterious rhythm of nature, he struggles to the surface, breaks open the nymphal case, and emerges as a winged fly. He is from this instant draining the precious stock of life stored up on the stream bottom, for nature has atrophied his mouth and he cannot feed again. The insect now has only one function: to mate, to drop eggs into the stream, and then to die.

TOPIC SENTENCE AT THE END

My table stands by the lattice door that leads to the veranda, so that I may get as much as possible of the light evening breezes. The palms rustle quietly while the crickets and toads make loud music. From the jungle come dreadful and sinister cries. Caramba, the faithful dog on the veranda, growls gently to let me know he is there. A tiny dwarf antelope lies at my feet under the table. In this solitude I try to give form to thoughts that have been stirring in me since 1900, and to help in the restoration of civilization. **O solitude of the primeval forest, how can I ever thank you for what you have been to me.**[1]

The Concluding, or Clincher, Sentence

Sometimes a writer may wish to reemphasize the main point of a paragraph by restating it in a concluding sentence. This kind of restatement is sometimes called a *clincher sentence*. It is used to very good effect by skillful writers. A paragraph concluding with a clincher sentence has two statements of its topic: one in the topic sentence and one in the clincher.

Use clincher sentences sparingly. A clincher is unnecessary in a very short paragraph. A poor clincher is one that seems to be tacked on just for its own sake to a paragraph which is complete and effective without it.

In the following paragraph both the topic sentence and the clincher sentence are printed in bold-faced type.

Then in the cool long glade of yard that stretched four hundred feet behind the house he planted trees and grape

[1] From *On the Edge of the Primeval Forest* by Albert Schweitzer, The Macmillan Company, 1931. Reprinted by permission.

13b

vines. **And whatever he touched in that rich fortress of his soul sprang into golden life.** As the years passed, the fruit trees— the peach, the plum, the cherry, the apple—grew great and bent beneath their clusters. His grape vines thickened into brawny ropes of brown and coiled down the high wire fences of his lot and hung in a dense fabric upon his trellises, roping his domain twice around. They climbed the porch end of the house and framed the upper windows in thick bowers. And the flowers grew in rioting glory in his yard—the velvet-leaved nasturtium, slashed with a hundred tawny dyes, the rose, the snowball, the red-cupped tulip, and the lily. The honeysuckle dropped its heavy mass upon the fence. **Wherever his great hands touched the earth, it grew fruitful to him.**[1]

● EXERCISE 1: The topic sentence in each of the following paragraphs may be at the beginning, in the middle, or at the end. Examine each paragraph carefully to discover the topic sentence and the clincher sentence, if any; then copy these sentences.

1. This farm, which was situated two miles west of the village immediately won our love. It was a glorious place for boys. Broad-armed white oaks stood about the yard, and to the east and north a deep forest invited to exploration. The house was of logs and for that reason was much more attractive to us than to our mother. It was, I suspect, both dark and cold. I know the roof was poor, for one morning I awoke to find a miniature peak of snow at my bedside. It was only a rude little frontier cabin, but it was perfectly satisfactory to me.[2]

2. Academically talented students sometimes become dissatisfied because they cannot fit into their schedules certain elective courses they want to take. They ask, "Where and how can a good student broaden his field of studies beyond the courses required of him?" Summer school is the perfectly natural answer to this question, provided the school offers the right courses instead of limiting itself to helping students make up their

[1] From *Look Homeward, Angel* by Thomas Wolfe. Copyright 1929 Charles Scribner's Sons; renewal copyright © 1957 Edward C. Aswell. Reprinted by permission of Charles Scribner's Sons.

[2] From *A Son of the Middle Border* by Hamlin Garland. Copyright 1937 by The Macmillan Company. Reprinted by permission.

failures. For example, a capable student, busy with numerous activities, needs to take an advanced chemistry course to qualify for the college of his choice. But his academic program, outside activities, and the thirty-five-hour week keep him from doing this during the regular school year. Another student wishes to enroll in an art course because he enjoys painting, but he, too, cannot fit this extra into his program. Both students, however, would be glad to go to summer school. They would welcome the chance to do something valuable instead of wasting the summer just killing time.

3. The choice of how to make one's living is crucial, for the work a man does makes him what he will become. The blacksmith pounds the anvil, but the anvil pounds the blacksmith. The clam's shell turns golden in the brown depths of the ocean, and in far more subtle ways is a man's mind colored by the course of his life. So when a man chooses his labor, he chooses his future self.[1]

4. Limiting the field to experienced pilots was the first obvious step. It would be foolish—particularly in a semicrash program—to train astronauts in the basics of flying when a sizeable pool of trained pilots was available. But even this limitation left too unwieldy a group from which to winnow the final choices. And at no time was consideration given to throwing Project Mercury open to volunteers from among our considerable number of experienced pilots. Psychologists insisted, with some justification, that many of the men who would blindly volunteer to be fired into orbit would show signs of emotional instability. Thus it was determined to pre-select a rather small group from which volunteers would be sought after the program had been carefully explained to them.[2]

● EXERCISE 2.   Select one of the following topics and write a paragraph (100–150 words) on it. Underline the topic sentence and, if you use one, the clincher sentence as well.

1. A visit to an interesting place
2. A new discovery (or invention) and its importance

[1] From *To Catch an Angel* by Robert Russell. Copyright 1962 by Robert Russell. Published by The Vanguard Press, Inc. Reprinted by permission.

[2] From "Selecting the Astronauts" by Joseph N. Bell.

3. Reasons why students worry
4. Your opinion on a controversial issue
5. An example of happiness, democracy, or loyalty

DEVELOPMENT OF A PARAGRAPH

13c. A paragraph is usually developed by means of additional, detailed information given in support of the idea expressed in the topic sentence.

It is easy to make general statements; it is harder to find the specific details, examples, or reasons that are needed to back up such statements. The details may be of many kinds —facts, examples, incidents, or logical arguments. The details, however, must be there, and they must clearly support the topic sentence.

The following paragraph does not develop its topic sentence. Instead, it merely restates its main idea several times in different words. Saying something over and over does not, of course, make it any clearer or more true than saying it once. Details are needed to make a general statement stick.

A mother of young children belongs in the home, not in a business office. Grown-ups talk a great deal about delinquent children today, but there would not be so many delinquent children if mothers stayed at home and planned and supervised their children's activities. It is a mother's job to train her children to be good citizens. She cannot do this when she is away from them all day. A mother's most important job is to stay at home and take care of her home and family. Mothers do not belong in the business world when their children are young.

A paragraph that consists of a series of general statements without supporting information is little better than the one that keeps making the same statement over and over. One topic sentence is enough for a paragraph; once you have stated it, it is up to you to develop it. The following paragraphs deal with the same topic. Notice that the second one is more convincing and interesting than the first because it is more specific.

I

Baseball demands intelligence, especially behind the plate—because the catcher is the quarterback of baseball. He runs the team and is the one player who can never relax, whether his team is in the field or at bat. He has a wide variety of duties. He must keep track of the tactical situation on the field and see that the rest of the team knows it also.

II

Baseball demands intelligence, especially behind the plate—because the catcher is the quarterback of baseball. He runs the team and is the only man who sees every player on the field and every move that takes place. He calls the pitches and sometimes directs much of the defensive play. He is the one person on the team who can never for a moment relax, whether his team is in the field or at bat. He must know wind conditions in every ball park, and his duties vary from studying the opposing batteries, the mental condition of his own pitcher, and the spacing of the outfielders, watching runners on base, keeping track of the tactical situation and seeing that the rest of the team knows it also, to backing up third and first except when a runner is in a scoring position.[1]

The second paragraph is better because it gives the details that make the general statements interesting and meaningful. Always be specific and illustrate with appropriate details the points you want to make.

The Paragraph Outline

Like most human projects, a paragraph calls for planning. Before you begin to write, make a simple inventory of your ideas on the topic you have chosen. Jot down these ideas

13c

[1] From "Who's Catching?" by John R. Tunis, *The Atlantic Monthly.* Reprinted by permission of the author.

in any order they come to mind. The act of setting them down will suggest others, and these may in turn generate still others. Continue until you have a tidy list before you. Next, you can begin to arrange the ideas into some order and to cull out every idea that does not directly pertain to the subject in hand. The following is an outline of a paragraph:

TOPIC SENTENCE   People vary a great deal in the conditions they require for efficient study.

DETAILS   1. Some want silence and solitude.
2. Others want noise and company.
3. Some want the radio on.
4. Some want the same conditions day after day.
5. Some can study anywhere.

● EXERCISE 3.   Make a paragraph outline for each of the following topic sentences. The items in the outline need not be in sentence form. Copy the topic sentence first; then list the details you would use in your paragraph.

1. Anyone planning a trip from New York to San Francisco finds several ways to make the journey.
2. Luck is often the deciding factor in football (or in some other game).
3. In every home certain jobs should be delegated to the children.
4. You will find some of the same types of teachers in any high school.

Methods of Paragraph Development

A paragraph may be developed in a number of ways. Your skill as a writer will increase and your writing will become more effective as you gain proficiency in a variety of methods. Later you may wish to use several methods in the development of one paragraph. For the time being, you should study the specific types of development, experiment with each method, and do the exercises as directed.

13d. Master several different methods of paragraph development.

(1) Develop a paragraph with facts.

The most logical way to develop a topic is to supply additional factual information. Facts are much more convincing than your own unsupported opinions because they leave no doubt in the reader's mind. They are as reliable as the source—reference books, direct observation, or the words of an established authority. These facts may be used to illustrate the topic, to support the main idea, or simply to provide additional information. *Statistics* are collected facts stated in numbers.

> Not only has recreation expanded enormously, but it has been upgraded culturally. In 1900 there were 10 symphony orchestras in the country; today there are about 1,200. We have more than 1,500 local theater groups, most of them amateurs. People spend $500 million annually on concert tickets. In 1934, 500 records of Beethoven's *Ninth Symphony* were bought, and in 1954, 75,000. We expend $2.5 million annually for musical instruments, radios, and television sets. Twenty million of us play the piano, 4 million the guitar, 3 million the violin. There are 2 million "Sunday painters." [1]

● EXERCISE 4. Develop one of the following topic sentences with facts.

1. One of the greatest problems of our country is the scarcity of water.
2. It is a common but erroneous notion that most teen-agers are wild and irresponsible.
3. Many popular beliefs about wild animals are completely wrong.
4. Some folk sayings have an excellent basis in fact.
5. The increase in our school population has affected education in this community.

13d

[1] From "Using Our Leisure Is No Easy Job" by Bruce Bliven, *New York Times Magazine*, April 26, 1964. Reprinted by permission.

(2) Develop a descriptive paragraph by giving concrete details.

The details that make a description vivid are those that communicate sharp sensory impressions—the feel, look, taste, and touch of the object. Notice in the following paragraph how the author develops his idea by giving concrete details.

> It was agreeable upon the river. A barge or two went by laden with hay. Reeds and willows bordered the stream, and cattle and gray, venerable horses came and hung their mild heads over the embankment. Here and there was a pleasant village among the trees, with a noisy shipping yard; here and there a villa in a lawn. The wind served us well up the Scheldt and thereafter up the Rupel; and we were running pretty free when we began to sight the brickyards of Boom, lying for a long way on the right bank of the river. The left bank was still green and pastoral, with alleys of trees along the embankment, and here and there a flight of steps to serve a ferry, where perhaps there sat a woman with her elbows on her knees or an old gentleman with a staff and silver spectacles. But Boom with its brickyards grew shabbier every minute; until a great church with a clock, and a wooden bridge over the river, indicated the central quarters of the town.[1]

● EXERCISE 5.   Choose one of the following topics, and write a descriptive paragraph developed by concrete details. Begin with a general statement of the idea you will develop.

1. An agreeable or a disagreeable place
2. A sight you will always remember
3. A well-dressed person
4. Sunday dinner at your home
5. A busy air terminal

(3) Develop a paragraph by specific examples.

When the topic sentence contains a general idea that can best be supported by many particulars, the writer may give

---

[1] From *An Inland Voyage*, by Robert Louis Stevenson.

each particular in the form of an example. This is a natural way of illustrating or clarifying a topic sentence. Since clarity is a constant aim in all forms of writing, the use of examples is a good way to make the meaning clear.

Lord of the Flies is an interesting book, not only because it has an unusual plot but also because of the constant suspense Golding creates. For example, there is always the question as to whether or not the boys will find adult help before they destroy themselves. Then, too, there is the problem of the beast. Is the beast real or is it imaginary? If real, what kind of creature is it and how should it be dealt with? A third event which is full of suspense is the chase near the end of the book when Ralph is being hunted down by Jack and his band of savages.

● EXERCISE 6. Write a paragraph developed by examples to illustrate, or support, one of the following topics.

1. Classroom manners are sometimes bad manners.
2. Haste does not always make waste.
3. "Every neighbor is a teacher."   [Arab proverb]
4. A physical handicap sometimes proves to be a blessing.
5. A community can do many things to help its young people.

(4) Develop a paragraph by relating an incident.

The writer sometimes relates an incident to make his point understood. An incident follows the pattern of a story. It is brief and presents only the important details; if it is too long, it may divert the reader's attention from the point being illustrated. Notice how the incident related in the following paragraph illustrates the main point.

. . . After a spring tide there was also much high talk of treasure and no little search for it. We lived, indeed, on a coast that nurtured such fancies. Not far from us lay the very island which was rumored to hide within its sands the bulk of Captain Kidd's ill-gotten gains. Moreover, not so many years past, two boys who lived near us, following an old footpath through the woods during a storm, had rested against a small boulder beneath a pine tree. One of them, idly kicking the soft mold at the base of the rock, caught the glint of metal, tarnished yet still bright enough to be distinguished against the black earth. They dug farther, with feet and with hands, to discover at last an iron pot half filled with gold coins, coins marked by strange designs and a strange language. They proved to be French pieces of the seventeenth century, probably buried there, so the learned of our coast surmised, by escaping French traders and settlers of the nearby town of Castine when their fort was captured by the Dutch. What wonder that we scrutinized the wrack of spring tides and dug now and again in likely coves or beneath giant boulders![1]

● EXERCISE 7.   Compose a paragraph in which the main idea or topic is developed by an incident. Be specific about time, place, and characters.

1. There are times when it is simply impossible to put down a book until you have reached the end.
2. Disagreeable jobs are best done quickly.
3. "A soft answer often turneth away wrath."
4. It is nice at times to be appreciated.
5. The foolishness of some drivers is beyond belief.

(5) Develop a paragraph by giving reasons.

Quite often the main idea in a paragraph is developed by giving reasons for a certain belief or point of view.

We read fiction for several reasons. Probably the foremost reason is that a story is entertaining. From the latest mystery thriller to *War and Peace*, a book must be fun to read; otherwise only English teachers and literary critics would bother with it. Many of us seek escape in a book. Bored by our own lives or burdened by worries, we like to leave our narrow world and enter an imaginary world where we can identify with characters whose lives are more exciting than ours and whose experiences we can never hope to have. Although few people would read a dull story just for its ideas, many of us

[1] From *A Goodly Heritage* by Mary Ellen Chase. Copyright 1932 by Henry Holt and Company, Inc. Reprinted by permission of Holt, Rinehart and Winston, Inc.

do find in works of fiction ideas about life and its problems which help us in our effort to understand human beings better. Novelists know life. Their beliefs are often expressed in their novels, and by reading them, we broaden our own experience.

● EXERCISE 8. Compose a paragraph in which your topic sentence is developed by at least three reasons. Use one of the following:

1. A feature of your life at school which you like or dislike
2. A social condition in your community which you like or dislike
3. An aspect of television which you like or dislike
4. A widely held notion or idea which you think is right or wrong
5. An aspect of interscholastic sport which you like or dislike

(6) Develop a paragraph by contrast or comparison.

Paragraphs may be developed by offering a comparison or stating a contrast. A comparison shows how two things are alike; a contrast, how they are different. In both cases, facts, incidents, concrete details, or examples may be used to point out the similarities or differences. At times a writer may even wish to use both comparison and contrast to develop a single paragraph.

How extraordinarily different, again, are the attitudes of different people to their fellow men! One man, in the course of a long train journey, will fail entirely to observe any of his fellow travelers, while another will have summed them all up, analyzed their characters, made a shrewd guess at their circumstances, and perhaps even ascertained the most secret histories of several of them. People differ just as much in what they feel toward others as in what they ascertain about them. Some men find almost everybody boring; others quickly and easily develop a friendly feeling toward those with whom they are brought in contact, unless there is some definite reason for feeling otherwise. Take again such a matter as travel; some men will travel through many countries, going always to the best hotels, eating exactly the same food as they would eat at home, meeting the same idle rich whom they would meet at home, conversing on the same topics upon which they converse at their own dinner table. When they return, their only feeling is one of relief at having done with the boredom of expensive locomotion. Other men wherever they go see what is characteristic, make the acquaintance of other people who typify the locality, observe whatever is of interest either historically or socially, eat the food of the country, learn ·its manner and its language, and come home with a new stock of pleasant thoughts for winter evenings.[1]

● EXERCISE 9.   Write a paragraph presenting the differences or similarities between two persons, places, or things. Use comparison, contrast, or both.

● EXERCISE 10.   Consider the following topic sentences. Then, next to the proper number on your paper, write down your recommendation for the best method to develop each into a paragraph. You may recommend one or a combination of methods.

(1) facts and statistics	(4) an incident
(2) concrete details	(5) reasons
(3) specific examples	(6) contrast or comparison

1. Last year I got the fright of my life.
2. Automation is certain to create unemployment.
3. The differences between identical twins are often more surprising than the likenesses.
4. Personal freedom is never valued until it is lost.
5. Our democracy is far from perfect.
6. It is much easier to get along with men teachers than with women teachers (or the other way around).
7. My parents are unreasonable in expecting me to be better in school than they were.
8. The difference between a freshman and a sophomore is astonishing.

9. When does "sincerity" become just cruelty?
10. I like only two kinds of books.

● EXERCISE 11. Choose one of the topic sentences below, and write a well-developed paragraph. Begin your paragraph with the topic sentence. Use the type, or types, of paragraph development suggested in the brackets. Remember, the suggested length of a properly developed paragraph is about 150 words.

1. You do (or don't) need money to be happy. [reasons—examples—incidents]
2. Autumn, not spring, is the high school student's season to make a new beginning. [contrasts—facts—examples]
3. The roads leading into any community reveal a great deal about the inhabitants. [concrete details]
4. "A nickname is the hardest stone that the Devil can throw at a man."—WILLIAM HAZLITT. [examples—incidents]
5. "A boy is an appetite with a skin pulled over it."—ANONYMOUS. [examples—incidents—facts]
6. Like a coin, everything has two sides to it. [facts—examples—comparison and contrast]

UNITY IN THE PARAGRAPH

Suppose you are writing a paragraph describing the first voyage of Columbus to the New World. Suppose also that in addition to knowing the facts about the voyage itself, you also know that many scholars consider the Italian admiral a latecomer to the scene. Vikings, and perhaps others as well, came here before him. As interesting as these matters are, still they have no place in a paragraph describing the first voyage of Columbus. They are irrelevant and would destroy the unity of your paragraph. Before any bit of information qualifies for admission into your paragraph, you must submit it to a rigorous test: Does this information have a direct bearing on my main idea? If it does not, it must be excluded.

13e. A paragraph should be unified. Unity is achieved by discussing only one topic in a paragraph, the topic stated in the topic sentence.

A unified paragraph is a forceful unit because all of the sentences have a common purpose—to develop or support the general statement made by the topic sentence.

It is possible to measure the unity of a paragraph by testing the relationship of each sentence to the main idea. You should ask this question: "How is each detail or subordinate statement related to the topic sentence?" Study the following paragraph, noting how its unity has been violated.

1 One difference between dogs and cats as pets is that dogs can be taught obedience whereas most cats cannot.
(1) topic sentence

2 Dogs are easily taught not to get on the furniture and not to steal food left on the kitchen table when no one is around. 3 They can be taught to heel, to stay, and to do tricks.
(2–3) examples of dogs' obedience

4 Cats, on the other hand, do just exactly what they want to do in spite of their owners' efforts to discipline them. 5 Our neighbor has two Siamese cats. 6 No matter how many times she punishes them for getting on the furniture or stealing food, she knows that at any time she may find them curled up on the davenport, and she would never dare leave the cats alone in the house with any food lying around.
(4–6) examples of cats' disobedience

7 Many people are fond of cats because cats are beautiful and independent. 8 As kittens they are more entertaining than they are when full grown.
(7–8) unrelated statements violate unity

9 I have never heard of a cat
(9) an example

that had been taught to stay or to sit
or to roll over. [10] Dogs make more
satisfactory pets because they can be
taught to obey.

related to
examples 4–6
(10) clincher
sentence

● EXERCISE 12. Examine each of the following paragraphs to test its unity. There is one sentence in each that is not closely related to the topic. Find this sentence, copy it onto your paper, and be ready to explain how it violates the unity of the paragraph.

1

It is a mistake for teachers to assign large homework projects to be done over vacations at Christmas and Easter because students do not have time to do such assignments well. Many families use the school vacations for travel. Carrying a pile of books is impractical, especially on a plane trip, and sandwiching study into the busy routine of sightseeing and recreation is almost impossible. Some students use their vacations to earn money for their future education or to help the family income. Jobs not only leave little time for school work but also are likely to occupy the hours when the library is open. The student cannot, therefore, use the library for research. During the school term between vacations, a student must fit his big projects into his study program, which gives him good training in planning and budgeting his time. Some parents, during vacation, step up their own outside activities, knowing they can rely on the older children to be around and take charge of the household, a fact that makes it difficult to concentrate on studying. Since many students have less time for school work during vacation than during the term, it is unreasonable to expect them to have time to do large school assignments.

2

The most time-consuming job in painting a house is painting the trim and the little crosspieces of the windows. The man who thinks the job is half done when he has merely painted the walls is in for a surprise. Painting the windows will take twice as much time as painting the walls. A good brush and an extension

13e

ladder are essential for doing an efficient job. There are always many unexpected spots on the sill and sash which have to be scraped and sandpapered before any painting can be done. Finally there is the exacting task of painting the crosspieces without spreading paint all over the panes. Count the windows in your house and multiply by one hour, and you will have a fair idea of how long this part of the job will take you.

3

There are many things to learn about paddling a canoe. Since a canoe can be pushed from its course by a slight breeze, the paddler must sit in such a way that the bow will not be forced too high out of the water where it will catch too much wind. In calm weather, the canoeist should sit in the stern, but in windy weather, he should kneel just aft of the middle, for in this position he can control his craft with less effort. He should paddle on the side opposite the direction of the wind because the wind then actually helps him to hold to a straight course. A canoe should never be loaded with stones for ballast because the stones will sink the canoe, should it be swamped. Steering is done by a twist of the paddle at the end of each stroke, the extent of the twist depending upon the force of the stroke and the strength of the wind against the bow.

4

Many a poor boy has risen to high position. Abraham Lincoln was born in a humble log cabin, spent part of his life as a rail splitter, and later became the emancipator of the slaves and President of the United States. Louis Pasteur was born of poor parents, but through great struggle became world-renowned for his pasteurization process. Giuseppe Verdi was born poor in a small Italian village, and as a youth played an organ for the community church. In his later years, he wrote the unforgettable opera *Aïda*. In the present day Eddie Cantor was a man who was born in the New York slums and became a favorite actor. Both Theodore Roosevelt and Franklin D. Roosevelt were sons of wealthy parents, but they had to overcome handicaps in their rise to the Presidency. Indeed, there are many people in this world who were born of poor parentage, but as men or women made for themselves high positions in life.

5

Walking is more than an everyday necessity—it can be used for all kinds of reasons. As a recreation it serves to pass your leisure time. When you are feeling lonely and depressed, a long walk in the crisp air does heaps of good toward cheering you up. Then again, if you're filled with the glorious feeling that everything is perfect, you enjoy a walk outdoors where everything in nature seems to be happy with you. On hikes through wild country, campers make many wonderful and surprising discoveries. A nervous businessman, waiting to hear whether the stock market has gone down another point, puts his hands behind him and paces impatiently up and down the room. Riding in a car everywhere you go is faster but not so good for you as walking. Next time you're bored or happy or unhappy or worried, take a walk.

COHERENCE IN THE PARAGRAPH

13f. A paragraph should have coherence; that is, its ideas should be arranged according to a definite plan and should be linked clearly to one another.

Coherent paragraphs are easy to read. The relationship between the sentences is clear, and the train of thought, moving easily and naturally from one sentence to the next, is easy to follow. The two ways to achieve this coherence are (1) to arrange the ideas in a logical order and (2) to provide clear transitions, or links, between sentences.

Order of Ideas in a Paragraph

Three orders, or arrangements of the ideas in a paragraph, are commonly followed. The kind of order depends upon the nature of the paragraph.

(1) The details in a paragraph may be arranged in chronological order.

13f

Paragraphs developed by an incident and those that explain the steps in a process usually call for *chronological order* in arranging details. Chronological order is simply the order in which things happen or in which steps in a process should be done.

In building a brick wall, the builder must **first** prepare a bed which is perfectly horizontal. **At the same time** he must be sure that the bed is firm enough to hold a wall without sinking. For this purpose cement or cement blocks may be used. On this foundation the bricklayer **next** builds up the ends or corners several layers high. **After** he has got these absolutely true, he stretches a line between the corners at the exact height of his first layer of bricks, and **then** lays the entire row to fit this line. He lays only a few layers of brick at a time all around the building or the full length of his wall because bricks are liable to settle and so carry the work out of plumb. **Finally**, when his day's work is finished, the bricklayer covers his wall to protect it from excessive weathering during the drying process.

(2) The details in a paragraph may be arranged in spatial order.

Spatial order, the order of position, is often followed in descriptive writing. Although it is usually wise to make a selection of details in a description rather than enumerating every possible detail, you can often add clarity and coherence to an impression by showing the spatial relation of the various details. The simplest way to do this is to set up a logical plan that will enable you to move naturally from one part of the scene to another. In the following example, notice how the important details are stated in relation to the position of the narrator.

Football practice presents a lively and colorful picture. As I hurry down the gravel path toward the practice field, I can smell the crisp autumn air with its faint tinge of burning leaves. I hear **in the distance** the harsh cries of the coaches mingled with the high-pitched voices of the younger boys. I approach the field, and the scene, as I stop to take it in, presents a pageant of color and movement against a background of green grass and the orange glow of the setting November sun. On my left are the lightweights, scampering about, their shrill voices shrieking louder and louder. Leaping into position, they prepare for the play. One stout little fellow seems momentarily lost and stands bolt upright hesitating before he finds his place. In a sudden blur of colors, the play swings **toward the right** and ends abruptly in a splash of maroon and gray jerseys, a milling pile bristling with legs and kicking feet. I hear the insistent wail of the whistle and watch the referee dive hard down into the wriggling mass to find the ball.

(3) The details in a paragraph may be arranged in the order of importance.

When your paragraph is explanatory or argumentative, you may choose to put your facts or reasons in the *order of their importance*. In general, it is a good idea to begin with the least important details and build up to the most important ones, thus achieving a vigorous conclusion. In some situations, however, it may be appropriate to do just the reverse—to give the most compelling fact or reason first and then to support it with less important ones. In either case, the relative importance of the ideas should be clear to the reader.

I have very little use for the man who takes pride in his ability to keep himself aloof from other people and hides his talents from the world. Such a man not only exhibits a distastefully self-centered character but is a piece of useless timber in the social structure. For example, this hermit shows himself unwilling to pay for what he gets. I do not mean that he doesn't pay his bills. He must do that to avoid the law. I mean that all the things in civilization which make it possible for him to enjoy his comforts he owes to the efforts of others; yet he himself contributes nothing to others. He does not interest himself in the problems of society—in the poor, the suffering, the struggling. He does not strive to make the world any better. He creates nothing. As a result, he is of little good in the world or to the world. Therefore, I neither approve of him nor respect him.

Not all paragraphs, of course, follow these three common orders. A paragraph developed by facts or examples may not follow any particular order if the facts or examples are all of equal importance. Simple, easily understood facts should precede those that are hard to understand. Remember too, that many writers use not one method, but a combination of methods to produce an effective paragraph.

● EXERCISE 13.   The following paragraphs are developed by different types of orders. Examine each and determine its order of development: (1) order of time, (2) order of space or position, and (3) order of importance. Be able to explain your choice.

1. Over to the west of the Big Pond, at a distance of perhaps three hundred yards, Saline Creek flows down its wooded course, flanked on the far side by a high limestone bluff behind which the sun sets early. But a mile to the east, where Buford Mountain raises its rounded crest, the glow lingers for moments longer while purple shadows creep up the deep hollows on its slopes. It is the hour when tree and bank swallows come to harvest insects above the water, dipping now and then to break the surface. And high above them, still in bright sunlight, the night-hawks wheel and dive in graceful, erratic flight.[1]

2. I am convinced small high schools can be satisfactory only at exorbitant expense. The truth of this statement is evident if one considers the distribution of academic talent in the school which serves all the youth of the community. It will be a rare district where more than 25 per cent of a high school class can study with profit twelfth-grade mathematics, physics, and a foreign language for four years (assuming that standards are maintained). If a school has a twelfth grade of only forty and if indeed only a quarter of the group can handle the advanced

[1] From *The Country Year* by Leonard Hall. Copyright 1956 by Leonard Hall. Published by Harper & Row, Publishers, Inc. Reprinted by permission.

subjects effectively, instruction in mathematics, science, and foreign languages would have to be provided for a maximum of ten students. If the girls shy away from the mathematics and science as they do in most of the schools I visited, the twelfth-grade mathematics classes may be as small as six or seven. To provide adequate teachers for specialized subjects is extremely expensive. Furthermore, to maintain an interest in academic subjects among a small number is not always easy. Wide academic programs are not likely to be offered when the academically talented in a school are so few in number. The situation in regard to the nonacademic elective programs in a small high school is even worse. The capital outlay for equipment as well as the salaries of the special vocational instructors adds up to such a large figure in terms of the few enrolled as to make vocational programs almost prohibitively expensive in schools with a graduating class of less than one hundred.[1]

3. We sailed. We cleared the Hook, the land dropped down, the hard horizon of the sea encircled us. My life became a memory and the future broke against our prow and shimmered, and was foam and trailed behind us in the steamer's wake. There was no measure of time but days and nights, and the passage of these was forgotten in the contentment of their monotony, or concealed in the illusion of swiftly changing seasons as from the springtime of the north the steamer bore us southward through six weeks and seven thousand miles, through the midsummer of the equator to the July winter of the Strait of Magellan.[2]

● EXERCISE 14. The sentences in the following paragraphs are not in logical order. Study the paragraphs until you have discovered the correct order; then list the sentence numbers in the order in which they should be arranged. Indicate the type of order you have used: *spatial order, chronological order*, or *order of importance*.

[1] From *The American High School Today* by James B. Conant, McGraw-Hill Book Company. Copyright 1959. Reprinted by permission of Conant Studies, Educational Testing Service, Princeton, New Jersey.

[2] From "Why and Where" from *Voyaging—Southward from the Strait of Magellan* by Rockwell Kent, G. P. Putnam's Sons, 1924.

1

(1) In the middle distance Highway 86 wound through the valley like a thread, looping the blue saucer of Sullivan's Lake. (2) The view from Slide Mountain was superb. (3) Then the highway left the lake and dropped down through the gorge to where Willmington lay under a pall of woodsmoke. (4) We did not regret the hours spent toiling through the forest, picking our way over vast fields of broken talus, and the last scramble through wiry bushes to the summit. (5) Westward shimmered the vast expanse of Mooselukmeguntic, and in the far distance, serried rank upon rank, rose the dim ramparts of the White Mountains. (6) Directly below us, the red tile roofs of the lodge described a tiny horseshoe around the blue dot of the swimming pool.

2

(1) Second, weekend homework must be left until Sunday night unless you're one of those rare souls who, after five days of school, can settle down to the books on a Friday night in spite of the movies, the games, and the dates which Friday seems to inspire. (2) For instance, when are we going to work on the lawn for Dad, clean house or run errands for Mother, go shopping, get outdoors, see a show, or just read that book we have been waiting to get into? (3) There are several reasons why homework should not be assigned over the weekend. (4) First, five days out of seven devoted to school are enough for teenagers, who really do have other things to do besides study. (5) Finally, you come back to school on Monday fresher, more willing to start in again, if you have had a clean break from school for two days. (6) Then, too, weekend homework is so often either not done at all or so poorly done that teachers have nervous breakdowns all day Monday trying to work with students who don't have the vaguest idea what the lesson is all about. (7) In fact, it would be easier on everyone if the assignment had never been given at all. (8) A change is good for everyone, and anyone knows what all work and no play does to Jack.

Linking Expressions

Putting the ideas of a paragraph into a logical order improves its coherence. Another way to achieve coherence is to use linking expressions.

13g. Strengthen the coherence of a paragraph by using linking expressions and connectives which help the reader to follow the line of thought from one idea to the next.

The most useful words for this purpose are the pronouns: *he, they, this, that, these, those, them, it,* etc. When they appear in the paragraph, they serve to remind the reader of their antecedents, that is, the words, expressions, and ideas to which they refer. By doing this, they help to bind the ideas in the paragraph more tightly together.

(1) Keep the thought of a paragraph flowing smoothly from sentence to sentence by using pronouns which refer to words and ideas in preceding sentences.

As you read the following paragraphs, notice how the words in bold-faced type refer back to a preceding idea.

A hundred years ago, the average work week in the United States was about seventy hours. Today, **it** is about forty hours—and experts say that in the next decade or so **it** will be cut again, the predictions ranging from thirty-seven hours or thereabouts down to twenty or even less. **This reduction** might come as a shorter workday, or fewer workdays per week, or longer—very much longer—vacations.

What shall we do with all **that free time?** Many people are profoundly troubled about **this question. They** feel that, far from being a blessing, the change may prove a catastrophe. Certainly, the growth of leisure time is an extremely serious matter. **It** deserves far more attention than **it** is getting.[1]

(2) Keep the thought of the paragraph flowing smoothly from sentence to sentence by the use of linking expressions.

One infallible mark of a good prose style is care in the choice of linking expressions. Many expressions do approxi-

[1] From "Using Our Leisure Is No Easy Job" by Bruce Bliven, *New York Times Magazine*, April 26, 1964. Reprinted by permission.

13g

mately the same job. For instance, you can add still another idea to those already mentioned in a paragraph by introducing it with a "furthermore" or an "in addition." You can use "consequently" and "therefore" to show that one idea is the result of the preceding idea. You can use "however" or "nevertheless" to make clear that you are about to introduce a contrasting idea. Which connective you use depends on the logical relationship of the sentences. This relationship must be kept clear and distinct if you are to write well.

Read the following lists of linking expressions. Use the lists for reference when you write.

LINKING EXPRESSIONS

To add an idea to one already stated:

moreover	likewise	besides	too
further	also	and	again
furthermore	nor	and then	in addition
equally important	in the same fashion		

To limit or contradict something already said:

but	still	although
yet	nevertheless	otherwise
and yet	on the other hand	at the same time
however	on the contrary	

To show a time or place arrangement of your ideas:

first	meanwhile	next	here
second	later	presently	nearby
finally	eventually	at length	opposite to
at this point	sooner or later	afterward	adjacent to

To exemplify some idea or to sum up what you have said:

for example	to sum up	in any event
for instance	in brief	in any case
in other words	on the whole	as I have said
in fact	in short	as a result

● EXERCISE 15. Read the following paragraph. Select from it (1) all pronouns that you think add to the coherence of the paragraph, (2) all linking expressions. Copy them in order, placing before each the number of the sentence in which it appears.

1. Indiscriminate tampering with the balance of nature has often had unfortunate results. 2. A case in point is the Pacific Islands. 3. On the more remote of these, eons of isolation from the mainland masses had allowed an enormous variety of life forms to evolve. 4. Furthermore, the relationship between these life forms and their environment was precariously balanced. 5. One species of plant, for example, depended upon one species of insect for its pollination. 6. This insect not only served to reproduce the plant, but by feeding upon competing and more virulent growths protected the plant from being choked out. 7. In a like manner, one species of bird kept the insects in check, and on certain headlands, by its thousands of nests that blanketed the ground, provided the humus for still other varieties of plants. 8. This balance was violently upset by the first Polynesian settlers who brought with them pigs and, accidentally, rats. 9. Within a few centuries thereafter, hundreds of species of birds and plants had become extinct. 10. Later on, mongooses were imported from the East to control the rats which—without natural enemies of any kind—had decimated the bird population and threatened to overrun the islands. 11. These little heroes of Kipling's tales, however, found the ground-nesting birds much easier prey than the rats, and so the carnage goes on unimpeded to this day.

● EXERCISE 16. Read the following paragraph. You can see at once that the necessary connectives have been omitted. Consult the list on page 270, and next to the proper number on your paper, put down your choice for the correct connective.

It is rarely wise for a teen-ager to buy a car. (1) ——, the average teen-ager cannot pay cash; (2) ——, he must buy "on time." (3) ——, he must pay far more than merely the value of the car. (4) ——, he must commit himself to a long series of payments. Without a full-time job, none of these payments

is easy to meet. When, (5) ——, the monthly payment happens
to come at the same time as the inevitable and unlooked-for
repair bill, then the task of raising the necessary money becomes
difficult. (6) ——, this incessant anxiety over money can easily
sour whatever pleasure comes from owning the car.

Checklist for Paragraph Revision

PHRASING THE TOPIC SENTENCE

1. Is it concise, directly to the point? Does it make your topic narrow enough?
2. Will it arouse the reader's interest or curiosity? Will it produce agreement or disagreement?

DEVELOPING THE TOPIC

3. Does the paragraph have unity?
4. Have you used good examples, specific facts, sensory details, vivid comparisons, convincing reasons?
5. Does the paragraph have coherence? In what order are the details arranged? Are linking expressions and other connecting devices used properly?
6. Does the paragraph rise to a climax, come to a conclusion, reach a solution? Does it merit a summarizing, or clincher, sentence?
7. Is the paragraph adequately developed? By what method or combination of methods is it developed?

PROOFREADING YOUR PARAGRAPH

8. Did you check the spelling of every doubtful word and refer to a list of your own commonly misspelled words?
9. Have you looked for unnecessary words, for trite expressions?
10. Are you confident that the grammatical usage is correct?
11. Have you checked your own error chart, or earlier compositions, to see that your special weaknesses are not being repeated?

CHAPTER 14

Exposition

Planning and Writing
the Longer Composition

Writing a good expository composition entails many of the same procedures as writing a good paragraph. Like the paragraph, the composition has a central, controlling idea that must be developed by means of smaller, more specific ideas. These specific ideas must be carefully chosen and organized in a logical way, and their relation to each other and to the central idea made clear. Since the idea for a composition is necessarily broader than the main idea of a paragraph, a composition calls for more thought, more planning, and more writing. (A composition is also likely to require a certain amount of research.)

The main steps in writing a composition are listed below in the order in which they are performed. Each of them is important in successful expository writing. The letters designating the steps correspond to the rules in this chapter.

a. Choosing a subject
b. Limiting a subject
c. Planning the composition
d. Outlining
e. Writing the first draft
f. Revising
g. Writing the final draft

CHOOSING AND LIMITING A SUBJECT

14a. Choose a subject that interests you.

Good writing is possible only when you really know your subject. In addition to what you have learned in school, you have a great deal of knowledge that comes from other sources. Your own special interests have already taught you many things. Your interest in places has acquainted you with the people, the sights, and the experiences associated with another town, city, or country. Your hobbies—collecting stamps, coins, stones, or sea shells; practicing a musical instrument, singing, or dancing—all these have developed your interests and increased your knowledge. When the time comes to make a choice, such a familiar subject often makes an ideal point of departure.

You should not, of course, limit yourself to subjects you know well already. In addition to familiar material from your own experience, there may be topics that interest you and arouse your curiosity even though you do not know much about them. Such topics may make excellent material for compositions, providing that you are willing to acquire the information necessary to write about them. Writing is an intense and stimulating activity; new ideas that you have mastered sufficiently to write about are likely to become a permanent part of your stock of knowledge and can extend your interests. In other words, writing a composition is not just a way to show what you know already; it can be a way for you to learn new things.

Some compositions that you write will derive completely from your own experience; others will come mainly from reading and research. For your first composition this year, you will probably wish to choose a familiar topic. But give some thought to the other kind of topic as you read books in English and your other classes. Before long, you should have several interesting possibilities for use in later, more ambitious compositions.

● EXERCISE 1. Make a list of ten familiar subjects which you could develop into compositions. (If you wish, turn to the lists on pages 295–300 for ideas.) Submit your list to your teacher for his suggestions and comments. Then keep it in your notebook for future use.

● EXERCISE 2. Study the following list of unfamiliar subjects. Select five possibilities that you think you would enjoy studying and writing about. You need not limit your selections to this list. For each subject you choose, phrase several questions you think a composition on the subject should answer. Then submit your list to your teacher for his suggestions and comments. When he returns it, keep it in your notebook for future use.

EXAMPLE   1. Schools in Russia

> a. *How does one get to attend college in Russia?*
> b. *What is the normal tenth-year curriculum in Russian schools?*
> c. *Are the schools free to all?*
> d. *Is more or less expected of a Russian student than of us?*

1. Jet ejection systems
2. Skin diving
3. The trouble with "juvenile fiction"
4. Nobel prize winners in literature since 1960
5. Pop art
6. The new turbine car
7. Financing your own college education
8. High school dropouts
9. The tragic side of a comic character in a novel or play
10. Origins of place names in your area
11. Folk music
12. Famous American zoos
13. The importance of physical fitness
14. Wildlife conservation
15. From crystal sets to radio
16. Characteristics of science fiction
17. Novels popular with teen-agers
18. Changing tastes in teen-age dancing
19. American opera
20. New horizons in science
21. The future of the U.N.
22. How advertisers attract teen-agers

14a

14b. Limit your subject.

Most of your composition assignments will call for a paper of from 300–500 words, four or five paragraphs. You can see that if you choose a subject like "Skin diving" (about which whole books have been written), you must severely limit your treatment of it to some specific aspect of the sport to avoid uttering meaningless generalities. Even one aspect —the first experiments with underwater breathing gear carried out by the intrepid little band of French swimmers in Mediterranean waters after World War II—offers more to write about than can be covered by a short composition.

In fact, whenever possible, choose only a part of the subject. Better still, choose part of that part; then treat the matter thoroughly, refusing to be content merely to repeat what everybody knows about the subject already.

(1) Limit your topic to one part of the subject.

Notice how the following general topics may be subdivided into more limited topics. Any of these might be covered fully in a short composition, whereas the general topic, before being cut down, would demand several more pages of development. Think of the general topic as the title of a book and each of the subtopics as the chapters. Your composition then would make a very short chapter or even a part of a chapter.

GENERAL TOPIC   Skin diving

SPECIFIC TOPICS

1. Nitrogen poisoning: what it is and how to avoid it
2. Are sharks really dangerous?
3. The advantages of the wet suit
4. Scuba diving in nearby Marion Pond

GENERAL TOPIC   Sophomores

SPECIFIC TOPICS

1. Are sophomores "sophomoric"?
2. Some helpful hints on how to fail the tenth year

3. How a sophomore differs from a freshman
4. Sophomores: three familiar types

GENERAL TOPIC Walking

SPECIFIC TOPICS

1. Is the pedestrian outmoded?
2. What to look for when walking through the woods
3. Last summer's disastrous hike to Elk Creek
4. Walking in the city

● EXERCISE 3. For five of the following general topics, write three specific subtopics that are suitably limited for a short composition.

1. Cars
2. Sports
3. Family life
4. Our town
5. Clothes
6. Popularity and unpopularity
7. Things I wish were different
8. High school
9. Science
10. The Cold War

(2) **State the purpose of your composition.**

You can see from the examples above that it is hard to limit your subject without at the same time indicating what you are going to say about it. Now is the time to make your purpose even more clear and definite. Since almost every subject can be treated in a number of ways, a clear statement of how *you* intend to treat it helps you choose the ideas to use in your composition. Notice how the following topic admits four different purposes.

GENERAL TOPIC Autumn

SPECIFIC TOPIC Autumn Comes to Colp's Hill

To amuse   My purpose is to show the funny side of some typical fall activities in Colp's Hill, such as dressing up for Halloween, going out for football, and raking leaves.

To inform   My purpose is to show how a colony of yellow jackets in our woods prepares for and survives the coming winter.

14b

To persuade	My purpose is to persuade residents of Colp's Hill to take special care that their leaf fires do not spread out of control and threaten our forests.
To create a mood	My purpose is to convey the special quality of autumn in Colp's Hill.

● EXERCISE 4.   Select five of the following general topics and list for each three limited topics suitable for a short composition. Each of the limited topics should lend itself to a different one of the four purposes: (1) to amuse, (2) to inform, (3) to persuade, (4) to create a mood. After each topic, write the purpose you would have in writing about it.

EXAMPLE   High school   [general topic]
   Sophomore types   *to amuse*
   The intramural program   *to inform*
   More privileges for sophomores   *to persuade*

1. Money	6. Travel
2. Television	7. Jewelry
3. Books	8. Food
4. Hobbies	9. Movies
5. Politics	10. Pets

(3) Choose a title that reflects your purpose.

Once you have limited your subject to suitable length and drafted your statement of purpose, the title may suggest itself as a matter of course. A good title gives both subject and purpose in one phrase. It excites the reader's interest and lets him know what to expect. Take, for example, the sample topic given above, "Autumn Comes to Colp's Hill." Some possible titles are

1. "Autumn High Jinks in Colp's Hill"   [to amuse]
2. "The Winter Sleep of the Yellow Jackets"   [to inform]
3. "Let's Burn Leaves, Not Forests"   [to persuade]
4. "September Song in Colp's Hill"   [to create a mood]

If you cannot immediately think of the right title, it is no great matter. You will probably think of a suitable one later. The next step is far more important, for now you are asked to do most of the thinking that will go into your composition.

PLANNING THE COMPOSITION

14c. Plan your composition before writing it.

Planning a composition involves four steps: listing your ideas, grouping them under a few main headings, putting your ideas in proper order, and preparing an outline.

(1) List all the ideas you can think of that bear upon the subject and purpose of the composition.

The first step in planning a composition is to list on paper all the ideas you have on the subject. Write down these ideas as rapidly as they come to you without any regard for their order or importance. Later there will be plenty of time to rephrase and organize them. The important thing at present is to tap the reservoir of the mind for its freshest and most vivid impressions, notions, and memories on the subject and to get these down on paper. At first, the flow of ideas is likely to be strong, but before long—unless you happen to be very well acquainted with the subject—the flow will dwindle and then stop altogether. When this happens, you need not be content with what you have. If the subject is not entirely personal, you can replenish the flow by referring to a good encyclopedia or by reading a magazine article or by talking with your parents or friends about the subject.

Suppose, for example, you were assigned the topic "My Favorite Community" and asked to write a paper of 300–500 words. With this topic in mind, how would you limit it? What would your purpose be in writing it? Try the title

14c

"Pleasant Valley, Pennsylvania, Is a Nice Place." That sounds rather commonplace and would doubtless entail a catalogue of the things you liked about the town—a catalogue probably that everyone else is thoroughly familiar with. Think more deeply about the town you are discussing. Try to grasp its essential character—the character that sets it apart from all other towns. Suppose that while you are sorting out your first impressions, you are struck suddenly with the fact that the most vivid impressions are ones of age: the old houses, the great spreading elms, and all the lingering evidence of a greater but bygone age. Thereupon you know at once that, most of all, your favorite community is old-fashioned. And it occurs to you furthermore that it would make an interesting composition to explain why Pleasant Valley is old-fashioned. Having come to this decision, you draft your statement of purpose.

> My purpose is to explain why Pleasant Valley is old-fashioned by telling something of its history.

A title then comes to mind:

> Pleasant Valley: A Town Right Out of the Past

Next you open your notebook and settle yourself to recording every idea, impression, and recollection about the town that bears upon the subject and purpose. This list, which will constitute the raw material of your composition, is not merely the product of one session of silent thought but grows rather out of reading, talks with your parents and friends, and (perhaps in this case) even a telephone call or letter to your local historical society. For the sample topic the following list might be jotted down:

1. The town's air of deep repose
2. Fifteen miles by bus to high school
3. The great elms and the old houses
4. Early settlement by the Yankees
5. Great-Aunt Millicent's youth in Italy

6. The coming of bad times in Pleasant Valley and the closing of the mines
7. The Dunker, Moravian, and Mennonite farmers
8. P.V.'s preoccupation with the past as shown in its many historical societies
9. The ugly mill towns
10. Coal everywhere but Pleasant Valley
11. The orchards, greenhouses, and vegetable gardens as an example of the widespread love of nature
12. "Tourists" and "Guests" signs on the lawns
13. Pleasant Valley's great days after the Civil War
14. Miners' daughters at the normal school
15. Strikes, lockouts, and company towns
16. Great-Aunt Millicent's formal garden with its cypresses and cisterns
17. Great-Aunt Millicent's reminiscences of parties on the verandas
18. The decline of Pleasant Valley
19. The lack of vocational opportunity in Pleasant Valley
20. The steel industry's move to Pittsburgh
21. Pleasant Valley as a sanctuary from exhaust fumes and neon lights
22. The declining role of the farmer
23. Culture groups in Pleasant Valley
24. Modern emigration from small communities
25. The industrial retraining program

● EXERCISE 5. For one of the topics you have already chosen or entered in your notebook, draft a statement of purpose and select a suitable title. Then list as many items (facts, details, examples, incidents, impressions, reasons, recollections, etc.) as you can think of to develop the topic into a composition of from 300–500 words. Try to avoid repetition, that is, using the same idea in two different ways.

(2) Organize your list of ideas under a few main headings.

The second step is to scrutinize your list in order to sort out the three or four major ideas under which everything else may be included. Call these the main headings. In a composition intended to persuade, these main headings will be the dominant impressions you mean to leave with your reader. In an explanatory composition these headings will be the major steps in the unfolding of your explanation, and so forth. Under each of these headings, you will group whatever examples, incidents, facts, or observations are necessary to develop the main heading clearly.

For the sample list on the topic "My Favorite Community," such a sorting out of main headings is easy because the writer has decided to show how his town is old-fashioned by recounting its history, and history suggests the order of events.

    I. Early history of Pleasant Valley
   II. The isolation of Pleasant Valley
  III. The decline of Pleasant Valley
  IV. The timelessness of Pleasant Valley

● EXERCISE 6.   Examine the list of materials you prepared for Exercise 5. Look for relationships between the items. What general heading is suggested by several specific details? Formulate three or four main headings. If you have difficulty finding or phrasing these, it may be that you do not have enough material to develop your composition. If that is the case, give your initial list of materials more thought.

(3) Place your ideas in their proper order.

The third step is to arrange the main headings into the order in which you will discuss them in your composition. Usually this order will suggest itself merely from an examination of the main ideas in the light of your purpose. An argument, for example, proceeds logically—usually from least important argument to most important or vice versa. An explanation goes from simple to complex, and a description from small to large or from near to far, etc. An historical account, as in the example about Pleasant Valley, follows a chronological order—the order of events as they happened. Any composition is clearest when its elements are arranged in the right order; it is your task as the writer to determine what that order is.

Experiment with the raw material of your own list. Rearrange the items under your main topic until each has found its proper place and appears to belong nowhere else. Some will have to be rephrased, others combined, and still others —that cannot be fitted in anywhere or are too long and complicated to be treated adequately—will have to be eliminated entirely.

● EXERCISE 7. With the various orders in mind—order of time, order of position, order of simple to complex, and order of importance—examine the main ideas you formulated for Exercise 6, and place them in the most effective order. Be able to explain or to defend the position of each topic.

(4) Make a topic outline.

What you have so far produced is an outline. A formal topic outline differs from this only in form. The various items in a topic outline (main topics and subtopics) are single words or phrases, not complete sentences, and are arranged so that the main ideas stand out.

14d. Observe the rules for form in making a topic outline.

(1) Place the title and the statement of purpose above the outline.

(2) Use Roman numerals for the main topics. Subtopics are given capital letters, then Arabic numerals, then small letters, then Arabic numerals in parentheses, then small letters in parentheses.

14d

CORRECT OUTLINE FORM

I. main topic

   A.⎫
   B.⎬ subtopics of I

      1.⎫
      2.⎬ subtopics of B.

         a.⎫
         b.⎬ subtopics of 2.

            (1)⎫
            (2)⎬ subtopics of b.

               (a)⎫
               (b)⎬ subtopics of (2)

II. main topic

(3) Indent subtopics. Indentions should be made so that all letters or numbers of the same kind will come directly under one another in a vertical line.

(4) There must always be more than one subtopic because subtopics are divisions of the topic above them. When you divide, after all, you must have at least two resultant parts.

If you find yourself wanting to use a single subtopic, re-write the topic above it so that this "subidea" is included in the main topic.

WRONG   D. The study of French culture
            1. The study of the French language

RIGHT   D. The study of French culture and language

(5) For each number or letter in an outline, there must be a topic.

Never place an *A*, for instance, next to *I* or *1* like this: *IA* or *A1*.

(6) A subtopic must belong under the main topic beneath which it is placed. It must be closely related to the topic above it.

(7) Begin each topic and subtopic with a capital letter. You should not place a period after a topic because it is not a complete sentence.

(8) The terms *introduction*, *body*, and *conclusion* should never be included in the outline.

Of course, you may have an introduction and a conclusion in your composition, but these terms themselves are not topics you intend to discuss.

● Exercise 8.   Copy carefully the skeleton outline given at the right below and place each of the items in the list at the left in its proper position in the outline. The title is included among the topics.

Boots	*(Title)*
Snowplow turns	I.
Clothing	A.
Skiing	B.
Jumping	C.
Rope tows	D.
Skis	1.
Equipment	2.
Downhill technique	3.
Going straight downhill	II.
T-bar lifts	A.
Poles	B.
Turning	1.
Chair lifts	2.
Gloves	C.
Christie turns	III.
Parkas	A.
Ski lifts	B.
Ski pants	C.

● Exercise 9.   Prepare a detailed topic outline for the materials you developed in Exercises 5, 6, and 7. If this topic has been unsatisfactory, select a new one from the list in your notebook.

SAMPLE TOPIC OUTLINE

A Town Right Out of the Past

Statement of purpose:　To explain why Pleasant Valley is old-fashioned by telling some of its history

I. Early history of Pleasant Valley

    A. Yankee settlers from Connecticut

    B. Changes made by industrialization

        1. Mines and mills

        2. Industrial towns

        3. Immigration

II. The isolation of Pleasant Valley

    A. No industry

    B. The home of the rich

        1. Great houses

        2. Fashionable society

III. The decline of Pleasant Valley

    A. Causes

        1. Working out of the mines

        2. Replacement of coal by oil for heating

        3. Westward movement of the steel industry

    B. Effects

        1. Abandonment of Pleasant Valley to female relatives

        2. Closing of the houses

        3. Other uses for the houses

IV. The timelessness of Pleasant Valley

    A. Why young people leave

    B. What I hope for Pleasant Valley

WRITING THE COMPOSITION

14e. With your outline before you, write the first draft of your composition.

If you have been conscientious about the preceding steps, you will find that many of the problems of writing have been solved in advance. You know your topic and your purpose in writing about it. You have assembled the necessary material and have arranged it in the correct order for presentation. Now you can concentrate on the matter of how to say it: paragraphing, word choice, sentence structure, and transitions. These problems can best be understood in relation to the three parts of a composition—*introduction, body,* and *conclusion.*

The Introduction

Neither the introduction nor the conclusion of a composition appears as a heading on a topic outline. The outline is concerned only with the body of a composition. It is important, nevertheless, to make the right kind of beginning and ending.

The introduction should give the reader a preview of what the composition is about. It should clearly indicate the topic and your purpose in writing about it. In a short composition, the introduction may consist of only a sentence in the first paragraph. In longer compositions it is a good idea to allow a short paragraph for this purpose.

The Body

The body is the heart of the composition. It fulfills the promise of the introduction and consists of as many good paragraphs as may be needed to develop the topic. The nature of your subject and your purpose will determine the exact length of the body of your composition. As a general guide, however, you may think of the body as occupying about three fourths of your space and consisting of from two or three paragraphs for a short composition of 250 words to six or eight paragraphs for a longer one of 1000 words.

In Chapter 13 you considered the paragraph as a single unit of thought. Except for practice assignments in school,

14e

most pieces of writing consist of a number of paragraphs. So it is with the whole composition.

As you write your first draft, you must decide at which point a new paragraph must be started. The way you paragraph should show your reader the successive stages of your thinking. It may be that you can devote one paragraph in your composition to each of the main headings in your topic outline. This simple solution works out well in shorter compositions. In longer compositions, however, you will often find that you need to devote a paragraph to certain important subheadings in your outline. In any case, each of your paragraphs should be built around a single idea or aspect of your main topic. Every time you take up a new idea, begin a new paragraph. Do not start a new paragraph without a good reason for doing so.

The Conclusion

One way to end a composition is simply to stop writing. Although this method is an easy one, it has the disadvantage of suggesting that you have given up. A better way to end a composition is by recalling the purpose of the composition as expressed in the introduction and by summing up the information you have set forth in developing your topic. The conclusion may be only a few sentences or it may be a whole paragraph. In either case, it should tell your reader that you have finished your composition, not abandoned it.

Transitions Between Paragraphs

In a good composition the current of thought flows smoothly from introduction to conclusion. It is not interrupted by the divisions between paragraphs but is helped easily over these divisions by certain transitional devices. By their use, the writer informs his reader how the idea of the paragraph he has just read is related to the idea of the paragraph he is now beginning.

Linking expressions as transitional devices

LINKING EXPRESSIONS

therefore	furthermore
in spite of this	in the next place
consequently	however
accordingly	as might be expected
as a result of this	an example of this
similarly	finally
besides	lastly
nevertheless	also
on the contrary	meanwhile
on the other hand	soon
after all	in other words
such	in addition
likewise	then again

EXAMPLES   . . . And so day after day the drought continued.

On the thirtieth day, **however,** the wind changed. It blew cool against the face and carried a faint breath of something new . . .

. . . "Doe day" is dangerous for another reason too. When hunters are not compelled by law to distinguish bucks from does, they will frequently shoot at anything resembling a deer; and at this time, of course, the woods are more densely populated with hunters than with deer.

To restrict hunting only to bucks, **on the other hand,** means that the range will continue to be over-browsed . . .

Pronouns as transitional devices

EXAMPLE   . . . The child was overly nervous too. She started violently at unexpected noises and cried piteously when left alone.

This was not the worst burden on **her** mother, however . . .

Repetition of key words

EXAMPLES   . . . What is more, the car will accelerate from 0 to 60 miles per hour in only ten seconds.

This blistering acceleration, however, is not its best feature . . .

. . . A further advantage was that the Indian could shoot a dozen arrows while the desperate rifleman was recharging his musket.

Dodging **a dozen arrows** while carrying out an operation that, even at the best time was painstaking and slow, was often more than the untrained settler could manage, and therefore . . .

REVISING THE COMPOSITION

14f. Revise your first draft.

Shakespeare is supposed to have written whole plays and changed only a few lines. Unfortunately, that is not the way it goes for most of us. Most of the time, our second thoughts are better than our first ones; a thoughtful and critical reading of our first drafts produces a clearer and stronger final draft.

If possible, lay your first draft aside for a while before you begin the process of revision. Revising is different from writing; it requires a little detachment, which the passage of time helps you to achieve. The object in revision is to see the composition as much as possible through the eyes of a reader. Look for trouble: sentences that are awkwardly constructed; ideas that are not clearly expressed; errors in capitalization, punctuation, and spelling. Make whatever changes seem necessary. Do not hesitate to rewrite or add whole paragraphs. The checklist that follows will serve as a guide for revision. The important matter of writing the final draft is discussed immediately following the checklist for revision.

Composition Checklist

1. Does your introduction contain a clear statement of purpose?
2. Does each paragraph have only one main idea?
3. Are the main ideas developed by a variety of methods—factual details, concrete details, examples, reasons, and so forth?
4. Do you use transitions to bridge gaps between paragraphs?
5. Is each main idea in the composition related to the topic as a whole?
6. Does your composition follow a logical order of development?
7. Is your final draft free from errors in capitalization, punctuation, sentence structure, spelling, word choice, and grammar?
8. Is your title interesting and suggestive of the main idea in your composition?

14g. Write the final draft.

A composition requires a considerable amount of effort. By the time you come to the preparation of the final draft, most of this work is behind you. Your main concern now is to put your composition in a neat and attractive form that reflects the thought and care you have devoted to the whole undertaking. Follow the instructions for manuscript preparation in Chapter 25 or the specific instructions that your teacher gives you.

The final draft of the composition you have seen taking shape throughout this chapter is given below. Read it through, noting the general organization, the adherence to the outline (page 286), the paragraphing, the use of transitional expressions, and the divisions into introduction, body, and conclusion.

● EXERCISE 10. Read the following high school composition and discuss in class the following points:

**14
f-g**

1. The statement of purpose in the introduction
2. The topic sentence of each paragraph
3. The paragraph divisions. Is each paragraph the development of a main heading in the topic outline, or is the composition differently arranged?
4. The transitional devices that link one paragraph to another
5. The conclusion. What does it accomplish?

A Town Right Out of the Past

Pleasant Valley is a town right out of the past. It has no commercial places of entertainment—no movies, skating rinks, bowling alleys, or dance halls. These attractions are fifteen miles away in one of the modern towns. I miss them sometimes and occasionally resent the spirit of my town that has no interest in the future but dreams continually of its past: Why is Pleasant Valley old-fashioned? Why am I still glad it is my home? Let me explain.

Pleasant Valley was settled by Yankees from Connecticut in the last half of the eighteenth century. Pining for New England, they planted the old elms around the common that today bury the town in greenery and even at noon plunge the streets into an emerald twilight. Within two generations these Yankees, who were not farmers but craftsmen, had transformed the river

— introduction

statement of purpose

body

main topic I early history

valleys into industrial districts. Sleepy river ports turned into grimy mill towns, and the surrounding countryside took on a blasted look as if a great breath of fire had shriveled every green thing. As the towns prospered, Irish immigrants came, followed by Poles, Slovaks, and Italians. They became miners and mill hands and crowded their families into the ramshackle company towns.

Pleasant Valley, **however,** shared only the best of **this progress.** It became rich. Lacking coal, this valley was "unexploited." Its streams remained pure, its forests untouched, and its air untainted. Neither was Pleasant Valley touched by industrial strife. There were no torch-lit battles fought in the cinders of switchyards, no factory windows broken—because here there were no switchyards and no factories. All was gracious and elegant in Pleasant Valley. Although they made their fortunes elsewhere, the men of Yankee stock built their homes here. The lanes between the imposing houses became in the afternoons avenues of fashion. Ladies in silk with parasols, bound on polite errands, passed in the dappled shade. In the evening the soft, orange glow of Chinese lanterns on the verandas over-

transitions

main topic II
isolation

spread the lawns. Angry men might gather in the mill towns and stock prices might fall, but none of this was real in Pleasant Valley.

Thus, when the rest of Pennsylvania moved into the twentieth century, Pleasant Valley stayed in the nineteenth. Many of the mines were worked out; others were forced to close when oil replaced anthracite for heating. The steel industry had long since moved west to Pittsburgh. The men of Pleasant Valley had to sell their local interests and follow the industry west. Gradually the town was left to female relatives whose stocks and bonds could not long maintain the old elegance. Many of the homes were shut up for good. Gardens were first overgrown with weeds, then planted with vegetables. The greatest of the mansions became the normal school. Lesser ones were turned into funeral homes or convalescent homes. A few stayed open, their mistresses timidly setting out small signs on the lawns— "Tourists," "Guests."

A town **like this,** which clings to its past, offers no future to its children. When I graduate from high school, I shall, like other young people before me, leave Pleasant Valley. If I ever re-

transition

main topic III
decline

transition

turn (which is doubtful because few ever return now), I hope it will be then as it is now, a sanctuary from the world of superhighways, gas stations, and shopping centers. In the crisp, smoke- less air of morning, I hope the fox still barks sharply from the hillside; at noon the orchards will be sleepy with the humming of bees; and in the evening, as the trout begin to rise on the mill- pond, a deep stillness will fall on the streets where, long ago, stately ladies paused to exchange courtesies.

main topic IV
timelessness

—conclusion

TOPICS FOR COMPOSITIONS

The topics listed below are intended as suggestions. If you find one that you could use if it were changed slightly, change the topic to suit your wishes. Word your own title.

The Arts

1. The secret of taking fine photographs
2. Favorite rock groups
3. A good (bad) movie
4. Ceramics
5. How to refinish antique furniture
6. Making sense of new art
7. A musical instrument any- one can learn to play
8. Ballet vs. modern dance
9. The training of a balle- rina
10. Designing and building a stage set
11. The principles of stage lighting
12. The dress rehearsal
13. Qualities of a good feature writer
14. How to appreciate good music
15. What's great about great painting?
16. The origins of jazz
17. Interior decoration
18. Careers in fashion design
19. Violence on television
20. The use of watercolor
21. Modern filmmaking
22. The art of junk sculpture

Literature

1. A great American play-wright
2. Brutus and Cassius—allies and opposites
3. The importance of the minor characters in a Shakespearean play
4. Differences between Shakespeare's language and today's English
5. Sources of Shakespeare's plots
6. Some special features of the Elizabethan stage
7. Two very different poems on the same theme
8. A great American poet
9. Conflicting views of life as represented by two fictional characters
10. The novel as a force for social reform
11. The case against (or for) censorship
12. The qualities of a good short story
13. Can science fiction be good literature?
14. From book to movie
15. How to read a poem

Personal Opinions and Experiences

1. Moods that I can't help
2. On following the crowd
3. My chief ambition
4. My favorite meal
5. A look at my own personality
6. On sophistication
7. An embarrassing experience
8. The season that best suits my temperament
9. First impressions are rarely the best.
10. Why I want to be (any vocation)
11. Sports bore me.
12. I would like to redesign myself.
13. The uses and misuses of makeup
14. What is it to be mature?
15. My finest hour
16. What my country means to me
17. What does it mean to be true to yourself?
18. Three ways to overcome anxiety
19. Do "nice guys really finish last"?
20. The uses of adversity
21. "The world is too much with us . . ."
22. Why I hate injustice
23. Status-seeking among high school students
24. Three quick and easy routes to unpopularity
25. What is a really *great* man?
26. My bank account problems
27. A pleasant journey or holiday

28. My prejudices
29. Some people simply amaze me!
30. My happiest surprise
31. How to endure a terrifying exam
32. On being a big sister (brother)
33. A look into the distant future
34. The friends around me
35. How to deal with the weather
36. On being a nuisance
37. My greatest triumph
38. Daydreaming and the troubles it has caused me
39. The person I admire most
40. People I like

Right Around Home

1. Our family customs
2. Why my parents annoy (or criticize) me
3. Sunday dinners at our house
4. Our favorite family holiday
5. Wait till I have my own family!
6. The family car
7. Trials and tribulations of moving
8. Discipline and what it does to (or for) me
9. Two relatives too many
10. Ancestors as only I could know them
11. Chores that bore me
12. Guests who I wish would stay longer
13. Street games
14. "To grandfather's house we go . . ."
15. My dream house
16. Waiting for the doctor to come
17. Our worst accident
18. Our furniture
19. Backyard pests
20. Our family album
21. Landlords are often human
22. Oh, for a room of my own!
23. Our block is a tight little world.
24. Educational television
25. Ingenious uses for the fire escape
26. Network television
27. Neighborhood sounds

School

1. Fighting your way up the ladder
2. How to make grades and lose friends
3. Teachers' problems
4. My favorite seat
5. A trip to the infirmary
6. Waiting in line
7. "Miles to go before I sleep . . ."
8. On spelling (or any other subject)

9. Suggested changes in the curriculum
10. Struggling to win an election
11. Schools I have attended
12. My favorite subject
13. Arguments for (or against) busing
14. Advantages of the honor system
15. Once I tried to bluff . . .
16. Trying out for the class play
17. Teachers and their odd habits
18. A system for doing homework
19. My locker
20. High schools in the U.S. and in another country
21. Students come in three varieties
22. Appropriate school dress
23. Who should determine what is proper?
24. Typical sights in the corridor
25. My happiest (unhappiest) school experience

Hobbies and Leisure Time Activities

1. Raising hamsters (or any other pet)
2. Collections and how to arrange things
3. Just loafing around the house
4. An educational hobby
5. Mr. Fix-it, which is what I was *not!*
6. Bicycling
7. My favorite animal
8. Church work
9. How to spend a rainy Sunday
10. Friendship by mail
11. On learning to play a musical instrument
12. The game I play best
13. The do-it-yourself craze
14. What I do in my spare time
15. Training a dog
16. Low-cost improvements on a car
17. The fascination of bird watching
18. Fun on water-skis
19. Ham radio
20. Teaching boys to dance
21. Horror movies, or why is it fun to be scared?
22. The discriminating window-shopper
23. Television commercials
24. The unobserved observer
25. Organize your own rock group
26. Quick and easy ways to spoil a child
27. A lexicon of high school slang
28. On collecting a library of classical music
29. Profitable activities
30. On tour with the family

31. Sailing: racing and cruising

Far and Wide

1. The country fair
2. On the boardwalk
3. Customs I have observed in other people
4. Our strange neighbors
5. Virtue is rewarded.
6. How to enjoy an illness
7. Right up to the moon and beyond it
8. On borrowing and lending
9. On being lost
10. The art of fishing (or hunting)
11. On mountain climbing
12. Outdoor Christmas decorations
13. On looking up at the stars

Science

1. Pollution control
2. The Ice Age in North America
3. To Mars and beyond
4. Oceanography—an exciting new science
5. Why birds migrate
6. Rocks—the record of the earth's history
7. The exploding universe
8. The possibility of life in outer space
9. The uses of the laser beam
10. The dangers of insecticides
11. Easy experiments for the home workshop
12. Hybridization—a way to bigger crops
13. A community conservation project
14. The great sequoias of California
15. Landing on the moon
16. The internal combustion engine—miracle or menace?

Social Problems

1. The threat of Communism
2. The idea behind the UN
3. What is the balance of trade?
4. Why vote?
5. The tyranny of the automobile
6. Air pollution
7. Stream pollution
8. How to improve our schools
9. Will there always be wars?
10. Fewer and fewer farm jobs
11. The blessing (curse) of automation
12. Discrimination: the shame of our democracy
13. The need for more city parks
14. How Congress passes a law
15. Teen-agers and cars
16. The age of anxiety
17. Overcrowded schools

18. The continuing fight for civil rights
19. The nonmedical use of drugs
20. The promise of urban renewal
21. Our plundered natural resources
22. The future of Africa
23. Are demonstrations effective?
24. Juvenile delinquency
25. The chief problem of my home town
26. Population control
27. Divorce and the family
28. Problems of welfare
29. Educate everyone?
30. Freedom of the individual
31. A cure for unemployment
32. Our changing cities
33. Why we have strikes

CHAPTER 15

Specific Writing Assignments

**Explanations, Essay Answers,
Character Descriptions, Critical Reviews,
Essays of Opinion, Definitions**

The general principles of exposition discussed in Chapter 14 apply to most of the writing assignments you are likely to be given in school. There are, however, certain specific kinds of composition which come up often enough to require special treatment. Except possibly for the description of a character, the kinds of composition discussed in this chapter will play an increasingly important part in your classroom assignments from now on. Concentrate on one type at a time, always remembering that the general rules for planning and organizing a composition apply to all expository writing.

EXPLAINING A PROCESS

Explanation differs from description by focusing on a process or series of steps. The writer of a society column may *describe* a wedding cake. The writer of a cookbook must *explain* how to make one. A recipe, in fact, is one of the commonest examples of process explanation.

Hints for Writing the Explanation of a Process

1. *Choose a subject that lends itself to explanation.* Make sure it is a subject about which you are fully informed.

2. *Keep your reader in mind.* Don't assume that he knows more than he really does, but don't go to the other extreme and "talk down" to him. Try to anticipate his questions. Define briefly any terms that he might not understand.

3. *Be clear, accurate, and complete.* Don't omit any necessary step, or allow anything irrelevant to intrude.

4. *Begin effectively.* Identify the process you will explain; explain its purpose; explain when and by whom it is performed; clarify what value it will have when performed.

5. *If you are explaining how to make something, make clear to the reader what he will need to carry out the process* (*equipment, ingredients, skills, etc.*). You may use one paragraph to list and explain these materials all at once, or you may explain them as they come up naturally in the process.

6. *Break down the process into steps, and present these steps in chronological order.* Provide easy transitions between the steps, and put in whatever cautions are needed where missteps might normally occur ("Don't let the two wires touch").

7. *Conclude this type of composition by explaining what the results will be if the steps have been followed carefully.*

Read the following explanation of the process of preparing baked beans. Note the step-by-step organization, the clear instructions, the description of ingredients and equipment.

Now about the baking of the beans. Baked beans have to be baked. That sounds like a gratuitous restatement of the obvious, but it isn't. — introduction—process identified

Some misguided souls boil beans all day and call

the lily-livered result baked beans. I refrain from comment.

We use either New York State or Michigan white beans because we like them best, although yellow-eyes are very popular too. 1 I take two generous cups of dry beans, soak overnight, and put them on to boil early in the morning. When the skins curl off when you blow on them, they've boiled long enough. 2 Then I put in the bottom of the bean pot, or iron kettle with a tight-fitting cover, a six-by-eight inch square of salt pork with the rind slashed every quarter of an inch, a quarter cup of sugar, half a cup of molasses, a large onion chopped fairly fine, and a heaping teaspoonful of dry mustard. This amount of sugar and molasses may be increased or cut, depending on whether you like your beans sweeter or not so sweet. This is a matter every man has to decide for himself. 3 The beans are dumped in on top of this conglomerate, and enough hot water is added to cover. The baking pot should be large enough so that there's at least an inch of freeboard above the water. Otherwise, they'll boil over and smell to high heaven. 4 Cover tightly and put into a medium oven—about 350° is right.

materials needed

(1) first step

(2) second step

(3) third step

caution against misstep

(4) fourth step

They should be in the oven by half-past nine in the morning at the latest, and they should stay there until supper time, which in our family is at six.

So far there is no trick in making good baked beans. The trick, if it can be dignified by such a term, lies in the baking, and like a great many trade tricks, it consists only of patience and conscientious care. 5 You have to tend the beans faithfully, adding water whenever the level gets down below the top of the beans, and you have to keep the oven temperature even. If you're lazy, you can put in a lot of water and not have to watch them so closely. 6 But to get the best results, you should add only enough water each time to barely cover the beans. This means you'll give up all social engagements for the day, as you can't leave the baby for more than half an hour at a time. I think the results are worth it—but then, I haven't anywhere special to go anyhow. My beans are brown and mealy, and they swim in a thick brown juice. They're good. I always serve them with cornbread, ketchup, and pickles.[1]

(5) fifth step

(6) last step

conclusion: reward for following directions—delicious beans

[1] From "Baked Beans" from *We Took to the Woods* by Louise Dickinson Rich. Copyright 1942 by Louise Dickinson Rich. Reprinted by permission of J. B. Lippincott Company.

Checklist for Explanations

1. Is the explanation complete and clear? If carried out, is it likely to give the desired results?
2. Are the steps easy to follow from one to the next? Have you cautioned against missteps?
3. Did you list and explain unfamiliar terms and mention all of the materials needed?
4. Do the introduction and conclusion accomplish their special purposes of identifying the process and defining the end product?
5. Has the writer adapted the explanation to his intended audience?
6. Is the writing itself interesting to read?

● EXERCISE 1. (Suggested writing assignments)

1. *How to make something:* a birthday cake, a cement walk, a model airplane, a rock garden, a sweater, a crystal radio, a bookcase, a hot rod.
2. *How to do something:* organize a club, buy stereo equipment, build a library of your own, redecorate your room, write a news story.
3. *How a process works:* how green plants manufacture sugars, how lenses invert images, how storekeepers arrive at the price of their stock, etc.
4. *A humorous essay or explanation:* how to lose a job, how to antagonize your best friends, how to fail English, how to be a wet blanket.

WRITING THE ESSAY ANSWER

Most of the classroom tests you have taken so far have probably required one-word or short-paragraph answers. As you continue in school, however, you will find that you are more and more frequently asked to write longer essay answers to test questions. While the specific techniques will vary, there are some general techniques which will be helpful.

The essay answer is really an impromptu composition written under time pressure about a specific subject. All that you have learned about writing compositions, therefore, can be brought to bear on the writing of the essay answer. In addition, the following suggestions should be of help.

Hints for Writing the Essay Answer

1. *Read the test question slowly and carefully.* Watch for key terms used in the question and follow them exactly.

EXAMPLES *compare:* find likenesses

contrast: point out differences

criticize: find faults and merits

discuss: examine, analyze carefully, and come to a conclusion

explain: stress the how and why

summarize: condense the main points

trace: give a description of progress, sequence, or development

2. *Plan your time and your answer.* Calculate on the basis of the point value of the question and the total time of the test. Then jot down your ideas in a simple outline with usually not more than three or four major points.

TOTAL TEST TIME 40 minutes

Question 1. (60 points) allow 24 minutes

Discuss the question: Who is the real tragic hero of *Julius Caesar* —Brutus or Caesar?

OUTLINE (1) Brutus in all five acts; Caesar dies in third.
 (2) Brutus, not Caesar, is lamented at the end—"The noblest Roman of them all."
 (3) Inner conflict occurs in Brutus, not in Caesar.

3. *Write a good introductory paragraph in which you refer directly to the question, and state the main point, or thesis, of your answer.*

4. *Devote one paragraph to each main point, and begin it always with a topic sentence.* In this way your main points will stand out for the teacher who is reading your answer quickly.

5. *Illustrate and support what you say by specific details, examples, and references.* Teachers are not likely to admire unsupported generalities.

6. *Summarize what you have said in a good concluding paragraph.*

7. *Allow yourself a few minutes to proofread what you have written, checking carefully for spelling and usage errors.*

There is room for much honest debate as to whether Caesar or Brutus is the real tragic hero of Shakespeare's *Julius Caesar.*	reference to the test question
In my close reading of the play, however, I found three compelling reasons for believing that Brutus is the protagonist.	statement of answer
The first reason is that Brutus has a much bigger role than Caesar. Caesar dies in Act III; Brutus is present in every act.	first main point
It has been argued that Caesar's ghost continues to make his presence and influence felt throughout the rest of the play. Such an influence is at least quantitatively negligible: the ghost speaks only three times, a total of sixteen words. Even a master dramatist like Shakespeare cannot build a successful final two acts with the hero offstage. By the mere reason of his presence on the stage, it is Brutus' play.	supporting facts

The second reason is also concerned   second main point
with this matter of structure and pres-
ence. When the play ends, it is Brutus   specific example
to whom Antony and Octavius pay
tribute. Antony's final speech is especially significant here:

This was the noblest Roman of them
        all . . .
    Nature might stand up
And say to all the world, 'This was a
        man.'

The most compelling reason of all is
found in Brutus' own nature. It is he in
whom the moral issue of the play is   third main point
fought out. He is the person in the play
who experiences the most intense inner
conflict—and inner conflict in the tragic   specific details
hero is the essence of all great tragedy.
There is little of this in Caesar; he is a
man with few doubts and uncertainties,
a character who undergoes no change.
Brutus, on the contrary, is torn with
doubt and pulled apart by the moral
issue. The tragedy is the chronicle of
his rise and fall.

By reason of what happens on the   summary
stage and what takes place inside the
characters, Brutus is the tragic hero
of *Julius Caesar*.

Checklist for Essay Answers

1. Does the introductory paragraph make direct reference to the question and state the main thesis of the answer?
2. Are the key points referred to in the topic sentence of each paragraph?
3. Are the main points of the answer supported and illustrated by details and references to the text?
4. Does the concluding paragraph summarize what has been said?
5. Does the answer follow the directions of the question exactly?

● EXERCISE 2.   (Suggested writing assignments)

1. Compose your own essay question on a subject in the field of English, social studies, or science. Then write an essay answer for the question you have composed.
2. Ask your science or social studies teacher to give your class a practice essay question. When you have written your answer, submit it to both your English teacher and to the teacher who assigned it.

DESCRIPTION OF A CHARACTER

If you wanted to know what a person looked like and was like, the best way would be to meet him in the flesh. The second best way would probably be to see a motion picture of him in action. The third best way would be to read a character sketch of him that would show him speaking and acting.

Hints for Writing the Character Description

1. *Select an interesting character to describe.* Although a skilled writer can make any character interesting, you will do well to choose a character who, because of his appearance, idiosyncrasies, characteristics, or occupation, is intrinsically interesting. Observe him closely before you begin

to write; get to know him so well that you can see beneath the surface. Try to understand and reveal, not just what he seems to be, but what he really is.

2. *When you begin your description, place him in a setting that either reflects his personality or that serves as an effective contrasting background for him.* Don't describe the setting in too much detail; a few brief strokes should suffice. Whenever possible, details of setting should be woven naturally into the rest of the sketch.

3. *Decide on the dominant impression you wish to create.* Since you will ordinarily not be able to develop a character as fully in a 300-word sketch as a novelist would in an entire story, you can avoid painting a jumbled and confused picture by emphasizing one chief impression. Your character sketch thus becomes a study in depth of the outstanding quality of the subject.

4. *Show your character in action.* Remember we mentioned a moving picture, not a still life. Since action reveals character, show us, for example, how he walks, how he sits, how he gestures, how he holds his head, and how he acts when angry, amused, or confused.

5. *Use dialogue to contribute to the total picture.* What does his voice sound like? What characteristic idioms and expressions does he use? Does he slur endings, drop sounds from words, or enunciate with exaggerated precision? What does he say when he is upset, happy, moody, angry, or depressed?

6. *Select vivid details of his physical appearance that will individualize him.* Since it is impossible to say everything about a person's appearance, selection becomes necessary. Two principles will help you determine which details to select. Select those which contribute most to the dominant impression you are trying to create; select those which will best individualize and differentiate. In describing features, use striking comparisons whenever possible, but avoid clichés like "a nose like an eagle's," "waddled like a duck."

7. *Use sensory details for vividness.* In describing details both of the setting and the appearance of the character, choose sensory details that will help the reader see, hear, feel, and smell. Since we apprehend experiences through the senses, it is essential that any re-creation of experience rely heavily on depictions of these sense impressions.

8. *Pay special attention to word choice.* Always important in writing, word choice is crucial to good description. Use specific and concrete nouns (not "he wore a sweater," but "he wore a red wool cardigan"). Use active and sharp verbs (not "walked," but "ambled" or "strode" or "paced"). And use vivid adjectives too, but don't overuse them.

The family was at the very core and ripeness of its life together. Gant lavished upon it his abuse, his affection, and his prodigal provisioning. They came to look forward eagerly to his entrance, for he brought with him the great gusto of living, of ritual. They would watch him in the evening as he turned the corner below with eager strides, follow carefully the processional of his movements from the time he flung his provisions upon the kitchen table to the rekindling of his fire, with which he was always at odds when he entered, and onto which he poured wood, coal, and kerosene lavishly. This done, he would remove his coat and wash himself at the basin vigorously, rubbing his hands across his shaven, tough-bearded face with the cleansing and

character placed in a setting

dominant characteristic

character in action

details of physical appearance

male sound of sandpaper. Then he   vivid diction
would thrust his body against the door
jamb and scratch his back energetically
by moving violently to and fro. This
done, he would empty another half can
of kerosene on the <u>howling flame, lung-
ing savagely at it and muttering to him-   vivid diction
self.</u>

Then, biting off a good hunk of powerful apple tobacco, which lay ready to
his use on the mantel, he would pace
back and forth across the room fiercely,
oblivious to his grinning family who
followed these ceremonies with exult-
ant excitement, as he composed his
tirade. Finally, he would <u>burst in</u> on
Eliza in the kitchen, <u>plunging to the
heart of denunciation with a mad howl.</u>   vivid diction

His turbulent and undisciplined
rhetoric had acquired, by the regular
convention of his usage, something of
the movement and directness of classical epithet: his similes were preposter-
ous, created really in a spirit of vulgar
mirth, and the great comic intelligence
that was in the family—down to the
youngest—was shaken daily by it. The
children grew to await his return in the
evening with a kind of exhilaration.

<u>As he stormed through the house,</u> un-   vivid diction
leashing his gathered bolts, the children

followed him joyously, shrieking exult-   vivid diction
antly as he told Eliza he had first seen
her "wriggling around the corner like a
snake on her belly," or, as coming in
from freezing weather, he had charged
her and all the Pentlands with malevo-
lent domination of the elements.

"We will freeze," he yelled, "we will   quotation
freeze in this . . . cruel and God-for-
saken climate. . . . Merciful God! I
have fallen into the hands of fiends in-
carnate, more savage, more cruel, more
abominable than the beasts of the field.
. . . They will sit by and gloat at my
agony until I am done to death."

As his denunciation reached some
high extravagance, the boys would
squeal with laughter, and Gant, in-
wardly tickled, would glance around
slyly with a faint grin bending the
corners of his thin mouth.[1]

● EXERCISE 3.   (Suggested writing assignments)

1. Take a character from fiction whom you know well. Write a
   character sketch as if he were a real person.
2. Write a character sketch of yourself, but write it in the third
   person, as if you were looking at yourself from a detached
   point of view.
3. Write a character sketch of yourself—as you think your
   mother or father sees you.

[1] From *Look Homeward, Angel* by Thomas Wolfe. Copyright 1929
Charles Scribner's Sons; renewal copyright © 1957 Edward C. Aswell.
Reprinted by permission of Charles Scribner's Sons.

4. Write a character sketch of a close friend.
5. Write a character sketch of a town "character" who interests you.

Checklist for Character Descriptions

1. Do we see the character in action? Are gestures, movements, and responses vividly pictured?
2. Do we hear the character speaking? Is there effective use of speech to reveal character and feeling?
3. Is the setting sketched in so that it helps us see the character? Is the setting readily visualized?
4. Are the details of the description skillfully chosen so that we get a clear sense of the dominant characteristic of the character?
5. Does the description make an effective appeal to the senses? How do the sensory images contribute to the total effect of the description?
6. To what extent do word choice and diction contribute to the success of the description? Are there striking comparisons? Is there good use of precise, specific, and vivid nouns, verbs, and adjectives?

THE CRITICAL REVIEW

Reviews of nonfiction books (biography, history, science, current affairs) are written to enable other readers to decide whether or not they would enjoy a particular book. Your review, therefore, must summarize clearly the theme of the book, examine a few of the major arguments, and comment upon the author's conclusion.

While none of these jobs is easy, the last is hardest of all because you are expected to make impartial judgments upon matters you are likely to know little about. Under these circumstances, the only thing to do is to evaluate as best you can the author's reliability. If he seems—either through his experience or his sources—to be in a position to know what he is talking about, then his conclusions demand respect. To be modest in your appraisals is surely the wisest course.

Hints for Writing the Critical Review

1. *Begin the review by identifying the title, author, and publisher, and by indicating the book's general nature.*

2. *In the library look up the author's background, and from the information given there, discuss the author's qualifications in the early part of your review.* What else has he written? Does his job or position afford him any particular insight into the matter of the book, or, on the contrary, is it likely to prejudice him?

3. *Summarize—usually in not more than one or two paragraphs—the content of the book.* Focus particularly on those sections of the book that might be controversial.

4. *Discuss the author's purpose in writing the book.* For what kind of audience was the book intended—young readers, college students, the general public, or specialists in the field? Is the book broad or limited in coverage?

5. *Describe any special features of the book.* Is it well illustrated? Does it have a good index, a complete bibliography? Do the footnotes add interest or distract?

6. *Evaluate the overall effectiveness of the book.* Is it timely? Is it reliable; that is, are the generalizations supported by convincing evidence?

7. *End your review by giving your individual response to the spirit of the book.* Are you now aware and alive to things that formerly you did not know?

> *They Call It a Game*
> by Bernie Parrish
> Dial, $7.50

title, author, and publisher

Professional football, which monopolizes the television screen from the kickoff Friday night to the last play Monday evening, has proved to be a gold mine to the networks, to the sports owners, but not, according to

theme of book

Bernie Parrish, to the players, who take the beating.

By the time Bernie Parrish was ready for college, he had won the reputation for being one of the fiercest tacklers in Florida. As a candidate for All-American in both football and baseball, he left college to sign a $30,000-plus bonus contract with the Cincinnati Redlegs, but the minor leagues didn't appeal to him, he couldn't get his mind off football, and when the Cleveland Browns picked him as a rookie, he returned the unearned half of his bonus, and staked everything on football.   author's qualifications

Parrish loved playing; his speed, fierceness, and intelligence made him one of the best defensive cornerbacks in the business, and under Paul Brown's coaching, he was one of the main reasons why Cleveland won the world championship for 1964. He was elected to be the players' representative and then set out to organize the Players Association into a union with real bargaining power. At this point he was blacklisted, and as his suspicions mounted, the game turned sour. Parrish's description of professionals in training and in action, of the injuries and the doctors, of the punishment given and taken, and of the exhilaration of a winning team is the best that has been written, and I understand that he did most of the writing himself.   summary of contents

    evaluation

The crusading half of this book is a rugged indictment of how the billion-dollar monopoly of television, the owners, the coaches, and the press create a front which denies the possibility of unionization, opposes a fair cut of the annual profits for the players' pensions (the average playing expectancy is eleven years), and of how they rule out the rebels as Parrish himself was erased. Parrish names names and figures, and those who are prepared to believe him will look more cynically at the spectacle this autumn.[1]

final evaluation

Checklist for Reviews

1. Is the reader told enough about the book so that he has an accurate idea of its contents? Does the review give the overall theme of the book as well as discuss its specific parts?
2. Is the reader given enough information about the author's background and qualifications?
3. Does the review seem fair, and are the reviewer's judgments supported by quotations from the text?
4. Is the review well written?
5. Does the review help the reader decide whether or not he would enjoy the book or profit from reading it?

● EXERCISE 4.   (Suggested writing assignments)

1. Write a review of a nonfiction work that will prove to your teacher that you have read and understood the book.

2. Suppose you have been appointed to a committee to award a prize to the best nonfiction work written for high school students in the past year. Write a report to the committee in which you indicate your selection and defend your choice.
3. Find a published review of a nonfiction book which you have read. Write your own review and clip it to the published review. Be ready to explain how the two reviews differ, since they were intended for different purposes.

THE ESSAY OF OPINION

A familiar sort of essay of opinion is the "letter to the editor." It is a written statement of the writer's belief about an arguable subject, supported by evidence, and written to convince. Actually the essay itself is the culmination of a process all students are normally engaged in—an interest in controversial subjects, an examination of the pros and cons, and finally the formation of judgments about them.

Hints for Writing the Essay of Opinion

1. *Choose a debatable subject, one that permits of constructive controversy and disagreement.* Be sure that it is clearly stated, is concerned with only one issue, and is sufficiently limited in scope. A formal statement of the subject of an argument is called a "proposition"; for example, "All drivers of motor vehicles should be required to pass a physical examination."

2. *Jot down a list of the arguments that support your stand.* Cross out any that are self-evident, trivial, or irrelevant. The ones that remain should have two genuine sides to them. They are called "issues." In dealing with the issues, you should (if you have the time) anticipate and refute every argument unfriendly to your point of view.

3. *Begin effectively.*

Catch the reader's interest.

State the proposition fairly and clearly.

Define any terms likely to be misunderstood.

Indicate the issues to be discussed.

Consider (if important) the history and significance of the question.

4. *Support your point of view with evidence.*

When you quote from an authority, identify the authority.

If you cite facts, give the source.

When you use an example, do not claim that one example establishes a general rule.

Be logical and fair.

5. *Conclude your essay by summarizing your main arguments and indicating a future course of action.*

Driver Training for All

On a single weekend last month, there were three serious highway accidents in this county that involved teen-aged drivers. One of the results of this tragic weekend was a renewed public demand that high school students should be required to take a course in driver training before receiving their driver's licenses. True, most of the high schools in this area have offered driver-training courses for many years. But these courses have always been elective, rather than required; and sometimes only a small fraction of the student body has actually been enrolled in the course. It would be an excellent idea, as I see it, to make driver training a required course.

The opponents of this idea have argued that providing driver training for every student would be very expensive and that the results would not be worth the price. It is true that the courses would be costly. Our town school board has estimated that in order to provide driver training for every high school student, the school would need at least two more full-time instructors and two additional training cars, as well as extra lab space and equipment. While the cost of this program would be large, it must be weighed against the much greater cost—both in money and in human suffering—of continuing to allow inexperienced and poorly trained people to join the ranks of licensed drivers. An effective driver-training program would certainly be worth the expense.

I think there is little question that the driver-training course now offered at our school has been effective. According to Mr. Ames, the instructor in charge of the course, only two of the forty-three students who took and passed the course last year failed to pass the state driver's-license examination on the first try; both of them passed on the second try. This compares

consideration of opposing views

first argument supported by evidence

very favorably with the statewide average of nearly twenty percent failures on the examination. Furthermore, Mr. Ames reports that only one of the students who has completed the course during the past five years has been involved in a serious accident since getting his license, and that in this case the other driver was judged at fault. Although Mr. Ames does not have figures for accidents involving students who have *not* taken the course, he says that each year at least three or four such students from our school have been arrested for speeding, while no student who has completed the course has been arrested for any traffic violation.

Some people grant that driver-training courses are effective, but still do not feel that driving instruction should be a required subject in a public high school. I think, on the contrary, that if we are to turn out a future generation of well-trained drivers, the public school is the logical place to provide the training. Sixty years ago, driving an automobile may have been a hobby of the rich, but today it is an essential part of nearly every adult's workaday life. It would be in the public interest to train all citizens to drive well and wisely. The

second argument supported by reasons

only present alternative to teaching driving in the schools is to continue the haphazard practice of leaving the instruction to parents or older friends, a system that in too many cases has proved ineffective.

The schools have shown that they can train good drivers. Let's give them the job of teaching all students to drive well.

short summary statement

Checklist for Essays of Opinion

1. Is the question truly debatable; that is, are there genuinely two sides to it?
2. Does the writer take a definite stand, and is he fair to the contrary point of view?
3. Does the opening paragraph arouse the reader's interest, state the proposition, and provide the necessary background?
4. Are the arguments supported by ample evidence?
5. Does the writer refute or ignore evidence to the contrary?
6. Is the essay well written?
7. Does it convince?

● EXERCISE 5.   (Suggested writing assignments)

1. Write an imaginary letter to the editor of a school newspaper on some school issue, for example:
     Enlarged powers for the student government
     Freedom for the student press
     Class elections
     Greater freedom for students in choosing their courses
2. Write an essay of opinion on some community issue, for example:
     A youth recreation center should be established.
     Schools should be open six days a week, all year long.

A teen-age curfew should be enacted.

Traffic regulations should be changed.

The community should set up collection centers for bottles, cans, and other trash that can be recycled.

3. Write an essay of opinion about some historical issue, for example:

The Revolutionary War should not have been fought.

The U.S. should have joined the League of Nations.

We should not have dropped the atomic bomb on Japan.

4. Select a candidate in a school, local, or national election, and try to convince your readers that they should vote for him.

THE DEFINITION

Frequently larger issues cannot be debated until the contestants have first agreed on the meaning of certain terms. That is why definitions are so important and why it is necessary to take such care in composing them. A definition may be one sentence long, or it may require a long essay.

Limited Definition

A short definition in a single sentence follows a definite pattern:

EXAMPLE   A taxicab is a public vehicle, usually equipped with a meter, for carrying passengers.

In this sentence definition, taxicab is the *term;* the broad class into which the term is placed is called the *genus* (public vehicle); and the properties which differentiate the term from others in the genus are called the *differentiae* (equipped with a meter, for carrying passengers). These parts of a definition always occur in a specific order: the term, followed by *is* or *are;* the genus; and the differentiae.

       term   *genus*

EXAMPLE   A captain is a commissioned officer next in grade

differentiae
above a first lieutenant.

Avoid the following errors in sentence definitions:

(1) Irrelevant material

EXAMPLE   A taxicab is a vehicle for carrying passengers, usually wealthier people.

(2) Circular definitions (defining the term by using a different form of the same word)

EXAMPLE   Freedom is the state of being free.

(3) Differentiae that do not really set apart the term

EXAMPLE   Democracy is a form of government used in modern times.

(4) Differentiae that restrict the term too much

EXAMPLE   A university is an advanced school for liberal arts students.

(5) Differentiae just as puzzling as the term

EXAMPLE   Sapremia is a state resulting from the products of putrefaction in the blood.

Extended Definition

Complex terms or concepts are best defined by compositions which explore every aspect of the idea. You may begin with a sentence definition, but in all likelihood you will use the rest of your composition to explain why you have chosen the differentiae you have cited. In such an extended definition, you might use the following methods:

(1) Citing authority

EXAMPLE   Justice Holmes once defined democracy as . . .

(2) Using a dictionary definition (give title and publisher)
(3) Discussing the origin of the term
(4) Discussing the history of the term

EXAMPLE   *Gentleman* first signified one of gentle birth; next a person of refinement who put others at ease; now it is someone who takes his hat off in the elevator . . .

(5) Using comparison and contrast

EXAMPLE Baseball is a game similar in some ways to cricket . . .

(6) Using an anecdote

EXAMPLE To define what I mean by a "good neighbor," let me cite the parable of the Good Samaritan . . .

(7) Defining by telling what it is *not*

EXAMPLE A gentleman is not one who merely follows the rules of etiquette. He is not necessarily one who belongs to the best clubs . . .

(8) Defining by citing many examples

EXAMPLE A young mountain range is, for example, the Rockies or the Alps or the Himalayas . . .

A [1]melodrama is a kind of [2]play, usually with a happy ending, [3]in which the interest centers in the exciting and unusual things that happen fast and mysteriously. [4]The characters are likely to be stock figures—that is, types rather than strongly marked individualities— moved by elementary motives. [5]The good people in such a play are very good and very brave, qualities which they need if they are to survive the dangers into which they are plunged for no plausible reason except to provide another thrill for the audience. The bad people are very bad, with no redeeming feature unless tenacity of purpose may be so called. [6]Melodrama pays <u>almost no attention to human values,</u> and <u>its object is to give a thrill.</u>

(1) term (2) genus

(3–4) differentiae

(5) supporting details

(6) differentiae continued

It is not to be judged too seriously. If it supplies harmless entertainment, like *Broadway*, for instance, its purpose is achieved. The plot of *Hamlet*, as it originally existed, is melodramatic, but Shakespeare transformed the leading character from a figurehead of blood-and-thunder melodrama to a genuinely tragic human being.[1]

Checklist for Definitions

1. Does the definition place the subject in its class or genus?
2. Does the definition sufficiently distinguish the term from others similar to it?
3. Is the definition sufficiently clear so that no ambiguity remains and all exceptions are accounted for?
4. Is the definition sufficiently complete and inclusive so that no essential ideas or concepts are overlooked?

● EXERCISE 6. (Suggested writing assignments)

1. Without consulting a dictionary, write a one-sentence definition for the following nouns: wrist watch, shoe, cup, match, chair, glove, fountain pen.
2. Demonstrate your knowledge of any one of the following literary terms by showing how it is used in several literary selections: simile, metaphor, irony, alliteration.
3. Define the following pairs of words so that the difference between them is clear: conservative—reactionary; liberal—radical; melodrama—tragedy; democracy—capitalism.
4. Use a combination of methods to define as completely as possible any one of the following abstract terms: wit, progress, faith, success, common sense, courage, love, intelligence.

[1] From *Enjoyment of Literature* by Ralph P. Boas and Edwin Smith. Copyright 1934 by Harcourt, Brace and Company, Inc. Reprinted by permission of Harcourt Brace Jovanovich, Inc.

CHAPTER 16

Writing the Narrative

The Essentials of Story Writing

Among the dozens of compositions you have written so far in your school career, most have probably been narratives—written accounts of events that happened to you or to somebody you have known. You may even have tried your hand at writing stories. If you have, you know that stories too are narratives but narratives of a special kind. The first difference is that stories are not necessarily true. They need only *seem* to be true. The second difference is that stories, unlike factual reporting, aim for a single effect; and they secure this effect by telling, not what in fact *did* happen, but what the author thinks *should* have happened in order for the events to be as funny or as sad or as exciting or as meaningful as they could be. In other words, in stories, art improves upon life.

THE NATURE OF THE NARRATIVE

16a. Recognize the essentials of a good story.

Most good stories have three common elements and three common qualities. The common elements are the following: 16a

1. *The hero*—the central character. His experiences make the story. The "hero" is not necessarily bold and brave, of course, and may be a man, a woman, a band of persons, or even an animal. The only essential thing is that the hero should *act*. Otherwise, there is no story.

2. *The conflict*—the element that causes the hero to act. The conflict can be between the hero and some force outside himself—a storm, a mountain ledge, another person—or, as in many memorable stories, the conflict may be purely psychological and take place inside the hero.

3. *The climax*—the climax occurs when the tension built up by the conflict is *resolved*—in other words, when the hero wins out or is beaten by whatever opposes him. After the climax the tension of the story breaks off abruptly, and in a few lines the story ends.

You must not expect this conflict always to be obvious. On the contrary, it is often quite subtle. A famous story by a sixteen-year-old girl is a case in point.[1] In the first few lines of this story, the heroine introduces herself to the reader. She hastens to assure him that "she knows the score." She is sixteen; she is not giddy nor romantic nor given to daydreaming; and she is certainly not the type to misconstrue a boy's casual friendliness and think it the beginning of a romance. Nevertheless, on the very next evening, this is precisely what she does. She goes skating, and on the rink a boy makes her a casual gesture of friendliness. Abruptly, all of her good sense abandons her, and she loses herself in romantic fancies. The story's last scene shows the heroine keeping a heavyhearted and useless vigil by the telephone.

Where is the "conflict" here? It is, of course, entirely within the heroine, but it is no less real for that. Her good sense is pitted against the fatal tendency of many sixteen-year-old girls to see the world through rose-colored glasses

---

[1] "Sixteen" by Maureen Daly.

—not as it is, but as they would like it to be. This tendency, conspiring with the magic of the night at the skating rink, is sufficient to defeat her good sense and to bring on a bout of quite unnecessary sadness.

As you can see, the story does not end happily. In this conflict the heroine is defeated, but since this ending is much more likely than a happy one, it is truer to life, and therefore its appeal is much greater. Many of the best stories end this way—with the defeat of the hero. This does not mean, however, that they are bad stories. Only a sentimentalist needs to be constantly reassured that everything turns out for the best. For most readers the deepest appeal of any story comes from the abiding and inexhaustible interest everyone shares in other human beings and in what happens inside them. This is the interest that a storyteller seeks to arouse, and it is this interest that enables a story written by you about, say, the death of your dog or a quarrel with your brother to be just as fascinating as some swashbuckling tale of high deeds.

In addition to the three common elements mentioned above, every good story has certain common qualities:

1. *The sense of reality*—the quality that allows the reader to believe in the hero and in what happens to him. In order to capture this quality, storytellers take pains to create solid characters whom the reader can get to know. (It is very hard to care deeply about what happens to someone you don't know.) Next, storytellers are careful to make their characters act consistently and involve them in believable events. Miss Priscilla of Sunnybrook Farm, for example, could never become trail boss on the Chisholm drive, nor would Huck Finn ever be appointed Ambassador to France.

Last of all, storytellers use every device to assist the imagination of the reader to take an active part in the story —in a sense, to *live* the story rather than merely to view the events from outside. To this end, most conversation is reproduced in direct quotation rather than merely reported. Scenes are set carefully. The sense of time, place, and mood is made vivid by description. Characters in the story reveal their dominant traits in what they do and say rather than by what the author says about them. Finally, everything in the story is calculated to contribute to a single impression.

2. *The sense of drama*—the excitement that arises from the conflict and the uncertainty of its outcome. Good stories maintain this uncertainty right up to the climax; often the drama is most intense right before the issue is resolved.

3. *Significance*—the point of the story. This does not mean that each narrative must have a message or moral, but it does mean that every good story which is to rise above the level of commonplace gossip should at least suggest some insight into human nature that is not commonly perceived. In other words, a story with significance does more than merely entertain the reader; it *changes* him—making him more understanding, wiser, kinder, more patient, or more sensitive. Stories that achieve this quality in a high degree become literature.

STORY MATERIAL

Writing a short story is very much like writing any other kind of composition. You must first choose your subject. Next, you must limit the subject (although in the case of the story, you shape it for dramatic impact rather than limit it for economy). Next, you must plan it, and finally you must write and revise it.

The chief difference between a short story and a composition is in the planning. A story is planned *backward*, that is, from the climax back to the details and incidents that mount up to it. This is done so that every element in the story—character traits, conversation, incidents, even the introduction—contributes to the force of the last scene.

The first stage is to find something to write about.

16b. Recognize and record the story material around you.

Beginning writers who despair of finding material should realize that good material for narratives is all around them, and the real problem is knowing what to select from all the sources available.

1. *From your reading.* To begin with, you should read widely. This does not mean that you can legitimately "borrow" existing stories; it does mean that the sensitive reader will see ways in which a story can be modified or made to take a completely different turn. Did you read something in the newspaper that intrigued you or made you smile? Jot such items down in a notebook or journal for possible story ideas. Ancient myths are also good sources for ideas. They embody themes of such basic appeal that modern readers still respond to them after thousands of years. Finally, as you read stories, ask yourself why a given story succeeds while another fails, why one character is convincing while another is unbelievable. Most of our successful contemporary authors tell us that they have never had a course in writing but have learned to write from careful study of the masters.

2. *From your experience.* A better source than your reading, however, is your own immediate experience—the people you meet, the incidents you observe, the things that happen to you. We are more reliable reporters of events we experience directly. We write with more confidence and knowledge of the people, places, and events we know from firsthand experience. While these daily experiences of ours rarely make the headlines, they can provide the stuff of good narratives. Therefore, learn to see with a fresh eye; watch for the eccentric character, the everyday hero, the humor and tragedy of daily existence. And learn also to record what you see. Make it a practice to keep a writer's journal in which you capture fleeting impressions and flashing images.

Experience is the proper source of story material—vicarious experience (the things you read and hear about) and direct experience (the things you have known at first hand). The next problem is how to tap all this experience. What approaches can lead you into this mine of experience?

16c. Shape the general idea into a dramatic story idea.

Almost any idea you recover from your reading or experience has dramatic potential. All you need apply is a little imagination. After all, stories are fiction. They need simply to seem true. Cut out dull details, and add others right out of your imagination. Think of the things that *might* have happened instead of what did happen—events that would have made the incident mysterious, exciting, funny, suspenseful, or sad.

Some writers approach this task through theme. Nathaniel Hawthorne, we are told, usually began with an idea that intrigued him and tried to build a story around that idea. The danger here for beginning storytellers is that the theme can very easily become more important than the characters, resulting in a stiff and moralizing little fable. At times, however, a theme can suggest a story idea that does more than merely illustrate the theme. It can create a character and show him in action. Does the following theme suggest a story idea to you?

> It is sometimes said that if all our wishes were suddenly granted, we would wish for one more, namely, that everything be put back the way it was.

Other writers tell us they approach through character. One writer says, "I find a good strong character, imagine him faced with different situations, and just see where he takes the story." Quite often you will find it stimulating and productive to keep a notebook on just one person whom you know. Note the clothing he wears, the gestures he uses, the expressions he repeats, the way he laughs—all seemingly unimportant details which together help to flesh out his portrait if he should appear in a story of yours. Then try to imagine him faced with different kinds of situations. This speculation, you will find, often leads to the beginning of a story.

Many writers build a story out of a single incident. Most of Mark Twain's stories, it is said, are just a retelling of the events of his boyhood. We can see in Twain's notebooks, for example, how a seemingly insignificant episode in his life was later transformed into an important part of a novel.

Can you remember the first time you learned something important about yourself? What was your first big success, and how did you respond to it? Have you perhaps suffered the loss of a friend, and are you sufficiently removed from it so that you can write about it objectively? Can you think of a time when you caused someone else to suffer—and what your feelings were on this occasion? Such incidents involving conflict, failure, success, and understanding usually make good narratives.

● EXERCISE 1.　Try to recall an incident from your childhood or a more recent experience that illustrates any one of the ideas or themes listed below. Retell the incident so that the point comes through clearly for the reader.

1. Everyone masks his real self.
2. We all learn from failure.
3. A lie always comes out.
4. Many heroes come and go unrecognized.
5. Everyone needs attention and recognition.
6. True nonconformity is simply a matter of making up your own mind.
7. The greatest lies are those we tell ourselves.
8. It is always darkest before the dawn.
9. He laughs best who laughs last.

16c

10. A fool and his money are soon parted.
11. Misery loves company.
12. Time heals all wounds.

● EXERCISE 2. Any one of the following suggestions will give you practice in using your reading as a source for story ideas. Select one.

1. From a newspaper, cut out a clipping which you think has great human interest. Retell the news story as a narrative. Attach the original clipping to your story.
2. Select a myth or fable of Aesop or La Fontaine, and retell it as a modern narrative. Be sure to identify the specific tale you are using.
3. Take a character from fiction who appeals to you, and make him the hero of a new adventure.

● EXERCISE 3. Take one of the following suggestions for practice in using the experiences of others as a source of story ideas.

1. Talk to someone from another country, and ask him to tell you a story illustrating how life in his country differs from life in the U.S. Then retell this story as a narrative.
2. Interview someone in your community who you think has an interesting story to tell. Then write his story as if he himself were telling it.
3. Ask your parents to help you recall an incident from your childhood that they think others would find amusing. Retell this incident from the viewpoint of your parents.

PLANNING THE NARRATIVE

As noted before, a story is different from an exposition in that a story is planned "backward," that is, from the ending back to the events that lead up to it. The reason for this is that everything that happens in a story must build up to the climax of the last scene. You cannot know, of course, what to put in or leave out until you know how each bit of conversation, description, and incident contributes to the emotional impact of the last scene.

16d. Organize the story.

The best way to organize your story is to ask yourself the following questions:

1. How is the story going to end?
2. Where should the story begin?
3. Should the story be told in the first or third person?
4. Which parts or scenes should be written in the greatest detail?

(1) Decide upon the ending first.

At this stage you have only your essential "story situation" or basic plot in mind. Suppose it were the following:

> During lunch hour a girl finds ten dollars on the school grounds. In class she waits impatiently for the final bell so that she can hurry to the store and buy a sweater she has been coveting. Before the bell rings, however, she finds out who has lost the money.

The conflict here is obvious. It is one of conscience: will the heroine restore the money to its rightful owner, or will she spend it on herself? Now of course she must do one or the other of these two things; but if she does either *immediately*, that is, without taking thought, then there is no conflict and no story. In other words, the lucky girl cannot be either entirely selfish or entirely unselfish. She must feel both of these impulses—the selfish and the unselfish—at the same time and *with almost equal force*. Only in this third case is the conflict sharp enough to make a good story.

This consideration warns the storyteller that his story cannot succeed unless he creates a realistic character—neither all saint nor all sinner. Now to further define his main

16d

character, he must imagine the ending. Suppose it were the following:

> The girl gives back the money. She does it sadly and is not rewarded. (Only in Mother Goose does the beggar whom the hero befriends turn out to be the King in disguise.) Nevertheless, she is at peace with herself as she walks home.

As you can see, this ending allows the better nature of the heroine to prevail. It also means that the storyteller must make his story exciting by letting it appear—right up to the last moment—that the heroine will *not* give back the money but will buy the sweater. This is what is meant by planning a story "backward" from the ending.

(2) Begin the story as near to the end as possible.

With the ending of the story in mind, you must now determine where to begin. The best place, of course, is just at that point at which the tension has already begun to mount and only a few scenes lie between the beginning and the climax.

In the sample story the planner has decided to show the mounting tension in three scenes:

> 1. The girl is excited and impatient as she waits in class for the final bell. She manages to pass a few surreptitious notes to her best friend. These notes infect the other girl with her own excitement. The girl does not dare give her friend the details, but can only hint vaguely of a "great event" that is to come to pass right after school. At length, the impulse to confide grows so strong that both girls contrive to be sent down together to the girls' locker room on some errand.
>
> 2. The girls settle themselves on a bench, and the heroine prepares to divulge the great secret. This confidence is interrupted by the sound of someone crying softly behind the lockers. The girl in tears turns out to be someone whom, for her past rudeness, they both despise—a large, awkward, impudent girl whose present distress is so graceless both are moved to contempt by it. The friend questions the weeping

girl and finds that it is she who has lost the money. She finds further that the girl does not dare go home for fear of her parents' anger. The friend is not very deeply interested in this story; and so, dismissing the other from her mind, she turns eagerly to the heroine again. This time, however, she finds her changed. Where before she was brimful of her secret, now she is shy and abashed. Both girls then return to class—one perplexed and the other strangely silent.

3. In class once again, the heroine waits as before for the final bell. She still dreams of the sweater, of course, but her mind is now troubled by the memory of the girl's tears in the locker room. As the minutes pass, she arrives at a state in which she is quite unable to tell what she will do when the bell rings.

When it does finally ring, the heroine goes half-reluctantly to the store, buys the sweater, and tries it on before the mirror. The sweater is beautiful—everything she hoped for and more. As she admires it in the mirror, however, she chances to meet her own gaze in the glass. There stands a girl she only dimly recognizes and one whom in her heart she doesn't like. Accordingly, to the amazement of the shopgirl, the heroine returns the sweater; and with the money in her hand, leaves the store and makes her way back to school to look for the girl who lost the money.

These three scenes are just enough to let the conflict in the girl's conscience come to a climax. As for the introductory circumstances of the story—the time and place and the heroine's delight in first finding the ten dollar bill— these circumstances the storyteller sees at once he can impart in the first scene. He does not really need to tell of the discovery in a separate scene. It will *tighten* the story if he does not.

(3) Decide on the point of view.

The next question to decide is called the *narrative point of view*. That is, from whose viewpoint will the story be told? Will it be the main character who refers to himself as

"I" (first person method) or some onlooker who refers to all the characters as "he," "she," or "they" (third person method)?

Usually, short, "confessional" stories of dramatic inner change seem best suited to the "I" as storyteller. The narrator is inside the story, acting and being acted upon; and therefore his point of view is closest to the heart of the story. This makes the first person method intimate and vivid.

Many stories, on the other hand, cannot be told by an "I." Often incidents happen in stories that the hero could not know about. Conversations take place that he cannot possibly hear; changes occur around him that he doesn't understand. Yet it is often essential to such stories that the *reader* understand what the hero cannot or will not. Therefore, such stories must be told by a narrator who sees and understands all—in other words, by an omniscient author. Stories like this require the third person method. In this point of view, the author is like an all-seeing god who can look into the minds of all the characters and know what each is thinking.

No matter what point of view you choose, there is one thing you must keep in mind. You must be consistent. You cannot begin with an "I" and later switch to a "he." Nor can you step outside the consciousness of your hero when it suits your convenience to do so. When, for example (to take an extreme instance), your hero loses consciousness, your story must abruptly stop.

(4) Decide which scenes should be presented in greatest detail.

Obviously, the most important parts of the story should receive the most attention. But which parts are most important? Surprisingly, the most important scene is often *not* the climax. There is (to take the sample story as an example) nothing particularly unusual about restoring lost money to its rightful owner. Most sophomores would do it without any of the heroine's indecision. The only dramatic interest in the last scene of the sample story comes, not from what the heroine does, but from what she feels as she discovers before the mirror that nothing is really free. The reader, however, would have no inkling of the meaning of this moment in the store if he had not already participated in the girl's earlier crisis of conscience.

You can see, therefore, that the most important scenes are those which give the greatest insight into the character of the hero. It is on these scenes that you must take your greatest pains.

● EXERCISE 4.   Select any one of the following "scenes of quiet crisis" as the basis of a narrative. These scenes or incidents may help you devise your own original story.

1. A boy goes to his counselor because he is deeply disturbed by his relationship with his parents. The boy finds that his counselor completely misunderstands the situation and offers him only vague words of comfort.

2. A girl decides that she can no longer go steady with her boyfriend because their relationship has grown too serious. She tries to explain her feelings to him.

3. An honor student has been caught cheating. He reports after school for an interview with his teacher.

4. A shy boy sits alone at a cafeteria table. Suddenly, he finds that he is being teased by a group of football players.

5. A boy and girl have secretly liked each other for a few months. One afternoon they find themselves alone in the school newspaper office.

6. A boy has been dating a girl for months but has been very careful to keep her away from his home and his family because he is ashamed of both. One Saturday the girl drives up to his house for a surprise visit.

7. A member of a school club is attending a meeting in which new members are being considered. He hears the group discuss unfairly a friend of his who is a member of a minority group.

8. A boy is studying for a biology final with a small group of his friends. Another friend rushes up to the table and announces that he has found a carbon copy of the test.
9. A girl has been delayed in the locker room. She happens to see one of her best friends steal a watch from another girl's locker.
10. To gain prestige with his crowd, a boy has foolishly bought a car. He meets the first payment but, at the end of the second month, finds that he cannot possibly meet the next one.

16e. Make a story outline.

While you cannot outline your narrative in the sense of identifying major topics and subtopics, you can plan your story on paper in such fashion that your teacher can see where you need help before you begin to write. Use the outline form below to submit your story idea to your teacher for his suggestions and approval.

SAMPLE STORY OUTLINE

(1) Main character—Carolyn Tedesco, a high school sophomore
(2) Setting—A high school anywhere in the United States
(3) Basic story situation—A girl finds ten dollars on the school grounds.

During the afternoon before the final bell, she entertains herself with pleasant fancies of how she will impress her friends with the lovely sweater she intends to buy with the money. Before the final bell, she discovers the real owner of the money. A struggle ensues in the girl's conscience. She decides at last to restore the money.

(4) Minor characters—Susan Grimes, Carolyn's best friend; Nora Southey, the loser of the money
(5) The point of view—First person
(6) The point of the story—Everything has its price.

WRITING THE NARRATIVE

A story, like a composition, is best written out quickly while the details are fresh and vivid and jostle each other to be put down on paper first. Again, as with a composition, it is best to set the story aside for a little while so that you may come back to it later with new eyes and a mind refreshed. Then, attack it anew, making every change that seems to tighten the story.

As for style, try to achieve a narrative style that sounds like good informal talk. The story itself is the thing that should hold attention, not the "literary" quality of the way you tell it. This is summed up in the injunction—*Be natural.* You can always communicate more to your readers by what you leave out than by what you put in. A good story, after all, is dramatic; it *shows* things happening before our eyes instead of telling about them. Even when these things are emotional changes that are invisible, it is always more effective to show than to tell. Below are five suggestions that make for good storytelling.

16f. Use effective storytelling techniques.

(1) Establish the setting.

In a short narrative like the one you are writing, you should limit yourself to one setting—one definite time and place in which the story takes place. Establish the setting quite early in your narrative, either at the very beginning or right after the introduction of the main character. Don't feel you have to describe all aspects and details of the setting. It makes more sense to choose a few salient features of the setting to sketch in—distinctive odors, sounds, sights, and textures. Let the reader fill in the rest of the details in his own imagination.

Notice in the following excerpt how author Sally Benson is able to establish the setting with a minimum of carefully chosen details:

> Although the window by the breakfast nook was open, it was very warm. The yellow-and-white gingham curtains hung

16 e-f

still, and the blue oilcloth tie-backs showed beads of moisture. Even the painted table top felt damp and sticky, and Joe Grannis was conscious of the discomfort of the hard bench on which he sat.[1]

● EXERCISE 5.   Write a one-paragraph description of one of the following settings, being sure to include important sense impressions.

1. The boys' locker room after a game
2. The dining room at home
3. A farm kitchen at noon
4. The local snack shop or drugstore
5. The gym after a big dance
6. A favorite classroom
7. The cafeteria during lunch period
8. A lonely street corner on a wintry morning
9. The lobby of a movie theater
10. A quiet spot in the country

(2) Introduce the main character early.

The main character also must be introduced early in the story, either at the very beginning or right after the setting has been described. Again, don't overdescribe your main character. The more you try to particularize the face you see, the more you will destroy the one the reader's imagination is forming. Give the portrait a few broad strokes and let the reader complete the picture. Usually one vivid detail will prove more effective than a complete description. Give your main character a name that will be distinctive and yet will not call undue attention to itself. On the other hand, do not bother to name characters who merely walk on.

Show, do not tell. Give your main character life by showing his actions, his mannerisms, his features, and weave the description unobtrusively into the narrative.

[1] From "Profession: Housewife" by Emily S. Benson from *Short Stories from the New Yorker* by the Editors of the New Yorker. Copyright © 1960 by Simon & Schuster. Reprinted by permission.

POOR	BETTER
He was nervous.	He tore at the ragged cuticle on his thumb. His hand seemed to shake. His words tumbled out breathlessly.
He was tall.	He let his long legs stretch out over half the floor.
He was conceited.	He looked at himself in the mirror, carefully adjusted his tie, pushed a wave into his hair, turned his head half to the left, and smiled approvingly.

(3) Introduce the conflict early in the story.

The very beginning of the story must present or hint at a problem or a conflict. After establishing the setting and introducing the main character, you must indicate clearly to the reader what kind of conflict has developed or probably will develop.

> Carefully he arranged one black forelock so that it drooped over his temple. "But I don't want any breakfast, Mother," he called from behind the bathroom door. Idly he scraped at the film of dirt covering the washbowl and looked once more at that nose—too long, too sharp, too much nose.
> "But breakfast is your best meal, Billy."
> Oh, for the love of Pete, he thought, every morning we argue about breakfast and every morning she calls me "Billy."

Note here that in just a few sentences we know much already: the boy is worried about his appearance; his mother is not a very good housekeeper; she still thinks of him as a very young boy; and there has been a long-standing conflict between them.

(4) Use dialogue to reveal character and keep the story moving.

Dialogue is talk reproduced, not just reported, and accordingly is much more fascinating to read than straight narration. The characters reveal themselves much more intimately by what they say than by what is said about them.

Before you can write good dialogue, however, you must develop an ear for the way people talk. Listen carefully to the talk of people of all ages and sorts. Note their characteristic expressions, the constructions they use in speech, and the idioms they favor. Jot down in your journal or notebook scraps of dialogue that appeal to you and seem to be real clues to character. Try also to preserve the naturalness of the spoken language. Avoid long speeches and stilted structure, unless, of course, this is the way you intend a character to speak.

● EXERCISE 6.   Write a brief exchange of dialogue between the pairs of characters given below. See if you can write the dialogue so that a reader would know who is talking even though you failed to identify him.

1. A grandfather in his 70's and an eight-year-old boy
2. A teen-age boy and his four-year-old sister
3. A college freshman and a high school junior
4. A high school sophomore and an eighth-grader
5. A policeman and a woman driver

(5) End your narrative effectively.

Don't make your ending so abrupt that the reader turns the page expecting to find more. On the other hand, don't waste your reader's time with a long drawn-out ending. End the story just as soon as the central conflict has been resolved. Don't feel you have to tie up all loose ends. The conflict, after all, *is* the story.

Three kinds of endings are so poor that they should always be avoided:

1. The "miracle" ending—A poor boy finds a wallet with $100 in it.

2. The "fake" ending—"Then he woke up and realized it was all a dream."

3. The moralizing ending—"John realized then, deep in his heart, that honesty is the best policy."

REVISING THE NARRATIVE

At this stage, your story is down on paper. Read it now swiftly to see if it "reads" well. A story that "reads" well has a certain momentum; that is, it carries the reader's interest along in a smooth-flowing narrative current from the beginning to the end. Nothing intervenes to check that current—no unnecessary description, no superfluous incident, no loose ends, and of course no spelling or grammatical errors.

16g. Revise the first draft.

As you begin to revise, check your narrative against the list below. Any element in the story that fails to pass muster should now be rewritten. Then all that remains is to copy the final draft carefully according to your teacher's instructions.

Checklist for the Narrative

1. Does it have a good title—one that relates to the story, yet is not too trite or too general?
2. Is the setting—the time and place—given early in the narrative with a few significant sensory details?
3. Is the main character introduced early in the narrative with a few characteristics and features indicated?
4. Is the dialogue natural and consistent with the characters?
5. Is the point of view consistent?
6. Is the basic conflict given early in the narrative?
7. Is the theme or central meaning of the story clearly suggested?
8. Is the narrative free from spelling, usage, sentence structure, and punctuation errors? The punctuation of dialogue needs special care.

16g

CHAPTER 17

Letter Writing

A letter speaks for you in your absence. To do its job of representing you well, it must be clear, appropriate in tone, and attractive in appearance. Let us consider these three important qualities individually.

Clarity. Remember that you will not be present when your letter is being read to explain what you mean. The reader will not be able to ask you to clarify. Obviously, then, you must make your message unmistakably clear. It goes without saying that your letter should be easily legible, whether handwritten or typewritten.

Tone. When speaking face-to-face with someone, you use your tone of voice to reflect shades of meaning and attitude. Writing, too, has a tone, reflected largely in the words you choose. What will your letter sound like to the recipient? First, be sure that it sounds like *you*—that it speaks with your voice. Second, be sure that the tone will neither anger nor offend. Unlike spoken words, which are often readily forgotten, letters are permanent records of what you have said. An angry letter may make you feel better at the time of writing, but a few weeks later you may be sorry that you mailed it.

Appearance and form. Appearance and form are the "good manners" of letter writing. This chapter explains the conventions of letter-writing form. If you follow them carefully, even though they may seem unimportant to you now, your letter will have a much better chance of making a good impression. A letter that is neat, free of errors, and in good form will do a fine job of representing you—just as your speech and personal appearance do in a face-to-face relationship.

THE FRIENDLY LETTER

17a. Observe standard practice in writing friendly letters.

You have already written and received many friendly letters. The informality of the friendly letter means that it is subject to fewer "rules and regulations." Both these factors should make the writing of a friendly letter less of a problem for you. There are, however, a few suggestions about appearance and content which, if followed, should make your friendly letters better personal ambassadors for you.

Appearance

Even with a letter to a close friend, appearance is important. Use letter stationery, preferably white or lightly tinted, avoiding stationery of unusual shape or size. If your letters are handwritten, always use unlined paper. Blue or black ink is proper, but colored inks in combination with exotic shades of stationery are in poor taste. A typewritten letter is perfectly proper, but don't subject your friends to inaccurate and messy typing.

Arrange the letter so that it is centered well on the page. Keep margins even and equal on either side and on the top and bottom. Have at least three lines on the last page; never

17a

finish your letter on one page and put the closing and signature alone on the next page. If you use folded stationery, follow these rules:

1. If your letter is more than two pages long, use the page order of a book, with page two on the back of page one.

2. If it is only two pages long, write the second page on page three of your stationery.

Remember, however, that like standard practice in usage, grammar, and punctuation, standard practice in the writing of friendly letters recognizes a difference between formal and informal situations. While you need not observe all the details of standard letter form in writing the more informal of your letters, you will surely want to observe them carefully in writing to a new acquaintance or to your uncle in Hawaii whom you have never seen, for such people have only your letters by which to judge you. Follow the suggestions on standard letter-writing procedures on the following pages.

Parts of a Friendly Letter

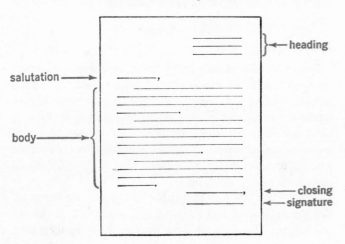

The Parts of a Friendly Letter

1. Heading

It is customary to write your complete address (unless you are sure the receiver knows it) and the date in three lines at the top right-hand corner of the page, with a comma between the town and the state, and a comma between the day of the month and the year. Begin the heading at least an inch below the top of the page. Do not put a comma between the state and the ZIP code.

EXAMPLES

Block Style	*Indented Style*
14 Brixton Road	14 Brixton Road
Dayton, Ohio 45403	Dayton, Ohio 45403
September 17, 1972	September 17, 1972

In general, it is better not to use abbreviations, but if you do use them, be consistent—abbreviate the word *street* as well as the state. An abbreviation is always followed by a period.

You may, if you prefer, put your address and the date at the end of the letter, in the lower left-hand corner, instead of at the top.

2. Salutation

The salutation of a friendly letter is easy to learn. The usual form is "*Dear* . . ." followed by a comma. Begin the salutation at the left-hand margin about a half inch below the heading.

Dear Dad,
Dear Dr. Riley,
Dear Roger,

3. Body

The body is the letter itself. Do not forget to divide it into paragraphs.

206 Elm Street
Haverford, Pennsylvania 19041
November 6, 1972

Dear Nancy,

Last night at the fall dance, Joe Smith asked me whether I had heard from you. I told him I still owed you a letter. Joe took Betty Calder to the dance, but I think he was wishing it was last summer and you were around. I went with Jack. He usually gives me a big pain, but he asked me first—nobody asked me second—and I decided a date with Jack would do better than no date at all. The dance was pretty good. Joan and Fred went with us. You know how crazy they are!

Sally, Becky, and I went bowling yesterday after school. What a riot! You've probably bowled a lot, being the athletic type, but this was my first time. I made 36 the first game, and Becky and Sally weren't much better. I got all the way up to 50 in my third game. Some boys from South High kept trying to help us and show us how to hold the ball and how to score and everything! They were sort of cute, too. One of them asked for my telephone number. I didn't give it to him, but now I almost wish I had. We bowled at Johnson's. It's a barnlike place out near Five Corners. My wrist is sore and my pocket book is flat. I spent $1.50 just to roll that ball—it weighs a ton—down the gutter. At least, it wasn't always the same gutter.

Pam came over Saturday and stayed all night. We got to sleep about one o'clock. Dad and Mom were out. Pam's going to New York for Thanksgiving. Maybe she'll look you up. I gave her your address. I wish I were going with her. Now you owe me a letter! Remember, Joe's waiting!

Love,
Jean

4. Closing

In a friendly letter there are many appropriate closings. Among these are *Sincerely yours*, *Sincerely*, *Cordially*, *With love*, *Affectionately*, etc., each of which is followed by a comma.

Avoid "clever" closings such as "Yours till Niagara Falls." They don't ever look as well as you think they will, and they are usually trite and in very poor taste.

Capitalize only the first letter of the closing. Do not use a business-letter closing such as *Very truly yours* on a friendly letter.

5. Signature

Below the closing, *write* your name. Even when your letter is typewritten, the signature is always handwritten.

The Envelope

Place the name and address on the lower half of the envelope about midway between the ends. Always write Mr., Mrs., or Miss before the person's name unless you are using some other title like Reverend, Dr., President, or Professor.

Jean White
206 Elm Street
Haverford, Pennsylvania 19041

　　　　　　Miss Nancy Brownlow
　　　　　　85 East Forty-ninth Street
　　　　　　New York, N.Y. 10017

At the time the ZIP code was adopted, the Post Office published a list of two-letter abbreviations for the states. You will find this list in the *World Almanac* in your school library. Put a comma between the city and the state. Your own name and address should be written in the upper left-hand corner of the envelope.

CONTENT OF A FRIENDLY LETTER

A friendly letter is like a conversation. An English textbook can no more tell you exactly what to say in a letter than it can tell you what to talk about.

The most important thing, of course, is to make your letter lively and interesting. When you write a friendly letter, ask yourself, "What would my correspondent be interested in hearing about?" You can add interest to your letter by giving him some details about recent experiences; general statements like "I'm having a wonderful summer" are meaningless to your friend unless supported with details about people, places, and activities. Don't go to the other extreme, however, and bore him with seemingly endless accounts of who wore what and who said what. Something interesting about mutual friends is always appropriate, but malicious gossip should be avoided.

Tone is important in a friendly letter. Avoid cuteness or cleverness; the expression which you consider to be the height of "smartness" when you write it may seem to your correspondent who reads it just ridiculous or offensive. Also, don't fall into the trap of using what some editors and writers call the "schoolgirl style": trite slang; excessive use of exclamation marks, underlining, and quotation marks; immoderate use of superlatives like "greatest," "terrific," "most wonderful." Be natural and be yourself.

A few special suggestions about beginning and ending your friendly letter may be of help here. Usually it is wise to begin with some enthusiastic comments about and reactions to a letter you have received from your friend; if you haven't heard from him for a while, you may wish to tease him about the fact, but don't sound hurt or critical. Beginning your letter with a series of questions may show your interest in the person to whom you are writing, but it can also be very dull and commonplace. The receiver wants a letter from you, not a questionnaire.

Ending a letter with such awkward statements as "I have to go now," and "Well, I can't think of anything else to say," is neither original nor graceful. If you are writing to a friend whom you haven't seen in some time, perhaps you can suggest he visit you. If the letter is going to someone to whom you have long owed a letter, you may wish to assure him you will try to do better next time. Make your closing appropriate to the person to whom you are writing as well as to the situation.

In friendly letters the most important things for you to think of are *to be interesting* and *to be yourself*.

● EXERCISE 1.   On a piece of regular letter stationery (your personal stationery if you have any), write a letter to a pen pal (real or imaginary) in a foreign country. Tell him about yourself and your community and express interest in learning about his country.

● EXERCISE 2.   Draw two envelopes on your paper and address them, using the following information.

1. *Sender:* Mr. John S. Scarlatti, 116 Courtland Boulevard, Newark, New Jersey   07102
   Receiver: Miss Juanita A. Martinez, Apartment 16B, Hyacinth Court, Valley Drive, San Mateo, California   94401
2. *Sender:* Miss Irma Potter, RFD #3, Mangrove Road, St. John, Florida   32950
   Receiver: Mr. Joseph D. Buckley, 16 Rue Ste. Supplice, Trois-Rivières, Quebec, Canada

● EXERCISE 3. Criticize the following letter from the standpoints of both form and content, and on your paper set down your criticisms in a numbered list.

October 3, 1972
411 Beach Ave.
Santa Barbara, California 93107

Dear Judy:

It's been ages since I've heard from you, but I imagine you're so busy going to dances and parties that you just can't find time to write to little me. Life here is a drag—nothing to do, nobody to see. I'm bored to tears and sick of this place. The only person my age who's down here is Elaine, and she's worse than nothing—but don't tell her I said that, because she thinks I think she's pretty nice. And her mother's just as bad. They're over here almost every day—wouldn't that kill you! I got a real cool bathing suit yesterday—wait till you see it! It's been so hot here that you could fry eggs on the pavement. My mother's calling me now to do the dishes, so I guess I had better stop here.

Sincerely
Ellen

THE SOCIAL NOTE

The social note is a short letter usually written for one of the following purposes: (1) to extend an informal invitation; (2) to accept or decline an informal invitation; (3) to thank someone for a gift or for entertaining you.

The form of the social note is very much like that of a friendly letter, with the address and the date either in the top right-hand corner or the lower left-hand corner, the salutation *Dear . . .*, and the informal closing.

The social note may be written on regular notepaper, on correspondence cards if the note is a short one, or on personal notepaper. White is preferred, although a pastel shade may be used. You may be proud of your violet-colored paper, and you may like to use white, brown, or green ink on it, but don't use that kind of thing for social notes. It's likely to brand you as a person who doesn't know the proper thing to do.

The Informal Invitation

Although the form and content of an invitation are very similar to those of a friendly letter, you do have to be careful to include the following:
1. Your full address
2. The date, time, and place (if other than your home)
3. Any necessary explanation regarding the kind of affair it is to be

Informal Invitation

---

14 Woods Road
Highland Park, Illinois 60035
May 5, 1972

Dear Ann,

How about a weekend in the country? It's time you gave your old friends a look at you. I'd love to have you come for the weekend of May 16. If you can come, I'm going to schedule a slumber party for the old crowd Saturday night. I think I won't tell them you're coming; that will be a wonderful surprise.

You can get a 4:30 train on Friday which will get you here in time for dinner. Bring some old clothes—no party dresses. Tell your family you will be back late Sunday.

Sincerely,
Alice

Replying to the Informal Invitation

Still another kind of social note is the one you write when accepting or declining an invitation that is informal. Perhaps a friend of yours has invited you to his summer home for the day, or he and his sister have planned a party in your honor. If the invitation is a written one, your acceptance or refusal should be written. Don't forget that it should be a gracious acceptance or a regretful refusal. Always remember the importance of politeness, even more particularly when you write than when you speak.

Informal Invitation

---

418 Bay Avenue
Riverhead, New York 11901
April 7, 1972

Dear Sam,

Bill Mercer came over the other night, and we started talking about last summer at camp. That reminded us of canoeing. I remembered how much you like canoeing, and Bill and I wondered whether you could go on a trip with us the last weekend of the month—the 28th and 29th.

We could leave here before noon on Saturday, camp out somewhere along the shore of the bay that night (I've managed to get an extra bedroll for you), and paddle back on Sunday. Bill is already bragging about what a good chef he is, and I guess I can stand his cooking if you can.

Try to get the 4 o'clock train from Penn Station Friday afternoon. You can go back on Sunday at 5:00. We hope you can come.

Sincerely,
Bob

Note of Acceptance

---

876 *Lake Road*
Chicago, Illinois 60621
May 8, 1972

Dear Alice,

Your invitation for the weekend of the 16th sounds like more fun than I've had all year. Mother said OK at once, and I'm counting the days. Dad will take me to the 4:30 train and will meet me at 6:30 on Sunday. The news can wait until I see you and the gang.

Sincerely,
Ann

Note of Regret

---

23 Morningside Drive
New York, New York 10027
April 10, 1972

Dear Bob,

Your invitation came in yesterday's mail, and how I hate to have to turn it down! I already have a big date with Linda for that Saturday. A bunch of us are going to the spring play at school.

A first-of-the-season canoe trip sounds great. You and Bill have fun. Give me another try sometime, will you?

Sincerely,
Sam

The Thank-You Note

Most of the social notes you have had to write so far are thank-you notes for a gift you have received. A gift should never go unacknowledged, as it represents a thoughtful gesture on the part of the person who gave it to you. Your thank-you notes should always be prompt, courteous, and appreciative. Always mention the gift by name and comment on its usefulness and appropriateness.

In your attempt to show appreciation, don't be too extreme or "gushy" in your gratitude. Telling five different people that each has given you "the nicest present I've ever received" is obviously insincere.

A special reminder is perhaps needed here for students who are awarded commencement prizes or other similar awards. Even though you may feel you have earned the award and do not consider it a gift, it still is good form to write a letter of thanks to the donor or sponsor.

Thank-you notes become more formidable the more you put them off. In many instances you should use the opportunity to write a full letter, but a brief thank-you note is often sufficient.

Thank-You Note

---

38 Crescent Avenue
Glenside, Pennsylvania 19038
February 20, 1972

Dear Aunt Alice,

Thanks a lot for the very good looking cuff links and tie clasp you and Uncle Bill sent for my birthday. Dad gave me a couple of shirts with French cuffs for Christmas, but I haven't worn them much because I didn't have any decent cuff links.

We—the whole family—went out to dinner and to the movies on my birthday, so everyone got in on the act. It was fun.

Mom says we'll be seeing you next month at the State game. We're all looking forward to a big get-together.

Love,
Harry

The "Bread-and-Butter" Note

Another type of social note is the thank-you letter you write after you have been entertained at someone's home. Commonly called a "bread-and-butter" letter, this kind of social note is sent to your hostess. If you have been visiting a friend of your own age, write your letter to his mother.

"Bread-and-Butter" Note

---

44 Appleton Road
Long Beach, California 90805
August 2, 1972

Dear Mrs. Fairben,

Thank you a lot for having me at your home over the weekend. You know what a good time Bruce and I had, and I hope I didn't make too much extra work for you. (Sometime would you tell my mother how you make apple pie?) It was wonderful of you to invite me, and I enjoyed every minute of the weekend.

Tell Bruce I'll write him soon.

Sincerely yours,
Larry

● EXERCISE 4. Write a social note covering the following situation: You have received an unusual gift for Christmas. Thank the person who gave it to you, and explain why you are glad to have it.

● EXERCISE 5. You have been entertained for a weekend at the cottage of your best friend. On Saturday it rained all day, but you all had a good time learning new card games and toasting marshmallows. Sunday the weather was perfect, and you were in the water almost all day. Write your friend's mother a "bread-and-butter" letter, thanking her for her hospitality and also for having been resourceful about keeping you entertained during the bad weather.

● EXERCISE 6. Write a note to an out-of-town friend, asking him to spend a day with you during Easter vacation. Give him a choice of either of two days. Tell him what you plan to do (a bicycle trip, a baseball game, fishing— are suggestions), and suggest a train or bus for him to take.

● EXERCISE 7. Answer the preceding invitation, either accepting or declining it. If you decline it, be sure to explain why you can't go.

THE BUSINESS LETTER

17b. Observe standard practice in writing business letters.

A business letter is usually written to a firm or an individual in a firm. It must be a combination of clearness, brevity, and courtesy.

Appearance and Stationery

Proper stationery is the first important consideration in a business letter. Businessmen much prefer that you type your letter, if possible, on the usual $8\frac{1}{2} \times 11$-inch, plain white paper. The typewritten letter is more legible and therefore more quickly read than a handwritten one. If you write the letter by hand, use the same stationery as for a typewritten letter. Also, remember to write carefully; your best penmanship is a courtesy you owe to anyone to whom you are writing.

Form

The form of a business letter follows a certain pattern. Whether your letter is typewritten or handwritten, the pattern is the same. The semiblock form is used in the illustrations which you will find later in this chapter; however, the full block and the block forms are also acceptable, and an illustration of these forms is also given.

The Letter Picture

Three frequently used forms for the business letter are the full block, the block, and the semiblock. In the full block all typed material is flush with the left-hand margin, and paragraphs are not indented. Such a form is easiest for the typist, since there is no indention to worry about. Some object to it, however, because it seems unbalanced to the left.

BLOCK

SEMIBLOCK

FULL BLOCK

17b

The only difference between the block and the full block is the placement of the heading, closing, and signature; in the block style these are placed just to the right of the center. In this chapter the semiblock style is used for both friendly and business letters. It is similar to the block except that it does use paragraph indention.

Before beginning your letter, judge the amount of space it will occupy on the page you are using. Center it as nearly as possible by making sure you have approximately the same margin at the top of your page as at the bottom, and the same margin on both the left- and right-hand sides. Never run your letter off the page at the right-hand side, and never finish the body of your letter at the end of a page so that you have nothing left for the second page except the complimentary close and your signature. If the letter is to be very short, it will look better on smaller stationery. Use the $5\frac{1}{2} \times 8\frac{1}{2}$-inch size, which is also acceptable for business letters. For a model letter, see page 363.

1. Heading

To begin your business letter, always put your *complete* address and the full date in the upper right-hand corner, beginning no less than one inch from the top of the page. It is better to write this heading without abbreviations.

EXAMPLES

49 Surrey Lane
Clinton, Iowa 57232
June 4, 1972

RFD 4
Cross Corners, Oklahoma 73028
September 27, 1972

2. Inside Address

This is the part of a business letter that is not a part of a friendly letter. Business firms file copies of the letters they write. Since the copies are filed under the name of the person

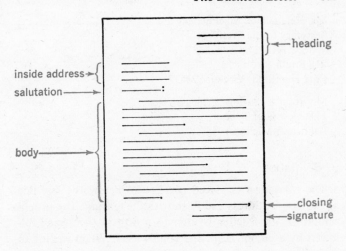

The Parts of a Business Letter

or firm to which they are written, it is necessary to have an inside address on every letter.

The inside address should be placed at the left-hand side of the page, flush with the margin and several spaces (at least four, if the letter is typewritten) lower on the page than the heading. It should include the full name of the company to which you are writing, as well as its full address. If you are writing to an individual in the firm, use his full name and title, with a comma between the two if they are on the same line; if the name and title are too long to be put on one line, put the title on the next line.

EXAMPLES

The James Mills Company
220–224 Center Street
Waukegan, Illinois 60085

Mr. James R. Joy, Vice-President
Newland and Company
40 Fifth Avenue
Lewiston, Maine 04240

Mr. Reginald B. MacPherson
Secretary to the President
Wilbur Field and Sons
218 South Street
Fort Hamilton, Virginia 24437

Mr. John E. Barlow, Principal
Lakeview High School
Lakeview, Michigan 48850

3. Salutation

The salutation is placed two spaces below the last line
of the inside address and flush with the margin. The proper
salutation for a letter written to a firm is *Gentlemen* followed by a colon. *Dear Sirs* is also used. When writing to
an individual within the firm, the correct salutation is *Dear
Mr. . . .* (or *Mrs.* or *Miss*) followed by a colon. If you are
writing to a professional man or woman, use his title instead of *Mr.*

EXAMPLES   Gentlemen:
               Dear Mr. Bowne:
               Dear Dr. Grayce:
               Dear President Tyson:

Sometimes you may be writing to an officer in a firm
without knowing his name. You may have just "Principal,"
"President," or "Secretary" on the first line of the inside
address. The proper salutation then is *Dear Sir* followed by
a colon.

4. Body

The form of the body of a business letter is the form followed in the body of any letter. A double space is used between paragraphs of a typed letter. If your typewritten letter
is short (7 lines or less), you may either put it on a smaller
sheet of stationery or double-space the entire body of the
letter on $8\frac{1}{2} \times 11$-inch stationery.

5. Closing

The closing of a letter comes between the body of the letter and the signature. In business letters, appropriate closings are limited, and the same ones you use in friendly letters will not do. *Very truly yours*, *Yours truly*, and *Yours very truly* are the ones most frequently used. *Sincerely yours* and *Yours sincerely* are also correct. The closing is placed just to the right of the center of the page, two spaces below the last line of the body of your letter. It is followed by a comma.

Avoid ending your letter with an outmoded phrase such as "I beg to remain," "Hoping to hear from you soon, I am," or "Thanking you in advance, I am . . ." End the body of your letter with a *period*, and then begin your closing.

EXAMPLES Very truly yours,
Yours truly,
Sincerely yours,

6. Signature

Sign your full name to your letter. Do *not* put *Miss* or *Mr.* before your name. An unmarried woman writing to a stranger should put *Miss* in parentheses before her signature.

EXAMPLE *(Miss) Margaret Hoyt*

A married woman signs her full name, and if she wishes, she may put her married name in parentheses directly below her signature.

EXAMPLE *Elsie M. Rhoad*
(Mrs. Robert L. Rhoad)

A signature should always be handwritten. If your letter is typewritten, type your name below your written signature, flush with the first letter of the closing and far enough below to allow room for your signature.

7. Envelope

For a letter on small stationery, use a small envelope (be sure the letter fits it). A letter on small single-sheet stationery is usually folded twice unless it fits into the envelope without any folding. The folds are made in this way: up from the bottom about a third of the way, then down from the top, so that when it is unfolded it will be right side up for the reader. Note paper or personal stationery is usually folded in half and inserted with the fold at the bottom.

Either a small or a large envelope may be used for a letter on large single-sheet stationery. If a large envelope is used, the folding is the same as that of a small sheet for a small

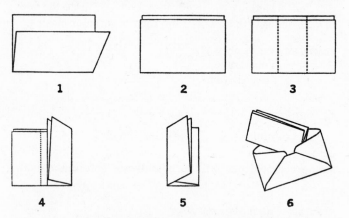

envelope. If the envelope is small, fold your letter up from the bottom to within a quarter of an inch of the top; then fold the right side over a third of the way; finally, fold the left side over. Insert in the envelope with the fold at the bottom of the envelope.

Your envelope should carry the same address as the inside address of the letter and also your own name and full address. You may put your return address on the back of the envelope, but the Post Office prefers that you put the return address in the upper left-hand corner of the envelope on the same side as the address to which it is going. Unless the address to which a letter is being sent is very long, you should start it about halfway down the envelope and place it midway between the ends.

The Post Office also requests that you use your ZIP code number in both the address to which the letter is going and in your return address. The ZIP code should appear on the last line of the address, following the city and state, with a double space left between the last letter of the state and first digit of the code. A comma should *not* be inserted between the state name and ZIP code. Note the examples in the model shown on page 351 and below.

Model Envelope

Theodore Jonas
303 Clayton Street
Huntington, West Virginia 25703

Executive Secretary
Chamber of Commerce
Mystic, Connecticut 06355

CONTENT OF THE BUSINESS LETTER

Clarity, tone, and form are perhaps even more important in the business letter than they are in the friendly letter, since business letters are customarily sent to firms or individuals who do not know you and who have a large bulk of mail to handle. No matter how routine your communication is, be sure that your letter speaks well of you.

Even though the tone will be more formal than that of the friendly letter, you still should strive for naturalness and simplicity of expression. Come right to the point in your letter; avoid wordy beginnings. Make sure you have supplied all the necessary information. Never use the old-fashioned clichés of business correspondence. Be very certain that you don't close with the expression, "Thanking you in advance." Such a phrase presumes that the recipient will grant your request and seems to indicate that you are too lazy to write a separate thank-you note if some special favor is received.

TYPES OF BUSINESS LETTERS

The Request Letter

You have had and will continue to have many occasions to write letters of request: sending for a college catalogue, requesting a free pamphlet, arranging for a speaker to talk to your club. First, be reasonable in your requests. If you are asking for information. be very specific about what you want. Don't make yourself look ridiculous by asking, "Please send me all you have about Indians." If asking for a free pamphlet, request only that number which you personally can use. If arranging for a speaker, be sure to write in plenty of time and give him all the information he will need about time, place, type of audience, etc.

Second, be courteous in the phrasing of your request. While you should avoid the "thanking you in advance" expression discussed above, it is good form to conclude the request letter with a polite acknowledgment like: "I shall certainly appreciate any help you can give me with this request." Finally, make your request simple and clear. Since the company to which you are writing is probably handling a large volume of mail, their employees cannot afford to waste time reading lengthy, chatty letters.

Model Request Letter

---

76 Brixton Place
Phoenix, Arizona   85008
July 8, 1972

Model Airways, Inc.
410—12 Second Avenue
Flagstaff, Arizona   86001

Gentlemen:

Will you please send me a copy of your
latest catalogue on model planes? I have
three of your models and would like to add
some of the later ones to my collection.

Very truly yours,

Frank Tyndall

Frank Tyndall

● Exercise 8.   Write to a college, asking for their catalogue. If you think the catalogue may not include all the information you need, ask specifically for whatever you wish to know.

Another type of request letter is the kind you write when you ask a firm to send a representative to your school for some purpose or other. This kind of letter is a little more complicated to write, because it is *you* who have to give the company information before they reply. Remember to include all the details necessary for the company's complete understanding of the situation.

● Exercise 9.   Copy in proper form the business letter given below.

420 Jackson Avenue, Iola, Texas   77861, January 8, 1972. Mr. R. F. Hawkins, Business Manager, Perry and Company, 480–96 Fuller Street, Fort Worth, Texas   76104. Dear Mr. Haw-

kins: Our junior class of 170 pupils in the Iola High School is to decide this month on our class rings and pins. We expect to have representatives from several companies here on Monday, January 21, to show us samples of the rings and pins their firms make, together with price lists. We'd like very much to have someone from your company here on that date, if possible. Your representative should come to Room 31, any time after 2:45. Very truly yours, Sarah Porter, Secretary of the Junior Class, Iola High School.

● EXERCISE 10.   Using the following information, set up this material in the form of a business letter. You must compose the letter.

Miss Elsie Dowing of 222 Twin Oaks Road, Carlsburg, Ohio 43316, writes on April 6, 1972, to the George C. Buckeye Company, 240 Lexington Avenue, Cleveland, Ohio 44102, stating that while shopping there the week before, she lost a valuable gold ring. It contained a diamond and two pearls in an old-fashioned setting. She would like to know if it has been found and if so, where she may call for it.

● EXERCISE 11.   As student assembly-program chairman, you wish to have a neighboring high school send its glee club to perform in one of your assembly periods. Give the time, date, place, length of program, type of song selection (if you wish), and any other information you think is necessary.

● EXERCISE 12.   You are interested in art. There is an exhibit to be given in the high school auditorium of a nearby city. Write to the art department of the high school, requesting information. Ask specific questions about what you want to know—time, admission price, dates the exhibit will be displayed, etc.

The Order Letter

If you are writing an order letter, you should list the items you wish, one below the other, with complete information (catalogue number, style, size, price, etc.) about each item. The price should be put at the right-hand side (flush with the right-hand margin) and each amount should be placed directly under the one above, to make it easier to add the prices. List the cost of shipping, if you know it, and include it in the total, unless you know the firm pays for it. Be sure to specify how the articles are to be paid for—check, C.O.D., etc.

Model Order Letter

---

58 Crane Street
Canton, Iowa 52542
December 1, 1972

Webb and Sons
140–156 Seventh Avenue
Des Moines, Iowa 50311

Gentlemen:

I should like to order the following articles, as advertised in the Des Moines Press of November 29.

2 white silk scarves, fringed, one with
  black initials A.J., the other with red
  initials M.W., @ $2.98 $5.96
1 size 15–34 Supercron white
  shirt, collar attached   6.50
                               Postage   .20
                               Total $12.66

I am enclosing a check for $12.66 to cover the total amount.

Very truly yours,

Amy Ladd

Amy Ladd

● EXERCISE **13.** Write a business letter to Marshall Field and Company, Chicago, ordering 2 long-sleeved cotton blouses, size 14, 1 plain white, the other French blue, at $4.98, 1 green "Betty Gaye" dress, size 13, at $11.95. Have them sent C.O.D.

● EXERCISE **14.** Write to Ritz Camera Center, 1147A Sixth Avenue, New York, N.Y. 10036, an order letter ordering the following: 1 Star D Model D–18 tripod, price $9.75; 3 rolls 35 mm. Kodachrome film at $1.75 a roll. Include $.25 postage. You are enclosing a money order for the amount.

The Letter of Application

The letter of application is one with which you have no doubt had very little experience to date. However, you soon may find that it is one of the most important types of business letter, for it is in the application letter that you try to convince an employer that it is to his advantage to hire you.

When you apply for a position, your letter of application comes before your personal interview with your prospective employer. It is the first contact you have with him. Therefore, you must "put yourself across" in a way which will make him feel confident that you can do the job called for. You will also have an added advantage if you can put some original, personal touch into your letter (but only if it comes naturally to you) to distinguish you, favorably, from the rest of the applicants this employer may be considering.

Remember to include the following:

1. Include a statement of the position you are applying for and how you learned about it.

2. Show that you know what qualifications are needed and that you believe you can fill them. State your age, experience, and education.

3. Give references as to your character and ability.

4. Request an interview at the employer's convenience.

98 Oxford Street
St. Cloud, Minnesota   56303
April 2, 1972

Mr. O. A. Lester, Director
Camp Carlson
Oneidaga Lake
Big Pines, Minnesota   56680

Dear Mr. Lester:

Ben Nichols, one of your regular campers, told me this week that you have a vacancy for a swimming counselor on your camp staff this summer, and I should like to apply for the position.

I am a senior at St. Cloud High School and am eighteen years old. For the last two years I have been the junior swimming counselor at Camp Winnebega, Cauhoga Falls, Wisconsin. I have just received my Examiner's badge in lifesaving and am now certified for the position of senior swimming counselor. If you have junior or senior lifesaving classes, I am also qualified to direct them.

The following gentlemen have given me permission to use their names as references:

Mr. J. B. Morse, Director, Camp Winnebega, Cauhoga Falls, Wisconsin.

Mr. Alexander B. Davis, Secretary, Y.M.C.A., St. Cloud, Minnesota.

Mr. Chester Roberts, Principal, St. Cloud High School, St. Cloud, Minnesota.

I shall be glad to come for a personal interview at your convenience.

Sincerely yours,

Frank Larson

Frank Larson

● EXERCISE 15.   You have learned from a friend that a woman she knows in another city is looking for a high school girl to spend the summer with her family at their summer home. She wants the girl to take care of her three children, ages two, four, and six. Write to the woman (make up a name and address) and apply for this job. State your qualifications. Try to make your letter interesting as well as informative.

● EXERCISE 16.   A drugstore in a neighboring town needs a delivery boy from 4:00 to 6:00 after school and all day on Saturdays. Write your letter of application.

PART FIVE

Speaking and Listening

CHAPTER 18

Public Speaking

Giving a Talk and Listening Critically

In high school you will often have to speak to groups of your fellow students. You will present your ideas in class, at club meetings, and at assemblies. You may be called upon to relate a personal experience, explain how to make or do something, or argue for or against a proposed plan. If you can speak clearly, easily, and forcefully, you will be able to take satisfaction in such experiences and possibly influence the ideas and actions of your classmates. The student who wants to become a leader must not only have good ideas but also be able to communicate them.

The ability to speak before groups is a valuable asset, but an equally important talent is the ability to listen. The skilled listener exerts his wits just as actively as the speaker. By *listening* to what is said and not just *hearing* it, he can grasp the gist of a speaker's remarks without the need for repetition. He can also distinguish fact from fancy and good sense from nonsense.

The principles of speaking and listening that you will study in this chapter will help you to acquire these two important skills. Both will be useful to you in school and in later years.

PREPARING A TALK

18a. Choose an appropriate topic.

If possible, choose a subject about which you already know a great deal. Doing so has two important advantages:

1. It restricts your choice to your own background and interests and encourages you to talk about things with which you have had direct experience—your hobbies, special talents, jobs, and unusual experiences

2. It also insures that you will speak with enthusiasm since it is hard to keep your feelings out of any subject that is close to you. If what you say engages your own interest powerfully, the chances are good it will interest your audience as well. Enthusiasm is contagious.

Choose your topic as far in advance as possible. Think about it daily—mulling over both the gist of what you will say and the way you will say it. The longer this sifting process goes on, the better the result.

● EXERCISE 1. List five possible subjects about which you feel yourself able to speak. Submit the list to your teacher for his comments and suggestions. When it is returned, put it in your notebook for future use.

18b. Limit your subject.

In the few minutes allotted to you, you may not be able to tell everything you know about your topic. Even if you could, your listeners might not be able to grasp all that you had to say, particularly if your subject happens to be complex. Narrow your topic so that you can cover it in the time allowed. For example:

TOO GENERAL	Modern Aircraft
SUITABLE SUBJECT	What makes an airplane fly?
	Vertical takeoff aircraft
	Why don't they mass-produce private helicopters?

18
a-b

● EXERCISE 2. Choose one of the topics you listed for Exercise 1 and limit it to a still narrower topic. Submit the new topic to your teacher for comments and suggestions.

18c. Have a purpose for your talk.

A speaker should have a definite aim. If you have a purpose and keep it steadily in mind, you can *calculate* the effect upon your audience of the remarks or gestures you are thinking of using. You can then eliminate every feature that does not seem to advance your purpose.

Furthermore, almost every subject can have different purposes. Three obvious ones are *to inform*, *to entertain*, and *to persuade*.

Suppose for example that the subject of your talk is western movies. If your purpose is to *inform*, you may decide to discuss the first westerns. Or you may explain how the tradition arose from the dime novel or describe stock characters and standard plots. You may want to point out how certain good movies—*High Noon*, *Shane*, *Stagecoach*, for example—used these common features to advantage; whereas the poorer movie merely made them ridiculous.

If your purpose is to *entertain*, you might tell the class about the life of the Hollywood stuntman who simulates all of the disastrous falls, crashes, collisions, and brawls in cowboy movies without injury to men or horses.

And if your purpose is to *persuade*, you might persuade the class to join you in composing an indignant letter to the movie makers, taxing them with insufficient respect for historical truth and the real traditions of the old West.

Therefore, as soon as you have determined your purpose, write it out in an explicit statement.

TOPIC   Two- and four-barrel carburetion systems

PURPOSE To inform. I shall explain clearly by the use of models and diagrams the functions and the advantages of two- and four-barrel carburetors.

● EXERCISE 3. Choose three subjects from the list approved by your teacher in Exercise 1. For each, compose an explicit statement of purpose and submit it to your teacher for his suggestions and comments.

18d. Gather material for your talk.

Where will you find material for a talk? Start with yourself. First consider the vast amount of information you already have in your head. You have within yourself a store of facts and opinions about many subjects. Explore this background before you look elsewhere. By doing this, you will give your talk a fresh and original viewpoint, and you will discover which phases of the topic you have chosen you will need to study further.

If you cannot find enough material for a talk from your own experience, go to outside sources such as your friends and acquaintances, newspaper and magazine articles, radio and television programs, and, of course, books.

Once your interest has settled upon some general subject, talk to your friends about it to widen and deepen your understanding of it. Listen to radio and television broadcasts for further information. Your school and neighborhood libraries are full of books and reference materials that your librarian will be pleased to show you.

18e. Outline your talk.

Avoid the temptation to write out your speech word for word and to memorize what you have written. Instead, outline the structure of your speech. You may, if you wish, write out and memorize the opening and concluding sentences, but no more than that.

The outline of an anecdote is quite simple, of course—just a reminder to yourself of the sequence of events you intend to tell about. An outline of an argument or explana-

**18
c-e**

tion is more detailed. Head the outline with the topic, and then, below it, write out the statement of purpose. After this comes the outline itself. Here is a typical outline for a persuasive talk.

TOPIC   Can We Stop the Slaughter on the Highways?

PURPOSE   To make listeners aware of the need for highway safety and some means of achieving it

I. Increasing toll of highway deaths
  A. More Americans killed on highway than in World War II
  B. Inadequacy of existing laws
II. Need for stricter state laws
  A. Compulsory courses in driver education
  B. Frequent medical examinations for drivers
  C. Annual automobile inspection
  D. Severe penalties for speeding and reckless driving
  E. Uniform traffic regulations in all states
III. Responsibility of automobile manufacturers
  A. Seat belts in all cars
  B. Improved visibility
  C. Improved headlights
  D. Other safety devices
IV. Responsibility of highway departments
  A. Legible road signs
  B. Elimination of dangerous curves and steep grades
  C. Removal of railway crossings

● EXERCISE 4. Make outlines for the three subjects worked on in the preceding exercises.

Make sure that your talk has a good introduction and conclusion.

In your introduction, try to arouse interest. Often you can do this with an arresting sentence or question. For example:

Baby-sitting may seem like a dull pastime, but the most exciting experience I ever had occurred on a quiet winter night when I was baby-sitting in a neighbor's house.

As for the conclusion, there are two disappointing ways for a talk to end: (1) to sputter to a stop like a motor out of gas and (2) to be checked in full course by the teacher's admonition, "Time's up." Do not allow your speech to end so. Conclude strongly by summing up what you have said or by leaving in the mind of your audience a dominant impression of your talk. For example:

> And so, my friends, my first baby-sitting experience came to an end. The "babies" were sprawled in the wreckage of their bedroom, sleeping the sleep of exhaustion; I was trembling and pale when the Joneses returned; and on the way home in the Joneses' car, my courage finally gave out and I started to cry. Never again!

● EXERCISE 5. Write an attention-getting introduction and an emphatic conclusion for one of the subjects worked on in the previous exercises.

GIVING THE TALK

So far we have been discussing the *content* of a good speech. This section will discuss the *technique*.

A good public speaker is interested in his audience. He talks about what concerns his listeners and looks at them as he talks. He has a friendly manner, speaks distinctly, and pitches his voice so that he is easily heard. Although he may be a bit more formal when addressing a large group, he speaks as naturally as he would if he were conversing.

If you look on public speaking as conversation with a large group and take every opportunity you can to speak in public, you will notice yourself growing in self-confidence and skill.

18g. Conquer stage fright.

Do not reproach yourself if you are somewhat tense. Even veteran actors and performers are tense before they go on. Tension is merely the body's signal that it is ready for whatever demands the next few minutes will make on it. Once you are on the "stage," excess tension will usually disappear.

The best antidotes for nervousness are these three:

1. *Know your subject.* Know your subject so thoroughly that it tells itself.

2. *Practice.* Practice imprints on your memory the sequence of your talk and makes it very hard to get "stuck."

3. *Relax.* Deep breathing helps. One well-known trick of professional orators and actors is to "sigh" deeply before inhaling. By forcing all the air out of your lungs, you will also relax your muscles.

18h. Develop a good platform manner.

1. *Rehearse your presentation.* Using your outline as a guide, practice your speech aloud at home. Do not write out or memorize what you are going to say. Each rehearsal will be different, and when you finally deliver your speech, it will differ from all your rehearsals.

2. *Use colorful language.* As you practice, search for colorful and accurate words and expressions which will make your talk more vivid to your listeners. Look for words that have life and sparkle. For example:

> My little sister squirmed onto the stool and let her coltish legs dangle.
>
> He toppled track records like rows of dominoes.
>
> They progressed by inches when they should have been taking seven-league strides.

3. *Watch your posture.* Stand comfortably erect. Keep your feet a few inches apart and parallel, weight primarily on the ball of one foot. The leg that does not bear the weight will be slightly bent at the knee. Keep your shoulders level.

You will find it helpful to imagine yourself held up by a string attached to your breastbone. Keep your neck and body free from tension and let your arms hang naturally.

4. *Look over your audience.* Listeners like speakers who are interested in them and who talk *to* them, not *at* them. A speaker should look at individuals in his audience, talk with them as individuals, and notice the way they respond. A speech is a communication, not a performance. After a talk, a good speaker is able to point out those who listened most attentively and who seemed to follow best what he had to say.

5. *Move about and gesture naturally.* Inexperienced speakers often appear to wish that their hands were invisible. Gesture naturally and fix your attention on any visual materials you may have brought to explain your topic better. Keep your eyes on your audience, glancing only from time to time at your model or chart when you are referring to a specific part of it. Above all, try to keep your mind off yourself. Teen-agers are especially prey to self-consciousness and they must struggle hard against it.

6. *Enunciate clearly and accurately.* While practicing, be sure to speak distinctly. Slovenly speech is caused by laziness of the lips and tongue. Be overprecise in practice, but when you speak before your classmates, concentrate on *what* you are saying rather than on *how* you are saying it. There will be some carry-over from the practice to the presentation.

LISTENING WITH A PURPOSE

Most listening is passive. That is, we *receive* all sounds, of course (this is just a matter of mechanics), but we do not truly begin to *hear* them until we fix our attention on what is being said. When our attention is fully engaged, as it is in a trained listener, then we no longer merely hear sounds, we *listen* to them and the process becomes active.

18h

This section will help you to become a more skillfull listener, that is, a listener able to apply his full attention to any matter that warrants it—to understand what is said; to sift fact from fancy, the weighty from the trivial; and to make wise and true judgments of what he hears.

18i.   Listen courteously.

As your classmates speak, remember that you owe them the courtesy of your attention. Good listening manners require that you listen and do nothing else. Do not let yourself be distracted. Be patient and quiet if a speaker experiences difficulty. You will be grateful for such treatment when your turn comes.

18j.   Listen accurately.

The greatest enemy to accurate listening is a wandering mind. You can often force your attention to stick to its job by giving it the following tasks:

1. *Listen to understand and recall what was said.* Of course we cannot recall everything, but memory can be trained, and by constant practice we can remember a lot more than we might suppose. Pay close attention to what is said and immediately afterward try to review it in your mind, rehearsing the main points and repeating them to yourself in the order given.

● EXERCISE 6.   Compose six questions similar to those below. Read them aloud, pausing about five seconds between each question to allow your classmates time to jot down their answers. When you have finished, your classmates will check their answers to determine how accurately they have listened.

1. In the series of numbers 8–9–4–3–1, the third number is ——?
2. In the list of words *on-off-at-or-in*, the fourth word is ——?

3. In the list of words *but-can-stop-then-until,* the word beginning with *c* is ——?
4. In the announcement "Send your replies to Box 665, Los Angeles, California 90047, before March 31st together with a box top from our product," the post office box number is ——?
5. In the statement "Joe will keep the score, Tom will be captain of one team, and Frank of the other, and Ed and Walter will pitch," what is Joe's assignment?
6. The letters f, g, h, i, j, k are in alphabetical order. What letter comes immediately after the first letter in this sequence?

● EXERCISE 7. Compose an announcement in which essential information is omitted. Read it aloud and test your classmates' attentiveness by asking them to point out the details you have forgotten.

EXAMPLE Tomorrow our basketball team will play one of the strongest teams in our county league. The game will be played at 4 P.M. Admission is free to all members of our Student Organization. Nonmembers can purchase tickets for fifty cents. This promises to be one of the most exciting games of the season. Everyone should attend. [Note that the announcement omits the name of the opposing team and whether the game will be played at home or away.]

2. Listen to understand the underlying structure of a talk or a lecture. This exercise trains your powers of analysis so that you can understand and recall the gist of a complicated talk by knowing what its main arguments will probably be. There is nothing magical in this; to an amazing degree it can be done from the signals a speaker gives in his opening remarks as to what his main ideas are going to be.

For instance, of the following two sets of opening remarks, the listener might ask, "What is the speaker's topic?" and then "How will the argument proceed?" He might then jot down the following notes.

18
i-j

There are two reasons, among others, for finishing high school: first, to get a better job, and second, to extend your interests and thus get more enjoyment out of life.

Notes Finish high school
1. Better job
2. Better person

This morning we pay tribute to Theodore Roosevelt as a conservationist, President, and advocate of the outdoor life.

Notes Theodore Roosevelt
1. As conservationist
2. As President
3. As physical culturist

● EXERCISE 8. Cut out the introductory paragraph of a short magazine article. Read it to the class, asking them what they think the main points of the article will be. Then compare these versions with the real one.

3. *Listen to grasp the main ideas.* As the speaker finishes his introductory remarks and develops his subject, the listener, pencil in hand, asks,

"What arguments support his main points?"
"What facts are offered as proof?"

A speaker's main points frequently stand out because of the emphasis given them. Forceful speakers punctuate each main idea by tone, gesture, and expression. They restate the arguments frequently, illustrating them, citing statistics in their support, and bringing in authoritative opinion in their behalf.

The transitions from one point to the next are signaled by words like *therefore, consequently, on the other hand, however,* etc., and should be carefully noted by the listener. Other clues to the development of an argument are words like *for example, for instance,* which usually indicate that the ideas that follow illustrate a point. Still others show that the speaker is about to summarize: *in conclusion, finally, to sum up,* etc.

● EXERCISE 9. Your teacher will lecture to you without interruption for ten or fifteen minutes, or he will read to you a brief magazine article for about the same length of time. As you listen, write an outline of the lecture or article; then compare it with the teacher's, which he will put on the board.

18k. Listen critically.

The critical listener is a judge. Like the accurate listener, he is careful to understand what is said, but he is not content only to understand; he insists upon evaluating what he hears. Critical listening, therefore, is the art of making distinctions.

1. *Learn to weigh the evidence.* To do this, you must distinguish fact from opinion.

FACT Abraham Lincoln was born on February 12, 1809.

OPINION Abraham Lincoln was the greatest President this country ever had.

FACT At sea level water freezes at 32° F.

OPINION Warm water is better for swimming.

FACT Weimaraners were first bred in Germany.

OPINION Weimaraners make better pets than any other breed of dogs.

You must distinguish between reliable and unreliable authority.

RELIABLE The U.S. Bureau of Public Health says cigarettes are harmful.

UNRELIABLE Wednesday Jones, the popular starlet, says that cigarettes are harmless.

You must distinguish between generalizations from sufficient evidence and those from insufficient evidence.

SUFFICIENT Decatur High's team won every game in our league; our team lost every game. Therefore, Decatur's team is better than ours.

18k

INSUFFICIENT I know three boys from Decatur High School. Each has red hair. Therefore, most Decatur boys have red hair.

You must distinguish between proper and improper comparison or analogy.

PROPER George, whom I can usually beat at bowling, beats Tom regularly. Therefore, I probably can beat Tom, too.

IMPROPER John, who lives next door, read *Quo Vadis* and didn't like it. Therefore, I shall probably not like it either.

2. *Learn to recognize and avoid unfair argument.* Because it is always easy to let emotion rather than reason control our judgments, the critical listener must be on guard against propaganda devices that encourage him to accept opinions he would not ordinarily agree with. Some of these propaganda devices are listed, with examples, in the following pages.

Prejudice. Opinions based on prejudice are really not opinions at all, for in most cases they are maintained in the face of contrary evidence which the prejudiced person simply ignores. Very often people cling to prejudice because they need to feel "better" than someone else or out of sheer laziness; and they will usually not change their minds because it is too much trouble to do so.

EXAMPLES Country man: City slickers are stuck-up, devious, and not to be trusted.

City man: Yokels are stupid, unimaginative, and suspicious.

Bandwagon appeals. Here the propagandist exploits the natural desire to go along with a popular cause and plays on the natural fear of being "different."

EXAMPLE All over the country people are switching to Warwicks. It is the thing to do.

Name-calling. By labeling complicated problems with

simple and emotionally charged names and slogans, the propagandist avoids rational argument. Name-calling can also damage someone's reputation by repeating false charges.

EXAMPLE Of government aid to foreign countries: "Yankee Imperialism Must Go!"

Of any political opponent: "Mr. Smith's election would help the Communist conspiracy."

Slogans. A favorite device of propagandists, catchy slogans are easily remembered, quickly shouted, and impossible to refute. Like name-calling, slogans are designed to take the place of sober reasoning.

EXAMPLES Millions for defense but not one cent for tribute!

Remember the Maine!

Snob appeal. Most people like to think of themselves as successful and deserving. Advertisers play on these feelings by trying to make their products status symbols—visible signs of success.

EXAMPLE For the man *who has made it*—drive the Frontenac luxury sedan!

The unproved assertion. Advertisers and speakers often make statements without proof. Unless a statement is supported by reasons, figures, examples, or the opinions of competent and unbiased authorities, it should be questioned. The following statements seem to prove a point but actually do not because no evidence is offered.

Cigarette smoking causes cancer. It injures body tissue. It irritates the lungs, poisons the blood, and affects digestion.

Cigarette smoking does not cause cancer. Smokers are not physically impaired. There is no danger to the throat, lungs, heart, or arteries. Smoking is harmless.

● EXERCISE 10. In the following statements you will find many examples of invalid and unfair argument. Identify each type of unfair argument and explain briefly how each violates the standards of good reasoning.

1. The Representative was against space travel for this reason: "If man was meant to fly, he would have been given wings."
2. Never cross a picket line, for it is well known that capitalists are the enemies of the working man.
3. The wise merchant will never employ a teen-ager. As any newspaper shows, teen-agers are undependable, dangerous, and larcenous.
4. My opponent is a demagogue. He promises pie in the sky to all but is destitute of fiscal responsibility. His philosophy is soak the rich. He and his kind will surely kill the goose that lays the golden eggs.
5. Olaf, Niels, and Karen are all blue-eyed, tall, and blond. They are Swedish. All Swedes are tall, blue-eyed, and blond.
6. Oneonta High won all of their games right after adopting a new cheer. For Heaven's sake, let's end our losing streak by adopting a new cheer, too!
7. Let's end foreign aid at once. Foreigners don't deserve our help. They don't believe in the American way and are so slick in diplomatic dealings that we, who have been taught always to call a spade a spade, are certain to lose our shirts.
8. The math test was terribly unfair! I spent three days reviewing for it and only got a *C*.
9. General Smith is certain to make a fine governor. After all, he had a brilliant military record and captured Kioga Atoll in three days.
10. Senator Jones failed to vote for the new super carrier. That shows he is soft on Communism.

● EXERCISE 11. Compose a brief, one-paragraph argument for or against some idea, in which you deliberately trespass against the rules for fair and honest thinking. Try to make your argument somewhat subtle so that your classmates must exercise their ingenuity to discover the abuse. If you cannot compose one yourself, look through a magazine, and cut out an advertisement making obvious use of some propaganda device. Bring it to class for discussion.

THREE SPEAKING AND LISTENING SITUATIONS

Although all speeches have certain things in common, you can use different techniques depending on the kind of speech you are giving. The most common speeches you will be called upon to deliver in school, and also later on, will probably be the narrative speech, the expository speech, or the persuasive speech.

The Narrative Talk

Often the easiest and most interesting kind of talk to make is the narrative talk, in which you tell about a personal experience or relate an anecdote. It is not difficult to find a subject for such a talk if you keep in mind that it is the *manner* and not just the subject matter that makes such talks interesting. A quarrel with your brother or a funny experience on the bus can be just as fascinating as the description of a Caribbean cruise.

18 l. Make your tale vivid.

1. *Begin with action.* After you have decided upon your purpose, plunge right into your story without any preamble.

1

Classmates, how many of you have been in a completely strange place and yet were unmistakably certain *that you had seen it all before*—perhaps in a dream? Eerie, isn't it? Well, it happened to me!

2

One day while Polly Garcia and I were riding the San Bernardino bus, an old man got on hauling a huge burlap bag after him. He sat down across the aisle from us, settled the bag between his knees, and kept all the while a firm grip on the top. All at once, something squirmed inside the bag and moaned.

2. *Maintain suspense.* Lead your listeners up to the climax, giving them no inkling until the last moment of how

the story will end. Then end it and take your seat. To linger after the end of the story, explaining away small, unimportant details weakens the dramatic effect you are aiming at.

● EXERCISE 12. *For Speakers.* Relate an unusual personal experience to the class. If you can, select an incident that illustrates a point. Arouse and maintain suspense. Use colorful language. Pay attention to your posture and your enunciation. Practice at home before delivering your talk. Limit your talk to three minutes.

● EXERCISE 13. *For Listeners.* With the rest of the class, draw up a rating sheet on which to record your criticisms of each speaker. Remember, criticism is not necessarily adverse. Listen courteously to each talk, record your comments, and rate each speaker in each category—A, B, C, etc. Then discuss your results in class. A possible rating sheet might be organized like the following:

Topic _____
   Choice_____
   Preparation _____
Delivery
   Posture _____
   Enunciation _____
   Poise _____
   Choice of language _____

● EXERCISE 14. *For Speakers.* Relate an experience or anecdote to illustrate a proverb. The following list is suggestive.

1. A stitch in time saves nine.
2. A rolling stone gathers no moss.
3. Waste not, want not.
4. An empty barrel makes the most noise.
5. A fool and his money are soon parted.
6. A watched pot never boils.
7. Easy come, easy go.
8. Pride goeth before a fall.

9. Spare the rod and spoil the child.
10. A cat may look at a king.

● EXERCISE 15. *For Listeners*. Rate the speakers as you did in Exercise 14; then discuss.

● EXERCISE 16. *For Speakers*. Relate an unusual incident in the life of a famous man or woman. Below is a list of suggested persons.

1. John F. Kennedy
2. General Douglas MacArthur
3. Julius Caesar
4. Dr. Jonas B. Salk
5. Dr. Enrico Fermi
6. Alexander the Great
7. The Apostle Paul
8. Abraham Lincoln
9. George Gordon, Lord Byron
10. Joan of Arc

● EXERCISE 17. *For Listeners*. Rate speakers as before.

The Explanatory Talk

From time to time you will be called upon to explain how to make or to do something. To explain so that your listeners will understand easily, you must plan carefully and observe certain principles of organization and delivery.

18m. Make your explanation clear.

1. *Limit your topic.* It is impossible to explain something clearly without first understanding it clearly. This is why it is important to restrict your choice to a topic you know (or can get to know) thoroughly. The narrower the topic, the more completely you can treat it in the time allowed.

INTEREST   Auto mechanics
CHOOSE   Reboring the cylinder head
INTEREST   Archery
CHOOSE   How to fletch your own arrows
INTEREST   American painting
CHOOSE   The paintings of Andrew Wyeth

18m

2. *Organize your explanation.* Your outline is all-important in a talk of this kind. In it you determine the arrangement of ideas in a step-by-step progression from the simple to the complex, the familiar to the unfamiliar, or in whatever order best suits your subject.

3. *Master all technical terms.* If you choose a subject which ordinarily uses technical terms, master this vocabulary so that you can explain technical terms as you go along. It would be absurd for a student to speak of a tennis racket as a "tennis bat," a distributor as "that little pot with all the wires going in," or of a chihuahua as "a skinny, naked little dog."

4. *Use visual aids.* If you can bring to class the object, tool, or device you are going to explain and demonstrate how to use it or how it works, it will go a long way toward making your explanation clearer. If you cannot bring to class an object or device, illustrate your talk by drawing a diagram on the chalkboard.

While you talk, hold the object you are going to demonstrate in front of you so that it may be clearly seen even by those in the back rows. If you use a diagram, stand to one side and refer to it with a pointer.

● EXERCISE 18.   *For Speakers.* Give an explanatory talk to the class. Your talk should last about five minutes. Use one of the topics from the list below or choose your own.

1. How to make a campfire
2. A science experiment that you can do at home
3. Balanced meals
4. Changes in football rules
5. The structure of a saxophone
6. How our local government is organized
7. Constructing a bench
8. How to maintain a motorcycle or a motorboat
9. Training a dog
10. How to drive safely

● EXERCISE 19.   *For Listeners.* Listen attentively to each speaker. Did you understand every step in his explanation? If not, question him at the end of his talk until you understand completely. Was each step in correct order? Did he omit any essential information?

If you completely understand what he said, you should be able to repeat the essential steps in correct order.

The Persuasive Talk

A speaker must plan carefully, arrange his arguments thoughtfully, and speak forcefully if he wants to persuade others to believe as he wants them to believe or act as he wants them to act.

18n. Make your talk convincing.

1. *Choose a truly controversial question.* Simple questions of fact are not arguable, but questions of policy are.

FACT   Presidents are elected by vote of the Electoral College.
POLICY Should we abolish the Electoral College?

2. *Arrange your arguments carefully.* Work and rework your outline until the speech it represents is logical, well supported, and hard-hitting. Remember that when you cite an authoritative opinion in support of your own, you must jot down the name, publication, and page number just as you would in a footnote for a composition.

3. *Rehearse your talk.* The chief advantage in rehearsing your talk in front of your parents or friends is the opportunity it gives them to raise questions and objections that you have overlooked. Once you are aware of these flaws in your argument, you can make changes to answer them. No argument is strong that ignores evidence to the contrary.

● EXERCISE 20. *For Speakers.* Give a persuasive talk to the class on some subject you think important. Choose one of the topics listed below or select one of your own.

1. Marijuana should be legalized.
2. Ernest Hemingway was *not* a great writer.

18n

3. The overemphasis on athletics in college is dangerous.
4. A free college education ought to be the right of all who can qualify.
5. Stringent laws against air and stream pollution are needed now!
6. Students are given too much homework.
7. Varsity letters should be awarded to the chess team.
8. Our cafeteria is poorly run.

● EXERCISE 21. *For Listeners.* Listen carefully to the persuasive talks of your classmates, jotting down the outline of the argument as you do. Head your paper with the topic, then list the main arguments in the order given and the evidence produced to support them. Note especially the use of invalid or unfair arguments. After the talk, exchange papers with your neighbor to mark the accuracy of your notes. The speaker will read his own outline for this purpose. Then, together with the class, discuss the speech.

CHAPTER 19

Group Discussion

Purposes and Techniques of
Group Discussion, Parliamentary Procedure

As a responsible person you are expected to cooperate with your fellow citizens in analyzing and solving problems confronting your town, state, and nation.

In a democracy, problems are solved through discussion and debate. Some questions are so complicated that no one person can settle them. The pooled judgment and experience of many people are needed. School groups, labor unions, clubs, and organizations of every kind hold meetings so that their members can have a voice in decisions affecting their welfare. Committees recommend solutions after studying, discussing, and hearing opinions of persons with specialized knowledge.

You must know the purposes and techniques of group discussion to participate effectively in making wise decisions. Through discussion you will learn the meaning of freedom of speech and the responsibilities that go with it. You will discover that persons with differing views can disagree in an atmosphere of mutual respect and can work together for the common good without abandoning their beliefs.

Even when discussion does not result in a solution, the time spent is seldom wasted because the participants may perceive the extent of a problem more clearly by exchanging opinions and may become more willing to compromise.

Group discussion differs from social conversation in the following ways:

Social conversation is private, unplanned, and touches lightly on many topics. It requires no leader, although a host or hostess may occasionally steer it. Its aim is enjoyment, persuasion, or instruction.

Group discussion may be informal or formal. Informal group discussion resembles social conversation except that it is usually more purposeful and deals with a single topic or a limited number of topics decided beforehand by the participants. An informal group, such as a small committee, may or may not be guided by a chairman.

Formal group discussion is public and planned. It considers many aspects of a single topic. It is directed and summarized by a chairman. Its aim is to reach an agreement, solve a problem, or start action.

A *debate* is public and planned, like formal group discussion, but considers only two sides of a question. The supporters of one side attempt to defeat their opponents by arguments. The victor is determined by a judge or group of judges.

A debate may grow out of a group discussion. The numerous solutions developed in a discussion may be narrowed to one, which is then offered to a wider public for acceptance or rejection.

PREPARATION FOR GROUP DISCUSSION

As you have seen, there are many kinds of "group discussion," from conversation that is purely social to a formal debate. This chapter, however, will deal only with those four kinds that are more formal than social conversation and less formal than a debate. All are characteristically *purposeful* and *planned*.

19a. Learn the characteristics of the various forms of group discussion.

The round table is a form of group discussion in which the participants exchange views around a table (not necessarily round) under the leadership of a chairman. The number of people usually does not exceed a dozen. The discussion is informal. There is no audience.

The most common example of a round-table discussion is the committee meeting. Most organizations conduct a large part of their business through committees. A committee considers matters referred to it and reports its findings and recommendations to the entire organization.

A forum is any type of speaking program which is followed by audience participation. For example, a lecture followed by questions from the audience is a forum. A forum is most successful when the audience is small; otherwise, people are reluctant to stand up and speak their minds.

A symposium consists of prepared talks by several speakers on different aspects of a single topic. When all the speakers have finished their presentation, the chairman invites the audience to ask questions, contribute additional information, or express agreement or disagreement with the speakers' views.

A panel discussion is like an overheard conversation. It consists of a chairman and from four to eight participants seated, usually in a semicircle, before an audience. The participants remain seated during the discussion. They speak in conversational style, generally not longer than one or two minutes at a time. They express opinions, disagree with and question one another. The chairman acts as a moderator, stimulating, directing, and summarizing the discussion. After a while the audience joins in the conversation. The panel discussion spills over, as it were, and engulfs the audience. The chairman summarizes the discussion before bringing it to an end.

19a

19b. Select a topic that lends itself to profitable group discussion.

Before selecting a topic for discussion, ask:
1. Is it worthwhile?
2. Is it timely?
3. Is it related to the needs, experience, and interests of listeners and speakers?
4. Is it stimulating?
5. Is it many-sided?

What are good sources of topics for group discussion? Your own experience may suggest some, for example, "Teen-age problems," "Fads in popular music," or "Learning by working after school hours." Your school courses may suggest others, for instance, "Why study mathematics and science?" "The most valuable subject in the curriculum," or "Is high school too easy?" Books, magazine articles, movies, and television programs can often stimulate discussion. Newspapers are another source. The discussion of current events, especially of controversial matters, can capture and hold an audience's attention.

A topic for discussion should be a question of policy rather than a question of fact. "Have we a supply of atomic bombs?" is a question of fact and hence not discussible. The only appropriate reply is a direct, factual answer. "Should we use atomic bombs in the event of war?" is a question of policy which should stir discussion.

Topics that are trivial, timeworn, have no audience appeal, do not evoke strong differences of opinion, or can be answered by *yes* or *no* are not suitable.

Select an up-to-the-minute controversial topic. For example:

What's wrong with today's teen-agers?
Who's to blame for juvenile delinquency?
How can we prevent another war?
Who should go to college?

19c. Prepare for a group discussion by thinking, talking, and reading about the topic.

Many discussions fail because of insufficient preparation by the participants.

If a discussion is to be more than a pooling of ignorance, everyone must think, talk, and read about the topic before the discussion takes place. When the topic is announced:

1. *Think about it.* What is your opinion? On what evidence is it based?

2. *Talk to others about it.* Discuss it with your friends and parents. If you know someone who is an authority on the subject, discuss it with him. Be ready to modify your previous opinion in the light of your new knowledge.

3. *Consult reference books, recent publications, magazine articles, and editorials.* Inform yourself as thoroughly as you can about the topic. Keep an open mind while you are learning.

19d. Learn the duties of the chairman of a discussion.

A chairman should:

1. *Know the subject thoroughly.*

2. *Know the backgrounds and special interests of each of the speakers.*

3. *Arrange a preliminary meeting of the speakers.* At this meeting the topic might be explored, points of agreement and disagreement revealed, and details of procedure settled.

4. *Arouse the audience's interest in the topic by a brief introductory statement.*

5. *Introduce the speakers to the audience, telling something of each one's background or the point of view he represents.*

6. *Ask questions to stimulate discussion.*

19
b-d

7. *Prevent fruitless digressions.*
8. *See that everyone has a chance to speak.*
9. *Summarize the discussion.*
10. *Thank the audience and the speakers.*

19e. Learn the duties of speakers in a round-table, forum, symposium, or panel discussion.

A speaker in a group discussion should:

1. *Know the subject thoroughly.*

2. *Listen intelligently.* When you agree with another speaker, listen to increase your store of information. When you disagree, listen to accept a different viewpoint if it is supported by sufficient evidence or to refute it by sound reasons if it is fallacious.

3. *Speak so that all may hear.*

4. *Recognize and admit the truth of what others say.*

5. *Be courteous always.* Sarcasm and ridicule are out of place. Self-control is a mark of maturity. Disagree reasonably—and with reasons.

19f. Learn the duties of members of the audience.

A member of an audience should:

1. *Know the subject thoroughly.* Prepare by thinking, talking, and reading about the topic.

2. *Listen with an alert mind.* Ask yourself: What proof is offered in support of each important argument? Take notes as you listen.

3. *Join in when the chairman invites the audience to participate.* Speak freely, briefly, sincerely. A discussion in which there is general participation is more stimulating and interesting than one in which only a few take part.

4. *Focus on the main issues.* Minor points of fact or opinion should be overlooked.

5. *Speak audibly.* While your remarks are addressed to the chairman, speak so that all may hear.

● EXERCISE 1.   List five topics suitable for group discussion. Test yours and those submitted by other members of the class against the criteria listed above. The topics may be related to school, community, state, national, or international affairs.

TAKING PART IN GROUP DISCUSSION

You can be more successful in communicating your ideas to others if you learn something about speaking and listening effectively in group discussions.

For Speakers

19g. Learn how to speak effectively in group discussion.

Put into practice the following principles:

1. *Think before you speak.* Know what you are going to say before you begin. Take a few seconds to organize your ideas before you start talking; clear thinking precedes clear speaking.

2. *Keep the other person in mind.* Try to understand the other person's point of view. Avoid sarcasm and ridicule; they hurt unnecessarily and are a sign that your own arguments are weak. In the midst of heated discussion, remain calm. Your calmness will show up in your tone of voice, facial expression, and rate of speaking.

3. *Be brief.* Omit long and unnecessary explanations. Know the point you want to make and go directly to it. Speak simply but naturally and enthusiastically. Listeners like an enthusiastic speaker.

19
e-g

For Listeners

19h. Learn how to listen accurately and critically while taking part in group discussion.

In group discussion the interplay of personalities is often so interesting that you may permit your attention to wander from what is said or fail to recognize that a speaker's comments are not relevant to the topic.

You can often focus your attention by taking notes. Jotting down only those arguments that have direct bearing on the question at hand will enable you to see at a glance which points are put in only as an emotional issue. The following principles should be followed by anyone who tries to listen to a discussion with an open mind.

1. *Recognize and guard against your own prejudices.* Be alert to the possibility of letting emotions color your thinking. For example, your reactions to a speaker's appearance, accent, or gestures may affect your acceptance or rejection of his ideas. It is important that you recognize your own prejudices and guard against them. Think fairly and test the acceptability of ideas on rational, not emotional, grounds.

2. *Recognize a speaker's bias and take it into account.* When a speaker has an ax to grind, a listener must be particularly careful. The arguments he advances may be valid, but they may also be one-sided and rooted in prejudice. He may, for example, be financially interested in a proposal or averse to a new plan because it might disturb his status. He may be suspicious of persons whose backgrounds are different from his own. Ask yourself: Does his bias weaken the force of his argument or are his proposals still sound despite his special pleading?

3. *Make allowances for words, phrases, and attitudes that are emotionally loaded.* Some words report a fact objectively. They have few emotional overtones, if any. Others are loaded with emotion.

Compare the following pairs of words. Notice how one member of each pair is relatively colorless, while the other arouses feelings.

house	shack	dwelling	mansion
car	jalopy	defeat	rout
book	tome	recline	sprawl
reply	rebuke	failure	fiasco
verse	doggerel	sunrise	dawn
farmer	peasant	dog	mongrel
work	drudgery	boy	rascal

Loaded words carry positive or negative charges. A positively charged word creates a favorable reaction; a negatively charged word, an unfavorable one. Propagandists make use of loaded words to influence listeners. They employ positively charged words to sway you to their way of thinking and negatively charged words to make you reject what they oppose.

● EXERCISE 2. Number your paper 1–20. Indicate by plus or minus signs which of the following words affect you positively or negatively.

1. adorable	11. democracy
2. skinny	12. dictatorship
3. glamorous	13. noise
4. communism	14. music
5. fabulous	15. reactionary
6. fascism	16. glutton
7. miserly	17. sympathy
8. generous	18. sentimentality
9. crude	19. horse opera
10. rebellious	20. screech

4. *Be careful not to be misled by catchy slogans and generalized introductory statements.* Advertisers and political organizations often employ slogans to popularize ideas, candidates, or products. A complex argument cannot be summarized fairly in a capsule expression.

19h

EXAMPLES

See America first. [slogan promoting travel in the United States, as opposed to foreign travel]

Ask the man who owns one. [advertising slogan]

Generalized introductory statements often have no basis in fact, but they imply that disagreement with the statement that follows is impossible for a right-thinking person. Typical examples:

EXAMPLES

It is common knowledge that . . .
Everybody knows that . . .
No right-thinking person will deny that . . .

5. *Look for and weigh evidence for every important statement.* As you learned in Chapter 18, every major argument should be supported by adequate evidence. A speaker may be able to prove a point by describing one or two examples and by quoting an eminent authority or by citing statistics.

If a speaker offers no evidence, ask for it. If he offers insufficient evidence, ask for more.

● EXERCISE 3.   Conduct a round-table discussion on a topic which concerns all the participants. The student chairman, appointed beforehand, will end the discussion after twenty minutes, summarize, and invite class discussion. Suggested topics:

1. The school yearbook
2. Improving the student organization
3. Building school spirit
4. Improving the school cafeteria
5. Assembly programs

● EXERCISE 4.   Conduct a symposium on discipline. The speakers should represent the viewpoints of a young person, a parent, a law enforcement officer, an educator, and a community leader.

● EXERCISE 5. Divide the class into groups. Each group will select a chairman and present a panel discussion on any one of the following topics. (The list is suggestive only. Choose a topic of your own if you prefer; be sure it is of interest and concern to all.) Each panel should meet beforehand to settle matters of procedure and scope.

1. Modern manners
2. Radio and television advertising
3. Comic books
4. Youthful crime
5. Violence on the screen
6. Vandalism
7. Should Latin be dropped from the curriculum?
8. Prejudice—and how to overcome it
9. The impact of the young voter
10. The ideal school
11. Choosing a vocation
12. The honor system of conducting examinations
13. Professional vs. amateur sports
14. Extracurricular activities
15. Our foreign policy
16. Problems of the small farmer
17. Ways of preventing war
18. Selecting a college
19. The kind of world I'd like to live in
20. Why read novels?

● EXERCISE 6. Conduct a class discussion on one of the following topics. After a number of pupils have expressed their opinions, call on someone to summarize. Consider whether the summary is complete and accurate.

1. Ways of improving our school
2. Traffic accidents
3. An eleven-month school year
4. Why go to college?
5. Why I prefer to live in a small town (or large city)

● EXERCISE 7. Why should you be particularly careful in listening to each of the following speakers?

1. The president of a college fraternity speaking about the advantages of fraternity life
2. A movie actress advertising a cold cream
3. A candidate of a political party speaking about his party's platform

4. A radio announcer delivering a commercial
5. A parent of a failing student criticizing a school

EVALUATION OF GROUP DISCUSSION

19i. Evaluate a group discussion by asking key questions about it.

Consider the merits and deficiencies of each group discussion after it is over. By such evaluation you can learn to improve future discussion programs. The following questions will help you estimate the worth of a group discussion.

1. Was the discussion purposeful? Were the causes of the problem considered? Were various solutions proposed and analyzed? Did the discussion ramble, or did it proceed in an orderly fashion?

2. Were the outcomes worthwhile? A group discussion need not reach a solution or agreement. It may be successful if it brings areas of disagreement into the open.

3. Were the participants thoroughly familiar with the problem? Did they present facts, instances, statements of competent and unbiased authorities, and statistics to support their opinions?

4. Was the discussion lively and general? Was there a give-and-take of opinion in an atmosphere of mutual respect? Did all participate? Did anyone monopolize the meeting, or did everyone speak briefly and to the point?

5. Did the participants reach a solution justified by the evidence? Do you agree with the solution? Why?

6. Were the audience's questions thought-provoking? Did the speakers answer them directly and fully?

7. Was the discussion courteous? Did each speaker exercise self-control by refraining from interrupting when another was speaking? Were statements and objections phrased courteously?

8. Was the chairman competent? Did he arouse interest

by his introductory remarks? Did he guide the discussion so as to prevent valueless digressions? Did he encourage everyone to join in? Did he summarize?

● EXERCISE 8. Criticize a radio or television discussion you have heard. Consider such matters as choice of topic, the speakers' familiarity with the topic, the quality of the discussion, and audience participation. In what ways could the discussion have been improved?

PARLIAMENTARY PROCEDURE

All organizations, except those which are very small and informal, conduct their meetings according to a code known as *rules of order* or *parliamentary procedure*.

Parliamentary procedure protects the rights of all and enables individuals to work together efficiently. It is a means of determining the will of the majority and at the same time safeguarding the rights of the minority.

Elections

When a club is organized, the founding members draw up a constitution with its by-laws. This document sets forth the name and purpose of the club and the rules by which it will operate. Among these rules is one regulating the election of officers.

19j. **Officers are elected according to the method prescribed in an organization's constitution and perform duties set forth in the constitution.**

Officers may be nominated by a nominating committee or members may make nominations from the floor. Nominations need not be seconded. Elections are usually held immediately after nominations are closed.

19
i-j

A majority vote is usually required for election unless a by-law states otherwise. If no one receives a majority, a new vote must be taken, limited to the two candidates who received the highest number of votes on the first ballot. Depending upon the constitution of the organization, officers may be elected by either an open or a secret ballot.

Duties of Officers

The president presides over meetings, appoints committees, calls special meetings if necessary, and sees that the organization's constitution and by-laws are observed.

The vice-president acts in place of the president if the latter is absent. He may have other duties specified in the constitution.

The secretary notifies members of meetings, takes the minutes, keeps a record of attendance, and answers letters as the president directs.

The treasurer receives dues and other income, pays the club's bills, and keeps a record of all receipts and disbursements. At every meeting he gives a report of the organization's current financial status.

Club Business

19k. The regular procedure at meetings is called the order of business.

The following is a typical order of business:

(1) Call to order
(2) Roll call
(3) Reading of minutes of previous meeting
(4) Treasurer's report
(5) Committee reports
(6) Unfinished business
(7) New business
(8) Adjournment

191. A motion is a proposal offered to the membership for discussion and action.

EXAMPLES I move that we purchase new uniforms for the basketball team.

I move that we publish a monthly bulletin.

I move that this question be referred to a committee of three appointed by the chair.

I move we adjourn.

An organization transacts all its business at meetings through motions.

Steps in Making a Motion

1. A member requests and receives recognition by the chair. If two or more members rise at the same time, the chair recognizes the one who addressed him first.

MEMBER "Mr. Chairman."
CHAIR "Mr. Jones."

2. The member states his motion.

MEMBER "I move that our club hold a skating party."

3. Another member seconds the motion. All motions must be seconded before they can be considered. The purpose of a second is to show that more than one person is interested.

ANOTHER MEMBER "I second the motion."

4. The chair repeats the motion using the original words.

CHAIR "It is moved and seconded that our club hold a skating party. Is there any discussion?"

5. The members discuss the motion.
6. When the discussion is finished, the chair repeats the motion.
7. The chair puts the motion to a vote.

CHAIR "All those in favor, say 'aye.' Those opposed, 'nay.'"

19
k-l

8. The chair announces the result.

CHAIR　"The motion is carried."

If the vote is taken by a show of hands or by ballot, the chair may announce the exact count.

CHAIR　"By a vote of 25–8, the motion is carried."

● EXERCISE 9.　Practice the steps in making a motion. With one class member acting as chairman, the others will offer various main motions. Suggested subjects for motions:

1. Abolition of homework
2. Class picnic
3. Purchase of books
4. Petition to principal
5. Field trip
6. Publication of class newspaper

19m. Motions are of two kinds: main motions and procedural motions.

A main motion brings new business before a meeting. It has to do with matters of substance. Motions to run a bazaar, stage a show, or purchase equipment are main motions. Main motions can be debated and amended. Only one main motion can be considered at a time.

A procedural motion concerns the procedure of a meeting or ways of handling main motions. Motions to postpone consideration of a question or to adjourn are examples of procedural motions. Most procedural motions cannot be amended. There may be several procedural motions before a meeting at one time. The most important procedural motions are:

(1) Adjourn
(2) Lay on the table
(3) Close debate
(4) Refer to committee

Amending a Main Motion

Main motions may be amended. Not more than one amendment can be considered at a time. Another amendment may be proposed when the first has been disposed of.

19n. **A main motion may be amended by adding, striking out, or substituting words.**

EXAMPLES   I move to amend the original motion by adding the word "monthly" before "dance."

I move to amend the original motion by striking out the word "new."

I move to amend the original motion by substituting the word "semiannual" in place of "annual."

● EXERCISE 10. Practice making and amending main motions using the topics listed in Exercise 9 or others of your own devising.

Procedural Motions

Motion to adjourn. The purpose of this motion is to bring the meeting to an end. It cannot be debated or amended and must be put to a vote as soon as seconded.

I move we adjourn.
I move that this meeting adjourn.
I move that this meeting do now adjourn.

Motion to lay on the table. The purpose of this motion is to stop consideration of a main motion at least for the time being. If a motion to lay on the table is passed, the main motion is put aside indefinitely. It may be reconsidered at some future time if a motion "to take from the table" is passed. A motion to lay on the table cannot be debated or amended.

I move to lay this motion on the table.
I move that this motion be tabled.

19
m-n

Motion to close debate. The purpose of this motion is to cut off discussion and bring a question to a vote. This motion used to be called the Previous Question, but because the term was confusing it is now called the motion to close debate.

The motion to close debate may not be debated or amended. It requires a *two-thirds* vote for adoption. (Notice that any motion which restricts freedom of speech requires a two-thirds vote in order to protect minority rights.)

I move that debate on the pending motion be closed and that we vote at once.

I move to close debate and vote on this question at once.

Motion to refer to committee. The purpose of this motion is to assign a question to a committee for study and report. Unlike the foregoing procedural motions, the motion to refer to committee can be debated and amended.

MOTION   I move that this question be referred to committee.

AMENDMENT I move that the motion be amended by adding the words "and that the committee report its findings at our next meeting."

19o. A point of order is an objection to a violation of parliamentary procedure.

Its purpose is to require members to comply with the rules of order.

Since a point of order is not a motion, it requires no second and no vote. Typical points of order are: absence of a quorum, irrelevant remarks by a speaker, motion which violates club's constitution.

MEMBER   Mr. Chairman, I rise to a point of order.

CHAIR   State your point of order.

MEMBER   I make the point of order that the meeting is so noisy the speaker cannot be heard.

CHAIR   The point is well taken and the meeting will come to order.

● EXERCISE 11.   Practice the following procedures in class.

1. Proposing, discussing, and voting on a main motion
2. Rising to a point of order
3. Adjourning a meeting
4. Nominating and electing officers
5. Proposing a procedural motion

● EXERCISE 12.   With one class member acting as chairman, other members of the class will propose, discuss, and vote upon humorous motions. For example:

1. That the members purchase a yacht for the custodian-engineer
2. That students be allowed to arrive late without penalty
3. That examinations be abolished
4. That the teacher invite the class to a party
5. That ice-skating be permitted on the school roof

● EXERCISE 13.   Attend a meeting of a club, council, or association, and report orally on the way the meeting was conducted. What did you learn about parliamentary procedure that you did not previously know?

● EXERCISE 14.   Read one of the following references and report on it. Explain a topic not taken up in this chapter so clearly that everyone understands. (Some suggested topics: duties and rights of members, reading and approving minutes, the motion to postpone, the motion to reconsider.)

1. Cushing's *Manual of Parliamentary Practice*
2. Eliot's *Basic Rules of Order*
3. Robert's *Rules of Order*
4. Sturgis' *Standard Code of Parliamentary Procedure*

● EXERCISE 15.   Two features of parliamentary procedure are freedom of discussion and majority rule. Of the two, which is the more important? Why?

190

PART SIX

Mechanics

CHAPTER 20

Capitalization

Standard Uses of Capitalization

Capital letters are used mainly to individualize what we are writing about. When we capitalize a word, we serve notice on the reader that we are referring to some *particular* person, place, or thing rather than to the general class. Custom determines the use of capital letters, and it is the wisest course to conform to customary or standard usage.

Occasionally, however, publications adopt slightly varying styles of capitalization to serve their own purposes. Newspapers may use the "down" style, in which words like *avenue, river, county,* etc., are not capitalized as they are in standard usage when used with a particular name. In the columns of your newspaper, you might see *Fifth avenue, Bergen county,* and *Red river;* and in some publications which condense much information into very small space, you might note even fewer capital letters. Advertisers, on the other hand, frequently use capital letters for every word of their messages. It is clear, therefore, that styles of capitalization do indeed differ, but in ordinary writing we are justified in hewing to the rules of standard usage, that is, the rules outlined in the following chapter. It is useful to know the rules, of course, but nothing can replace the habit of carefulness. Always read over your written work to check for correct use of capitals.

Take the following diagnostic test to see how much you have to review.

Diagnostic Test

If you can make 100 percent on the following quiz, you may work through this chapter very rapidly. If you make a lower score, you should learn the uses of capital letters and do the exercises so that you will be able henceforth to use capital letters correctly.

Number your paper 1–25. In each of the following items, you are to choose the correct one of two forms. After the proper number on your paper, write the letter of the correct form (*a* or *b*).

1. a. Last summer we hiked along the Adirondack Trail.
   b. Last Summer we hiked along the Adirondack Trail.
2. a. the Amazon River
   b. the Amazon river
3. a. the Morrison Hotel
   b. the Morrison hotel
4. a. They took the wrong exit on San Mateo Boulevard.
   b. They took the wrong exit on San Mateo boulevard.
5. a. Hofstra university is in Hempstead.
   b. Hofstra University is in Hempstead.
6. a. Is he a Senior this term?
   b. Is he a senior this term?
7. a. The junior prom was a huge success.
   b. The Junior Prom was a huge success.
8. a. My brother thinks that Reed is a fine college.
   b. My brother thinks that Reed is a fine College.
9. a. I enjoy french and trigonometry.
   b. I enjoy French and trigonometry.
10. a. the Mediterranean sea
    b. the Mediterranean Sea
11. a. She graduated from high school last year.
    b. She graduated from High School last year.
12. a. a package of Wise potato chips
    b. a package of Wise Potato Chips
13. a. a speech by the President of the United States
    b. a speech by the president of the United States
14. a. Mr. Allen, the chairman of that department
    b. Mr. Allen, the Chairman of that Department

15. a. They prayed to God for guidance.
    b. They prayed to god for guidance.
16. a. the Bijou Theater
    b. the Bijou theater
17. a. Jupiter was a Roman God.
    b. Jupiter was a Roman god.
18. a. Are you Canadian?
    b. Are you canadian?
19. a. We import tea from Asia.
    b. We import tea from asia.
20. a. a german shepherd puppy
    b. a German shepherd puppy
21. a. Forty-Second Street
    b. Forty-second Street
22. a. They drove West for twenty miles.
    b. They drove west for twenty miles.
23. a. We spent our vacation in the Far West.
    b. We spent our vacation in the Far west.
24. a. the Douglas Aircraft Company
    b. the Douglas Aircraft company
25. a. Everyone feared a civil war.
    b. Everyone feared a Civil War.

20a. Capitalize the first word in every sentence.

This is one of the first rules a schoolchild learns. It is usually broken only by students who have trouble telling where one sentence ends and another begins.

WRONG   Copenhagen is known as the Paris of the North. the residents of this beautiful city prefer to call Paris the Copenhagen of the South.

RIGHT   Copenhagen is known as the Paris of the North. The residents of this beautiful city prefer to call Paris the Copenhagen of the South.

WRONG   Helping himself to another plate, Tim said, "this spaghetti is marvelous."

RIGHT   Helping himself to another plate, Tim said, "This spaghetti is marvelous."

NOTE   It is customary to capitalize the first word in any line of poetry.

EXAMPLE   Cast a cold eye
On life, on death.
Horseman, pass by!—W. B. YEATS

20b. Capitalize the pronoun *I* and the inter-jection *O*.

WRONG   Bowing, i said, "Greetings, o Master."
RIGHT   Bowing, I said, "Greetings, O Master."

The common interjection *oh* (Oh, yes!) is capitalized only when it appears at the beginning of a sentence.

20c. Capitalize proper nouns and proper adjectives.

A *proper noun* is the name of a particular person, place, or thing.

How a proper noun differs from an ordinary, common noun, which is not capitalized, can be seen from the following lists.

COMMON NOUN	PROPER NOUN
city	New Orleans
river	Colorado River
mountain	Lookout Mountain
man	Socrates

Do not confuse proper nouns, which are *names*, with nouns which merely state kind or type. For instance, *convertible* is not the name of a particular automobile company (like Ford, Chrysler, etc.) or of a particular automobile model (like Impala, Thunderbird, Model T). The word *convertible* is merely a general name for a type of automobile.

20
a-c

WRONG When I can afford a car, I hope it will be a Ford Convertible.

RIGHT When I can afford a car, I hope it will be a Ford convertible.

WRONG The deer hunter has a Winchester Carbine.

RIGHT The deer hunter has a Winchester carbine.

A *proper adjective* is an adjective formed from a proper noun.

PROPER NOUN	PROPER ADJECTIVE
England	English tweed
America	American people
Ireland	Irish linen

Compound adjectives are frequently a source of trouble. In most cases, only that part of a compound adjective is capitalized which is itself a proper noun or adjective.

EXAMPLES French-speaking Canadians, God-given liberty
pro-Western alliance, anti-British, pro-American
Italian-American, Anglo-Saxon

Study carefully the list which follows. It classifies under seven headings the most frequently used kinds of proper nouns and adjectives.

(1) Capitalize the names of persons.

GIVEN NAMES James, Evelyn, Joseph
SURNAMES Johnson, Powers, Goldstein, Mangano

In some surnames, another letter besides the first should be capitalized. This practice varies; to be sure you are right, check a reference source.

EXAMPLES MacReady, O'Donnell, LeClerc, O'Casey

The abbreviations *Jr.* and *Sr.* (*junior* and *senior*) should always be capitalized when they follow a name.

EXAMPLES Gregory E. Burke, Jr.
Warren Grattan, Sr.

(2) Capitalize geographical names.

Cities and Towns Detroit, Perryville, Carson City
Counties and Townships Hamilton County, Atlanta County, Oyster Bay Township
States Georgia, Arizona, California
Countries France, United States of America, Mexico
Continents Africa, Asia, South America
Islands Catalina Island, Fire Island
Bodies of Water Caribbean Sea, Atlantic Ocean, Nile River
Mountains Sangre de Cristo Mountains, Mount Everest, Rocky Mountains
Streets Grand Street, Post Avenue, Northern State Parkway, Thirty-second Street. [In a hyphenated number, the second word begins with a small letter.]
Parks Sequoia National Park, Hamilton County Park, Jones Beach State Park
Sections of the Country the East, the Middle West, the Great Plains

◆ NOTE Do not capitalize *east*, *west*, *north*, and *south* when they merely indicate direction. Do capitalize them when they refer to commonly recognized sections of the country. The modern tendency is to write nouns and adjectives derived from capitalized *East*, *West*, *North*, and *South* without capital letters (a *southerner*, *southern fried chicken*).

EXAMPLES We headed west for five miles and then turned north. My grandmother spends the winter in the South.

When an adjective indicating direction is *part of the name* of a recognized region or political unit, capitalize it. When such an adjective merely indicates some portion of a region or political unit, do *not* capitalize it.

EXAMPLES South America [a continent], Eastern Samoa [a territory], southern Mexico, northern Idaho

● EXERCISE 1. Copy the following, using capital letters wherever they are required.

1. yellowstone national park
2. the bering strait
3. pro-british
4. a bracelet of mexican silver

5. at eagle lake
6. a house on block island
7. near the chattahoochee river
8. in schurtz county
9. the oklahoma oil fields
10. the bay of fundy
11. an east wind
12. danish pastry
13. pennsylvania farmers
14. on fifty-third street
15. john d. rockefeller, jr.
16. the east side of the canyon
17. the pacific northwest
18. the rocky mountains
19. some swedish glassware
20. spanish-american

● **EXERCISE 2.** Copy all words requiring a capital, and be sure to capitalize them. Before each word, write the number of its sentence.

1. My brother, who lives on the eastern coast of florida, has asked us to visit his home in the south.
2. We should leave manhattan island, point the car south on the newest turnpike, forget about going to raquette lake in the adirondack mountains, and let the road map guide us to kenansville, florida.
3. With my dad's sense of direction, east, west, north, and south are all the same; if you told him westbury pond was great salt lake, he might almost believe it.
4. He often has trouble finding his way through new york city to the george washington bridge.
5. Usually he does not drive to manhattan at all; instead, he catches a train which takes him to pennsylvania station on thirty-third street.
6. Dad kept insisting that he had to visit washington, d.c., situated on the banks of the potomac river, and that from there he wanted to drive through some of the mountains in virginia.
7. Mother said that if he was so interested in mountains, he should take a cruise up the hudson river to visit bear mountain in the catskills.
8. She added that she wanted to spend some time with her cousin in nichols, south carolina.
9. We decided to cross from new jersey to delaware over the delaware memorial bridge, cross the chesapeake bay bridge in maryland, and then get into the south.

10. Incidentally, we never did drive to florida; we drove to kennedy airport and took a plane from there.
11. From the air i was able to recognize the washington monument and the lincoln memorial.
12. While we were flying over cape hatteras in north carolina, we were served lunch.

● EXERCISE 3.   Read the following paragraphs and list in a column all words requiring capitals. When two or more capitalized words belong together, list them together: *East Shore Drive, Windsor Square,* etc. Number your list according to the numbers of the sentences. Do not list words already capitalized.

EXAMPLES   1. Our dog ran away from our home on east shore drive, and somebody found him wandering around windsor square.

               1. *East Shore Drive*
                 Windsor Square

              2. How he ever got across fulton street and park boulevard without being hit by a car is a mystery to me.

               2. *Fulton Street*
                 Park Boulevard

· 1. Our school is located in the heart of macon county, but the exact location really isn't very important. 2. The students and teachers could be dropped into any school in the north or the south, the east or the west; and, except possibly for regional accents, nobody would notice the difference. 3. There are blonds, brunets, and redheads whose ancestors may have come from finland, italy, england, or spain. 4. There are some who live on farms on the west side of town, and there are others who live in apartments on franklin avenue. 5. There are some whose parents take them to europe, to mexico, or on caribbean cruises, and there are others who have never been farther north than tanners pond or farther south than winslow park. 6. A few of us may become captains of industry and work in san francisco or new york, and some might even become celebrities on broadway or in hollywood. 7. Even our homes could be found anywhere in the u.s.a.

8. Stroll along cherry street, and you will notice cape cod cottages that look as if they were transplanted from a new england village overlooking an atlantic beach. 9. Turn left on smith street, and you will see ranch houses that would look right at home in nevada or texas. 10. In short, we are a fairly typical cross section of the united states.

(3) Capitalize the names of organizations, business firms, institutions, government bodies.

Organizations and Clubs Jericho Country Club, Elks Club, Ladies' Aid Society, National Honor Society

♦ NOTE Do not capitalize such words as *democratic, republican, socialist*, etc., when these words refer only to types of societies rather than to specific parties. The word *party* in the name of a political party may be capitalized or not; either way is correct: *Republican party, Republican Party.*

EXAMPLES Mr. Jones, formerly a Democrat, has now joined the Republican party.

Most of the new African nations have adopted republican forms of government.

The democratic nations of the West cherish many of the same ideals.

Business Firms Eastman Kodak Company, Ford Motor Company, Aluminum Greenhouses, Inc., United Aircraft Corporation

Institutions and Buildings St. Charles Hotel, the Empire State Building, Rivoli Theater, Colby College, Chester High School, Friends Academy, St. Mary's Hospital

♦ NOTE Do not capitalize such words as *hotel, theater, college, high school* unless they are part of a proper name.

EXAMPLES Carroll College   a college in Wisconsin
Eastland Hotel   a hotel in Portland
Great Falls High School   a high school in Montana
Helen Hayes Theater   a theater in New York

Government Bodies   House of Representatives, the Supreme Court, Congress, the Securities and Exchange Commission

(4) Capitalize the names of historical events and periods, special events, and calendar items.

Historical Events and Periods   the Renaissance, World War II, the Battle of Gettysburg, the Middle Ages, the San Francisco Conference, the Atomic Age

Special Events   the Junior Prom, the Mercy League Ball, the Meadowbrook Dog Show, the National Amateur Tennis Championships, the World Series

Calendar Items   Wednesday, February, Easter, Labor Day, Fourth of July

◆ NOTE   Do not capitalize the names of the seasons: summer, winter, spring, fall.

(5) Capitalize the names of nationalities, races, and religions.

EXAMPLES   Japanese, Hungarian, Negro, Indian, Roman Catholic, Methodist

(6) Capitalize the brand names of business products.

EXAMPLES   a Chrysler automobile, Coldspot refrigerator, Maxwell House coffee

NOTE   Do not capitalize the nouns which often follow a brand name.

RIGHT   Sunbeam toaster, Kroflite golf balls, Vicks cough drops, Schrafft's candies

(7) Capitalize the names of ships, planes, trains, monuments, awards, heavenly bodies, and any other particular places, things, or events.

EXAMPLES   the *Queen Mary* (a ship), a Constellation (a plane), the Purple Heart (a medal), *Mariner II* (a space vehicle), Jupiter, Orion (heavenly bodies)

◆ NOTE   Do not capitalize *earth*, *sun*, or *moon*.

20d. Do *not* capitalize the names of school subjects, except names of languages and course
names followed by a number.

English, Spanish, Latin, French, mathematics, social studies,
history, Mathematics II, History II

◆ NOTE Do not capitalize *senior, junior, sophomore,* and *freshman* unless these words are part of a proper noun or are used to
designate a *specific* organization.

EXAMPLES The juniors invited the seniors to the Junior Prom.

The Freshman Class cordially invites all sophomores
to its first play.

● EXERCISE 4.   List in order all words requiring capitals.
When two capitalized words belong together, list them together. Number your list according to the numbers of the
paragraphs. Do not list words already capitalized.

1. The hawaii visitors bureau spends thousands of dollars
   each year to lure visitors from the mainland to sample the
   delights of the hawaiian islands, located in the pacific.
2. Whether you travel on the *mariposa,* the matson line's
   glamorous ship, or by japan air lines, the hawaiian hotel
   association will be delighted to welcome you.
3. The original settlers of hawaii probably arrived from asia by
   way of the malay peninsula.
4. According to hawaiian folklore, pele, the goddess of vol-
   canoes, is responsible for the craters that dot the islands. In
   hawaii national park is mauna loa, a volcano that has made
   news since the days of captain cook and the christian mis-
   sionaries from new england.
5. The most densely populated of the islands is oahu. To the
   south of the hawaiian islands are samoa and tahiti, to the
   north are the aleutian islands, and to the west lies guam.
6. Honolulu, on oahu, is famed throughout the world. Waikiki
   beach has been known to tourists for years. The most famous
   landmark near the city is diamond head, a promontory
   jutting into the pacific. The best view of the harbor is from a
   skyscraper in downtown honolulu.

7. Visitors to oahu may not be interested in bishop street, the center of the financial district in downtown honolulu, but they are interested in the bronze statue of king kamehameha on king street.

8. Prospective college freshmen may be interested in the university of hawaii, located in manoa valley. The university offers degrees in botany, french, english, and many other fields.

9. The japanese attack on pearl harbor was responsible for the united states' entry into world war II.

10. Hawaii is a year-round resort, and the honolulu chamber of commerce hopes that the image of the carefree life will attract thousands of people.

● EXERCISE 5. List in order all words requiring capitals. When two capitalized words come together, list them together. Number your paper according to the numbers of the sentences.

1. Edmund is a senior at calhoun high school and expects to attend a university in the west next fall.

2. Every thursday the club meets at winthrop hall on chestnut street.

3. The painting was shipped from the louvre, a museum in paris, to the National art gallery in Washington, d.c.

4. Will the kiwanis club hold its halloween party in the Salisbury theater or at the herrick country club?

5. The hilton fife and drum corps will lead the parade down main street on memorial day.

6. The wilton memorial library is on the corner of fulton avenue and jefferson street, near a baptist church.

7. Last tuesday, march 8, I stayed after school for extra help in french and english; but I really should have stayed for help in geometry and social studies.

8. The century theater, located on Sheridan road just outside evansville, shows the latest pictures from hollywood as well as films from europe.

9. Every morning for breakfast, Hank has some danish pastry and a bowl of corn flakes.

10. Johnson & jackson, inc., buys most of its office supplies from Hillman's Supply company.

20d

● EXERCISE 6.   As you did in Exercise 3, list all words requiring capitals in the following sentences. Do not list words already capitalized.

1. Last fall Fred came to midville high school from a small town in the midwest. 2. On labor day his family said farewell to oak falls, indiana, and moved to wilson avenue in midville. 3. It wasn't easy to start his senior year in high school without knowing anybody, but if the Carter manufacturing company had sent his father to the shores of lake okeechobee in florida or to an indian reservation in wisconsin, Fred would have had to go along, of course.

4. Fred spent a day or so being interviewed by the guidance counselor in our school and was assigned to classes in french, intermediate algebra, social studies, physics, and english. 5. That's not exactly the easiest program in the world, but since he wants to go to the United States Military academy at west point, he needs to concentrate on math and science. 6. Although a member of the Varsity club showed Fred around school the first day, he ended up in latin class when he should have been in physics. 7. Now that he's been here a few months, he could take a member of the Midville Board of education on a tour and even give a declamation on the monument in memorial park that was built after world war I.

8. Fred was in for a surprise when he saw the peach trees behind the brentwood arena. 9. Fred is now thoroughly accustomed to suburban life, even though for him the spanish moss in baker park can never replace the oak and hickory forests of indiana.

20e. Capitalize titles.

(1) Capitalize the title of a person when it comes before a name.

EXAMPLES   General Eisenhower, Dr. Foster, President Adams

(2) Capitalize a title used alone or following a person's name only if it refers to a high official or someone to whom you wish to show special respect.

EXAMPLES   The President spoke from the White House. [When it refers to the highest official of the United States, *President* is always capitalized.]

Charles Evans Hughes, Chief Justice of the Supreme Court from 1930 to 1941, served during one of the most interesting periods of the Court's history. [The office of Chief Justice is a high one.]

Who is principal of your school?

Mr. Montgomery is president of the new firm.

The new traffic commissioner will be sworn in tomorrow.

Mrs. Deering, chief dietician for the city's junior high schools, has her office in Elm Street School.

◆ NOTE   When an official is directly addressed by his title, it is customary to capitalize it.

EXAMPLES   Do you intend, Captain, to lead your men?
Mr. Secretary, will you read the minutes?

(3) Capitalize words showing family relationship when used with a person's name but *not* when preceded by a possessive.

EXAMPLES   Grandfather Scott, Aunt Martha, Uncle Chet, my brother Arthur

◆ NOTE   When family-relationship words like *uncle*, *cousin*, and *grandfather* are customarily used before a name, capitalize them even after a possessive noun or pronoun.

EXAMPLES   My Grandfather Finch is going to retire to Florida next month.

Did you notice my Uncle Ned's picture in the paper? [You customarily call these men *Grandfather Finch* and *Uncle Ned*.]

My sister Claire graduates from high school next June. [You do not customarily call her *Sister Claire*.]

◆ NOTE   Words of family relationship may be capitalized or not when used *in place of* a person's name.

20e

EXAMPLES   Hello, Father. *or*   Hello, father.   [Father is used in place of the man's name.]

(4) Capitalize the first word and all important words in titles of books, periodicals, poems, stories, movies, paintings, and other works of art.

Unimportant words in a title are *a*, *an*, and *the* and short prepositions and conjunctions (usually those under five letters long).

EXAMPLES   *Harper's Bazaar* (magazine), Turner's *Crossing the Brook* (painting), *The Return of the Native* (novel), Treaty of Versailles, the Charter of the United Nations, the Talmud, "Under the Lion's Paw" (short story), "The Tuft of Flowers" (poem)

The words *a*, *an*, and *the* written before a title are capitalized only when they are part of the title. In a composition they are usually not capitalized before the names of magazines and newspapers.

EXAMPLES   *The Mayor of Casterbridge* (book), *A Nation of Sheep* (book)

Rob reads the *Times* and the *Reader's Digest*.

(5) Capitalize words referring to the Deity.

EXAMPLES   God, Father, His will

● EXERCISE 7.   List all words requiring capitals. Number your list according to the numbers of the sentences. Do not list words already capitalized.

1. One of el greco's finest paintings, *saint martin and the beggar*, is in the mellon collection in washington, d.c.

2. In the january edition of the *reader's digest*, my father read an article called "the crisis in u.s. transportation."

3. Mr. west, the chairman of the school music department, told us that a play produced on broadway in 1931 called *green grow the lilacs* was turned into the musical *oklahoma!*

4. My uncle joe enjoyed ellery queen's book *the chinese orange mystery* more than he did *the murderer is a fox*.

5. Last christmas aunt harriet, the family sculptress, gave my grandmother a statue called *the captive warrior;* but this statue will never be a serious threat to *the thinker* by rodin.

6. I enjoyed reading clarence day's *life with father*, and I particularly liked the chapter "father lets in the telephone."

7. Mr. commissioner, would you care to confirm the report that mayor douglas and senator giacomo have asked you to resign?

8. The president has invited protestant, catholic, and jewish leaders to a conference in the White House.

9. Bill Gomez, president of our high school's conservation club, introduced deputy inspector rogers of the new jersey fish and game commission.

10. In the school auditorium, while the principal introduced the winner of the american legion award, I spotted commissioner murphy, superintendent adams, and mayor digiorgio.

● REVIEW EXERCISE. List all words that should be capitalized. Number your list according to the numbers of the sentences.

1. Because I don't know a waltz from a tango and am not in the least ashamed of my ignorance, I refused to take lessons at the diane dance studio on maple avenue.

2. The gee cee rhythm band may not sound exactly like charlie barnett, but when they play "smoke gets in your eyes," our gym turns into the savoy plaza ballroom.

3. Twice a year, dr. carter, the dentist whose office is on butler street, reminds me to pay him a visit; and twice a year, I read old copies of the *national geographic* in his waiting room and hope that daily brushings with zing toothpaste have prevented any new cavities.

4. The *nina II*, a replica of christopher columbus' smallest ship, was towed to nassau from san salvador last tuesday.

5. After world war II thousands of veterans flocked to colleges and universities all over the country.

6. Whether you want japanese cultured pearls or norwegian skis, you will find these items at perkins & company's new store, located at the corner of twenty-first street and maple avenue.

7. In his last lecture in hadley hall, professor jennings said that man, from the dawn of history to the present, has always been able to laugh at himself.

8. Without looking up a copy of the declaration of independence, I cannot name five of the original signers; but I do know that the document was first signed at independence hall in philadelphia.

9. The president left the white house early and drove to the capitol to deliver his address to congress.

10. The lutheran minister who spoke at our christmas program reminded us to give thanks to god.

11. I enjoyed reading *to kill a mockingbird*, a novel about life in a small town in maycomb county, alabama.

12. *The harvesters* is a painting by pieter brueghel, a sixteenth-century artist.

13. One of the cities of the incas, machu picchu, lay hidden among the peaks of the andes in peru and was never discovered by the spanish conquerors.

14. Each year more than a million visitors flock to holland state park, a preserve on lake michigan, west of grand rapids.

15. Last saturday a fire, fanned by a brisk northwest wind, destroyed the meadtown lumber company.

16. Traffic along powell avenue had to be rerouted when a gray lincoln sedan rammed a truck.

17. Julie anderson, the president of her nursing class, joined the peace corps last july and is now working as a nurse in pakistan.

18. Because bruce took advanced courses in english, chemistry, and mathematics at washington high school in st. paul, minnesota, he had little difficulty with his freshman courses at duke university.

19. When my grandfather retires, he expects to spend his winters at sea island, georgia, and his summers at lake manota in the northern part of minnesota.

20. Between halves of the football game between lincoln high school and milbridge academy, the band marched down the east side of the field, played stirring marches composed by john philip sousa, and exited through the main gate.

Summary Style Sheet

NAMES OF PERSONS

Shirley, Shirley O'Neil	the girl next door
Mrs. William McAndrew, Jr.	a family friend

GEOGRAPHICAL NAMES

Carson City	a city in Nevada
Yosemite National Park	a national park
the San Mateo Mountains	a mountain in New Mexico
the Pacific Ocean	an ocean voyage
the Savannah River	the banks of a river
living in the South	the south side of town
the Caribbean Sea	a sea voyage
the Gaspé Peninsula	a long peninsula

ORGANIZATIONS, BUSINESS FIRMS AND PRODUCTS, INSTITUTIONS, GOVERNMENT BODIES

the Press Club	a club for writers
the Union Coal Company	a coal company
the Commodore Hotel	the newest hotel
Chevrolet	an automobile
Erasmus High School	a large high school
the Supreme Court of Nebraska	a Nebraska court

HISTORICAL EVENTS AND PERIODS, SPECIAL EVENTS, CALENDAR ITEMS

the French and Indian War	wars on the frontier
the Renaissance	the sixteenth century
Memorial Day	a day in May
the Junior Prom	a junior in high school
the Winter Carnival	in the winter

NATIONALITIES, RACES, RELIGIONS, LANGUAGES

Canadian	a nationality
Negro	a race
Lutheran	a religion
Spanish	a language

SHIPS, PLANES, TRAINS, MONUMENTS, AWARDS,
HEAVENLY BODIES, AND PARTICULAR PLACES,
THINGS, OR EVENTS

the Mary Deere	a schooner
the Orient Express	a train
the P-51 Mustang	a fighter plane
the Washington Monument	a monument in Washington, D.C.
Saturn and Venus	the sun, earth, and moon
the Congressional Medal of Honor	the highest award of the nation
Friendship VII	a space vehicle

TITLES

Mayor Winthrop	Mr. Winthrop, the mayor
the President, the Chief Justice (high government officials)	the president of the club a senator's duties
Praise God for His blessings	the gods of the ancient Greeks
Aunt Sarah	his aunt
Go with Grandfather.	my grandfather
A Tale of Two Cities	
"Ode on a Grecian Urn"	
"Smoke Gets in Your Eyes"	

CHAPTER 21

Punctuation

End Marks and Commas

The sole purpose of punctuation is to make clear the meaning of what you write. When you speak, the actual sound of your voice, the rhythmic rise and fall of your inflections, your pauses and hesitations, your stops to take breath—all supply a kind of "punctuation" which serves to group your words and to indicate to your listener precisely what you mean. Indeed, even the body takes part in this unwritten punctuation. A raised eyebrow may express interrogation more eloquently than any question mark, and a knuckle rapped on the table shows stronger feeling than an exclamation point.

In written English, however, where there are none of these hints to meaning, simple courtesy requires the writer to make up for the lack by careful punctuation. Examine the sentences below. If you heard them spoken, you would know exactly what was meant; but as they stand, with no punctuation to show where one thought ends and another begins, they are confusing.

Into the new washing machine she put the clothes and Mother then turned the water on.

The children munched happily on the various courses soup vegetables and meat salad rolls and butter pie and ice cream.

He settled wearily onto the first chair which was not strong enough to hold him.

437

Don't overpunctuate. A sentence that bristles with commas, colons, dashes, and brackets within parentheses doesn't need the services of a punctuation expert. It needs to be rewritten. Use a mark of punctuation for only two reasons: (1) because the meaning demands it, or (2) because conventional usage requires it. Otherwise do not use punctuation.

The rules for the correct use of end punctuation and commas are listed on the following pages. Learn the rules. Do the exercises. Read over carefully whatever you have written once or twice before handing it in, each time inserting whatever punctuation is necessary to make the writing clear and taking out those marks that are unnecessary. Above all, *apply what you learn about punctuation to everything you write.*

PERIODS, QUESTION MARKS, AND EXCLAMATION POINTS

21a. A statement is followed by a period.

EXAMPLES   Dad worked for years in Gary, Indiana.
From out of the cave came a low growl.
"Yes, I'll be there," Barbara said.

21b. A question is followed by a question mark.

EXAMPLES   Where are you going?
Who broke my record?
What did you say?

Sometimes the way in which a writer intends a sentence to be read determines whether it is a statement or a question.

STATEMENT   You mean you are not going.   [Read with falling inflection.]

QUESTION   You mean you are not going?   [Read with rising inflection.]

21c. An exclamation is followed by an exclamation point.

EXAMPLES What a fight!
How wonderful!
Whew, isn't it hot!

21d. An imperative sentence is followed by either a period or an exclamation point.

EXAMPLES Put the book down, please. [calmly]
Put the book down! [with strong feeling]

It is not hard to use the question mark and the exclamation point correctly. The sound of your own voice as you read your sentences under your breath gives you sufficient clues to where these marks go. It is much harder to know where to put the period. You can never be certain of this until you are certain of what a sentence is and where it ends. (Chapters 1–4 and Chapter 11 of this book should help you to recognize a sentence and therefore to know where to put the period.)

Perhaps the most common cause of end-mark errors, however, is simply carelessness. There is only one cure for this. Always take time to read over everything you write.

● EXERCISE 1.   In this exercise all end marks have been omitted. On your paper, write the final word of the sentence with the proper end mark, followed by the first word of the next sentence, if any.

EXAMPLE   1. Theodore Roosevelt, the twenty-sixth President of the United States, was attracted to the outdoor life afflicted with asthma and eye trouble as a child, he resolved to become physically strong to this end he spent years on a ranch in the West
    1. *life. Afflicted*
    strong. To
    West.

21
a-d

1. Chet was assigned a report on knighthood, and he undertook the assignment eagerly he knew from the stories he had read that knights were spotless champions of God and womanhood he knew also that a long apprenticeship preceded the honor of knighthood, and that young boys of the nobility entered upon this training as soon as they were able to wield a sword or draw a bow

2. When a lad completed his training as a page, he was promoted to the rank of squire in this capacity he accompanied his lord into battle, fighting at his side and caring for the knight's horse and equipment at long last the squire himself was deemed fit to become a knight he was accorded this honor, however, only after several honorable wounds and some show of gallantry on his part had impressed the sovereign with the lad's readiness to uphold the code of chivalry

3. When the sovereign considered him ready, a day was appointed for the ceremony how long had the youth waited for this glorious hour how many times had he rehearsed in his fancy every step in the stately ceremony now that it was at last at hand, he could scarcely believe his good fortune he resolved to comport himself always as a perfect knight—to bear true and faithful allegiance to his lord, to bow his head meekly before misfortune, to succor the weak, to chastise the unrighteous, and to be terrible and swift in answer to any insult offered to his honor

4. These things about knighthood Chet knew already as he entered the library and opened the encyclopedia what a surprise lay in store for him he found first of all that the chivalry of Europe arose from a simple economic circumstance the first chevaliers were those rich enough to afford horses *chevalier* in French and *Ritter* in German mean "knight," but these words also mean "rider" this fact suggests that the first knights were merely those Frankish warriors who rode into battle while their humbler fellows walked behind in the dust

5. When the cavalry of Charlemagne became the foremost military force in Europe, his way of ordering the forces was adopted by all other nations the class of soldiers composing the cavalry became, therefore, an elite class or an aristocracy

with special privileges but also with special obligations they were supported in peacetime, for example, by the labor of the rest of the population however, when the state was in danger, they were obliged to rally immediately underneath the royal standard and there to offer their courage, their property, and their lives to the royal cause

21e. An abbreviation is followed by a period.

EXAMPLES

Gen. General
Calif. California
A.D. *anno Domini*
Feb. February
oz. ounce
T. S. Eliot   Thomas Stearns Eliot

◆ NOTE   Abbreviations of government agencies are often written without periods.

FBI   Federal Bureau of Investigation
AEC   Atomic Energy Commission

Most abbreviations are capitalized only if the words they stand for are capitalized.

COMMAS

The comma is mainly used to group words that belong together and to separate those that do not. Some other uses of the comma are merely customary ways of punctuating sentences and have little to do with meaning.

Items in a Series

21f. Use commas to separate items in a series.

WORDS IN SERIES   The examination proctor distributed scrap paper, test booklets, blotters, and copies of the test. [nouns]
The cat spits, bites, scratches, and sheds. [verbs]

21
e-f

PHRASES IN SERIES   We have a government of the people, by the people, and for the people.

SUBORDINATE CLAUSES IN SERIES   I can go camping in Yellowstone National Park in June if my grades are high, if my mother gives her approval, and if my father has enough money.

♦ NOTE   When the last two items in a series are joined by *and*, you may omit the comma before the *and* if the comma is not necessary to make the meaning clear.

CLEAR   She washed, set and dried her hair.   [clear with comma omitted]

UNCLEAR   The following courses will be added next year: Physics II, Composition II, conversational French and French literature.   [Not clear with comma omitted. How many courses, three or four?]

CLEAR   The following courses will be added next year: Physics II, Composition II, conversational French, and French literature.

Some words appear so often paired with another that they may be set off in a series as one item.

EXAMPLES   bacon and eggs, pork and beans, bread and butter

(1) If all items in a series are joined by *and* or *or* (*nor*), you need not use commas to separate them.

EXAMPLES   We danced and sang and listened to records.

You may scrub the floor or polish the silverware or wash the dishes.

(2) Independent clauses in a series are usually separated by semicolons. Short independent clauses, however, may be separated by commas.

EXAMPLES   We played records, we danced, and we watched television.   [short clauses]

I finished my examination in forty minutes; I checked my answers carefully; and I handed my paper in to the proctor in the front of the room.

21g. Use a comma to separate two or more adjectives preceding a noun.

EXAMPLE Billy was an energetic, mischievous lad.

When the last adjective before the noun is thought of as part of the noun, the comma before the adjective is omitted.

EXAMPLE We found an old wooden chest in the attic.

Here the adjective *wooden* is so closely associated with the noun *chest* that the two words are considered a unit, a single word, or what is called a *compound noun*. Therefore, the adjective *old* modifies, not just *chest*, but *wooden chest* and is not to be separated from it by a comma.

To determine whether it is right to put commas between two adjectives in a series of adjectives modifying a noun, substitute the word *and* for the doubtful comma. If the *and* sounds wrong, then you don't need a comma.

PROBLEM A single electric bulb illuminated the long hallway. [comma before electric?]

USE <u>AND</u> A single and electric bulb illuminated the long hallway. [obviously wrong!]

SOLUTION A single electric bulb illuminated the long hallway. [no comma]

● EXERCISE 2. On your paper, copy each word after which a comma is needed and then add the comma. Some sentences will not need commas.

1. Abe Dick Gene and I played ice hockey last winter.
2. A picturesque old riding stable was torn down and replaced by a new macadam parking lot.
3. Give your money to the treasurer today tomorrow or Wednesday.
4. The dusty sore and weary hikers returned about 7 P.M.
5. We need a person who can sing dance and act.
6. Hank sharpened his pencil took out a clean sheet of paper made a few notes and finally started the first draft of his composition.

21g

7. Irving was a tall lean clean-shaven young man.
8. The conductor took my ticket punched it and handed me the stub as a receipt.
9. Neither wind nor rain nor sleet nor snow keeps the mailman from his appointed rounds.
10. The following people will report to the main office at the end of the period: Peter Stone Richard White Roger Gelder Terence Ward and Eric Robinson.
11. You can't eat drink and be merry when you are on a diet.
12. My hands were cold my feet were cold and my ears were cold.
13. In a bulky winter coat Norma was muffled against the strong March wind.
14. Beneath it she wore a blue summer dress.
15. For the outing she had washed her hair scrubbed her face pressed her dress and polished her shoes.
16. Mitch Miller's chorus sang songs from the thirties the forties and the fifties.
17. A tow-headed little boy in faded blue jeans emerged from the shrubbery to stare unwinkingly at the postman.
18. The postman came to an abrupt halt cleared his throat nervously and finally muttered, "Sorry, mister, no mail for you."
19. Sylvia is a fan of the great women novelists: Jane Austen the Brontë sisters Ellen Glasgow Willa Cather Elizabeth Bowen George Eliot and many others.
20. In the meadow were an amazing number of wild flowers: red and yellow columbines black-eyed Susans purple asters buttercups Indian paintbrush sweet peas pink wild roses Queen Anne's lace and tall tiger lilies.

● EXERCISE 3. Write five sentences, each sentence illustrating one of the following uses of the comma.

1. Two or more adjectives preceding a noun
2. Nouns in a series requiring a comma before the *and* between the last two items
3. Phrases in a series
4. Short independent clauses in a series
5. A sentence containing a series joined by conjunctions, requiring no commas

Comma Between Independent Clauses

21h. Use a comma before *and, but, or, nor, for,* and *yet* when they join independent clauses.

EXAMPLES Do your homework every day, and you certainly will pass the course.

There wasn't much to be done, but there wasn't much time in which to do it.

◆ NOTE Independent clauses joined by *and, but, or,* or *nor* need not be separated by a comma when they are very short. If the clauses are joined by the conjunctions *yet* or *for*, they must be separated by a comma.

EXAMPLES We knocked and Jed opened the door. [Clauses are too short to require commas.]

Laura pulled hard, yet the lid stayed on the jar. [Clauses are short but are separated by the conjunction *yet*. Therefore, a comma is required.]

I remained there, for Jim hadn't come. [Comma is needed because clauses are joined by *for*.]

Do not be misled by compound verbs, which often make a sentence look as though it contained two independent clauses.

SIMPLE SENTENCE Russ took the makeup examination and passed it with ease. [one independent clause with a compound verb]

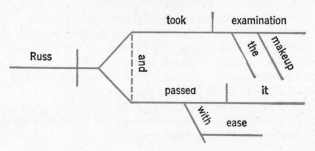

21h

TWO CLAUSES   Russ took the makeup examination, and he
passed it with ease.   [two independent clauses]

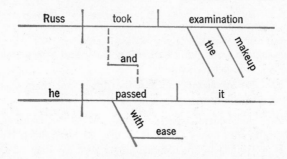

● EXERCISE 4.   The sentences in this exercise contain independent clauses joined by the conjunctions *and, but, or,
for, nor,* or *yet.* Number your paper 1–15. Decide where
the commas should go, and write on your paper after the
proper number the word preceding each comma. Add the
comma and the conjunction following it. Do not be misled
by compound verbs.

EXAMPLE   1. Shields tossed the ball neatly into the basket and
the crowd went wild with excitement.
1. *basket, and*

1. I was assigned a term paper about clipper ships and I went
to the library to do the research.
2. I didn't have any trouble obtaining books for nobody else
in my class was assigned a paper on this topic.
3. Clipper ships didn't interest Vic and Marcia was more concerned with the philosophy of Emerson and Thoreau.
4. We haunted the library for days yet the librarian never be-
trayed the slightest sign of impatience and was always ready
to help us find a needed book.
5. Our papers must have reflected much time and planning or
Mr. Hagen would not have given us such high grades.
6. Clipper ships were developed by U.S. shipbuilders during the
first half of the nineteenth century yet by the end of the
century they had become obsolete.

7. Nobody knows where the expression *clipper ship* originated but the expression "going at a fast clip" may be partly responsible for the name.

8. The *Ann McKim*, the first large clipper ship, was built in Maryland in 1833 but smaller ships of similar design had been built previously.

9. The discovery of gold in California swelled the demand for fast ocean travel and within four years 160 new clipper ships slipped down the ways to join the trade.

10. Americans wanted speed and they got it.

11. The building of clipper ships wasn't confined to America for many fine clippers were built in British shipyards.

12. Clippers were swift and easily manageable yet they were soon outmoded by steamships.

13. The steamships were built very differently from the clippers and they could carry a great deal more cargo.

14. The clippers had been sturdily constructed of oak and expensive hardwoods but trim and narrow hulls had left little space for cargo.

15. The development of steamships and the opening of the Suez Canal drove the clippers out of existence but even today these ships are famous for their grace and beauty.

● EXERCISE 5. Write six compound sentences each illustrating the use of a different one of the following six conjunctions to join independent clauses: *and, or, but, nor, for,* and *yet.* Punctuate your sentences correctly.

21i. Use a comma to set off nonessential clauses and nonessential participial phrases.

A nonessential[1] clause is a subordinate clause that is not essential to the meaning of the sentence. Such clauses serve only to add some extra information or to explain something further; they could be omitted without altering the fundamental meaning of the sentence. An essential[2] clause,

---

[1] A nonessential clause is sometimes called a nonrestrictive clause.
[2] An essential clause is sometimes called a restrictive clause.

21i

on the other hand, is one that cannot be omitted without changing the meaning of the sentence.

NONESSENTIAL   Robert Brill, **who lives across the street,** graduated from Mepham High School three years ago.

Since you know without the clause who it was that graduated from Mepham High School three years ago, the clause is not necessary to identify Robert Brill. It merely adds information about him. It is a nonessential clause and should be set off by commas. *Most adjective clauses which modify proper nouns are nonessential and require commas.*

ESSENTIAL   All boys **that march with the honor guard** are required to be over six feet tall.

The clause *that march with the honor guard* is essential because it tells which boys are required to be over six feet tall. Omitting the clause would change the meaning of the sentence into something absurd. Since the clause is an integral, or essential, part of the sentence, it is not set off by commas. (Adjective clauses introduced by *that* are almost always essential.)

EXAMPLES   The boy **whom we saw last week** drives the delivery truck for the florist. [essential]

Keith Barton, **whom we saw last week,** drives the delivery truck for the florist. [nonessential]

The bold sea raider **who helped destroy the Spanish Armada** was Sir Francis Drake. [essential]

Sir Francis Drake, **who was a bold sea raider,** helped destroy the Spanish Armada. [nonessential]

A magazine **that has good news coverage** helps me in social studies. [essential]

Life, **which has good news coverage,** helps me in social studies. [nonessential]

The subject **that I like best** is biology. [essential]

Biology, **which I like best,** will be my major in college. [nonessential]

Sometimes the writer of a sentence is the only one who knows whether the clause he uses is nonessential (commas) or essential (no commas). Accordingly, he will either make use of commas to enclose the clause or abstain from their use in order to make his meaning clear.

NONESSENTIAL   My uncle, **who lives in Mississippi,** sent me a check for my birthday. [The clause is not needed to identify this uncle. Since it is nonessential, it requires commas.]

ESSENTIAL   My uncle **who lives in Mississippi** sent me a check for my birthday. [I have several uncles. The clause is necessary to tell which uncle I am talking about. It should not be set off by commas.]

The same principles govern participial phrases. You will remember that participles are of two kinds: present participles ending in *–ing* and past participles ending usually in *–ed.* A participial phrase is a group of words in which a participle is the chief word. When such a phrase is nonessential—not necessary to the sentence—the phrase is set off by commas. When it is essential, no commas are used.

NONESSENTIAL   Arlene, **picking her way carefully along the icy sidewalk,** slipped when she reached the corner.

ESSENTIAL   The woman **picking her way along the sidewalk** is Arlene.

NONESSENTIAL   Carla and I, **dressed as Minnie and Mickey Mouse,** won first prize at the party.

ESSENTIAL   The two students **dressed as Minnie and Mickey Mouse** won the first prize.

● EXERCISE 6.   After the proper number, write all words in the sentence that should be followed by a comma. Write the comma after each word. Be prepared to explain your answers. Some sentences do not need commas.

1. The hat that I fashioned out of the raccoon pelt made me look like Daniel Boone.
2. Nobody recognized the boy wearing the gray jacket.

3. The Taj Mahal which is one of the most beautiful buildings in the world was built by Shah Jahan.

4. Will the students who ride the bus be sure to have their bus passes with them?

5. Their first trip which was in June lasted three weeks.

6. Any student making a perfect score on the preliminary test will be excused from taking the final test.

7. People who get seasick are not fond of ocean travel.

8. Louis Sullivan who designed some of America's first skyscrapers was an imaginative and influential architect.

9. My youngest brother enraged me by tracking mud all over the floor that I had just scrubbed.

10. A man who enjoys winter sports might not be happy in Florida.

11. A letter that is sent by airmail between Chicago and New York may arrive no faster than a letter sent by regular mail.

12. Lou who is unable to learn even the simplest dance steps is a master of fancy footwork on the basketball court.

13. Many people are startled by the ferocious growls that issue from our tiny Pekingese.

14. Carolyn Baker who is a honey-blonde is the most attractive girl I know.

15. Many people who do not wear glasses should wear them or get contact lenses.

16. My closest friends who should know better think I am bright.

17. All students submitting late papers will be penalized ten points.

18. Marty and Dot submitting late papers to Mr. Johnson were surprised to find their marks reduced by ten points.

19. Our math teacher who is also the wrestling coach never has any discipline problems.

20. The houses that are built by the Bennet Company are in great demand.

● EXERCISE 7. Write two sentences containing nonessential clauses, two containing essential clauses, two containing nonessential phrases, and two containing essential phrases. Label each sentence according to the kind of phrase or clause it contains.

Introductory Elements

21j. Use a comma after certain introductory elements.

(1) Use a comma after words such as *well, yes, no, why,* **etc., when they begin a sentence. Exclamations like** *wow, good grief, gee whiz,* **etc., if not followed by an exclamation mark, must also be set off by commas.**

EXAMPLES No, you can't go.
Well, I've heard that story before.
Why, he isn't old enough to drive!
Wow, this pavement is hot!

(2) Use a comma after an introductory participial phrase.

EXAMPLES **Looking at the clothes in her closet,** Liz heaved a sigh of boredom.

Determined to get along with what she had, she decided to wear her blue silk dress again.

(3) Use a comma after a succession of introductory prepositional phrases.

EXAMPLE **At the next tick of the clock,** you may start the examination. [Two prepositional phrases precede the comma.]

A single introductory prepositional phrase does not usually require a comma unless the comma is necessary to make the meaning of the sentence clear.

EXAMPLES **At dawn** the Indians attacked.
In our library, books are arranged according to the Dewey decimal system. [The comma is needed so that the reader does not read "our library books."]

(4) Use a comma after an introductory adverb clause.

An introductory adverb clause is a subordinate clause preceding an independent clause.

21j

EXAMPLES **Whenever a partridge flushes from beneath my feet,**
I am so startled I fire wildly.

If I shoot the bird on the ground, I feel ashamed.

Aunt Florence roasted the birds; and **when all of us
sat down to supper,** she served them with dumplings
and gravy.

● EXERCISE 8. The sentences in this exercise contain
introductory clauses and phrases. Decide where a comma
should be used. Copy on your paper the word preceding
each comma, and place the comma after it. Number your
answers to accord with the numbers of the sentences.

EXAMPLE 1. With a few flips of the dial Claire focused the
picture.
1. *dial,*

1. When the newspapers and magazines commented about the
severity of the winter over the entire Northern Hemisphere
we knew that the Arctic weather was here to stay.
2. After the temperature had hovered around zero for days a
forecast of more snow and continued cold added little joy
to the lives of millions of shivering people.
3. Since rivers and harbors from London to Tokyo were choked
with ice many maritime industries had come to a standstill.
4. While storms howled incessantly people complained about
the wind, snow, and cold.
5. Although specialists in weather explained that erratic jet
streams of air from the Arctic caused the misery this news
did not alleviate any of the suffering.
6. While the jet streams from the Pacific normally do curve
up into Canada nobody expected them to plunge into the
Arctic and then to bring down such bitter cold to our
normally temperate land.
7. By some strange freak of nature twenty inches of snow fell
in sunny Sicily.
8. In parts of the western United States ski resorts suffered because of the lack of snow.
9. In some parts of Japan it snowed for the first time in forty-
three years.

10. Swamped by demands London coal dealers were unable to deliver enough fuel to their shivering customers; and at the last report from England Londoners were carting coal home in whatever conveyance was handy.

11. Isolated by huge accumulations of snow many towns in the United States waited for snow plows to connect them again with the outer world.

12. Basking in the relative warmth of fourteen-degree weather Moscow could boast that its temperatures were higher than those in Atlanta, Georgia.

13. To the people in Georgia zero weather was unfamiliar and unwelcome.

14. For many people in Canada spring never arrived.

● REVIEW EXERCISE A.   This exercise covers all uses of the comma that you have studied so far. Decide where commas should be used in these sentences. Copy on your paper the word preceding the comma. Place the comma after the word. Number your answers according to the numbers of the sentences.

EXAMPLE   1. When the famous painting was exhibited in the museum thousands flocked to see it.
　　　　　1. *museum,*

1. Hal Barnes who won varsity letters in football basketball and track is also an excellent tennis player.

2. Before you begin to type the letter be sure you have made the proper margin adjustments.

3. Whenever the phone rings my sister hoping for a call from one of her boyfriends breaks track records in her haste to answer it.

4. Advancing across the room in her high heels Joanne clung to her escort's arm.

5. Nobody in the family is ever very eager to clear the table do the dishes or walk the dog.

6. Although Lynn insists that she eats like a bird very few birds could pack away that much food and still fly.

7. Since the roads were very icy motorists were urged to stay home.

8. The magazine always arrives on time but it usually arrives in a disheveled condition.

9. Although the plumber had made some temporary repairs to the furnace the noises issuing from the cellar did not reassure us.

10. The men had been working day and night yet they responded immediately to our emergency call.

11. If you need a new pen you can always buy one from the Student Store.

12. Whenever Dad starts working on his income tax we tiptoe around the house and try to stay out of sight.

13. After the judge had banged the gavel for order the noise in the courtroom subsided.

14. Father wants to go to the North Woods but the rest of us would prefer a vacation at the shore.

15. When I remember those long cool quiet summer evenings at the lake I become sentimental.

16. Well social studies isn't a hard course but it does require a lot of reading and writing and memorizing.

17. Throwing caution to the winds the cat leaped on Mother's new chair but our shouts persuaded him to beat a hasty retreat.

18. Yes a few students thinking they could get away with it skipped assembly.

19. In the first game of the doubleheader both teams used four pitchers five outfielders and five infielders.

20. Midge kissed her mother and her boyfriend stood to one side waiting to be introduced.

21k. Use commas to set off expressions that interrupt.

There are three kinds of "interrupters" which you should be able to recognize and punctuate properly.

(1) Appositives and appositive phrases are usually set off by commas.

An appositive is a word or group of words which follows a noun or pronoun and means the same thing as the noun or pronoun. An appositive usually identifies or explains the noun or pronoun that precedes it.

EXAMPLES   Coyotes, canny **cousins** of the wolf, are a plague to sheepmen.

The Aegean Sea, the **highroad** of ancient Greece, is sprinkled with small islands.

I lost my watch, a **present** from my grandfather.

In these sentences *cousins, highroad,* and *present* are appositives.

When you set off an appositive, you include with it all the words which modify it. An appositive, together with its modifiers, is an appositive phrase.

EXAMPLES   Julio Falabella**, a rancher near Buenos Aires,** raises miniature horses that are only thirty-six inches high at maturity.

I enjoyed *At Home in India***, a book by Cynthia Bowles.**

An attractive girl, Jennifer O'Neill was the Junior Prom Queen.

Sometimes an appositive is so closely related to the word preceding it that it should not be set off by commas. Such an appositive is called a "restrictive appositive." It is usually a single word.

EXAMPLES   my sister **Gail**
the sculptor **Michelangelo**
my old dog **Gypsy**
Edward **the Confessor**

● EXERCISE 9.   Copy the following sentences containing appositives, inserting commas where needed.

1. The *Mona Lisa* a painting by Leonardo da Vinci is a prize possession of the Louvre.
2. The painting a portrait of a young Florentine woman is slightly cracked from temperature changes.
3. In 1911 an Italian house painter Vincenzo Perugia stole the painting from its frame.

21k

4. For two years the Paris police some of the cleverest men in the world were baffled by the crime.
5. Since its recovery the painting one of the most valuable portraits in the world has been protected carefully.

(2) Words used in direct address are set off by commas.

EXAMPLES **Ben,** shut the window.
Yes, **Virginia,** there is a Santa Claus.
Won't you run for office, **Mr. Perkins?**

(3) Parenthetical expressions are set off by commas.

These expressions are often used parenthetically: *I believe* (*think, suppose, hope,* etc.), *on the contrary, on the other hand, of course, in my opinion, for example, however, to tell the truth, nevertheless, in fact.*

EXAMPLES The movie, **in my opinion,** was terrible.
The book, **on the other hand,** was excellent.

These expressions are not *always* used as interrupters.

EXAMPLES He promised **to tell the truth.** [not used as an interrupter]

I don't remember, **to tell the truth,** what he was talking about. [used as an interrupter]

I think Bart was elected. [not used as an interrupter]

Bart, **I think,** was elected. [used as an interrupter]

◆ NOTE A contrasting expression introduced by *not* is parenthetical and must be set off by commas.

EXAMPLE Samuel Johnson, **not James Boswell,** was called the literary dictator of the eighteenth century.

● EXERCISE 10. Number your paper 1–10. Copy after the proper number the words in each sentence that should be followed by a comma, placing a comma after each word.

1. One of my brother's friends a sergeant in the army is stationed at Ft. Riley, Kansas.
2. No Neil your answer I'm sorry to say isn't correct.

3. Once I had given my oral report an analysis of Julius Caesar's personality my legs stopped shaking.
4. Why you certainly must know Charlie Steubens the president of the Student Council.
5. To come right to the point Mr. Harken we don't like the design of the class rings.
6. Of course Betsy I knew the report was due Friday.
7. Yes it was Esther I think who was elected secretary.
8. When school ends however I feel as if Mr. Herner the principal had given us all a parole.
9. No that was I am sure a case of mistaken identity.
10. Brian old fellow you haven't even begun to work.

211. Use a comma in certain conventional situations.

(1) Use a comma to separate items in dates and addresses.

In addresses the street number and the name of the street are not separated from each other by a comma. Neither are the name of the city and the postal zone nor the name of the state and the ZIP code number which follows it. Similarly, in dates the day of the month and the month itself are considered one item. Commas do go between the date and the year and the city and the state.

EXAMPLES On June 30, 1963, my father's business moved to 837 Main Street, Seattle, Washington 98104.

Send your check or money order to Richard Stevenson, 981 Dartmouth Street, Newport News, Virginia 23602.

Our trip last summer to Tucson, Arizona, was most enjoyable.

On Wednesday, January 20, I shall be sixteen years old.

Our address is 718 Alvern Street, Los Angeles, California 90045.

211

As you can see from the last example, the use of the ZIP (Zoning Improvement Plan) number makes the use of the postal zone number unnecessary, for the latter is incorporated into the ZIP code number.

(2) Use a comma after the salutation of a friendly letter and after the closing of any letter.

EXAMPLES   Dear Roy,   Dear Aunt Martha,
            Affectionately yours,   Sincerely yours,
            Yours truly,

(3) Use a comma after a name followed by *Jr., Sr., Ph.D.*, etc.

EXAMPLES   Mrs. Juanita Montez, Ph.D.
            John Q. Adams, Jr.
            Joseph Scarlatti, M.D.

21m. Do not use unnecessary commas.

Too much punctuation is a greater impediment to easy reading than too little. Do not use a comma unless a rule specifically calls for it or unless the sentence would be unclear without it. When in doubt, leave it out.

● EXERCISE 11.   Number your paper 1–10. Copy after the proper number the words in each sentence that should be followed by a comma, placing a comma after each word.

1. We drove one hundred miles to visit my cousin at 418 Glendale Street Dayton Ohio.
2. On June 27 1972 the firm moved from 44 Rush Drive to a new building on Center Street.
3. We flew to Seattle Washington on September 9 1973 and flew back on October 9 1973.
4. Our friends sold their home at 237 Liberty Avenue Glens Falls New York and rented an apartment at 19 Circle Drive New York New York 10010.
5. The building at 29 Victory Drive Butte Montana was destroyed by an explosion on August 10 1970.

6. Address your letters to Mr. John Billings Jr. 18 Third Avenue San Francisco California 94118.
7. The letter from J. D. Harriman 16 Melbourne Road Seattle Washington 98177 was dated January 28 1973 but did not arrive until February 15 1973.
8. After baking Lily gave her brother Jimmie a piece of fresh bread.
9. To tell the truth Jeanne's resolution was prompted by the fear of being caught in an embarrassing white lie.
10. After the mutiny Captain Bligh the tyrannical master of the *Bounty* was put adrift in a boat with those of the crew who had remained loyal to him.

● REVIEW EXERCISE B. Number your paper 1–12. After the proper number, rewrite the sentence, inserting commas where necessary. Do not use unnecessary commas.

1. Last Tuesday we learned about the Pharos at Alexandria one of the wonders of the ancient world. It was I believe one of the largest lighthouses ever built.
2. The lighthouse situated on an island two hundred yards from the mainland was one of the tallest buildings of its time.
3. The rulers of Alexandria then one of the most powerful cities in the world built the lighthouse at the entrance of the city's harbor.
4. This magnificent lighthouse built entirely of marble stood for sixteen hundred years.
5. The Pharos a blocklike structure contained a military barracks at its base. Its huge lamp which was fueled by wood or oil cast a powerful beam far away into the night.
6. Donkeys carried a daily supply of fuel up the broad ramps that rose at an easy grade from one story to another. These animals so we are told often carried visitors who were anxious to view the huge beacon.
7. In the fourteenth century an earthquake destroyed the lighthouse.
8. Archaeologists tell us that traces of the lighthouse remained for centuries; but we could not I suppose reasonably expect to see signs of the ancient ruin today.

21m

9. Yes Pat today there is a lighthouse at Alexandria.

10. The city itself as its name suggests was founded by Alexander the Great in 332 B.C.

11. The Heptastadium a mile-long mole connecting the island of the Pharos to the mainland provided a way of escape for Caesar when after the Battle of Pharsalia he was driven out of the city by the mob.

12. Alexandria became a great and prosperous city rivaling Rome itself in magnificence and far surpassing it as a center for learning.

● REVIEW EXERCISE C. Select from the following sentences all words which should be followed by a comma. List these words on your paper, placing a comma after each. Number your answers according to the numbers of the sentences.

EXAMPLE   1. We all of course make mistakes once in a while.
1. *all, course,*

1. Yes as a matter of fact Ray does have a cold.

2. As the season progressed the team piled up one victory after another.

3. Miss Barrett send this letter to the Allied Chemical Corporation 61 Broadway New York New York   10006.

4. We watched the parade for an hour but couldn't decide which one of the floats was the best for they all looked beautiful to us.

5. Take the garbage out Todd and be sure to put the cover back on the pail.

6. Alan Bev and Martin served as ushers at the graduation exercises last year.

7. On June 6 1965 we closed the doors of our house at 16 Washington Street St. Paul; and on June 8 1965 we opened the doors of our new home in Durham North Carolina.

8. As soon as we heard the crunch of the tires on the gravel in the driveway we rushed out to inspect Dad's new car a Pontiac station wagon.

9. Although it was four years old the car had been very well cared for by its former owner a seventy-year-old lady.

10. That at least was the story the salesman told.

Summary of the Uses of the Comma

21f. Use commas to separate items in a series.
  (1) If all items in a series are joined by <u>and</u> or <u>or</u> (<u>nor</u>), do not use commas to separate them.
  (2) Independent clauses in a series are usually separated by semicolons. Short independent clauses may be separated by commas.

21g. Use commas to separate two or more adjectives preceding a noun.

21h. Use commas before <u>and</u>, <u>but</u>, <u>or</u>, <u>nor</u>, <u>for</u>, and <u>yet</u> when they join independent clauses.

21i. Use commas to set off nonessential clauses and nonessential phrases.

21j. Use commas after certain introductory elements.
  (1) Use a comma after such words as <u>well</u>, <u>yes</u>, <u>no</u>, <u>why</u>, etc., when they begin a sentence.
  (2) Use a comma after an introductory participial phrase.
  (3) Use a comma after a succession of introductory prepositional phrases.
  (4) Use a comma after an introductory adverb clause.

21k. Use commas to set off expressions that interrupt the sentence.
  (1) Appositives and appositive phrases are usually set off by commas.
  (2) Words used in direct address are set off by commas.
  (3) Parenthetical expressions are set off by commas.

21 l. Use commas in certain conventional situations.
  (1) Use a comma to separate items in dates and addresses.
  (2) Use a comma after the salutation of a friendly letter and after the closing of any letter.
  (3) Use a comma after a name followed by <u>Jr.</u>, <u>Sr.</u>, <u>Ph.D.</u>, etc.

21m. Do not use unnecessary commas.

● Review exercise D. Copy after the proper number the words in each sentence that should be followed by a comma, placing a comma after each word.

1. Whenever Vinnie watches Laurel and Hardy he doubles up with laughter.

2. In past years Broadway has exported a number of hit plays and musicals to London. This year strangely enough many shows are playing on Broadway that originated on the other side of the Atlantic.

3. As knives forks and spoons clattered to the floor Mother darted from the living room to see what had happened in the kitchen.

4. Dad who was discharged from the Army on January 30 1946 celebrates his release from the service each year by trying to squeeze into his old uniform.

5. My brother Mark is in his own opinion a genius in science. The teachers oddly enough do not share his opinion about his scientific aptitude.

6. "Walt for pity's sake," Mother shouted, "turn down the television sound or the neighbors will be banging on the walls again!"

7. "Yes Ruth Uncle Charles is a professor of English literature at Hofstra University, which is in Hempstead New York," said my father.

8. We intend to stay in Portland Oregon from Monday June 2 to Saturday June 7.

9. Broiled on the new grate the steak looked and smelled delicious.

10. An athlete who breaks the coach's training rules soon slips from the peak of condition a lapse which is hardly fair to the rest of the team.

11. Aristophanes whom the ancient Greeks considered the greatest of comic dramatists wrote *The Clouds* and *The Frogs*.

12. Sophocles often regarded as the greatest dramatist of all times is credited with almost a hundred plays of which only eight have been recovered.

13. Although the play was acclaimed by the critics the public did not like it and refused therefore to recommend it to their friends.

14. Leaning over the ship's rail Mel the cabin boy idly watched the flying fish disport themselves among the waves

15. Of course if you find it impossible to attend the Student Council meeting Anita who was elected an alternate delegate will take your place.

● REVIEW EXERCISE E. *End Marks and Commas* Copy the following sentences, inserting end marks and commas as needed. Remember to capitalize the first word of any sentence.

1. What else I wondered could possibly happen

2. Buzzy the cook on our camping trip liked ham and eggs every day; therefore we had no choice about what we would have for breakfast

3. Arnie rose to his feet was recognized by the chairman and asked what had happened to the treasury

4. Why Karen how beautiful you look in your new dress

5. On Friday April 10 the sophomores will have a special assembly program on Monday April 13 the juniors will I understand report to the gym for a class meeting

6. Despite a losing streak of seven games Mr. Miles the baseball coach thought we had a good chance of winning the next game

7. At the barbecue Vivian served a green salad baked potatoes hamburgers and rolls and berry pie

8. Flo who is supposed to be on a diet had second helpings of rolls and pie and ice cream

9. The old gypsy who read my palm at the fair in St Cloud Florida said that I would be taking a journey I never suspected however that it would turn out to be a trip to the principal's office

10. If you have some writing ability if you are willing to work and if you are interested in the school paper the staff of the *Echo* can use you

11. Of course I don't know a thing about wiring but if somebody would teach me I could learn

12. James Boswell wrote a long detailed biography of Dr. Samuel Johnson an outstanding author critic and conversationalist of the eighteenth century

13. If you can't sing or dance or act you can make yourself useful by selling tickets to the play
14. When Louise had collected her prize a lovely alligator handbag she and Maria departed quickly for 670 Church Avenue Lake Forest Illinois their home
15. Imprisoned without warning or explanation the two reporters were held if I remember correctly for two months in spite of the efforts by England France and the United States to effect their release

CHAPTER 22

Punctuation

Semicolons and Colons

THE SEMICOLON

The semicolon [;] is a very useful mark of punctuation. It says to the reader, "Pause here a little longer than you do for a comma, but not so long as you do for a period."

22a. Use a semicolon between independent clauses in a sentence if they are not joined by *and, but, or, nor, for, yet.*

EXAMPLES   The President was concerned about the international situation; he called a special meeting of his Cabinet.

Arthur Murray must have struggled to teach Floyd dancing; I've never known a clumsier boy.

When the thoughts of the clauses are *very closely connected*, a semicolon is better than a period.

22b. Use a semicolon between independent clauses joined by such words as *for example, for instance, that is, besides, accordingly, moreover, nevertheless, furthermore, otherwise, therefore, however, consequently, instead, hence.*

EXAMPLES   We waited in line for an hour; **however,** the movie was exciting and well worth the wait.

22
a - b

465

Winnie dresses strangely; **for example,** today she wore riding boots to school.

Wayne does not want to be president; **furthermore,** he refuses to take any part in the nominations.

The principal was a fine speaker; **therefore** he was often invited to address civic groups.

When the connectives mentioned in this rule are placed at the beginning of a clause, the use of a comma after them is frequently a matter of taste. When they are clearly parenthetical (interrupters) they are followed by a comma. The words *for example, for instance,* and *that is* are always followed by a comma. The word *however* is usually followed by a comma.

22c. A semicolon (rather than a comma) may be needed to separate the independent clauses of a compound sentence if there are commas within the clauses.

EXAMPLES   My parents bought our home ten years ago, but now they have decided to sell it. [A comma between the clauses is sufficient.]

My parents bought our home, a modified Cape Cod cottage, ten years ago; but since they now need more room, they have decided to sell it. [Additional commas make the semicolon preferable.]

22d. Use a semicolon between items in a series if the items contain commas.

EXAMPLES   The volcano has erupted three times: January 2, 1610; March 15, 1823; and May 8, 1945.

The meeting was called by Jim Cusco, president of the senior class; Nancy Blake, president of the junior class; and Marvin Celler, president of the sophomore class.

● EXERCISE 1. List on your paper (in the order in which they appear in the sentences below) all words you think should be followed by a semicolon or a comma. After each word, place the mark of punctuation you decide on. Number your list by sentences, keeping the words from each sentence together.

1. The scientific names of animals are often informative for example *Procyon lotor*, the scientific name for the raccoon, names two traits of the animal.

2. *Lotor*, which means "washer," refers to the raccoon's habit of dunking his food in water and *procyon*, which means "before the dog," indicates that the animal is a favorite quarry for hunters and their hounds.

3. Weighing about twenty-five pounds at maturity, the raccoon looks like a little bear indeed, "little bear" is precisely what the Indians call him.

4. The raccoon is usually a nocturnal animal that is, he begins to prowl for food at sundown and hunts only at night.

5. If the suburbs encroach upon the ponds and streams where he finds food, he rapidly adjusts to the changed environment for instance, he will make his home in attics, boathouses, and garages when he cannot find other lodgings to suit him.

6. His preferred diet consists of crayfish, frogs, mice, birds' eggs, fruit, and corn however, when these are in short supply, he will not hesitate to raid garbage cans and hen houses.

7. Raccoon fur coats, once very popular, have gone out of style consequently, the raccoon population has increased greatly in recent years.

8. Baby raccoons make excellent pets they are easily tamed and rarely bite or scratch.

9. Older animals are usually surly and ill-tempered accordingly it is very unwise to attempt to pet a grown raccoon.

10. The raccoon's front paws are marvelously dexterous in fact, his tracks along the muddy banks of streams look exactly like the prints of a baby's hands.

11. Raccoons are smart otters, on the other hand, are even smarter.

12. Most wild animals are very businesslike their search for food is almost incessant, interrupted only by the need to sleep.

22
c-d

13. Otters, on the contrary, do not spend all their waking hours hunting for food instead, they prefer to spend most of their time amusing themselves.
14. Unlike raccoons, otters detest civilization therefore, they are very rarely seen except in the deep woods.
15. Bill has seen them on only three occasions: on a fishing trip to Port Kent, Maine on a vacation trip to the Okefenokee Swamp in Georgia and on a canoe trip through Superior National Forest, Minnesota.
16. On the last occasion Bill had an odd assortment of gear in the canoe: a feather-light nylon sleeping bag a Hudson's Bay ax three new, valuable fishing rods a map case and compass a brass-bound grub box and a newly bought, expensive gasoline stove.
17. When a large otter surfaced suddenly in the water beside the canoe, Bill was so startled he upset the canoe luckily the water was shallow and none of his gear was lost.
18. Otters build long mud slides along the banks of streams then, having polished the slides to a perfect slickness, whole families of otters gather and pass the day in wild merriment.

THE COLON

The usual purpose of the colon is to call the reader's attention to what comes next. A colon means "notice the following."

22e. Use a colon to mean "note what follows."

Use a colon before a list of items, especially after expressions like *as follows* or *the following*.

EXAMPLES   We visited four states last year: Nevada, Idaho, Montana, and Colorado.

My little brother's vocabulary is limited to four words: "no," "daddy," "out," and "scram."

For the camping trip Fred bought the following: a two-burner stove, a lantern, an ax, and a new tackle box.

◆ NOTE   When a list comes immediately after a verb or preposition, do not use a colon.

WRONG   In the zoo can be seen: an Indian elephant, two giraffes, four gnus, and a rare Himalayan snow leopard.

RIGHT   In the zoo can be seen an Indian elephant, two giraffes, four gnus, and a rare Himalayan snow leopard. [The list follows the verb *can be seen.*]

RIGHT   Most interesting to me were the sea lions, the pandas, the chimpanzees, and the snakes.

RIGHT   Letters of congratulation came from relatives, friends, business associates, and government officials.

22f. Use a colon before a long, formal statement or quotation.

EXAMPLE   Thomas Paine's first pamphlet in the series *The American Crisis* starts with these famous words: "These are the times that try men's souls. The summer soldier and the sunshine patriot will, in this crisis, shrink from the service of their country; but he that stands it *now* deserves the love and thanks of man and woman." [1]

22g. Use a colon in certain conventional situations.

(1) Use a colon between the hour and the minute when you are writing the time.

EXAMPLES   8:45 P.M.
3:07 this afternoon

(2) Use a colon between chapter and verse in referring to passages from the Bible.

EXAMPLES   Proverbs 15:3
Romans 2:11

[1] For further discussion of the use of long quotations in a composition, see pages 474–75.

22
e-g

(3) Use a colon after the salutation of a business letter.

EXAMPLES   Dear Mr. Raymond:
Dear Sir:

Use a comma after the salutation of a friendly letter.

EXAMPLE   Dearest Janice,

● EXERCISE 2.   Decide where colons should be used in the following sentences. On your paper, write the word preceding the colon, then add the colon. If a sentence needs no colon, write *C* for correct after its number. Be able to explain your answers.

1. Mr. Bryant wanted a report on one of the following men Thomas Paine, Alexander Hamilton, Benjamin Franklin, or Thomas Jefferson.
2. Look, Randy, if you want to do well in her class, take my advice hand in your homework on time, take notes, pay attention, and keep quiet.
3. The following students will report to the principal at the end of the first period Anna Crossan, Nelson Finn, Mary Aspland, and Steven Shaw.
4. The performance was scheduled to start at 8 10, but technical difficulties held up the opening until 8 45.
5. At the picnic everybody enjoyed the french fries, the potato salad, the corn, and the hamburgers.
6. The story of Moses and the Pharoah's daughter is told in Exodus 2 5-10.
7. The president of the Student Council opened the special meeting with these words "It has been brought to my attention that many of the students are dissatisfied with the ban on senior privileges."
8. There are three reasons why we have chicken for dinner so often Dad likes it, Mom likes it, and it's cheap.
9. The principal began his announcement as follows "Good afternoon. Here is a list of the afternoon activities for Green Bay High School."
10. Tom's favorite authors are Ernest Hemingway, Willa Cather, C. S. Forester, and Jules Verne.

CHAPTER 23

Punctuation

Underlining (Italics) and Quotation Marks

UNDERLINING (ITALICS)

Italics are printed letters which lean to the right, such as the following:

These words are printed in italics.

When you are writing or typing, indicate italics by under-lining the words you want italicized. If your composition were to be printed, the typesetter would set the underlined words in italics. For instance, if you typed

```
All sophomores in our school read The Good
Earth, by Pearl Buck.
```

your sentence would be printed like this:

All sophomores in our school read *The Good Earth*, by Pearl Buck.

23a. Use underlining (italics) for titles of books, periodicals, works of art (pictures, musical compositions, statues, etc.), planes, trains, and so on.

EXAMPLES The Red Badge of Courage
the Mona Lisa
the Reader's Digest
the Santa Maria

23a

471

◆ NOTE   The words *a*, *an*, and *the* before a magazine or newspaper title are not underlined. Notice, however, that in titles of
books these words are underlined if they are part of the title.

EXAMPLES   the <u>Atlantic</u>   [magazine]

the <u>Washington Post</u>   [newspaper]

<u>The Wings of the Dove</u>   [book]

<u>The Return of the Native</u>   [book]

23b. Use underlining (italics) for words, letters, and figures referred to as such, and for foreign words.

EXAMPLES   How many <u>and</u>'s are there in this sentence?

There is only one <u>c</u> in the word <u>recommend</u>.

His phone number has three <u>7</u>'s in it.

Common poison ivy (<u>Rhus toxicodendron</u>) is to be
avoided.

● EXERCISE 1.   List on your paper all words and word
groups which should be italicized. Underline each.

1. In Arts Club we have no program; we just talk about things
that are crafted. By this word crafted we mean not only works
of art but also useful things that happen to be beautiful.

2. This definition admits things like the yacht Challenger on the
same basis with works like Brancusi's famous sculpture Bird
in Space.

3. Most of the boys think that mechanical things are beautiful—
for example, the train El Capitan. Some boys admire things
for the romance that surrounds them—for example, Mississippi
steamboats like the Grey Eagle, The Maid of New Orleans,
and the doomed Robert E. Lee or clipper ships like the Cutty
Sark, the Nightingale, and the Thermopylae.

4. Books, however, are usually the chief topic of our talks. The
boys vote for adventure—books like Guthrie's The Big Sky,
Ernest Thompson Seton's Two Little Savages, Willa Cather's
Death Comes for the Archbishop, Defoe's Robinson Crusoe,
and Johann Wyss's The Swiss Family Robinson.

5. The girls prefer books of another sort—books like Emily Brontë's Wuthering Heights, Edna Ferber's Showboat, Marjorie Kinnan Rawlings' The Yearling, and Jessamyn West's The Friendly Persuasion.

6. Notice that Miss West spells her first name with a y rather than an i. This practice is now widely adopted: Alice becomes Alyce and Caroline becomes Carolyn.

QUOTATION MARKS

Quotation marks are used mainly to show the reader that someone's *exact words* are being reproduced. Accordingly, quotation marks come in pairs—one set marking the beginning of the quotation and the other the end.

23c. **Use quotation marks to enclose a direct quotation—a person's exact words.**

Do not use quotation marks to enclose an indirect quotation—not a speaker's exact words.

DIRECT QUOTATION   Marie said, "I have an hour's detention for being late for homeroom." [Marie's exact words]

INDIRECT QUOTATION   Marie said that she had an hour's detention for being late for homeroom. [not Marie's exact words]

◆ NOTE Place quotation marks at both the beginning and the end of a quotation. Omission of quotation marks at the end of a quotation is a common error.

WRONG   "I can't budge this piano alone, said Dan. [second set of quotation marks left out]

RIGHT   "I can't budge this piano alone," said Dan.

23d. **A direct quotation begins with a capital letter.**

EXAMPLE Ed asked, "What time does the bus leave?"

23
b-d

♦ NOTE If the quotation is only a fragment of a sentence, not intended to stand alone, do not begin it with a capital letter.

EXAMPLE He resented Bob's remark that he was "never there when needed."

23e. When a quoted sentence is divided into two parts by an interrupting expression such as *he said* or *she replied*, the second part begins with a small letter.

EXAMPLES "I know," said Joan, "the solution to our problem."
"All we have to do," she continued, "is raise some money."

"Let's hear your ideas," replied Ann, "because the treasury is sadly depleted."

If the second part of a broken quotation is a new sentence, it begins with a capital.

EXAMPLE "Start from the beginning," said Greg. "The joke doesn't make sense to me."

23f. A direct quotation is set off from the rest of the sentence by commas or by a question mark or an exclamation point.

EXAMPLES "Where will it all end?" asked Ernest.
"Let me do that!" exclaimed Harold.
"There is no specific homework assignment for this weekend," announced Mrs. Levitt, "but remember that your term papers are due next Friday."
"Has anyone in this class," asked Mr. Lukas, "seen a performance of *Julius Caesar?*"
Of the Spitfire pilots the Prime Minister said, "Never in the field of human conflict was so much owed by so many to so few."

♦ NOTE A long quotation in your composition is usually introduced by a colon and is set off by itself from the text by wider margins and by single-spacing instead of double-spacing (unless your teacher instructs otherwise). This practice so clearly identifies the passage as a quotation that no quotation marks are needed.

> After the collapse of Europe and the tragedy of Dunkirk, the German dictator thought he had penned the British lion in its home islands and that, weakened as it was by its losses on the continent, it would easily succumb to an invasion. The British Prime Minister, voicing the grim resolve of the whole nation, warned him against such a move:

> > We shall defend every village, every town and every city. The vast mass of London itself, fought street by street, could easily devour an entire hostile army; and we would rather see London laid in ruins and ashes than that it should be tamely and abjectly enslaved.

23g. Other marks of punctuation when used with quotation marks are placed according to the following rules.

(1) Commas and periods are always placed inside the closing quotation marks.

EXAMPLE   "I've got a report due tomorrow," he said, "so don't count on my being at the meeting tonight."

(2) Colons and semicolons are always placed outside the closing quotation marks.

EXAMPLES   Miss Kendall said, "Write your answers on one side of the page"; however, I wasn't paying attention and put mine on both sides.

23
e-g

The following students in our homeroom have, according to Mrs. Cahill, "hit the honor roll jackpot": Vic Chapman, Mary Arnold, and Jack Biggane.

(3) Question marks and exclamation points are placed inside the closing quotation marks if the quotation is a question or an exclamation. Otherwise, they are placed outside.

EXAMPLES   "Are you sure this is the assignment?" asked Pete.
Did I hear you say, "Get lost"?
Never say, "I'll put it off until tomorrow"!
Suddenly Ben yelled, "Three cheers for the coach!"

● EXERCISE 2.   Copy the following sentences, inserting the necessary punctuation. Watch carefully the placement of commas and end marks in relation to quotation marks, and capital letters for the beginning of direct quotations.

1. I'm afraid said the man you've made the wrong turn.
2. You're headed toward Newton now he added, but if you make a right turn on Route 200, you'll come to your destination.
3. Did you say I should turn right on 200 asked Jake.
4. Wow, look at that house exclaimed Sue. Did you ever see anything spookier?
5. You shouldn't read only fiction said Mr. Werner. You should try an occasional biography.
6. The following sophomores have, in the words of Coach Balcolm, brought honor to their class and school: Al Hawthorne, Eunice McCarthy, and Irving Levin.
7. Eric shouted give him air!
8. Did you hear Mr. Lopez say hand in your papers?
9. Yes, I heard him say that answered Sheila I wish I hadn't because I'm far from finished.
10. In a crowded place never shout fire! unless you mean it.
11. Mr. Timpanaro asked if anyone knew the beginning of Alexander Pope's line which ends with the words where angels fear to tread.
12. He asked how old I was, and I replied I'm old enough to know better.

23h. When you write dialogue (two or more persons having a conversation), begin a new paragraph every time the speaker changes.

EXAMPLES "Hello, mates," said Captain Handy softly, "what can I do for you now?"

"You can turn over the ship to me," replied the first mate, his voice filled with tension.

Handy looked with deliberation at the crowd of mutineers. "So it's mutiny, is it, you blackguards? You can't get away with it!" he roared.

"We have got away with it, sir," replied the mate.

23i. When a quoted passage consists of more than one paragraph, put quotation marks at the beginning of each paragraph and at the end of the entire passage.

EXAMPLE "Fellow sophomores," said Theresa, opening the meeting, "permit me first of all to thank you for turning out in such good numbers. Despite our dismal showing so far, I think this packed room proves beyond any doubt that the Sophomore Class is determined not to take second place to the freshmen.

"Up to now, we have simply not been ourselves. As you know, the freshmen have more people on the honor roll than we. More freshmen than sophomores play on all school teams. Perhaps we are ready to change all that."

23j. Use single quotation marks to enclose a quotation within a quotation.

EXAMPLES Margaret whispered, "Mr. Burns just said, 'Do the first three examples.'"

Dick said, "I don't understand the poem 'My Last Duchess' very well."

23
h-j

23k. Use quotation marks to enclose titles of short stories, poems, songs, chapters, articles, and other parts of books and periodicals.

EXAMPLES   "Mending Wall" is my favorite poem by Robert Frost.

Did you read the article "America on Ice" in *American Heritage?*

The assignment for Wednesday is Chapter 16, "Egypt and the Fertile Crescent."

♦ NOTE   The length of a written work determines whether the title should be italicized or enclosed in quotation marks. Book-length works are italicized; shorter works usually are not. However, the titles of poems long enough to be divided into books, cantos, or sections—like Longfellow's *Evangeline*, Coleridge's *The Rime of the Ancient Mariner*, and Hardy's *The Dynasts*—are italicized.

23l. Use quotation marks to enclose slang words, technical terms, and other expressions that are unusual in standard English.

EXAMPLE   Pat's taste in clothes was "way out."

Putting slang expressions within quotation marks amounts to apologizing for them. If you are doubtful about the appropriateness of a word, do not use it.

● EXERCISE 3. Using quotation marks correctly, write one original sentence containing each of the following.

1. A direct quotation beginning with *he said*
2. A direct quotation ending with *he asked*
3. An indirect quotation
4. A direct quotation not beginning with a capital letter
5. A direct quotation interrupted by *he replied*
6. A question mark inside quotation marks
7. A question mark outside quotation marks
8. The title of a short poem within a direct quotation

CHAPTER 24

Punctuation

Apostrophes, Hyphens, Dashes, Parentheses

APOSTROPHES

The possessive case of a noun or a pronoun is used to indicate ownership or relationship.

OWNERSHIP   the **boy's** car

                 his dog [The dog is *his*.]

RELATIONSHIP **her** crying

                 this **evening's** program

In the English language the possessive case of *nouns* is formed by adding an apostrophe and an *s* or, with some words, merely an apostrophe, to the noun.

EXAMPLES a **child's** toy

             Bert's paper

             two **ladies'** umbrellas

Making a word possessive is very easy. *Remembering* to do so, however, may be hard. When you are in doubt whether or not to use an apostrophe, try an "of" phrase in place of the word. If the "of" phrase makes good sense, then an apostrophe is called for.

EXAMPLE a half hours work [An apostrophe in *hours?*]

           work "of a half hour" [This makes good sense, therefore . . .]

           a half **hour's** work

23
k-l

479

24a. To form the possessive case of a singular noun, add an apostrophe and an *s*.

EXAMPLES   a day's work
Sam's dog
cat's whiskers

◆ NOTE   Many writers prefer to make proper names ending in *s* possessive by adding the apostrophe only. They do this to avoid too many *s* sounds at the end of a word, making it difficult to pronounce (Socrates' death, Themistocles' oration). Some singular nouns ending in *s* need the apostrophe and the *s* since the added *s* must be pronounced as a separate syllable to make the meaning clear (waitress's uniform). In general, adding an apostrophe and an *s* is a correct way to make any singular noun possessive.

24b. To form the possessive case of a plural noun ending in *s*, add only the apostrophe.

EXAMPLES   boys' club
turkeys' feathers

◆ NOTE   The few plural nouns that do not end in *s* form the possessive by adding an apostrophe and an *s*.

EXAMPLES   men's hats
children's games

Take care not to use an apostrophe to form the *plural* of a noun.

WRONG   The four hour's passed swiftly.
RIGHT   The four hours passed swiftly.

WRONG   The dog's barked all night long.
RIGHT   The dogs barked all night long.

Study the following examples of the application of these rules for forming the singular and plural possessives of nouns. Be able to explain how each possessive was formed.

SINGULAR	SINGULAR POSSESSIVE	PLURAL	PLURAL POSSESSIVE
girl	girl's ticket	girls	girls' tickets
Mr. Jones	Mr. Jones's house	the Joneses	the Joneses' house
ox	ox's hoof	oxen	oxen's hooves
nurse	nurse's uniform	nurses	nurses' uniforms
lady	lady's gloves	ladies	ladies' gloves
clerk	clerk's desk	clerks	clerks' desks
monkey	monkey's paw	monkeys	monkeys' paws
lawyer	lawyer's office	lawyers	lawyers' offices

● EXERCISE 1.   On your paper, make a four-column chart listing the singular, singular possessive, plural, and plural possessive of the following words:

1. army	4. baby	7. deer
2. florist	5. mouse	8. rose
3. governor	6. book	9. fireman

Pronouns in the Possessive Case

24c. **Possessive personal and relative pronouns do not require an apostrophe.**

The lists below show the nominative and possessive forms of personal and relative pronouns. Note that there are no apostrophes.

NOMINATIVE CASE	POSSESSIVE CASE
I	my, mine
you	your, yours
he	his
she	her, hers
it	its [1]
we	our, ours
they	their, theirs
who	whose

[1] The common form *it's* is not possessive; it is a contraction meaning *it is*. See page 519.

24 a-c

24d. Indefinite pronouns in the possessive case require an apostrophe and *s*.

EXAMPLES   everyone's books
              nobody's name

If you need to review indefinite pronouns, see the list on page 6.

Compounds in the Possessive Case

24e. In compound words, names of organizations and business firms, and words showing joint possession, only the last word is possessive in form.

COMPOUND WORDS	sister-in-**law's** children
	commander-in-**chief's** order
	board of **directors'** report
NAMES OF BUSINESS FIRMS	Heywood and **Bigalow's** Department Store
	Remson and **Doyle's** office
JOINT POSSESSION	Doug and **Walter's** boat
	Jill and **Barbara's** house
	Peter's and **my** car [exception: noun and possessive pronoun]

24f. When two or more persons possess something individually, each of their names is possessive in form.

EXAMPLES   **Art's** and **Chuck's** report cards
              Sally's and **Jane's** toothbrushes

● EXERCISE 2.   Some of the following expressions need apostrophes; some are plurals that do not need apostrophes. Copy each expression, inserting apostrophes where needed.

1. a months delay
2. two cars in the garage
3. three pairs of gloves
4. a childs toy
5. a peoples choice
6. curtains in the breeze
7. a candidates speech
8. among four boys
9. the girls gym
10. seven loaves of bread
11. the sound of trumpets
12. two days work
13. the hands of the clock
14. Ulysses travels
15. two pairs of glasses
16. a ships cargo
17. Two cars collided.
18. Elaines keys
19. rivers of mud
20. my mothers cooking

● EXERCISE 3. List on your paper in the order in which they appear in the numbered sentences the words requiring apostrophes. After each word with an apostrophe, write the thing possessed. Remember that plural nouns ending in *s* require an apostrophe only.

EXAMPLE   1. At Stellas request we decided to visit George Washingtons home.
  1. *Stella's request*
     George Washington's home

1. At Midges party last week, my friends plan for this summers vacation didn't receive everyones approval. 2. Tims brother had been on a three weeks trip with the American Youth Hostels, and his brothers enthusiasm had infected Tim.

3. For this years trip somebodys suggestion was to go to Fishers Lake; but since nobody greeted this with shouts of approval, we listened to more of Tims idea. 4. He recognized the fact that a bicycle trip wasn't some peoples idea of fun, but it was at least something new and different. 5. Tim said that all one needed was to drag out the kid brothers bicycle, invest a few dollars in camping equipment, and pedal off to see our countrys scenery. 6. I agreed to go along with his suggestion, provided that first we all take a days bicycle trip to nearby Orchard Beach as preparation for the long trip.

7. I thought that after five years neglect my bike would probably need some repair, and a trip to the cellar soon confirmed this surmise. 8. Hidden behind my sisters old carriage, the bike looked rusty and in need of a mechanics skilled touch.

24
d-f

9. Dads tool kit was nearby, and with a little elbow grease and my brothers advice, I made the old heap look like a cyclists dream.

● EXERCISE 4. List in order after the number of the section the words requiring apostrophes. After each word with an apostrophe, write the thing possessed.

1. With my mothers advice and my fathers laughter ringing in my ears, I was at Joes house at the crack of dawn. The suggestion that we meet there was his. 2. Soon the whole gang arrived. Everyones bike was in good working order. 3. Helens idea that we agree to go slowly met with the girls approval. Before long we left the Greens house and started the first lap of the sixteen-mile round-trip. 4. Our groups spirit was high. Since everyones intention was to make the trip pleasant, we started to sing some of our schools songs. 5. There wasn't much traffic to worry about at that hour, and we soon passed the mens club building, Harris and Cosgroves store, and the policemens booth on the outskirts of town. 6. Of course, we had a long way to go, but sixteen miles seemed like childs play. 7. Luckily, no ones bike developed mechanical difficulties. Even Pegs and Julies bicycles held together, which surprised us because theirs were old models.

8. After about five miles of steady pedaling, my legs began to get tired, and somebodys suggestion that we take a short break seemed like a good idea. 9. The girls stamina proved to be equal to ours. 10. We all raided Julies supply of candy, and after a few minutes we were off again. 11. Before we reached our destination, Midges face was beginning to get a little sunburned, and Mikes brow was damp with perspiration. 12. Tired and dusty, we finally arrived at Orchard Beach and had a swim, a lunch, and a few hours relaxation. 13. The groups plan was to leave at two o'clock. If my legs had been tired early in the morning, now they were ready to fall off.

14. When we arrived at Freds house late that afternoon, everyones muscles were aching, but everybodys spirits were still high. 15. At Freds house Pegs bicycle at last collapsed. 16. Its front wheel detached itself suddenly from the frame and wobbled away. Pegs weariness overcame her and she began to giggle.

17. Soon everybodys restraint dissolved, and we all laughed so hard that the tears rolled down our faces.   18. After Pegs recovery, Joe offered her his bike while he walked beside her and carried hers. This arrangement of theirs worked nicely, and eventually everyone got safely home.   19. If your club decides on a days bicycle trip, I hope yours is as much fun as ours was.

Contractions

Contractions are shortened forms of certain words or certain word groups that commonly go together. The apostrophes in contractions are to indicate that letters have been left out.

24g.   Use an apostrophe to show where letters or numbers have been omitted in a contraction.

EXAMPLES you have   you've
we are   we're
it is   it's

What words or figures have been contracted, and what letters or numbers have been omitted from the following?

Readin', 'ritin', and 'rithmetic are the three R's.

You're too young to drive.

It's a long story.

The winter of '62 set records for cold weather.

● EXERCISE 5.   Study the following contractions. Be able to write them when your teacher dictates to you the uncontracted expressions.

1. shouldn't	should not	8. weren't	were not
2. they've	they have	9. that's	that is
3. o'clock	of the clock	10. hasn't	has not
4. isn't	is not	11. she'll	she will
5. they'd	they would	12. he's	he is
6. haven't	have not	13. I'm	I am
7. we're	we are	14. they'll	they will

24g

15. let's	let us	18. they'd	they had
16. who's	who is	19. doesn't	does not
17. he'd	he would	20. didn't	did not

● REVIEW EXERCISE A. Copy the following sentences, inserting apostrophes wherever necessary.

1. Youve got to finish todays assignment.
2. Theyre going to the principals office.
3. The girls gym wasnt painted this year.
4. One cats whiskers werent singed.
5. Im not so sure you cant do it.
6. Certainly hed met Jerrys uncle, but he didnt remember his name.
7. Youll have to pay a fine if your book isnt found.
8. At four oclock, lets see if theyre still in the gym.
9. Vivians sister wont be able to attend Elsies party.
10. Dont you want to tell us whos going to be there?

Do not confuse possessive pronouns with contractions.

POSSESSIVE PRONOUNS	CONTRACTIONS
its roof	it's = it is *or* it has
your house	you're = you are
their house	they're = they are
whose house	who's = who is

● EXERCISE 6. This exercise is to give you practice in distinguishing between possessive pronouns and contractions. You should be able to do the exercise perfectly. After each number, write the correct word from the pair (or pairs) in parentheses.

1. (Its, It's) true the plant has already lost (its, it's) leaves.
2. (Whose, Who's) the girl (whose, who's) record player you borrowed for the party?
3. (Their, They're) not really very suitable records for a party.
4. (You're, Your) sure (they're, their) not too loud?
5. (Who's, Whose) the vocalist on this one? (Its, It's) not labeled.

6. (Its, It's) one of the best by Connie May and the Singing Six. (Their, They're) very good.
7. (You're, Your) sure to like it. (Their, They're) accompanied by seven drums and a bass.
8. (Whose, Who's) orchestra do they use?
9. (Your, You're) parents may not like the record. (Its, It's) sound is something (they're, their) not used to at all.
10. (Whose, Who's) (your, you're) favorite singer?

24h. Use an apostrophe and *s* to form the plural of letters, numbers, signs, and words referred to as words.

EXAMPLES There are two *m*'s, two *t*'s, and two *e*'s in *com-mittee.*

There are four *3*'s in my phone number.

The +'s and 0's belong on your paper, not in the book.

Your sentences have too many *and*'s.

● EXERCISE 7. List on your paper all words and symbols needing apostrophes. List them according to the sentences in which they appear. Supply the needed apostrophes.

1. Youre sure they have two *t*s in their name?
2. The Joneses mill burned down in 29, the year of the crash.
3. Youve forgotten the childrens shoes.
4. Deers, elks, and goats hooves are all cloven.
5. Whose car did you say this was, your sister-in-laws?
6. So far Ive got six 90s on these spelling tests; I mightve done better on this one.
7. The speakers delivery was marred by too many *ah*s and *um*s.
8. His is red, ours is green, theirs is blue.
9. Youve not told me whos coming.
10. *Aint* is in the dictionary, but its considered substandard by most educated people.
11. Whos in the girls locker room?
12. The equation contained two ∞s, which my glossary told me were symbols for infinity.

24h

13. Theyre not nearly as good as they pretend to be.
14. Georgias dog wags its tail continuously; its very friendly.
15. *And*s and *so*s occur too often in students compositions.
16. Beth shouldve recognized the handbag as Judy Johnsons; after all, its monogramed with two *J*s.
17. *Oh*s and *ah*s greeted the starlets appearance on the stage.

HYPHENS

24i. Use a hyphen to divide a word at the end of a line.

Division of words at the end of a line in order to maintain an even margin should be avoided but is sometimes necessary. A hyphen is used between parts of words divided in this way. Never divide one-syllable words. When you divide a word of more than one syllable, follow these rules:

1. Divide a word between its syllables.

WRONG   Katherine, the captain, is a fo-
         rceful speaker.

RIGHT   Katherine, the captain, is a force-
         ful speaker.

2. Words containing double consonants should be divided between the double consonants.

    ban-nister, recom-mend

See Rule 3 for exceptions like tell-ing and call-ing.

3. Words with a prefix or suffix should usually be divided between the prefix and root or the root and suffix.

    per-form, tell-ing, call-ing, accept-able

4. Divide an already hyphenated word only at the hyphen.

WRONG   She is also quite self-reli-
         ant.

RIGHT   She is also quite self-
         reliant.

5. Divide a word so that at least two of its letters are carried forward to the next line.

WRONG   Dave always takes his camer-
            a with him.

RIGHT   Dave always takes his cam-
            era with him.

6. Do not hyphenate a proper name or separate a title, initials, or first name from a surname.

WRONG   At the end of the period, Mr. Led-
            better collected the papers.

RIGHT   At the end of the period,
            Mr. Ledbetter collected the papers.

● EXERCISE 8. Assume that the following words come at the end of a line and have to be divided. Copy each word, indicating by the use of hyphens how it might be divided.

1. ravioli
2. inexplicable
3. squirrel
4. anti-British
5. approximately
6. delicious
7. accompaniment
8. happy-go-lucky
9. recognize
10. beginning

Compound Words

Hyphens are used to join together the parts of some compound words. There are three kinds of compound words in our language: solid compounds (bookkeeper), hyphenated compounds (self-satisfied), and open compounds (disc jockey). Every year a great number of new compound words come into the language.

Most new compounds are first written as two words (*nose cone, launching pad*). Often, as they become more familiar, they begin to be written with hyphens and then as single words.

Only dictionary makers can keep track of this progression from open to solid compounds. Therefore, to be sure about the correct form, consult an up-to-date dictionary.

24i

24j. Use a hyphen with compound numbers from *twenty-one* to *ninety-nine* and with fractions used as adjectives.

EXAMPLES   seventy-six trombones

a two-thirds majority [*Two-thirds* is an adjective modifying *majority*.]

nine tenths of the boys [*Nine tenths* is used as a noun.]

24k. Use a hyphen with the prefixes *ex-, self-,* and *all-,* with the suffix *-elect,* and with all prefixes before a proper noun or proper adjective.

EXAMPLES   self-assurance, all-encompassing, ex-champion, president-elect, mid-July, post-Reformation, late-Renaissance, anti-American

24l. Hyphenate a compound adjective when it precedes the noun it modifies. Do not use a hyphen if one of the modifiers is an adverb ending in *-ly.*

EXAMPLES   a well-planned campaign (But: "The campaign was well planned.")

an after-school job

a heavily laden burro

● EXERCISE 9. In the following sentences many compound words need hyphens. Find the words that should be hyphenated, and list them, correctly punctuated, after the proper number on your paper.

1. The self confidence of a scout comes from his deliberately cultivated self reliance.
2. Suzy wore three quarter length gloves to the fancy dress ball.
3. The mayor elect was a forty eight year old ex senator.

4. Two thirds of the vote was an expression of antibond sentiment.
5. Julius chipped a neatly hit shot directly onto the green.
6. Anti French sentiment was strong in nineteenth century England.
7. The self taught cabinetmaker finished the piece in mid July.
8. A well known ex champion is Jersey Joe Walcott.
9. His love of Europe was all embracing: he was pro British, pro French, pro Spanish, and pro Italian.
10. A well rehearsed minuet was staged by the French Club.

DASHES

24m. Use a dash to indicate an abrupt break in thought.

EXAMPLES   I invited Margie—she's the new girl in town—to the Winter Carnival.

The dog skidded on the linoleum—his nails acted like ice skates—and crashed into the kitchen table.

24n. Use a dash to mean *namely, that is, in other words,* etc., before an explanation.

EXAMPLES   The newspaper boy is the best we've ever had—he always puts the paper inside the door on rainy days. [*that is*]

The roses looked beautiful but were expensive and impractical—they lasted only two days before the petals began to fall. [*in other words,* or *that is*]

We visited three national parks—Grand Canyon, Yosemite, and Yellowstone. [*namely*]

♦ NOTE   The dash and the colon are frequently interchangeable in this type of construction.

In typewritten work you indicate a dash by striking the hyphen key twice.

24
j-n

PARENTHESES

24o. **Use parentheses to enclose matter which is added to a sentence but is not considered of major importance.**

EXAMPLES   Mrs. Henderson works all day long in her garden (she is a very particular woman) and is forever pruning, mulching, and weeding.

Several of the speaker's stories (they were very dull) pointed out the need for a good memory.

Put punctuation marks within the parentheses when they belong to the parenthetical matter but outside the parentheses when they belong to the sentence as a whole.

EXAMPLES   Charlie's exclamation when the gorilla came on the screen ("Oh, look, a monkey!") amused us all.

When the king met Bolingbroke (afterwards Henry IV), he charged him with treason.

◆ NOTE   Commas, dashes, and parentheses may all be used to enclose incidental words or phrases that interrupt the sentence and are not considered of major importance. Commas are much more commonly used in this way than dashes or parentheses.

EXAMPLES   We fished in the muddy stream, a brown torrent after the downpour. [a slight pause]

We fished in the muddy stream—a waste of time! [a stronger break in the sentence]

We fished (or should I say drowned worms?) in the muddy stream.   [two strong breaks]

● EXERCISE 10.   Colons, dashes, and parentheses are omitted in the following sentences. To show where each mark of punctuation belongs, copy the word or number that should precede the mark, write the mark, and then write the word or number that should follow it.

1. If anybody ever asked me what I wanted to do, I'd say this I want to make the world a better place in which to live.

2. Ted has heard a great deal about the Peace Corps a fine organization from all reports and hopes to join this group.
3. The dance committee always has one big problem everybody wants to decorate, but nobody wants to clean up the next day.
4. Rushing to catch the 3 45 train, Betsy broke the heel on her shoe she always wears heels at least three inches high and didn't arrive at the meeting in Greensville until 5 07.
5. Pacing up and down, Mark Antony addressed the people of Rome "Friends, Romans, countrymen, lend me your ears."
6. Harriet has a beautiful speaking voice Mrs. Jeffers raves about it in speech class but she can't sing a note.
7. Frank had many things to do yesterday buy the tickets, rent a tuxedo, arrange transportation, and order the flowers.
8. Hank agreed to serve on the committee what a surprise! if we really needed him.
9. Many spring flowers tulips, hyacinths, daffodils, crocuses should be appearing soon.
10. We approached the dog what an ugly looking hound he was! with caution.
11. My marks a subject for endless discussion in my home are never very high.
12. I received the following gifts for my birthday two shirts, a pair of cuff links, three books, and ten dollars.
13. Sam's father bought him a car something I've wanted for years as a graduation present.
14. Marcia is on a diet and has stopped eating candy, cake, ice cream, and potatoes.
15. If you miss the 3 05 bus after school, you can take a later one at 4 05 or 5 10.
16. I found my other gym shoe good grief, how long had it been missing? in the next locker.
17. There are many more people backstage than the average audience knows electricians, prop boys, scenery movers, prompters, wardrobe mistresses, and stand-ins.
18. Clearing his throat, the speaker began to quote "Ladies and gentlemen, we are here today for a serious purpose . . ."
19. Many imported products English bicycles, Italian motor scooters, Japanese toys are now available.

240

20. We grabbed our hats somebody had thoughtfully mixed them all up on the piano and ran out the door.

● REVIEW EXERCISE B. Copy the following sentences on your paper, inserting all necessary punctuation and any necessary capital letters.

1. Last weeks edition of the Echo our school newspaper contained a review of the play
2. Every morning I wake up at six o clock every morning I hate to get out of bed
3. Yes the first bus to Midvale leaves at 10 15 but you can always catch a later one at 11 10
4. Do you asked Mother always have to do what Anne Charlotte and Carol do
5. Bowers Candy Store our gangs meeting place is always crowded however Mr. Bower wont tolerate much noise
6. If you wash the dishes Irene Ill dry them I promised before we sat down to dinner
7. Whats the rush Steve I asked youve still got plenty of time before youre marked late
8. To tell the truth Eileens favorite flowers are roses not carnations
9. Why Gene exclaimed Mimi I havent seen you for ages where have you been
10. Right here in town he mumbled looking at the ground who wants to know
11. My cousin Harold who must be at least seventeen years old lives in Torrance California
12. The letter was dated August 15 1965 it was addressed to Larry Melton 1163 High Street Tulsa Oklahoma
13. Scratching your head wont help you Charles said Mrs. Marshal the French teacher what you need is a little more study
14. Frightened by the sound of the explosion the dog ran under the table and all the coaxing in the world couldnt persuade him to come out
15. Students who are taking examinations in the gym must bring the following items with them pens pencils rulers and compasses

16. An article entitled Three Steps to Happiness appeared in last months Readers Digest
17. A list of those students who made the honor roll was posted in the lobby last week the list of seniors with special privileges will be posted today at 3 10
18. Give the little lady a great big hand urged the master of ceremonies then he handed Rose her prize a transistor radio
19. Racing down the hall Ken was stopped by a monitor stuttering and stammering he tried to explain that he was late for class but the excuse fell on deaf ears
20. Your penmanships terrible Phil exclaimed Mr Mann who is very particular I cant tell your es from your is or your ts from your ls please rewrite your book report on Hardys novel The Return of the Native

● REVIEW EXERCISE C.   Copy the following paragraph, inserting all necessary punctuation and capital letters.

Frankly if Mr Lawrence hadnt forgotten to collect todays compositions my average in English would have hit a new low his unnatural lapse of memory I thought was the miracle of the century for hes the type who never forgets to dot is and cross ts all during homeroom period which had been extended until 9 30 because of some special announcements I had worked on an outline but the outline was far from perfect science French and social studies came the following periods and you know that it is impossible to do homework in those classes how I regretted reading my new detective story The Strange Case of the Missing Sub last night homework forgotten I had been lost in the terror laden spine tingling story and before you could say outline rough draft and finished copy it was 12 o clock what a lucky break for me that Mr Lawrence a strict teacher forgot to collect the themes

● REVIEW EXERCISE D.   Copy the following sentences, inserting capital letters and punctuation as needed.

1. Diane Johnston who is our homerooms representative to the student council read the minutes of last tuesdays meeting
2. The warm waters of the gulf stream from the south eventually meet the cold waters of the labrador current from the

north and the result is that some areas of the north atlantic are covered with fog

3. The sinking of the titanic off the grand banks of newfoundland on april 15 1912 at 2 20 am has been described in Walter Lords book a night to remember

4. On my last trip to Joffones grocery store I bought several items that were on sale tomatoes pears eggs and coffee

5. Tiny belgium which has only about ten million people is bounded on the north by the netherlands and the north sea on the southwest by france and on the east by germany

6. To tell the truth I dont remember what he looked like said the witness all I can recall is that he was wearing a black homburg hat however I do think that he had a scar on his cheek

7. The hamilton nurseries on jericho turnpike always sell the finest shrubs each plant according to the coltsville gazette is guaranteed to grow or youre given a refund

8. If alice arrives promptly at 6 30 in her new plymouth convertible we should be at your house by 7 oclock and have plenty of time to drive to the rivoli theater to see a movie

9. In spite of last summers heat wave we thoroughly enjoyed visiting the grand canyon yellowstone national park and a hopi indian reservation

10. Having graduated from ford high school with a straight a average harry stead who won every award in science last year thought he would find college a snap

● REVIEW EXERCISE E.   Copy the following, inserting all necessary punctuation.

1. Rembrandt the famous Dutch painter was born in Leyden Holland on July 15 1606.

2. When Rembrandt had finished his early schooling his father a well to do miller hoped he would become a lawyer and entered the young man in the University of Leyden.

3. However when it became apparent that the boy was determined to paint the wise miller made no serious objections to his sons choice of a career.

4. The painters Jacob Von Swanenbrach Pieter Lastman and Gerard Honthorst aided in his early training and soon Rem-

brandts works attracted the attention of art lovers in Amsterdam the great commercial center of Holland urged by their calls and interested in attaining commissions the young painter moved to Amsterdam in 1630.

5. Rembrandt whose paintings were in great demand married in 1634 much has been written about his wife Saskia she was beautiful she was wealthy she came from a fine family and few deny that she became the center of his life and art.

6. Paintings such as the Night Watch and the Anatomy Lesson enhanced his reputation and gold flowed into his pockets he in turn had many expenses a large house and a love of antiques paintings and engravings.

7. With the death of his wife however his paintings and his financial position underwent a change. Although he was still a master of reality his paintings became more calm more intimate and more introspective and he became less interested in sheer description his habits of free spending forced him into bankruptcy.

8. Selling just about everything he owned Rembrandt found that 5,000 florins about 150,000 dollars in todays money couldn't satisfy his creditors who even wanted to attach his future output this scheme was prevented by some legal manipulations but he remained poor for the rest of his life.

9. Although Rembrandts financial position wasnt good important commissions still came in and his career did not end in obscurity it is true nevertheless that debts and the death of his son made his last days unhappy.

10. On October 8 1669 he died a poor man in Amsterdam but his paintings almost 1,000 have been attributed to him which are found in museums in London Paris and New York attest to the fact that he was rich in genius.

CHAPTER 25

Manuscript Form

Standards for Written Work

A *manuscript* is any typewritten or handwritten composition, as distinguished from a printed document. More and more frequently in your school years ahead, you will be asked to hand in well-prepared manuscripts. Therefore, you should learn correct form for your written work now, and prepare all future written work accordingly.

25a. Follow accepted standards in preparing manuscripts.

Your teacher will find it easier to read and evaluate your papers if they are properly prepared. Although there is no single way to prepare a paper correctly, the rules given below are widely used and accepted. Follow them unless your teacher requests you to do otherwise.

1. Use lined composition paper or, if you type, white paper 8½ by 11 inches in size.

2. Type on only one side of a sheet of paper. Follow your school's policy about writing on both sides of composition paper.

3. Write in blue, black, or blue-black ink, or typewrite. If you type, double-space the lines.

4. Leave a margin of about two inches at the top of a page and margins of about one inch at the sides and bottom. The left-hand margin must be straight; the right-hand margin should be as straight as you can make it.

5. Indent the first line of each paragraph about one-half inch from the left.

6. Write your name, the class, and the date on the first page. Follow your teacher's instructions in the placement of these items. You may put them on three separate lines in the upper right-hand corner of the sheet, or write them in one line across the top of the page. Either way, they should begin about two inches down from the top of the page.

7. If your paper has a title, write it in the center of the first line. Skip a line between the title and the first line of your composition. (Double-space twice if you are typing.)

8. If the paper is more than one page in length, number the pages after the first, placing the number in the center of the line, about one-half inch down from the top.

9. Write legibly and neatly. If you are using unlined paper, try to keep the lines straight. Form your letters carefully so that your *n*'s do not look like *u*'s, *a*'s like *o*'s, and so on. Dot the *i*'s and cross the *t*'s. If you are typing, do not strike over letters or cross out words. If you have to erase, do it neatly.

25b. Learn the rules for using abbreviations.

In most of your writing, you should spell out words rather than abbreviate them. A few abbreviations, however, are commonly used.

The following abbreviations are acceptable when they are used before or after a name: *Mr.*, *Mrs.*, *Dr.*, *Jr.*, and *Sr.* If they do not accompany a name, spell out the words instead of using abbreviations.

**25
a-b**

EXAMPLES   **Mr.** Rugelli   **Dr.** Loesster

Mrs. Corning   John S. Wilbur, **Sr.**

She has an appointment with the **doctor.**

The **senior** law partner was consulted.

The abbreviations A.M. (*ante meridiem*—"before noon"), P.M. (*post meridiem*—"after noon"), A.D. (*anno Domini*— "in the year of our Lord"), and B.C. (*before Christ*) are acceptable when they are used with numbers.

EXAMPLES   The *Queen Mary* is scheduled to sail at 9:00 A.M.

Octavian (63 B.C.–A.D. 14) is now known as Augustus Caesar. [Notice that the abbreviation *A.D.* precedes the number, while *B.C.* follows it.]

Abbreviations for organizations are acceptable if they are generally known.

EXAMPLES   My brother and I joined the **Y.M.C.A.** [or **YMCA**]

Thousands visit the **UN** headquarters in New York.

The **FBI** cooperates closely with state police agencies. [Abbreviations for government agencies are usually written without periods.]

25c. Learn the rules for writing numbers.

Numbers of more than two words should be written in numerals, not words. If, however, you are writing several numbers, some of them one word and some of them more than one word, write them all the same way.

EXAMPLES   Edith traveled **675** miles on her trip to Minnesota.

Marlene weighs **ninety-seven** pounds.

To the north we have **750** acres, to the south **340,** to the west **182,** and to the east only **47.**

A number at the beginning of a sentence should be written out.

EXAMPLE   **Thirty-five hundred** pairs of terns were counted in the rookery.

Write out numbers like *eleventh, forty-third,* and so on. If they are used with a month, however, it is customary to use numerals only.

EXAMPLES My brother came in eleven [not *11th*] in the race.

School closes on **June 6.** [or *the sixth of June;* not ***June 6th***]

25d. Learn the rules for dividing words at the end of a line.

Sometimes you do not have room to write all of a long word at the end of a line. It may look better to start the word on the next line; however, if doing that would leave a very uneven right-hand margin, you should divide the word, using a hyphen after the first part. Learn the rules for dividing words (see pages 488–89). Remember that you should try to avoid dividing words if possible. A slightly irregular margin looks better than a hyphenated word.

25e. Learn the standard correction symbols.

In correcting your papers, your teacher may use some or all of the symbols given below. If you memorize these symbols, you will understand at once what is wrong in your paper. What you are to do about each marked error is explained after the given meaning of the symbol. If you are not sure how to correct your error, use the index of this book to find the section that you need to review.

All errors requiring rewriting of one or more sentences should be numbered (1, 2, etc.) in the margin where the symbol occurs. Then on a separate "correction sheet" (or on the final page of your composition if there is room), you should rewrite the incorrect sentence, numbering it to correspond with the numbered symbol. Errors that do not require rewriting a whole sentence are to be corrected on the composition itself at the place where the error appears.

CORRECTION SYMBOLS WITH INSTRUCTIONS

ms   *error in manuscript form or neatness*
Rewrite the sentence or paragraph neatly on correction sheet.

cap   *error in use of capital letter*
Cross out the incorrect letter, and write the correct form above it.

p   *error in punctuation*
Insert punctuation, remove it, or change it as required.

sp   *error in spelling*
Cross out the word; write the correct spelling above it; write the word five times correctly spelled on your correction sheet.

frag   *sentence fragment*
Correct the fragment by changing punctuation and capital or by rewriting on correction sheet.

rs   *run-on sentence*
Correct it by inserting the necessary end mark and capital.

ss   *error in sentence structure*
Rewrite the sentence on your correction sheet.

k   *awkward sentence or passage*
Rewrite the sentence or passage on your correction sheet.

nc   *not clear*
Rewrite the sentence or sentences on your correction sheet.

ref   *unclear reference of pronoun*
Cross out the error, and write the correction above it.

gr   *error in grammar*
Cross out the error, and write the correct form above it.

w   *error in word choice*
Cross out the word, and write a better one above it.

¶   *Begin a new paragraph here.*
This cannot be corrected but should be carefully noted.

t   *error in tense*
Cross out the error, and write the correct form above it.

∧   *You have omitted something.*
Insert omitted words above the line.

COMPOSITION PASSAGE MARKED BY THE TEACHER

p

gr

p

sp   *p*
w

r s

    "All is grass, said Heracli-
tus." By this he meant that
all animals including man depends
upon green plants to store up
the suns energy in forms they
can use. The sun shines on all
equaly, but it's energy would be
quickly dissipated (unless) the
green leaves of plants did not
take the three inorganic ma-
terials--water, carbon dioxide,
and sunlight--and transform them
into food even electricity is a
form of energy first trapped and
stored in green leaves. The
coal burned to make steam to
drive generators is energy
trapped by the leaves of ancient
carboniferous plants.

COMPOSITION PASSAGE CORRECTED BY STUDENT

p

gr

    "All is grass," said Heracli-
tus." By this he meant that
all animals including man depends
upon green plants to store up

p

the sun's energy in forms they
can use. The sun shines on all
equally
~~equaly~~, but it's energy would be
quickly dissipated *if* ~~unless~~ the
green leaves of plants did not
take the three inorganic ma-
terials--water, carbon dioxide,
and sunlight--and transform them
into food. *E*ven electricity is a
form of energy first trapped and
stored in green leaves. The
coal burned to make steam to
drive generators is energy
trapped by the leaves of ancient
carboniferous plants.

sp   p
w

rs

equally, equally, equally,
equally, equally

CHAPTER 26

Spelling

Improving Your Spelling

You must have heard the words "I never could spell" in the course of your high school career, and you probably realize that this is just another excuse for poor spelling. Naturally good spellers are rare people. If you belong to this group, you are indeed fortunate. If you do not and know you have difficulty, now is the time to do something about it. You can improve your spelling if you want to and if you are willing to make the effort. No one else can be of much help to you. *Learning to spell is your responsibility.*

GOOD SPELLING HABITS

There is no one way to learn to spell. What works for one person may not work for you, but careful observation and good visual memory will help no matter what method you use. By using a combination of several methods, you can in time become a good speller. Some of the ways that have helped others to spell are listed below. Read them over; put them into practice.

1. *In your notebook, keep a list of the words you misspell.* Set aside a few pages in your notebook and jot down all the words you misspell in your written work for all subjects. At first, this job of entering word after word will seem wearisome and never-ending; the list itself, as it daily grows

longer, will threaten too to preempt your whole notebook and leave room for nothing else. Nevertheless, you can take heart, for as the therapy takes effect, fewer and fewer words will need to be added to the list, and the day will come eventually when weeks will pass before another mistake forces you to open your notebook to this dismal page.

A three-column spelling sheet is best. In the first column, correctly spell the word you have missed and circle the troublesome part. In the second column, divide the word into syllables. This insures against misspelling the word by first mispronouncing it. In the third column, jot down any little counsel to yourself, warning, or trick of association that may help you to spell the word.

1. Feb(ru)ary	Feb-ru-ar-y	Pronounce correctly.
2. di(sa)pproval	dis-ap-prov-al	Study Rule 26c.
3. can(di)date	can-di-date	Word has three small words in it: *can, did, ate.*

2. *Get the dictionary habit.* Don't guess at the spelling of a word. There is no consistency in guessing. You may guess right today and wrong tomorrow and be no better off. Actually the simple operation itself of opening the dictionary, leafing through it, and searching down the page until you come upon your word fortifies your memory with its correct spelling and makes it much more unlikely that you will misspell it again. Then again, you can hardly fail to come across some of the cognate forms of the word you are looking for, and by making the acquaintances of these "cousins" to the word in question, you deepen your knowledge of the word itself. It is much harder to misspell *denomination* after you know its kinship with such words as *nominate, nominal, denominator,* etc.

3. *Learn to spell words by syllables.* If you divide a word into small parts which can be pronounced by themselves, you divide a word into syllables. Even the hardest words look easy when they are broken down into syllables. For

example, the word *pul'sate* has two syllables; the word *bul'le tin* has three syllables; the word *en vi'ron ment* has four syllables.

4. *Avoid mispronunciations that lead to spelling errors.* Careful pronunciation will help you to spell many words. The boy who says *sup rise* for *surprise* will probably spell the word incorrectly. He will leave out the letter *r*. The person who says *mod ren* for *modern* will also probably misspell the word. You need to learn the correct pronunciation of a word in order to spell it right.

Study the pronunciation of the words in the following list. Notice how incorrect pronunciation leads to incorrect spelling.

e*s*cape	(*not* e*x*cape)
ri*d*iculous	(*not* re*d*iculous)
en*t*rance	(*not* ent*e*rance)
temper*a*ment	(*not* tem*p*erment)
equi*p*ment	(*not* equi*pt*ment)
a*thl*etic	(*not* ath*a*letic)
main*ten*ance	(*not* main*tain*ance)
rec*o*gnize	(*not* rec*o*nize)
heig*h*t	(*not* heigh*th*)
*per*spiration	(*not* pr*e*spiration)

5. *Proofread your papers before handing them in.* *Proofreading* is the process of rereading carefully for errors whatever you have written. Proofreading is the best cure for carelessness in punctuation, capitalization, spelling, and grammar. It takes only a few minutes, yet it makes a great difference in the correctness of your work.

SPELLING RULES

Our English language owes its richness to the vast number of words it has borrowed from foreign sources. The payment for this richness, however, is the very wide variety in spelling. Words that sound alike are, only too often, not spelled alike. Nevertheless, there are strong family likenesses among many words, and the simple rules describing them are easy to learn. Learn these rules and you will be saved many trips to the dictionary.

ie and ei

26a. Write *ie* when the sound is long *e*, except after *c*.

EXAMPLES   piece, belief, niece, deceive, receive, conceive

EXCEPTIONS   either, seize, neither, weird

Write *ei* when the sound is not long *e*, especially when the sound is long *a*.

EXAMPLES   neighbor, weigh, veil, freight, forfeit, height

EXCEPTIONS   friend, mischief, conscience

● EXERCISE 1.   Write the following words, supplying the missing letters (*e* and *i*) in the correct order. Be able to explain how the rule applies to each.

1. ach...ve	7. y...ld	13. conc...ve
2. rec...pt	8. gr...f	14. sl...gh
3. p...rce	9. c...ling	15. v...l
4. bes...ge	10. dec...t	16. th...r
5. rel...f	11. rec...ve	17. h...ght
6. w...ld	12. dec...ve	18. f...rce

–cede, –ceed, and –sede

26b. Only one English word ends in *–sede*—supersede; only three words end in *–ceed*—exceed, proceed, and succeed; all other words of similar sound end in *–cede*.

EXAMPLES   recede, concede, precede

Adding Prefixes

A prefix is one or more letters or syllables added to the beginning of a word to change its meaning.

26c. When a prefix is added to a word, the spelling of the word itself remains the same.

il + legible = illegible   dis + advantage = disadvantage
in + sensitive = insensitive   dis + similar = dissimilar
im + partial = impartial   mis + lead = mislead
un + usual = unusual   mis + spell = misspell
un + necessary = unnecessary   over + run = overrun
re + capture = recapture   over + look = overlook

Adding Suffixes

A suffix is one or more letters or syllables added to the end of a word to change its meaning.

26d. When the suffixes *–ness* and *–ly* are added to a word, the spelling of the word itself is not changed.

EXAMPLES usual + ly = usually   mean + ness = meanness

EXCEPTIONS Words ending in *y* change the *y* to *i* before *–ness* and *–ly:* steady—steadily, sloppy—sloppiness. One-syllable adjectives ending in *y*, however, generally follow Rule 26d: shy—shyness, dry—dryly.

● EXERCISE 2. Spell correctly the words indicated.

1. *accidental* with the suffix *ly*
2. *heavy* with the suffix *ness*
3. *satisfied* with the prefix *dis*
4. *mean* with the suffix *ness*
5. *legal* with the prefix *il*
6. *appear* with the prefix *dis*
7. *understand* with the prefix *mis*
8. *sincere* with the suffix *ly*
9. *nerve* with the prefix *un*
10. *complete* with the suffix *ly*
11. *qualified* with the prefix *un*
12. *kind* with the suffix *ness*
13. *literate* with the prefix *il*
14. *ordinary* with the suffix *ly*
15. *ability* with the prefix *in*

26
a-d

16. *mature* with the prefix *im*
17. *consider* with the prefix *re*
18. *adequate* with the prefix *in*
19. *appoint* with the prefix *dis*
20. *sudden* with the suffix *ness*
21. *use* with the prefix *mis*
22. *stated* with the prefix *mis*
23. *noticed* with the prefix *un*
24. *special* with the suffix *ly*

26e. Drop the final *e* before a suffix beginning with a vowel.

EXAMPLES   dine + ing = dining
sense + ible = sensible
use + able = usable

EXCEPTIONS   Keep the final *e* before a suffix beginning with *a* or *o* if necessary to retain the soft sound of *c* or *g* preceding the *e*.

serviceable, advantageous, manageable
dye + ing = dyeing   [to prevent confusion with dying]

26f. Keep the final *e* before a suffix beginning with a consonant.

EXAMPLES   use + ful = useful
advertise + ment = advertisement
care + ful = careful

EXCEPTIONS   true + ly = truly
argue + ment = argument

● EXERCISE 3.   Write correctly the words formed as indicated.

1. guide + ance
2. scare + ing
3. courage + ous
4. approve + al
5. desire + able
6. separate + ing
7. nine + ty
8. taste + less
9. retire + ing
10. advance + ing
11. pronounce + able
12. compare + able
13. defense + less
14. hope + ful
15. whole + ly
16. true + ly
17. achieve + ment
18. use + ing
19. severe + ly
20. continue + ous

26g. With words ending in *y* preceded by a consonant, change the *y* to *i* before any suffix not beginning with an *i*.

EXAMPLES   lively + ness = liveliness
 bury + ing = burying
 bury + al = burial

● EXERCISE 4. Write correctly the words formed as indicated.

1. happy + est	11. pity + ful
2. friendly + est	12. pity + ing
3. merry + est	13. mercy + ful
4. marry + ing	14. satisfy + ed
5. marry + ed	15. try + ed
6. prophesy + ing	16. pretty + ness
7. prophesy + ed	17. busy + ly
8. carry + er	18. busy + ing
9. beauty + ful	19. gory + ness
10. spy + ing	20. glory + fied

26h. Double the final consonant before a suffix that begins with a vowel if both of the following conditions exist:

(1) the word has only one syllable or is accented on the last syllable.

(2) the word ends in a single consonant preceded by a single vowel.

EXAMPLES   win + ing = winning   [one-syllable word]
 omit + ed = omitted   [accent on the last syllable]
 begin + er = beginner   [accent on the last syllable]
 differ + ence = difference   [accent on the first syllable]
 droop + ed = drooped   [single consonant ending preceded by a *double* vowel]

26
e-h

● EXERCISE 5. Write correctly the words formed as indicated.

1. hit + er
2. propel + er
3. shovel + ing
4. beg + ing
5. refer + ed
6. refer + al
7. repel + ent
8. confer + ed
9. confer + ence
10. deter + ent
11. develop + ed
12. hope + ing
13. hop + ing
14. shop + ed
15. remit + ance
16. control + er
17. big + est
18. prefer + able

The Plural of Nouns

26i. Observe the rules for spelling the plural of nouns.

(1) The regular way to form the plural of a noun is to add an *s*.

EXAMPLES   dog, dogs   pencil, pencils

(2) The plural of some nouns is formed by adding *es*. Words ending in *s*, *x*, *z*, *sh*, and *ch* form the plural by adding *es*.

The *e* is necessary to make the plural form pronounceable.

EXAMPLES   waltz, waltzes   trench, trenches
            bush, bushes   glass, glasses

(3) The plural of nouns ending in *y* following a consonant is formed by changing the *y* to *i* and adding *es*.

EXAMPLES   city, cities   spy, spies
            enemy, enemies   penny, pennies

(4) The plural of nouns ending in *y* following a vowel is formed by adding an *s*.

EXAMPLES   turkey, turkeys   essay, essays

(5) The plural of most nouns ending in *f* or *fe* is formed by adding *s*. The plural of some nouns ending in *f* or *fe* is formed by changing the *f* or *fe* to *v* and adding *es*.

EXAMPLES   Add *s:*

belief, beliefs   chief, chiefs
roof, roofs   cliff, cliffs

Change *f* or *fe* to *v* and add *es:*

wife, wives   wolf, wolves
knife, knives   thief, thieves
                   leaf, leaves

(6) The plural of nouns ending in *o* preceded by a vowel is formed by adding *s*. The plural of most nouns ending in *o* preceded by a consonant is formed by adding *es*.

EXAMPLES   *o* preceded by a vowel:

patio, patios   radio, radios

o preceded by a consonant:

tomato, tomatoes   hero, heroes   Negro, Negroes

EXCEPTIONS   Words ending in *o* that refer to music form the plural by adding *s*:

alto, altos   piano, pianos
soprano, sopranos   solo, solos

(7) The plural of a few nouns is formed in irregular ways.

EXAMPLES   child, children   man, men   mouse, mice
            ox, oxen   tooth, teeth

(8) The plural of compound nouns consisting of a noun plus a modifier is formed by making the noun plural.

In the following examples, the phrases *in-chief* and *in-law* and the adjective *on* are all modifiers. It is the nouns modified by them that are made plural.

26i

EXAMPLES   editor-in-chief, editors-in-chief
son-in-law, sons-in-law
looker-on, lookers-on

(9) The plural of a few compound nouns is formed in irregular ways.

EXAMPLES   drive-in, drive-ins   two-year-old, two-year-olds
standby, standbys

(10) Some nouns are the same in the singular and the plural.

EXAMPLES   Chinese, Chinese   trout, trout   sheep, sheep
deer, deer   salmon, salmon

(11) The plural of foreign words is sometimes formed as in the original language.

EXAMPLES   alumnus [man], alumni [men]
alumna [woman], alumnae [women]
vertebra, vertebrae
parenthesis, parentheses
datum, data
monsieur, messieurs

♦ NOTE   The plural of other foreign words may be formed either as in the foreign language or in the regular way in English by adding *s* or *es*. Sometimes the English plural is preferred. For such words, consult the dictionary.

EXAMPLES   formula, formulae or formulas [preferred]
index, indices or indexes [preferred]
concerto, concerti or concertos [preferred]

(12) The plural of numbers, letters, signs, and words considered as words is formed by adding an apostrophe and *s*.

EXAMPLES   In the equation are two *t*'s.
There are three 7's in my address.
Please don't use so many *and*'s.

● EXERCISE 6.   Write the plural form of each of the following nouns and the number of the rule that applies.

1. cupful
2. girl
3. valley
4. oasis
5. calf
6. porch
7. sky
8. goose
9. π
10. monkey

11. Japanese
12. ox
13. father-in-law
14. deer
15. solo
16. self
17. board of education
18. alumnus
19. loaf
20. hero

● EXERCISE 7.   Write the plural form of each of the following nouns and the number of the rule that applies.

1. alley
2. old-timer
3. lieutenant governor
4. half
5. donkey
6. theory
7. handkerchief
8. bacillus
9. gallery
10. echo

11. justice of the peace
12. stitch
13. radio
14. plateful
15. roof
16. burglary
17. mouthful
18. *b* (the letter)
19. man
20. gas

● EXERCISE 8.   By referring to the rules you have learned, explain orally the spelling of each of the following:

1. crises
2. deceive
3. writing (*e* dropped)
4. believe
5. sopranos
6. misstep
7. meanness
8. noticeable
9. relief
10. cities

11. unhonored
12. data
13. beautifully
14. weird
15. typing (*e* dropped)
16. overrun
17. overflows
18. neighbor
19. wives
20. dissimilar

WORDS FREQUENTLY CONFUSED

---

affect   [verb] *Affect* is usually a verb meaning *to influence*.
Did that tearful movie *affect* you?

effect   [noun or verb] As a verb, *effect* means *to accomplish*.
New glasses *effected* a remarkable change in his vision.
As a noun, *effect* means the *result of some action*.
What *effect* did the rain have on the garden?

---

all right   [This is the only acceptable spelling. The spelling *alright* is not acceptable.]

---

already   *previously*
We have *already* painted the sets.

all ready   *all are ready*
We were *all ready* to play.

---

all together   *everyone in the same place*
The boys were *all together* in the gym.

altogether   *entirely*
I am not *altogether* convinced.

---

brake   [noun or verb] *to slow yourself down* or the device you use to do so
At the curve, Georgia *braked* the speeding car.

break   [noun or verb] *to fracture* or the fracture itself
Don't *break* the speed limit.

---

capital   [Correct spelling for all uses except when the word means a *government building*.]
What is the *capital* of Colorado?
You need *capital* to start a business.
Begin all sentences with *capital* letters.
Do you believe in *capital* punishment?

capitol   *government building* [frequently capitalized]
We could see the *capitol* from our hotel.

choose [verb, present tense]
Alicia and Katherine *choose* partners now.

chose [verb, past tense]
When the signal was given, the girls *chose* two seniors.

coarse *rough, crude*
When he spilled the *coarse* salt, he used *coarse* language.

course *path of action;* also used with *of* to mean *as was to be expected*
Of course, you are always right.
He skipped the first *course* at dinner.
The *course* in speech helped my diction.
A new golf *course* opened last week.

complement [noun or verb] *to make whole or complete* or *that which makes whole or complete*
The *complement*, or full crew, is six hundred men.
The *complement* of 60° is 30°.

compliment [noun or verb] *respect, affection,* or *esteem*
Convey my *compliments* to the captain.
I *complimented* him on his success.

consul [noun] *a diplomat appointed by a government to reside in a foreign country and look after the interests of fellow citizens traveling or doing business there*
The American *consul* in Rangoon arranged for my trip to the interior.

council, councilor [noun] *a group meeting to discuss and take action on official matters; a member of such a group*
The *councilors* on the Security *Council* voted for the Canadian resolution.

counsel, counselor [noun or verb] *advice* or *to advise; an adviser*
Sue's aunt *counseled* her to refuse the invitation.
Ask your guidance *counselor*.

---

des'ert	*a dry region*
	The car crossed the *desert* at night.
desert'	*to leave*
	The rats *deserted* the unlucky ship.
dessert	*the last part of a meal*
	For *dessert* we had custard.

● EXERCISE 9.   Number your paper 1–15. Write after the proper number the correct one of the words given in parentheses in the sentences below.

1. The illness had a strange (affect, effect) on Margie.
2. Our family hasn't been (all together, altogether) for a reunion in years.
3. My small cousin knows the (capitol, capital) city of every state in our country.
4. The (coarse, course) material made her skin itch.
5. Of (course, coarse), Abby burned the (desert, dessert) again.
6. The British (council, consul) removed his pince-nez and (counciled, counseled) Marlowe to leave Stanleyville before the rains came.
7. It seemed as if we had walked miles before we reached the main door of the (capital, capitol).
8. Your answer isn't (all together, altogether) correct, but you're on the right track.
9. After all his worry, everything turned out (all right, alright).
10. Our four fast ball-handlers are (complimented, complemented) perfectly by an exceedingly tall pivot man.
11. A typing (coarse, course) is recommended for anyone planning to go to college.
12. We traveled for three days across the (desert, dessert).
13. The actors were (all ready, already) to audition for the play.
14. Owing to defective (brakes, breaks), the bus rolls down the hill and (breaks, brakes) through the guard rail.
15. Let's all (choose, chose) partners for the gavotte.

● EXERCISE 10.   Write sentences in which you use correctly each of the words just studied.

formally   *in a formal manner*
For funerals, weddings, and christenings, one should dress *formally*.

formerly   *previously*
The high ridges of the Blue Ridge Mountains were *formerly* the bed of an ancient sea.

hear   *using your ears*
You will have to speak louder; I can't *hear* you.

here   *this place*
You can't sit *here;* this section is only for juniors.

its   possessive of *it*
The town hasn't raised *its* tax rate in three years.

it's   *it is*
It's not time to get up.

lead   [present tense] *to go first*
You *lead* because you know the way.

led   [past tense of *lead*]
He *led* us five miles out of the way.

lead   [pronounced led] *a heavy metal;* also *graphite in a pencil*
These books are as heavy as *lead*.

loose   *free, not close together*
Put all the *loose* papers in the folder.
His little brother has two *loose* teeth.

lose   [pronounced looz] *to suffer loss*
Do not *lose* your tickets.

miner   [noun] *a collier* or *worker in a mine*
Miners' canaries told them when the air grew bad in the deep shafts.

minor   *lesser* or *under legal age*
In some states *minors* may not operate a vehicle after dark.

moral	*good;* also *a lesson of conduct*
	We admire a *moral* person.
	The *moral* of the story is to look before you leap.
morale	*mental condition, spirit*
	After three defeats, the team's *morale* was low.
passed	[verb, past tense of *pass*]
	We *passed* the papers to the front.
past	[noun or adjective or preposition]
	To understand the present, you must study the *past*.
	Adele read the minutes of the *past* meeting.
	The dog walked *past* the cat and never noticed it.

● EXERCISE 11. Number your paper 1–15. Write after the proper number the correct one of the words given in parentheses in the sentences below.

1. Where did you (here, hear) that story?
2. You can (lead, led) a horse to water, but you can't make him drink.
3. If you (lose, loose) the directions, we'll never get there.
4. For the (passed, past) week he has done nothing but work on his term paper.
5. The general spoke to the troops to improve their (moral, morale).
6. While the heir was still a (minor, miner), the estate was held in trust.
7. Our horse (lead, led) all the others around the track.
8. In only a few minutes the guest speaker will be (hear, here).
9. If (it's, its) not too much trouble, would you mail this package for me?
10. After she went on a diet, her clothes were too (lose, loose).
11. (Formerly, Formally), California was part of New Spain.
12. After the house had been painted, (it's, its) appearance was vastly improved.
13. When the little birds sickened and died, the (minors, miners) were warned to get out of the pits.

14. (Its, It's) not every day that his father lets him use the car.
15. After two years of struggling with French I, Barney finally (passed, past) the course.

● EXERCISE 12. Write sentences in which you use correctly each of the words just studied.

personal	*individual* The manager gave the customer his *personal* attention.
personnel	*a group of people employed in the same place* The management added four new employees to the *personnel*.

principal	*head of a school;* also an adjective, *main* or *most important* The *principal* of our school is Mr. Grebinar. The *principal* export of Brazil is coffee.
principle	*a rule of conduct;* also *a main fact* or *law* His *principles* are very high. On what *principle* did you base your argument?

quiet	*silent, still*
quite	*wholly* or *rather* or *very* Are you *quite* sure the studio is *quiet* enough to record?

shone	[past tense of *shine*] The star *shone* in the sky.
shown	*revealed* or *demonstrated* The slides were *shown* after dinner.

stationary	*in a fixed position* One of the desks is movable; the other is *stationary*.
stationery	*writing paper* Amanda's purple and perfumed *stationery* is in bad taste.

---

than   [a conjunction, used for comparisons]
               He is smarter *than* I.

then   [an adverb or conjunction] *at that time* or *next*
               We swam for an hour; *then* we went home.
               They didn't know me *then*.

---

their   [possessive of *they*]
               Their new car is a Plymouth.

there   *a place;* also an expletive
               I haven't been *there* in ages.
               There is too much crab grass in your lawn.

they're   *they are*
               They're singing off key.

● EXERCISE 13.   Number your paper 1–15. Write after the proper number the correct one of the words given in parentheses in the sentences below.

1. He doesn't understand any of the (principals, principles) of physics.
2. The sun (shone, shown) all day.
3. All during the inspection of the judges, the dogs in the ring remained (stationery, stationary).
4. He acts much older (than, then) he really is.
5. He spoke in a (quite, quiet) voice, (quite, quiet) out of keeping with his usually raucous manner.
6. You ask too many (personnel, personal) questions.
7. A collection of his paintings was (shone, shown) to the public last week.
8. You should never bother the animals when (their, they're, there) eating.
9. "Haven't you any (principals, principles)?" the judge asked the thief.
10. (Quite, quiet) soon after the strange uproar, all became (quite, quiet) again.
11. The book store is having a big sale on (stationery, stationary).
12. We are going to (there, their, they're) house.

13. All the (personal, personnel) in the store received a bonus at Christmas.
14. If you see the (principle, principal) in the hall, tell him he is wanted in the main office.
15. I don't care what (their, they're, there) parents let them do; you still aren't going to come in so late at night.

● EXERCISE 14. Write sentences in which you use correctly each of the words just studied.

---

to	[preposition; also part of the infinitive form of the verb]
	You must return the books *to* the library.
	He began *to* whistle.
too	[adverb] *also, too much*
	Barry plays the trumpet, and Wes plays it *too*.
	You are *too* young to drive.
two	*One plus one*
	I will graduate in *two* years.

---

waist	*the midsection*
	She wore a sash around her *waist*.
waste	[noun or verb] *to spend foolishly* or *a needless expense*
	Waste not; want not.

---

weather	*conditions outdoors*
	The *weather* has been perfect all week.
whether	[as in *whether or not*]
	He didn't know *whether* or not his parents would let him go hosteling.

---

who's	*who is, who has*
	Who's been using my socks?
	Who's there?
whose	[possessive of *who*]
	Whose book is that?

---

your	[possessive of *you*]
	Your coat is in the closet.
you're	*you are*
	You're never on time.

● EXERCISE 15. Number your paper 1–15. Write after the proper number the correct one of the words given in parentheses in the sentences below.

1. Around his (waste, waist) he wore a handmade leather belt.
2. (You're, Your) guidance counselor wants to see you today.
3. (Weather, Whether) or not you can take six subjects next term depends upon your grades this term.
4. There was (too, to, two) much traffic on the road, and we didn't enjoy the ride.
5. (Whose, Who's) going to buy his ticket now?
6. (Your, You're) going to have to work harder if you want to be a junior next year.
7. It really doesn't matter (whose, who's) fault it is.
8. You (to, two, too) can be a good speller if you really have the desire.
9. "(Whose, Who's) been fooling around with my razor?" shouted Dad.
10. (Weather, Whether) or not it rains or snows, we will be there.
11. This is fine (whether, weather) for sailing.
12. (Your, You're) sure that Mr. Thompson wanted to see me?
13. I don't know (whose, who's) slower, Brad or you.
14. We never can have (two, too, to) many people working on the decorations for the dance.
15. The list on the bulletin board will tell you (whose, who's) on the honor roll.

● EXERCISE 16. Write sentences in which you use correctly each of the words just studied.

● REVIEW EXERCISE. Number your paper 1–33. Select the correct one of the words in parentheses in each sentence, and write it after the proper number.

1. The dome of the (Capitol, Capital) could be seen from every part of the city.
2. If you want to win the election, you will have to plan your (coarse, course) of action now.
3. The paint has (all ready, already) begun to peel.
4. After reentry the capsule is (breaked, braked) by a huge parachute.
5. If you think (its, it's) too warm, turn the heat down.
6. My (morale, moral) sank to a new low when I failed the Latin test.
7. Since I've got you (all together, altogether), I want to tell you some good news.
8. Do you remember (whether, weather) or not Mr. Allen gave us a homework assignment?
9. You must start proper nouns with a (capitol, capital) letter.
10. I had (already, all ready) finished ten problems in algebra when I realized we had to do only five.
11. Bonnie addressed us (formerly, formally): "Ladies and gentlemen of the sophomore class."
12. Whenever you (lead, led) the way, we always get lost.
13. (Their, There) hasn't been a drop of rain in months.
14. He keeps his (loose, lose) change in a cup in the china closet.
15. (Their, They're, There) are two *m*'s in *recommend*.
16. The spotlight (shone, shown) on the actress as she walked to the center of the stage.
17. Can't you write better (than, then) that, Philip?
18. Where do you think (your, you're) going?
19. Because Chris is on a diet, she always skips (desert, dessert).
20. He has a (principal, principle) part in the play.
21. After two days at sea, he knew he wouldn't feel (alright, all right) until the boat docked.
22. The lion broke (loose, lose).
23. Slung about his (waste, waist) was a brace of enormous .44's.
24. (Whose, Who's) responsible for this mess?
25. If you haven't (all ready, already) bought your tickets, you should do so now.
26. Whenever (you're, your) in doubt about the spelling of a word, consult the dictionary.

27. Don't you (dessert, desert) me in my hour of need.
28. The navy was testing (it's, its) newest submarine.
29. Her coat was made from a very (course, coarse) tweed.
30. Crossing the (desert, dessert) at night, we avoided the hot rays of the sun.
31. The Town (Counsel, Council) ordered the contractor to repair the roads at once.
32. Every morning at 8:40, the (principle, principal) reads the announcements of the day.
33. He had a (personal, personnel) interview with the President.

ONE HUNDRED SPELLING DEMONS

ache	early
again	easy
always	enough
among	every
answer	existence
any	February
been	forty
beginning	friend
believe	grammar
blue	guess
break	half
built	having
business	hear
busy	here
buy	hoarse
can't	hour
choose	instead
color	just
coming	knew
cough	know
could	laid
country	loose
dear	lose
doctor	making
does	many
done	meant
don't	minute

much	though
none	through
often	tired
once	tonight
piece	too
raise	trouble
read	truly
ready	Tuesday
said	two
says	very
seems	wear
separate	Wednesday
shoes	week
similar	where
since	whether
some	which
straight	whole
sugar	women
sure	won't
tear	would
their	write
there	writing
they	wrote

THREE HUNDRED SPELLING WORDS

absence	adequately	apparatus
absorption	administration	appearance
abundant	adolescent	appropriate
acceptable	aggressive	approximately
accidentally	agriculture	arousing
accommodation	amateur	arrangement
accompaniment	ambassador	
accurate	analysis	ascend
accustomed		association
achievement	analyze	athlete
	angel	bankruptcy
acquaintance	annual	basically
actuality	answered	beneficial

benefited
bicycle
breathe
brilliant

calendar
category
changeable
characteristic
chemistry
chief
circumstance
civilization
cocoon
commencement

commissioner
committed
comparative
comparison
competition
conceivable
confidential
confirmation
conscientious
consciousness

consequently
considerable
consistency
continuous
controlled
controversial
cordially
corps
correspondence
criticize

curiosity

curriculum
definition
delegate
denied
develop
difference
disastrous
disciple
dissatisfied

distinction
distinguished
dividend
dominant
dormitory
earnest
easily
ecstasy
eighth
eliminate

embroidery
endeavor
enemy
enormous
equipment
especially
essential
estimation
etiquette
exaggeration

examination
exceedingly
exceptional
excitable
executive
exercise
exhaustion

exhibition
expense
extension

extraordinary
fallacy
fantasies
favorably
fiery
financial
foreigner
forfeit
fragile
fulfill

fundamentally
gasoline
grammatically
grateful
guidance
gymnasium
handkerchief
happiness
heroic
hindrance

humorist
hygiene
hypocrisy
illustrate
imitation
immense
inability
incidentally
indispensable
influential

innocence
inquiry

institute
intellect
interference
interpretation
interruption
interval
irrelevant
irresistible

island
jealousy
journal
laborious
liability
lightning
likelihood
liveliest
locally
luxury

magnificence
maintenance
maneuver
mansion
martyr
maturity
medical
merchandise
merit
miniature

mischievous
missile
misspelled
monotony
mortgage
municipal
narrative
naturally

neighbor
noticeable

nuisance
obstacle
occasionally
occupy
odor
offensive
omitted
opinion
opposition
optimism

ordinary
organization
ornament
pageant
pamphlet
parachute
parallel
pastime
peaceable
peasant

peril
permanent
persistent
perspiration
pertain
phase
picnic
pigeon
playwright
pleasant

poison
politician
positively

possibility
practically
practice
precede
precisely
predominant
preferred

prejudice
preliminary
preparation
primitive
priority
prisoner
procedure
proceedings
procession
prominent

proposition
prosperous
prove
psychology
publicity
purposes
qualities
quantities
questionnaire
readily

reference
referring
regard
register
rehearsal
religious
remembrance
representative
requirement

resistance

resolution
responsibility
restaurant
ridiculous
satisfactorily
security
senator
sensibility
sheer
sheriff

significance
simile
situated
solution
sophomore
souvenir

specific
specimen
spiritual
strenuous

stretch
studying
substantial
subtle
succession
summarize
superintendent
suppress
surgeon
suspense

syllable
symbol
symphony

technique
temperature
tendency
tournament
traffic
twelfth
tying

tyranny
unanimous
undoubtedly
unforgettable
unpleasant
unusually
vacancies
varies
vengeance
villain

PART SEVEN

Aids
to Good
English

CHAPTER 27

The Library

Arrangement of the Library; Important Reference Books

During the Renaissance, some scholars set themselves the task of mastering all knowledge. Today no one imagines that one man can know all there is to know. There is simply too much information. As a result, the modern scholar is not expected to know all of the answers, but he is expected to know how to find the answers that he needs.

This is where the library comes in. A library contains information on most of the matters that modern man has found it worthwhile to know about. To avail yourself of this great store of knowledge, you must have a clear idea of the contents of your library and how they are arranged.

ARRANGEMENT OF BOOKS IN THE LIBRARY

27a. Learn the arrangement of books in your library.

Libraries are sufficiently alike so that when you are familiar with one library you can find your way in others.

Fiction

The fiction section contains novels and stories about imaginary people, places, and things. Here the books are arranged alphabetically according to the author's last name. Jane Austen's famous novels, for example, will come near the beginning of the section. If the library has several of her novels, they will be arranged under *Austen* alphabetically by *title*. For example, *Pride and Prejudice* will come before *Sense and Sensibility*.

Nonfiction

Since nonfiction includes so many kinds of books on so many subjects, the simple method used for arranging fiction will not do. Instead, most libraries use a system invented by an American librarian named Melvil Dewey.[1]

The Dewey decimal system classifies all nonfiction under ten major subject areas. Each of these ten classifications is assigned an identifying number which is printed on the spine of the book near the bottom.

The classifications and the numbers that stand for them are as follows:

000–099	General Works (encyclopedias, periodicals, etc.)
100–199	Philosophy (including psychology, behavior, etc.)
200–299	Religion (including mythology)
300–399	Social Sciences (including economics, government, law, etc.)
400–499	Language (dictionaries, grammars, etc.)
500–599	Science (mathematics, chemistry, physics, etc.)
600–699	Technology (agriculture, engineering, aviation, etc.)
700–799	The Arts (sculpture, painting, music, etc.)
800–899	Literature (poetry, plays, orations, etc.)
900–999	History

Within each of the ten major classifications, there are an unlimited number of subdivisions. A work of history, for example, bears a number in the 900's. Since, however,

[1] Many larger libraries use a somewhat different method of classification developed by the Library of Congress. This system is not described here, but if a library in your area uses this system, the librarian will tell you how it works.

27a

history is such a vast field and even a small library might well contain several hundred books on history, the 900's must be further broken down.

The Dewey decimal system accomplishes this by creating many subdivisions within each major class. For example, it breaks down the general class *History* in the following way:

900–999   History
   910–919   Geography, Travel
   920–929   Biography (arranged alphabetically according to the name of the person written about)
   930–939   Ancient History
   940–949   European History
   950–959   Asian History
   960–969   African History
   970–979   North American History
     971.0–971.99   Canadian History
     972.0–972.99   Mexican History
     973.0–979.99   United States History
       974.0–974.99   History of the Northeastern States
       975.0–975.99   History of the Southeastern States
       976.0–976.99   History of the South Central States
          etc.

Therefore, a book bearing the number 972 will be generally a work of history (900), specifically a work on North American history (970), and still more specifically a work on Mexican history (972). This number, called *the call number*, may include a decimal point and additional identifying numbers to indicate a smaller division of the subject, such as a particular period of history. Large libraries find it necessary to use many numbers after the decimal point, but in smaller libraries the author's initial is usually printed under the call number to distinguish the book from other works on the same subject. For example, the call number $\frac{972}{P}$ may be used to designate William Prescott's famous history, *The Conquest of Mexico;* it will appear not only on the spine of the book itself, but also on every card in the card catalogue referring to it.

Once you have learned the call number, you may either go directly to the proper shelf and pick out the book; or, if the stacks are inaccessible to the public, have the librarian get the book for you.

LOCATING INFORMATION IN THE LIBRARY

The Card Catalogue

27b. Learn the uses of the card catalogue.

In every library there is a cabinet of small drawers containing cards. These cards list every book in the library alphabetically. In the average library there are usually three cards for each book: a *title card*, an *author card*, and at least one *subject card.*

1. *The author.* On the *author card*, as you can see on page 536, the author's name appears on the top line, last name first. If you wanted a book by a particular writer, you could look it up in the card catalogue under the author's last name. All books by an author are listed on similar cards and are arranged under his name in alphabetical order of their *titles.* All books *about* an author (critical studies of his work, biographies, etc.) are listed on cards coming after the cards for his own books.

2. *The title.* The title of the book is printed at the top of the *title card.* Title cards are arranged alphabetically according to the first letter of the title. If this first word is an article, however—an *a, an,* or *the*—then the card is filed according to the *second* word of the title. Jack London's story *The Call of the Wild* would come under the *C*'s, not the *T*'s.

3. *The subject.* The subject is printed at the top (usually in red) on the *subject card.* This kind of card is a great time-

27b

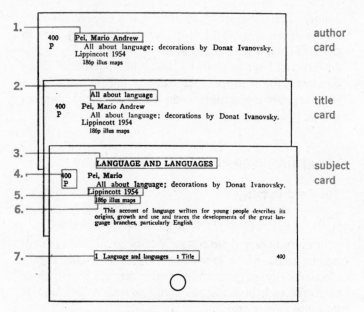

Sample Library Cards

saver when you come into the library to look up information on a general topic with no particular book in mind. Subject cards direct you to whatever books in the library deal with your topic. Among the subject cards, you frequently find still other subject cards dealing with different aspects of the main topic. For example, under the subject "Languages," you may find cards labeled "Linguists," "Orthography," "Composition," as well as "see" or "see also" cards. These "see also" cards refer you to yet another part of the catalogue for the information you are seeking. Under the topic "Ellis Island" you might find a card saying, "See United States—Immigrant Station, Ellis Island"; or under "Communism," another card saying, "See also Anarchism and Anarchists."

4. *The call number.* This Dewey decimal number appears on every catalogue card referring to the book.

5. *The publisher and the date of publication.* This information is important to students who wish to make sure they are consulting the latest information on any subject. A book on atomic physics published in 1960 would be vastly different from one published in 1930.

6. *The description of the book. All About Language,* for example, has 186 pages; the book is illustrated, and it has maps.

7. *The headings in the card catalogue under which the book is listed.*

● EXERCISE 1. Remembering that books are catalogued by title, author, and subject, answer the following questions by using the card catalogue in your library.

1. Does the library have these books?
   The Good Earth   *Vanity Fair*
   To Kill a Mockingbird   *The Adventures of Sherlock*
   The Swiss Family Robinson   *Holmes*
2. Does your library have any books written by John Steinbeck, Thomas Mann, Marjorie Kinnan Rawlings, and John Dos Passos? If it does, write the title of one book by each.
3. Give the title, author, publisher, and publication date of a book about Abraham Lincoln.
4. Does your library have any books by Winston Churchill? If so, give the title and call number of one of them.
5. What is the most recent book about electronics in your library? Give the call number.
6. Find the author, title, publisher, and call number of the following books:
   a. A book about American artists
   b. A book about American Indians
   c. A book by Jonathan Swift
   d. A book giving information about Jonathan Swift
   e. A book about photography

The Parts of a Book

Once the card catalogue has helped you find your book on the shelves, and you have it in hand, a quick glance at certain standard parts will tell you if it contains the information you seek.

27c.   Learn the parts of a book.

Not every book has all the parts described here, but all books have some of them. They are very useful in that they enable you to get acquainted with a book with no loss of time. Every careful reader should be familiar with them.

1. *The frontispiece.* A full page illustration usually facing the title page.

2. *The title page.* A page giving the complete title of the book, the complete name of the author (or authors), the name of the publisher, and the place of publication.

3. *The copyright page.* A page on the reverse side of the title page telling when the book was listed at the United States copyright office to protect the author's rights of ownership. The copyright page also tells by whom the book was copyrighted (sometimes the author, sometimes the publisher).

The copyright date is important when you want to know if the book's information is up-to-date. A book may be many times reprinted (each time with a new publication date) and yet be unchanged in form and content. A new copyright date, on the other hand, informs you that new material has been added. Do not confuse the copyright date with a date of reprinting. Copyrights often appear as a list of dates.

EXAMPLE   Copyright © 1965, 1963, 1959

4. *The preface, foreword,* or *introduction.* A section at the beginning of a book in which the author speaks directly to the reader. In this place he may comment about

the writing of the book, acknowledge the help he has received from others, indicate the purpose of the book, and generally prepare the reader for what is to come.

5. *The table of contents.* A table at the beginning giving, usually, the title of chapters, their subdivisions, and the number of the page on which each begins. The table of contents gives a general view of the book. Accordingly, it enables you to determine whether the book contains the information you want without leafing through the entire book. Works of fiction, of course, usually have no table of contents.

6. *List of illustrations.* A list telling what graphic materials (maps, diagrams, charts, etc.) are provided in the book and where they are found.

7. *The appendix.* A section containing material not included in the body of the book which the author nevertheless considers relevant. The appendix may include charts, maps, lists, statistics, or even long quotations from other works on the same subject. A text on American history might include the *Declaration of Independence* and the *Constitution* in the appendix.

8. *The glossary.* A dictionary section, usually at the end of the book, in which technical or difficult words and expressions are explained.

9. *The bibliography.* A list of books, periodicals, films, and other sources which the author has consulted in his preparation of the text. Many books have bibliographies at the end of each chapter listing books which the author recommends. Others have a single bibliography at the end of the book.

10. *The index.* A guide to all information in the book. It lists alphabetically the topics treated in the book. It is much more detailed than the table of contents and gives the exact page on which a topic is discussed. For those in search of specific information, it is doubtless the most important part of the book other than the text itself.

27c

11. *The end papers.* Pages pasted inside the front and back covers of the book. Maps, diagrams, charts, and illustrations are sometimes there. For example, the end papers of a history of California might have a map of the state.

● EXERCISE 2. Write on your paper the answers to the following questions.

1. List the parts of a book of nonfiction that you would probably not find in a work of fiction.
2. Explain the importance of the copyright date.
3. Why is a glossary more useful in a book about stagecraft than in a collection of modern plays?
4. What is the difference between a table of contents and an index?
5. Would a typical novel be likely to have an index?
6. By what company was this textbook published?
7. How many pages are devoted to the index of this book?
8. What copyright dates are given for this book?
9. What do you find on the end papers of this book?
10. Skim the preface of this book and briefly explain its main purpose.

The Readers' Guide

27d. Learn to use the *Readers' Guide to Periodical Literature*.

Often in writing a report or in doing an assignment for one of your other subjects, you will have occasion to use a story, article, or poem published in a magazine. To find it conveniently, you will need to use the *Readers' Guide to Periodical Literature*, an index to the contents of more than one hundred magazines. The *Readers' Guide* is published roughly twice a month—twenty-two times a year—and at regular intervals these booklets are combined into a cumulative volume.

Magazine stories are listed in the *Readers' Guide* by title

and author; poems and plays are listed by author and under
the headings POEMS and DRAMAS. A sample excerpt
from the *Readers' Guide* is reproduced below. You can
probably figure out the meaning of the various abbreviations. If not, all of them are explained in the front of the
Readers' Guide itself.

PAVEMENTS, Asphalt ———————————————— subject entry
  New strength for old asphalt; Chino, Calif.
    E. T. Lynch. il Am City 79:90-1 F '64 ——— title of magazine
PAZ, Octavio
  Pause; Here; Girl; poems, tr. by J. F. Nims.
    Atlan 213:99 Mr '64
PEABODY college. See George Peabody college
  for teachers, Nashville, Tenn.
PEACE
  Teaching war prevention. S. H. Mendlovitz. — title of article
    Bul Atomic Sci 20:19-22 F '64
PEACE corps. See United States—Peace corps
PEARSON, Lester Bowles
  Canadian Prime Minister visits Washington;
    U.S. and Canada agree on Columbia River
    development and establishment of Cam-
    pobello Park; joint communique; with joint   articles about a
    statements and texts of agreements, Janu-   public figure
    ary 21-23, 1964. Dept State Bul 50:199-206
    F 10 '64
  Pearson's progress. W. H. Hessler. il Re-
    porter 30:24-9 Mr 12 '64
PEAT moss
  What do you know about peatmoss? J. M.
    Patek. Horticulture 42:50-1+ Mr '64 ——— volume and page
PEDESTRIAN of the air; drama. See Ionesco,   numbers
  E.
PENANCE, Sacrament of. See Confession ——— cross reference
PENCE, Audra May
  Local associations take responsibility for pro-
    fessional behavior. NEA J 53:22-3 F '64 — author entry
PENGUINS
  Navy issues orders: save that penguin! Sci
    N L 85:150 Mr 7 '64 ——————————————— date of magazine
PENNSYLVANIA
  Pennsylvania; reproduction of paintings. D.
    Schwartz. Fortune 69:84-91 F '64
      Economic conditions
  Scranton of Pennsylvania. R. A. Smith. il   divisions of
    Fortune 69:80-4+ F '64   main subject
      Politics and government
  Scranton of Pennsylvania. R. A. Smith. il
    Fortune 69:80-4+ F '64
PENSIONS
  See also
  Income
PERCH fishing
  Who's teaching whom? D. Llewellyn. il Out- — author's name
    door Life 133:66-8 Mr '64

27d

From *Readers' Guide*, March 25, 1964. Reprinted by permission of
The H. W. Wilson Company.

● EXERCISE 3.   Using the *Readers' Guide* in your school or public library, look up the answers to the following questions.

1. Choose one of the topics and look up in the *Readers' Guide* three recent articles about it. Give complete information: title and author, magazine, date, and page numbers.

France	Poetry
Horses	Recreation
Photography	Scholarships

2. Select one of the topics above, look it up in the *Readers' Guide*, and list on your paper five articles *that you could get in your library* on the subject.
3. Choose a prominent man or woman whom you admire, and in the *Readers' Guide* look up an article about him. Give author, title, and source.
4. Suppose you are writing an essay on the President. How many articles about him were published last month? List three that you could get in your library and give the information from the *Readers' Guide*.
5. How many articles about folk music are listed in the *Readers' Guide* you are using? List them.

The Vertical File

27e. Learn the nature and proper use of the vertical file.

Useful information on current topics is often to be found in pamphlets — brief treatments of a subject, usually bound in paper covers. They are published by government agencies, industrial concerns, museums, colleges and universities, radio stations, welfare organizations, etc. The librarian files pamphlets in a special cabinet, usually referred to as the vertical file, and can help you to find material on your subject, especially if it is of contemporary interest.

In the vertical file the librarian also stores interesting pictures and significant clippings from newspapers.

REFERENCE BOOKS IN THE LIBRARY

27f. Acquaint yourself with the reference books in your library.

In every library there is a section known as the reference section. Here the librarian keeps together those ready reference volumes which are designed to help you look up brief articles giving various kinds of information. You will find acquaintance with certain of these reference books to be very valuable.

Special Dictionaries

Belonging to the reference section of a library are various dictionaries of the English language such as those described on pages 555–57. In addition, there are many special dictionaries written to help you with specific problems of word choice, correct usage, etc. Very often a writer has some trouble thinking of the exact word with which to express his meaning. Often, too, he has used the same word so many times in a composition that he wishes to find a synonym for it to avoid repeating. The two books described below, as their titles suggest, will help a writer to find the words he needs.

Roget's Thesaurus of English Words and Phrases

The word *thesaurus* derives from a Latin word meaning "treasure," so that literally a thesaurus is a storehouse or treasury. The contents of this storehouse are synonyms and antonyms. While the thesaurus can be useful to a writer, it is also a dangerous book to use. Since the synonyms are listed without definitions or other indication of differences in meaning, it is easy to choose an inappropriate word. For example, all of the following synonyms are given for the verb *change: alter, modulate, veer, swerve,* and *deviate.* All of these synonyms have something to do with the gen-

27
e-f

eral idea of change, but each has a specific shade of meaning that would make it unsuitable for most of the contexts in which *change* appears.

Make it a rule to use a thesaurus only as a memory aid— a reminder of words you already know. Do *not* use an unfamiliar synonym you find in a thesaurus without checking its meaning in a reliable dictionary. A strange word that you hope will sound impressive is likely to strike your reader as absurdly inappropriate.

Webster's Dictionary of Synonyms

Much safer to use because of its detailed distinctions between synonyms, *Webster's Dictionary of Synonyms* can be a great help to a writer in search of a word.

Encyclopedias

An encyclopedia offers informative articles on a wide range of subjects. The articles in an encyclopedia are arranged alphabetically, but many facts and references can be found only by using the index. For example, the *Encyclopædia Britannica* has a long entry on the "Olympic Games," but there are a number of references to this topic elsewhere in the encyclopedia which you can find only by using the index.

Encyclopedias are designed for quick reference. Because they give a general background in a subject, they are a good place to begin research on an unfamiliar subject. Remember, however, that encyclopedias should be the starting point, not the end of research. Limitations of space prevent encyclopedias from treating their topics in depth. A report based entirely on encyclopedia entries is likely to be too general to be of any real merit.

Most reliable encyclopedias are kept up to date through frequent revisions. In addition, yearbooks are published to supply information on important developments of the preceding year.

The following encyclopedias are well known and widely used:

General Encyclopedias

Collier's Encyclopedia

  24 volumes
  Index in Volume 24
  Publishes *Collier's Yearbook*

Encyclopædia Britannica

  24 volumes
  Index and atlas in Volume 24
  Publishes the *Britannica Book of the Year*

Encyclopedia Americana

  30 volumes
  Index in Volume 30
  Publishes the *Americana Annual*

Encyclopedias for Young Readers

The Book of Knowledge

  20 volumes
  A Dictionary Index at the end of each volume
  Publishes the *Book of Knowledge Annual*

Compton's Pictured Encyclopedia

  15 volumes (One third of space is devoted to pictures.)
  Fact Index (an index which itself gives information) at the end
    of each volume
  Yearbook and annual supplement

World Book Encyclopedia

  20 volumes
  Reading and study guide
  Publishes an annual

Encyclopedias of Scientific Information

The McGraw-Hill Encyclopedia of Science and Technology

  15 volumes
  Index in Volume 15
  Publishes an annual

Van Nostrand's Scientific Encyclopedia

A large, one-volume encyclopedia easier to use than the *McGraw-Hill Encyclopedia* but much less complete in coverage

Encyclopedias of Historical Information

Langer's *Encyclopedia of World History*

An excellent one-volume work with a complete index at the end

Biographical Reference Books

Besides the standard encyclopedias there are many reference books which give biographies of famous persons.

Webster's Biographical Dictionary

A one-volume work with very short entries giving the basic facts of the person's life

The New Century Cyclopedia of Names

A three-volume work, the *Century Cyclopedia* gives short biographies as well as information about people, places, things, events, and literary characters.

Current Biography

Published monthly, *Current Biography* is the best source of information about prominent people in the news. A picture of the subject usually heads the biography. The monthly pamphlets are bound together into a book each year, and a cumulative index is provided. Using these indexes, the student can often follow the career of an important person from early issues of *Current Biography*, at which time the celebrity first attracted public attention, to the latest issues of the magazine, in which his later achievements are reported.

Who's Who and *Who's Who in America*

These volumes give important data about prominent *living* persons. *Who's Who* is a British publication dealing mainly with famous Englishmen; *Who's Who in America* provides similar information about famous Americans. In both works the biographical entries are fairly short, giving such data as parentage, date of birth, positions held and honors received, principal achievements, names of immediate family, and present address. *Who's Who* is published annually; *Who's Who in America*, every two years.

Reference Books About Authors

Some books are devoted exclusively to literary men and women. If your library has any of the famous "author" books by Stanley Kunitz, you will find them valuable sources of information about writers. Often the biographies are headed with a picture of the subject.

> *British Authors of the Nineteenth Century* by Kunitz and Haycraft
> *British Authors Before 1800* by Kunitz and Haycraft
> *American Authors 1600–1900* by Kunitz and Haycraft
> *Twentieth Century Authors* by Kunitz and Haycraft
> *Twentieth Century Authors: First Supplement* by Kunitz and Haycraft
> *European Authors 1000–1900* by Kunitz and Colby

Atlases

An atlas is chiefly a collection of maps, but it may contain, as well, a wealth of statistical material about industries, raw materials, trade routes, rainfall, air and sea currents, and many other kinds of information. Any of the following are good atlases and are likely to be found on the shelves of your library.

> *Collier's World Atlas and Geography*
> *Goode's World Atlas*

Hammond's Standard World Atlas
Rand McNally Cosmopolitan World Atlas
The Encyclopædia Britannica Atlas

Three historical atlases of particular interest to students of world history are listed below. These atlases represent graphically historical changes from the earliest times, showing the rise and fall of empires, the movement of peoples, and the spread of culture.

Heyden's *Atlas of the Classical World*
Rand McNally Atlas of World History
Shepherd's *Historical Atlas*

Almanacs and Yearbooks

For factual information on the world today, the most useful of all reference books are the almanacs. Three popular ones are *The World Almanac and Book of Facts*, the *Information Please Almanac*, and the *New York Times Encyclopedic Almanac*. All are published annually and are full of information and statistics about current events—sports, industry, agriculture, science, entertainment, and census information. In addition, almanacs contain articles on significant events and issues of the past year. They also contain much historical information. Indeed, in these handy volumes you can find items as diverse, for example, as the batting record of Roger Maris and the names of the original signers of the Constitution.

The Statesman's Yearbook

This fat volume is published annually and contains a compilation of statistical information about the economies of the nations of the world. Most of the information is in quantitative form (i.e., number of bales of cotton produced, balance of foreign payments, etc.), but some of the information is political, governmental, etc., and can be understood without much knowledge of economics.

Literature Reference Books

Bartlett's *Familiar Quotations*

Occasionally you will need to know a quotation or the author of a quotation. In such a case, the place to look is Bartlett's famous *Familiar Quotations*.

The quotations in Bartlett's are arranged chronologically by author; that is, William Shakespeare comes long before Robert Frost. At the end of the work, there is a huge index in which every quotation is listed alphabetically by its first (and every important) word. For example, if you wished to find out who wrote

> Know then thyself, presume not God to scan;
> The proper study of mankind is man.

You would find this quotation by Alexander Pope indexed under the words *know, presume, God, scan, study, mankind,* and *man.*

Stevenson's *The Home Book of Quotations*

Used for somewhat the same purpose as Bartlett's book, Stevenson's *The Home Book of Quotations* is, however, arranged differently. The quotations in this book are arranged by subjects. You can also find the author of a quotation, although, since the book is not arranged by authors, you will find the book less efficient for this purpose than Bartlett's. Stevenson's book is especially helpful if you want a quotation on a certain subject. For instance, if you want one on love or happiness or Christmas, you will find many listed under each of these topics.

Granger's *Index to Poetry*

Granger's *Index* contains no poems. It tells you in what books you can find almost any poem or recitation (popular prose passage) you wish. If you know the title of a poem or its author, yet do not know in what books you will find the poem, look it up in Granger's. There you will find a list of books in which, for example, "The Highwayman" can be found. The names of these books, however, are abbreviated; and in order to make sense of them, you must consult the list of abbreviations in the front of Granger's. Suppose, for example, that you find "The Highwayman" listed as appearing in BLV. A glance at the key to abbreviations tells you that BLV means the *Book of Living Verse.* Then it is a simple matter to check the card catalogue to see whether the library has the book. Granger's also indexes poems and recitations by their authors and by the first word in the line.

Stevenson's *The Home Book of Verse* and Stevenson's *The Home Book of Modern Verse*

These anthologies, containing well-known poems, are so large that you are almost certain to find the poem you wish in any one of them. They are indexed in three ways—by title, by author, and by first word. The poems themselves are collected under general headings like *Poems of Youth and Age, Poems of Nature, Familiar Verse,* and *Poems, Humorous and Satiric.* These headings are useful to students in search of a suitable poem on certain subjects.

● EXERCISE 4.   Your teacher may assign you to give a brief description of the books in the following list with which he thinks you should be familiar. Tell what sort of material the book contains, how the material is arranged, and how best to use the book.

Special Dictionaries

   Roget's Thesaurus of English Words and Phrases
   Webster's Dictionary of Synonyms

Encyclopedias

   Collier's Encyclopedia
   Encyclopædia Britannica
   Encyclopedia Americana

Compton's Pictured Encyclopedia
World Book Encyclopedia
The Book of Knowledge
The McGraw-Hill Encyclopedia of Science and Technology
Van Nostrand's Scientific Encyclopedia
Langer's *Encyclopedia of World History*

Biographical Reference Books

Webster's Biographical Dictionary
The New Century Cyclopedia of Names
Current Biography
Who's Who
Who's Who in America

Reference Books About Authors

British Authors of the Nineteenth Century
British Authors Before 1800
European Authors 1000–1900
American Authors 1600–1900
Twentieth Century Authors
Twentieth Century Authors: First Supplement

Atlases

Goode's World Atlas
Collier's World Atlas and Geography
Hammond's Standard World Atlas
Rand McNally Cosmopolitan World Atlas
The Encyclopædia Britannica Atlas

Historical Atlases

Heyden's *Atlas of the Classical World*
Rand McNally Atlas of World History
Shepherd's *Historical Atlas*

Almanacs and Yearbooks

The World Almanac and Book of Facts
Information Please Almanac
New York Times Encyclopedic Almanac
The Statesman's Yearbook

Literature Reference Books

Bartlett's *Familiar Quotations*

Stevenson's *The Home Book of Quotations*
Granger's *Index to Poetry*
Stevenson's *The Home Book of Verse*
Stevenson's *The Home Book of Modern Verse*

● EXERCISE 5. Disregarding dictionaries and encyclopedias, decide what reference book would be the best in which
to look up the following items of information. Number
your paper 1–10, and after the corresponding number, write
the title or titles of the reference book.

1. A picture of the modern author Harper Lee
2. The population of important world cities
3. A biography of someone recently risen to prominence
4. Facts about the president of Harvard
5. The poem "Patterns"
6. Several quotations from William Wordsworth
7. A number of quotations about loneliness
8. The title of a book containing Alan Seeger's poem "I Have
a Rendezvous with Death"
9. A short explanation of the meaning of "atomic number"
10. A map showing the first centers of civilization in the Near
East

● EXERCISE 6. Follow the directions for the preceding
exercise.

1. A brief, authoritative biography of Theodore Roosevelt
2. A list of the Presidents of the United States
3. The gross national product of France
4. Some interesting information about the poet Carl Sandburg
5. The rest of the quotation beginning "A robin redbreast in
a cage . . ."
6. The author of the poem "Abraham Lincoln Walks at Midnight"
7. A picture and biographical sketch of the nineteenth-century
American poet William Cullen Bryant
8. The name of the present governor of the state of Oklahoma
9. A record of the last five annual games in the Rose Bowl
10. The titles of several books in which the poem beginning
"All I could see from where I stood . . ." can be found

● EXERCISE 7. Name the reference book best suited as a source for the following information. You may include the dictionary and the encyclopedia. Be prepared to explain your choice.

1. A list of words meaning *knowledge*
2. An account of the construction of the Panama Canal
3. A very short biographical sketch of Woodrow Wilson
4. An explanation of the difference in meaning between two common words often used interchangeably—*pretty* and *beautiful*
5. A number of pictures of San Francisco
6. The years American tennis teams won the Davis Cup
7. The site in Asia Minor of ancient Troy
8. The average annual precipitation in Ghana
9. A clear explanation of Johann Kepler's laws of planetary motion
10. The principal exports of Argentina
11. A detailed map of Soviet Russia
12. A detailed map of the Holy Roman Empire in 1500
13. The meaning of the Latin phrase *carpe diem*
14. An account of Enrico Fermi and the "Chicago pile"
15. The special meaning of the word *absorption* in the study of the behavior of gases

CHAPTER 28

The Dictionary

Arrangement and Content of Dictionaries

A dictionary is a report on words and their uses. In a sense, a good dictionary is also a report on the civilization of the users of the language it deals with. "Languages," observed Dr. Samuel Johnson, "are the pedigrees of nations." A good dictionary gives a complete account of that pedigree. In addition to the present meaning and spelling of a word, dictionaries tell what a word has meant in the past, how it came to be a part of English, what other words it is related to, and other useful facts about its history. For those who know how to use it, a good dictionary contains a wealth of information about the history of English and attitudes of English-speaking people over the centuries.

In earlier years you learned how to find words in a dictionary by means of the alphabetical arrangement and the guide words at the top of each page. Being able to find a word is an essential dictionary skill, but it is not the only one. It is equally important to know how to interpret the information a dictionary gives you about a word. This chapter is intended to help you develop this second important skill.

554

KINDS OF DICTIONARIES

28a. Know the kinds of dictionaries.

Dictionaries have been prepared for many special purposes: for specialists in history, the sciences, and other special studies; for crossword puzzle enthusiasts; for poets and others with special interests. This chapter deals only with general dictionaries—those intended for the general public. There are two main kinds of general dictionaries: *unabridged* and *college* dictionaries.

The Unabridged Dictionary

An unabridged dictionary is one that is not based on a still larger dictionary. Although a large library may have several different unabridged dictionaries, the one that is best known and is most likely to be found in even the smallest library is *Webster's Third New International Dictionary*, which has been kept up-to-date through recent revisions. The newest unabridged dictionary is the *Random House Dictionary of the English Language, Unabridged Edition*.

An unabridged dictionary may contain almost a half million words. For many words, it gives uncommon or historical, but now old-fashioned, meanings. It clarifies some of the meanings of a word by quoting examples of its use by prominent writers of the past and present. It contains fuller discussions of the distinctions in meaning between words whose meanings may seem to be very similar.

To see how unabridged and college dictionaries differ, compare the two entries reproduced on page 556.

The College Dictionary

A college dictionary is a shorter work, designed for anyone's convenient reference but especially for the use of students. Such a dictionary may contain from 125,000 to 150,000 words, as well as some special sections giving abbreviations, biographical information of famous people,

28a

²cel·e·brate \-,brāt, *usu* -ād·+V\ *vb* -ED/-ING/-S [L *celebratus*, past part. of *celebrare* to frequent, celebrate, fr. *celebr-, celeber* much frequented, famous; akin to L *celer* swift — more at CELERITY] *vt* **1** : to perform (a sacrament or solemn ceremony) publicly and with appropriate rites : SOLEMNIZE ⟨~ the mass⟩ ⟨~ a marriage⟩   **2 a** : to honor (as a holy day or feast day) by conducting or engaging in religious, commemorative, or other solemn ceremonies or by refraining from ordinary business   **b** : to demonstrate grateful and happy satisfaction in (as an anniversary or event) by engaging in festivities, indulgence, merrymaking, or other similar deviation from accustomed routine ⟨as though he had had a drink or two — which indeed he might have had in reality, to ~ the occasion —Joseph Conrad⟩   **3** : to proclaim or broadcast for the attention of a wide public ⟨that bloody nationalism which *celebrated* itself on so large a scale in 1914-1918 —Francis Hackett⟩   **4 a** : to portray with a high valuation and usu. in enhanced or poetic form or in exalted interpretation in a way to contribute to public awareness, edification, or enjoyment : hold up or play up for public acclaim or homage : EXTOL, GLORIFY ⟨verses *celebrating* the personal idiosyncrasy of the Yankee farmer⟩ ⟨American fiction had regularly *celebrated* the American village as the natural home of the pleasant virtues —Carl Van Doren⟩   **b** : to commemorate in appreciative interpretation for posterity esp. in some literary or art form ⟨his birthplace, *celebrated* by him in his early poetry —Padraic Colum⟩ ⟨the sort of beauty that is *celebrated* by the heroic male sculptures in the fountains of Rome —Tennessee Williams⟩ ~ *vi* **1** : to observe a holiday, perform a religious ceremony, or take part in a festival ⟨in an Eastern liturgy several priests may ~ together⟩ ⟨in the Western mass, the priests ~ in the Latin fashion⟩   **2 a** : to observe the occasion of an achievement, reunion, anniversary, or other notable occasion with gaiety   **b** : to engage in hilarious festivities usu. including drinking   syn see KEEP

cel·e·brate \'sel-ə-,brāt\ *vb* [L *celebratus*, pp. of *celebrare* to frequent, celebrate, fr. *celebr-, celeber* much frequented, famous; akin to L *celer*] *vt* **1** : to perform (a sacrament or solemn ceremony) publicly and with appropriate rites ⟨~ the mass⟩   **2 a** : to honor (as a holy day or feast day) by solemn ceremonies or by refraining from ordinary business   **b** : to demonstrate satisfaction in by festivities or other deviation from routine   **3** : to hold up for public acclaim : EXTOL ~ *vi* **1** : to observe a holiday, perform a religious ceremony, or take part in a festival   **2** : to observe a notable occasion with festivities   syn see KEEP — cel·e·bra·tion \,sel-ə-'brā-shən\ *n* — cel·e·bra·tor \'sel-ə-,brāt-ər\ *n*

articles on spelling and punctuation, and other useful information. As the sample entries reproduced above suggest, a college dictionary does not attempt to report as fully on a word as an unabridged dictionary does. On the other hand, college dictionaries are likely to be revised more frequently and consequently are often better able to give up-to-date information on the meaning and uses of words.

Since all dictionaries must pack a great deal of information into relatively little space, they make extensive use of abbreviations, special signs and symbols, and other short-cuts. These space-saving devices are always explained in the front part of a dictionary and are usually easy enough to understand. However, each dictionary has its own system of abbreviations and symbols, and you cannot always assume that you know what one of them means because you once looked it up in a different book.

● EXERCISE 1.   Open to the table of contents at the front of your own dictionary. Notice where to find the introductory notes, the beginning of the definitions, and the special tables, charts, and illustrations. Then on your paper, write down the page numbers on which each of the following items of information can be found.

1. An explanation of the way syllables are divided in the dictionary entries
2. The meaning of the abbreviation *NATO.*
3. The population of Moscow
4. The capital of Venezuela
5. The dates (birth and death) of Thomas Jefferson
6. An explanation of the metric system
7. The meaning of the abbreviations *n., adv., v.t.,* and *v.i.*
8. The meaning of the word *slalom*
9. A guide to capitalization
10. An explanation of the treatment of prefixes

KINDS OF INFORMATION IN DICTIONARIES

28b. Become familiar with the kinds of information in your dictionary and the method by which the information is presented.

As you study the following kinds of information that dictionaries contain, examine the sample column from a college dictionary on page 559.

28b

Spelling

The bold-faced word at the very beginning of a dictionary entry gives you the spelling. If there are two or more accepted spellings for a word, the various spellings are given. If one spelling is more common than another, the common one is given first. When in doubt, you will always be safe in using the first spelling given.

EXAMPLES   judgment, judgement   theater, theatre

If some grammatical change in the form of a word is likely to create a spelling problem, this form is given. For example, a dictionary gives the plural of a word if the plural is formed irregularly—*hero, heroes;* it gives the present and past participle forms of *refer*, showing that the final *r* is doubled—*referring, referred;* it gives the comparative form of *nervy*, with the *y* changed to *i*— *nervier.*

Capital Letters

Proper nouns and proper adjectives are given with capital letters in college dictionaries. If a word is capitalized in certain meanings only, a dictionary labels these meanings *cap.*

EXAMPLE   **pres·i·dent** (prez′ə·dənt)   *n.* **1.** One who is chosen to preside over an organized body. **2.** *Often cap.* The chief executive of a republic. **3.** The chief executive officer of a government department, corporation, society, board of trade or trustees, or similar body. **4.** The chief officer of a college or university. **5.** The chairman of a meeting conducted under parliamentary rules. Abbr. *P. Pres.* [< OF < L *praesidens, -entis,* ppr. of *praesidere.* See PRESIDE.] **— pres·i·den·tial** (prez′ə·den′shal) *adj.* **— pres′i·dent·ship′** *n.*

Division of Words into Syllables

When it is necessary to divide a word at the end of a line, the word should be divided between syllables. Most

in·fec·tive (in·fek′tiv) *adj.* Liable to produce infection; infectious. [< L *infectivus*]

in·fe·cund (in·fē′kənd, -fek′ənd) *adj.* Not fecund; not fruitful; barren. **— in·re·cun·di·ty** (′in′fi·kun′də·tē) *n.*

in·fe·lic·i·tous (in′fə·lis′ə·təs) *adj.* Not felicitous, happy, or suitable in application, condition, or result. **— in′fe·lic′i·tous·ly** *adv.* **— in′fe·lic′i·tous·ness** *n.*

in·fe·lic·i·ty (in′fə·lis′ə·tē) *n. pl.* **·ties** 1. The state or quality of being infelicitous. 2. That which is infelicitous, as an inappropriate remark, etc. [< L *infelicitas, -tatis*]

in·feoff (in·fef′), **in·feoff·ment** (in·fef′mənt) See ENFEOFF, etc.

in·fer (in·fûr′) *v.* **·ferred, ·fer·ring** *v.t.* 1. To derive by reasoning; conclude or accept from evidence or premises; deduce. 2. To involve or imply as a conclusion; give evidence of: said of facts, statements, etc. 3. Loosely, to imply; hint. **— *v.i.* 4. To draw an inference. [< L *inferre* to bring into < *in-* in + *ferre* to bring, carry] **— in·fer′a·ble** *adj.* **— in·fer′a·bly** *adv.*

♦ **infer, imply** *Infer* and *imply* both mean to involve as a necessary consequence, and in this sense they are often used interchangeably: An effect *infers* a cause; an effect *implies* a cause. In other senses the two words differ. *Infer* also means to derive or conclude by reasoning: I *inferred* from the noise that you were at home. *Imply,* on the other hand, means to suggest implicitly something that might be *inferred* by an observer: The noise *implied* that you were at home. *Infer* stresses the use of reason in reaching a conclusion, whereas *imply,* the more general term, may be applied also to conclusions that are suggested or presumed.

in·fer·ence (in′fər·əns) *n.* 1. That which is inferred; a deduction or conclusion. 2. The act or process of inferring. 3. Loosely, a conjecture. [< Med.L *inferentia* < L *inferens, -entis,* ppr. of *inferre.* See INFER.]

— Syn. 1. *Inference, induction,* and *deduction* are processes of reasoning. *Inference* is the comprehensive term for the formal drawing of conclusions; it includes both *induction* and *deduction*. *Induction* is the *inferring* of a universal or general rule from particular instances. *Deduction* is the reverse process of drawing a conclusion as to a particular instance from general premises.

in·fer·en·tial (in′fə·ren′shəl) *adj.* Deducible by inference. **— in′fer·en′tial·ly** *adv.*

in·fer·i·or (in·fir′ē·ər) *adj.* 1. Lower in quality, worth, or adequacy. 2. Lower in rank or importance. 3. Mediocre; ordinary: *an inferior wine.* 4. *Biol.* Situated below or downward, as an organ or part. 5. *Bot.* Growing below some other organ. 6. *Astron.* **a** Between the earth and the sun: an *inferior* planet. **b** Below the horizon; below the celestial pole. 7. *Printing* Set below the line. **— n. 1.** A person inferior in rank or in attainments. 2. *Printing* An inferior character. Abbr. *inf.* [< L, lower, compar. of *inferus* low]

in·fe·ri·or·i·ty (in·fir′ē·ôr′ə·tē, -or′-) *n. pl.* **·ties** The state or quality of being inferior.

inferiority complex 1. In Adlerian psychology, a neurotic condition arising from the child's repressed anger and fear at being inferior, especially in some physical aspect. 2. Loosely, an exaggerated sense of one's own limitations and incapacities, sometimes compensated for by aggressive behavior.

in·fer·nal (in·fûr′nəl) *adj.* 1. Of or pertaining to the mythological world of the dead, or to hell. 2. Diabolical; hellish. 3. *Informal* Damnable; hateful. [< OF < L *infernalis* < *infernus* situated below < *inferus* low] **— in·fer′nal·ly** *adv.*

infernal machine An insidious explosive device.

in·fer·no (in·fûr′nō) *n. pl.* **·nos** 1. The infernal regions; hell. 2. Any place comparable to hell. [< Ital.]

entry word
pro-
nunciation
part of
speech
numbered
definitions
spelling of
verb forms
derivation
usage note
synonym
entry
illustrative
example
subject
labels
primary and
secondary
accents
usage label
spelling of
plural

dictionaries indicate a break between syllables with a centered dot (el·e·va·tor). Syllable division is indicated in the bold-faced entry word.

Pronunciation

Dictionaries indicate the pronunciation of words by means of accent marks and respellings which show clearly how the words should sound. The respellings are necessary because our alphabet uses more than two hundred combinations of letters to represent the forty sounds of English. Each letter or special symbol used in the respellings always stands for the same sound. The sounds represented by the various letters and other symbols in the respelling are shown in a key that usually appears at the front of the dictionary and at the bottom of every pair of facing pages. Since different dictionaries use different systems of indicating pronunciation, it is essential that you familiarize yourself with the key and notes on pronunciation in your own dictionary. The more detailed presentation of pronunciation which begins on page 566 of this book shows several different systems in wide use.

Part of Speech

After each word listed in the dictionary, an abbreviation tells what part of speech the word is.

noun	*n.*	adjective	*adj.*
verb	*v.*	preposition	*prep.*
adverb	*adv.*	conjunction	*conj.*
pronoun	*pron.*	interjection	*interj.*

Since many words may be used as more than one part of speech, some entries will contain several part of speech labels. In the sample column on page 559, for example, the first seven definitions for *inferior* are labeled *adj.* (for *adjective*) and the last two are labeled *n.* (for *noun*). Verbs have, in addition to the label *v.*, the labels *v.i.* and *v.t.* (See the entry for *infer* on page 559.) The label *v.i.* stands for "intransitive verb," and *v.t.* stands for "transitive verb."

Meaning

The principal function of a dictionary is to give the meaning of words. Since a single word may have many different meanings, many dictionary entries contain a number of different definitions, which are distinguished from one another by means of letters and numbers. Numbers usually indicate important differences in meaning, and letters indicate differences within the numbered definitions.

In some dictionaries, these separate meanings are listed in historical order—the earliest recorded meaning first, the latest last. Other dictionaries give meanings in order of the frequency of their use—from the most common meaning to the least common. The following definitions illustrate these two methods of ordering meanings. The first is in historical order, and the second in order of use.

> **hec·tic** \'hek-tik\ *adj* [ME *etyk*, fr. MF *etique*, fr. LL *hecticus*, fr. Gk *hektikos* habitual, consumptive, fr. *hekt-* (akin to *echein* to have) — more at SCHEME] **1** : of, relating to, or being a fluctuating but persistent fever (as in tuberculosis) **2** : having a hectic fever **3** : FLUSHED, RED **4** : marked by feverish activity : RESTLESS —

By permission. From Webster's Seventh New Collegiate Dictionary
Copyright, 1963
by G. & C. Merriam Co., Publishers of the Merriam-Webster Dictionaries.

> **hec·tic** (hek′tik) *adj.* **1.** Characterized by great excitement, turmoil, haste, etc.: a *hectic* trip. **2.** Denoting a particular condition or habit of body, as in wasting diseases. **3.** Pertaining to or affected with hectic fever. Also **hec′ti·cal**. [< F *hectique* < LL *hecticus* < Gk. *hektikos* consumptive < *hexis* state of the body < *echein* to have] — **hec′ti·cal·ly** *adv.*

Quoted by permission from *Funk & Wagnalls Standard ® College Dictionary*. Copyright 1968 by Funk & Wagnalls Company, Inc.

Derivation

Most dictionaries indicate the history of a word. They show by means of abbreviations what language the word originally came from and what its original meaning was. English is unusual among languages for the vast number of words it has taken from other languages. The source of newly coined words is also given. Knowing the source and original meaning of a word is often a great help to you in understanding the word's present meaning and correct use.

The abbreviations used to indicate the languages from which words derive are explained in front of your dictionary under the heading "Abbreviations Used in This Book" or another heading of essentially the same meaning. The derivation of *geography* is given as follows in the *Standard College Dictionary:*

$$[< \text{L } geographia < \text{Gk.} < g\bar{e} \text{ earth} + graphein \text{ to write, describe}]$$

The sign < means "from." If written out, this etymology would read "From Latin *geographia* from Greek *gē* earth and *graphein* to write, describe."

Restrictive Labels

Most of the words defined in a dictionary belong to the general vocabulary of standard English. Some words, as well as some special meanings of otherwise standard words, require special treatment, and these usually appear with a label. There are three main kinds of labels: *subject* labels, which specify that a word has a particular meaning in a certain field: *Law, Med., Aeron.* (Aeronautics), etc.; *geographical* labels, which indicate the area in which a particular word, meaning, or pronunciation is principally used: *Brit., SW U.S.* (Southwest U.S.); and *usage* labels, which characterize a word as to its level of usage: *informal, slang, substandard,* etc. As the following examples show, however, different dictionaries may not agree about giving a label:

egg·head \'eg-,hed, 'ag-\ *n* **:** INTELLECTUAL, HIGHBROW

egg·head (eg′hed′)   *n.*   *U.S. Slang*   An intellectual; high-brow: often derisive.

Quoted by permission from *Funk & Wagnalls Standard ® College Dictionary*. Copyright 1968 by Funk & Wagnalls Company, Inc.

Usage labels provide a good general guide to usage, but every writer should learn to make his own judgments. Assigning a label such as *slang* or *informal* is necessarily a subjective judgment on the part of the definer, and not all dictionaries agree about labeling the same word (for instance, the first example has no label).

Synonyms and Antonyms

For some entries in the dictionary, synonyms or antonyms, or both, are given. A synonym is a word having nearly the same meaning as the word being defined: *brave—courageous*. An antonym is a word having the opposite meaning: *brave—cowardly*. See the entry for *inference* on page 559.

Illustrations

If the meaning of a word can best be shown by a picture, the dictionary may give an illustration. While you, of course, cannot depend on finding a picture of the thing you may be looking up, there is a chance that you might find one, especially if the object cannot be easily described.

OTHER INFORMATION IN THE DICTIONARY

Biographical Entries

Who was Clara Barton? When did Edison die? What was Chopin's nationality? What were the dates of Queen Elizabeth I's reign? For what is Anthony Van Dyck famous? What was George Eliot's real name? How do you pronounce Hippocrates? The answers to such simple fact questions about famous persons can probably be found in your dictionary.

Some dictionaries devote a special section called *Biographical Names* to famous persons. Others give names of persons and places in a section called *Proper Names*. Sometimes these names are included in the body of the book. You can easily discover which method your dictionary uses.

The following common pieces of biographical information are usually given in a dictionary:

1. *Name:* spelling, pronunciation, first name
2. *Dates:* of birth and death and of reign if a king or queen, or term of office if head of a government
3. *Nationality*
4. *Why famous*

The following is a typical dictionary entry for a famous person.

> **Byrd** \'bərd\ Richard Evelyn 1888–1957 Am. admiral & polar explorer

Mythological and Biblical characters, as well as some literary characters, are often listed in the body of the dictionary: *Odysseus, Lancelot, Naomi, Romeo,* etc.

Geographical Entries

Like the biographical entries in the dictionary, the geographical entries are sometimes given in the body of the book and sometimes in a special section. This section may be called a gazetteer—a geographical dictionary.

In general the following information is given about a place:

1. *Name:* spelling, pronunciation
2. *Location*

3. *Identification:* whether a city, country, lake, mountain, river, etc.

4. *Size:* population, if a city or country (usually given in thousands—225 = 225,000); area in square miles, if a country or territory or body of water; length, if a river; height, if a mountain, etc.

5. *Importance:* If a city is the capital of a state or country, this will be indicated by a star or an asterisk. The capital city of a country or state will also be given under the name of the country or state.

6. *Historical or other interesting information of importance:* Thus for Hampton Roads, Virginia . . . "battle of *Merrimack* and *Monitor*, March 9, 1862." For Lake Mead, formed by Hoover Dam in the Colorado River, the dictionary says "the largest man-made lake in the world."

7. *Governed or controlled by what country:* For Wake Island, the dictionary says "belongs to U.S.A."

Miscellaneous Information

Most good dictionaries include the following kinds of information, either in separate sections or in the body of the dictionary itself:

1. *Foreign words and phrases:* spelling, pronunciation, meaning

2. *Abbreviations:* a list of abbreviations of all kinds, giving the words in full

An unabridged dictionary and some of the larger student dictionaries include

3. *Signs and symbols:* Not all dictionaries include a section of this kind, but some do, and if yours does, you should study the section to familiarize yourself with its content.

4. *Spelling rules*

5. *Punctuation rules*

6. *New words*

● REVIEW EXERCISE A. When your teacher gives the signal, look up the answers to the following questions in the dictionary you have. Write the answers on your paper. Accuracy is more important than speed, but speed *is* important.

1. Who was Copernicus and for what is he famous?
2. When did Sir Francis Bacon live?
3. Give the meaning of the abbreviation WCTU.
4. Copy the pronunciation of *de facto* and *de jure*, and distinguish between the meaning of these two Latin phrases.
5. Who was Prometheus?
6. What is the derivation of *hippopotamus?*
7. What is the height of Mont Blanc and where is this mountain?
8. What is the area of Lake Erie?
9. What is the capital of Ghana?
10. Where is the island group called the Hebrides and to what country does it belong?

● REVIEW EXERCISE B.   Look up in your dictionary the answers to the following questions.

1. Give the pronunciation and meaning of *dolce far niente*.
2. Who was Eurydice?
3. Give the more usual pronunciation of *apparatus*.
4. Of what country is Djakarta the capital?
5. What is the population of Copenhagen?
6. What is the length of the Rhine River?
7. What is the derivation of *gypsy?*
8. What country governs the Falkland Islands?
9. Who was Mrs. Malaprop? For what is she famous?
10. What is the meaning of the abbreviation *CIF?*

PRONUNCIATION

28c. Use your dictionary for pronunciation.

You learn the pronunciation of most words from your parents, your teachers, and the other people you talk with.

Ordinarily, you consult a dictionary only for the pronunciation of words that you encounter in books but do not hear in normal conversation.

Dictionary makers try to provide a suitable pronunciation for every word, but since the same word may be pronounced quite differently in various parts of the country, this task is not always easy. The sound represented by the *a* in *water* is pronounced one way in Boston, another way in New York, and in still other ways in Richmond, Chicago, and Portland. There is no one correct way of making that sound—each different version of the vowel *a* is the right one for that area. For this reason, you may sometimes find that your dictionary tells you one thing about the sound of a word and that you hear it spoken quite differently in your part of the country. In such a case, ask your teacher about the acceptable pronunciation of the word in your area. Do not assume that the pronunciation you hear is wrong just because you cannot find it in the dictionary.

Because the actual spelling of many English words does not clearly indicate how they are pronounced, dictionaries use simplified respellings to indicate the sound of a word. Moreover, since there are more sounds in English than there are letters to represent them, special symbols called *diacritical marks* must be used to show different speech sounds represented by the same letter. The following pair of words illustrates both respelling and the use of diacritical marks:

knit (nit)   knife (nīf)

Notice that in both respellings the silent letters are dropped—both silent *k*'s and the *e*. Notice also that the different sounds of the *i*'s are distinguished. The *i* in *knit* is unmarked, and the *i* in *knife* is written with a straight line above it.

Indicating pronunciation is one of the dictionary maker's most difficult tasks, and it is not surprising that there is

28c

some disagreement as to how it should be done. The systems used in various dictionaries differ in a number of details. You will see some of these differences in this chapter. However, when you have need of a pronunciation, you will not need to know all the different ways of indicating it. What you will need to know is how to interpret the pronunciation given in your own dictionary. To do this, you must familiarize yourself with the explanatory notes dealing with pronunciation and with the pronunciation key. Most dictionaries explain in the introductory pages the system they use. A full key is usually given inside the front cover. Many dictionaries print a shorter key on each page or each set of facing pages. The key illustrates the use of each letter and symbol used, by means of simple examples that everyone knows how to pronounce.

Consonant Sounds

The sounds that a speaker makes by squeezing or cutting off his stream of breath are called *consonants*. The last sounds in *with*, *this*, and *itch* are made by forcing the breath through a narrowed passage at one point or another between the throat and the lips. The last sounds in *first*, *wasp*, and *break* are made by cutting off the breath momentarily.

Consonants present few problems in representing pronunciation because most of them are pronounced in essentially the same way in all words. In some cases, ordinary English spelling uses one letter for two different consonant sounds. For example, the letter *c* stands for two quite different sounds in *cake* and *cell*. In giving the pronunciation of these words, the dictionary would spell the first with a *k* and the second with an *s*.

Two closely related sounds, the first one in *thin* and the first one in *then*, are distinguished in different ways in different dictionaries. For example:

	NCD	SCD [1]
thin	/thin/	(thin)
then	/t̲h̲en/	(t̶h̶en)

Notice that both of these dictionaries use plain "th" for the sound of the consonant in *thin* and that they differ only in the symbol they use for the related sound in *then*. Whichever dictionary you use, the sound represented by the plain letters will be the one in *thin, thimble,* and *thank*.

Vowel Sounds

The sounds that a speaker makes when he does not squeeze or stop his flow of breath are called *vowels*. Although we use five letters (*a, e, i, o, u*) and sometimes a sixth (*y*) in representing vowel sounds in writing, there are actually nine different vowels that are used by most speakers of English in America. To indicate these sounds, dictionary makers use the letters above in combination with diacritical marks.

Long Vowels

The long straight mark over a vowel is called the macron. When the macron appears over a vowel, the vowel is said to have the sound of its own name. Such vowels are called *long vowels*.

EXAMPLES   late (lāt)
sheep (shēp)
tide (tīd)
bone (bōn)
cube (kūb) [2]

Short Vowels

The vowels in the words *hat, bed, pig, odd,* and *up* are called *short vowels*. There are two common methods of

[1] The abbreviations stand for *Webster's Seventh New Collegiate Dictionary* and *Standard College Dictionary*, respectively.

[2] The long *u* sound is also represented by *yo͞o* or *yü:* kyo͞ob, kyüb.

showing the sound of short vowels. One uses this symbol (˘), the breve, over the vowel; the other method leaves the short vowels unmarked:

EXAMPLES   **add** (ăd) or (ad)
            end (ĕnd) or (end)

Other Vowel Sounds

The remaining vowel sounds, which cannot be classified either as long or short, are represented by the letter and one of several other diacritical marks:

KEY WORD	NCD	SCD
order	ô	ô
urn	û	û
took	u̇	o͝o
pool	ü	o͞o

In addition, a number of sounds usually considered to be a single unit are in fact combinations of two other vowel sounds. Such combinations are usually represented by two letters:

KEY WORD	NCD	SCD
oil	oi	oi
house	ou	ou

The Schwa

Modern dictionaries use an *e* printed upside down (ə) to represent the indistinct sound of vowels in unaccented syllables. This symbol, called the *schwa* (shwa), is used in such words as the following:

against   (ə·genst′)
banal   (bā′nəl)
correct   (kə·rekt′)

Some dictionaries make more use of the schwa than others. Those that do, use this symbol for the same sound when it appears in accented as well as in unaccented syllables:

bun   (bən)
serpent (sər′ pənt)

● EXERCISE 2. Look up the pronunciation of each of the following words. On your paper, copy the word after the proper number, enclosing the respelling in parentheses.

1. consummate
2. cultural
3. genuine
4. hog
5. hypothetical

6. irrevocable
7. Themistocles
8. thistle
9. those
10. Worcester

Accent

In words of more than one syllable, one syllable is pronounced louder than the other or others. The syllable stressed in this way is said to be *accented* and is marked with an *accent mark*. Dictionaries mark accents in two main ways: with a heavy accent mark (′) after the accented syllable or with a mark (') before the syllable.

KEY WORD	NCD	SCD
compete	kəm'pēt	kəm·pēt′
pony	'po-nē	po′nē

Some longer words have two accented syllables—one receiving a heavy, or primary, stress and the other receiving a light, or secondary, stress. The following example illustrates ways of showing this difference in accent:

KEY WORD	NCD	SCD
elevator	'el-ə‚vāt·ər	el′ə·vā′tər

Sometimes the same word may be accented in different ways, depending upon how the word is used. The listed words are examples of how the accent shifts when the words are used as different parts of speech.

com′pact (noun)	com·pact′ (adjective)
con′duct (noun)	con·duct′ (verb)
con′tent (noun)	con·tent′ (adjective)
pro′test (noun)	pro·test′ (verb)

● EXERCISE 3.   Rewrite each italicized word, showing the accented syllables and the part of speech as given in your dictionary.

EXAMPLE   1. I *refuse* to carry out the *refuse*.
           1. (re fuse′) *v.*, (ref′use) *n.*

1. One cannot *object* to the *object* of trial by jury: to allow the guilt of an accused person to be judged by his peers.
2. The new track *record* was duly *recorded* in the book.
3. The Stamp Act caused the colonists to *rebel;* still, few of them yet considered themselves *rebels* against duly constituted authority.
4. Jeeves, *conduct* this gentleman to the door. His *conduct* has been intolerable.
5. To *console* his invalid sister, her brother bought her a huge mahogany *console*, housing both a television set and a record player.
6. Japan arranged to *import* quantities of scrap iron. The *import* of these shipments never did occur to those who could not imagine a war between Japan and America.
7. Of all my *subjects* I dislike algebra most. My total lack of comprehension *subjects* me to much ridicule in that class.
8. Although the police did not *suspect* him, the murderer sensed that to Mr. Philo Vance he was already a *suspect*.
9. Intense cold caused the plastic parts to *contract*, cracking many of them. A new *contract*, therefore, had to be negotiated with the supplier for better plastic.
10. The Queen's *consort*, the Duke of Essex, was known to *consort* openly with enemies of the crown.

● EXERCISE 4.   Using the pronunciation key in the front part of your dictionary, write the vowel markings above the vowels in the following common words. Place accent marks in the words of more than one syllable. The final silent *e*, of course, should not be marked.

1. stop	11. far
2. old	12. turn
3. lame	13. re make
4. like	14. pro test
5. rib	15. rob in
6. eve	16. com ment
7. send	17. loop hole
8. boil	18. look ing
9. us	19. un til
10. doom	20. out cast

● EXERCISE 5. Using the pronunciation key inside the front cover of your dictionary, respell the following words according to the system used by your dictionary. Make use of accent marks, diacritical markings, and divisions between syllables. When you have finished, check your work against the word as it actually appears in the dictionary.

1. beautiful	6. unnecessary
2. Chicago	7. apparatus
3. conduit	8. sough
4. bathe	9. sought
5. llama	10. rough

CHAPTER 29

Vocabulary

Learning and Using New Words

More and more these days, tests of one kind or another play an increasingly important role in our lives. They are used to measure success in school and often to decide who is accepted into a particular college or kind of job. These tests differ, but most of them place great importance upon vocabulary. To prepare for these tests, you will find it well worthwhile to take stock of your vocabulary right now and to consider ways of improving it.

The best way to increase your vocabulary is to read widely and thoughtfully. There is no other way of doing the job successfully. There are, however, ways in which to add to your vocabulary more of the new words you encounter than you may be adding now. This chapter will give you experience in using these techniques of word study.

Before you begin the chapter, take the following test to get a rough idea of how good your vocabulary is right now. Sixteen correct answers is about average for students of your age. Can you do better?

Diagnostic Test

Number your paper 1–25. After the proper number, write the letter of the word which is nearest in meaning to the italicized word at the left. Do not try to guess the correct answer.

1. *affluent*   a. verbose   b. wealthy   c. friendly
2. *assuage*   a. relieve   b. rub   c. make brighter
3. *brevity*   a. position   b. goodness   c. shortness
4. *circumvent*   a. evade   b. surround   c. open
5. *denizen*   a. lair   b. inhabitant   c. bear
6. *explicit*   a. proud   b. apologetic   c. definite
7. *flay*   a. arrange in line   b. cast a rod   c. strip off skin
8. *gregarious*   a. sickly   b. sociable   c. cheerful
9. *hierarchy*   a. system of ranks   b. sound of music   c. ancient manners
10. *indolent*   a. unrefined   b. sorrowful   c. lazy
11. *jeopardize*   a. risk   b. assist   c. stripe
12. *lucrative*   a. profitable   b. bright   c. creative
13. *miscreant*   a. sneak   b. hobo   c. villain
14. *nebulous*   a. indistinct   b. difficult   c. villainous
15. *onerous*   a. rich   b. burdensome   c. poor
16. *plebeian*   a. aristocratic   b. common   c. military
17. *preclude*   a. prevent   b. preview   c. prevail
18. *quaff*   a. guffaw   b. drink   c. tremble
19. *repugnance*   a. dislike   b. insolence   c. desire
20. *sinecure*   a. easy job   b. hard job   c. technical job
21. *subjugate*   a. sublet   b. submit   c. subdue
22. *turgid*   a. cloudy   b. unusual   c. swollen
23. *vacillate*   a. waver   b. impart   c. empty
24. *wreak*   a. destroy   b. inflict   c. stretch
25. *zenith*   a. heavenly body   b. highest point   c. tower

WAYS TO LEARN NEW WORDS

You have learned some of the words you know by looking them up in the dictionary, but the number of words you can learn this way is usually quite limited. The majority of words that you have in your vocabulary have come to you in other ways. You are constantly meeting new expressions in the course of your school work and your conversations, but you will never be able to make them a part of your own word list unless you become *word conscious*. Keep on the alert for new words, and when you meet them you will be able to add them to your collection.

29a. List new words with their meanings in your notebook, and use them in speech and writing.

Set aside a special part of your notebook for new words. Write down every new word that you find, together with its meaning. Thereafter, try to use it in speech and writing as often as you can in order to make it a permanent part of your vocabulary. Begin now. Enter every word you missed on the Diagnostic Test, and to these add the new words you learn from day to day.

Context

29b. Learn new words from their contexts.

If your teacher asks you what *cumulative* or *exotic* means, or if your younger brother looks up from a book and asks if you know what *grotesque* means, you won't be able to answer their questions unless the words are already in your vocabulary. However, most of the words you encounter will not be isolated; instead, you will find them surrounded by other words and used in specific situations that will help you guess their meaning. The total situation in which a word is found is called its *context*. The *verbal context* refers to the other words in the sentence or phrase, and the *physical context* refers to the circumstances in which the word is used.

By careful attention to the context of a word, it is often possible to make accurate guesses about its meaning.

Verbal Context

The words accompanying the new word usually provide plenty of "context clues" to its meaning. For example:

> Bills relating to taxation must originate in the House of Representatives.
>
> The dust particles gravitated slowly to the bottom of the pool.

In the first example the verbal context clues (*relating to taxation, House of Representatives*) tell us that *bills* must certainly refer to laws or legislative acts and not some other meaning of the word such as "part of the head of a bird" or "a statement of debt." Likewise in the second example, it is not hard for us to think of what dust particles would naturally do in a pool and arrive at a good idea of the meaning of *gravitate*—something like "to move slowly downward."

Sometimes, of course, the other words surrounding the new word may mislead or even deepen our puzzlement. In this case, look further. Frequently the context clues missing in the sentence are contained in the paragraph. For example, read the following three paragraphs. Do not look up the meanings of the words in bold-faced type, but try instead to guess their meanings from the clues given in the selection.

> Through interplanetary space, there are countless pieces of stone and iron, most of them wheeling about the sun in long **elliptical** paths and some apparently sweeping into the solar system from the depths of **interstellar** space. On the average, they are no bigger than a few grains of sand, but there are those that are immense and weigh tons.
>
> More than 100,000,000 of them bombard the earth every day, pouring down on the atmosphere in a constant stream, and were it not for our surrounding blanket of air, they would pepper the ground in a ceaseless **barrage.** As it is, these meteors, as they are called, are **vaporized** or burned to a fine ash by heat resulting from friction with the air and settle

29
a-b

imperceptibly through the atmosphere to add themselves to the vast bulk of the earth. We see them usually for only a brief instant, when the heat has vaporized their surfaces into gaseous light-emitting envelopes that appear much larger and more brilliant than the original subject. Almost immediately, after that **fleeting** glimpse, the average meteor is gone, and we have seen a "shooting star."

Billions of these meteors appear to travel together in space along orbits that, in a number of cases, have been identified with the orbits of certain comets. The comets may or may not exist, but there is evidence that the meteors of this group are simply the **remnants** of comets which have **disintegrated** or are now in the process of breaking up and that the scattered comet-material thus formed is distributed along the comet's orbit. When the paths of the shooting stars in such a display are marked on a star map and traced backward, nearly all seem to **emanate** from the same section of the sky.[1]

● EXERCISE 1.   Number your paper 1–10 along the left-hand margin. After each number, copy the italicized word in each of the following sentences. Then examine the context clues, and write down what you think the word means. Do not look up the word in advance. You may check your answers in your dictionary after you have written them.

EXAMPLE   1. He was suffering from *insomnia*, and the doctor
                  gave him some sleeping pills.
              1. *insomnia—inability to go to sleep*

1. This word is *ambiguous;* it can have two meanings.
2. *Oblivious* of the terrible danger threatening him, he sauntered along absent-mindedly.
3. He was a very *astute* buyer, estimating values very carefully and never allowing himself to be deceived.
4. They wanted no *remuneration* in money or gifts; their only reward would be the knowledge that they had saved the child.

[1] From *New Handbook of the Heavens* by Bernhard, Bennett, and Rice. Copyright © 1948 by McGraw-Hill, Inc. Reprinted by permission of McGraw-Hill Book Company.

5. Although he profited greatly by the action, the king could not *condone* Delacy's murder of the baron.

6. The fearful crowd watched with great *trepidation* as the rescuers inched their way along the ledge.

7. The *epitaph* on his tombstone was brief: "Here lies one who died for his country."

8. After what seemed to the impatient children an *interminable* time, the boring hour came to an end.

9. The trapped animal struggled for hours but could not *extricate* himself from the snare.

10. After a *cursory* examination of only a minute or so, the doctor said that the child probably had not been seriously hurt.

● EXERCISE 2. Follow the directions for Exercise 1.

1. He was a *fastidious* dresser, always very neat and very particular about what he wore.

2. The business was an extremely *lucrative* one; in their first year their profits were five times the size of their original investment.

3. The fire threatened to spread to the *adjacent* houses.

4. To drive home his accusation by repetition, he *reiterated* that he thought Smithers was a liar.

5. Such an ointment is likely to *mitigate* the pain of the burn.

6. Smoking too much is likely to have a *pernicious* effect on one's health.

7. Marjorie looked at the dead roach on the shelf without trying to conceal her *repugnance*.

8. Wasting no words at all and being very brief, he gave a *succinct* account of his adventures.

9. He wanted to meet the new girl, but he was too *reticent* to try to speak to her without having been introduced.

10. The bad odor from the leaking gas connection *permeated* the whole house.

Kinds of Context Clues

There are a number of kinds of verbal context clues, but three in particular are extremely useful, clear, and helpful.

A writer is often aware that some of his words may not be immediately clear to all of his readers, and he insures complete understanding by adding little definitions or shorter synonyms. Usually these little definitions or synonyms are preceeded by *or*. A writer may put down "the old man's irascibility, or *bad temper*" or something similar. Sometimes wording like *that is* or *in other words* is used. A person writing about first aid may say "a tourniquet may be used to stop excessive bleeding." On reconsideration he may change this to "a tourniquet, that is, *a tightly twisted bandage applied above the wound*, may be used to stop excessive bleeding." Sometimes these explanations are made by the use of appositives or appositive phrases (see pages 79–80). Appositives that define are often punctuated with commas, as in the sentence "the opprobrium, *the deep public disgrace*, of his treason stayed with him all the years of his life." Here the word *opprobrium* is made clear by the following appositive.

● Exercise 3. Number your paper 1–10. Copy after each number the italicized word in the corresponding sentence. Then after it write the context clue that helps you to know what it means.

1. Many of the Romans were quite willing to *deify* their Caesars, to make gods of them.
2. Then the old mansion split apart and fell into the widening *abyss*, into the yawning chasm developing before it.
3. Baltimore County and the city of Baltimore are *coterminous;* that is, they have a common boundary.
4. Such preparations will *depilitate* the skin; in other words, they will remove the hair.
5. He gave us the most *succinct*, or brief, answers that he possibly could.
6. The others questioned the *veracity*—the truthfulness—of these reports.
7. Jenkins was too *hypercritical*, too given to constant fault-finding, to be a very good teacher.

8. These medical students have decided to become *pediatricians*, that is, doctors specializing in the care and diseases of children.
9. The *nomenclature*, or system of naming, now used in botany is in part the work of Linnaeus.
10. Officially these men were viewed as *regicides*, as murderers of their king.

Physical Context

To know the actual circumstances surrounding the use of a word, that is, its *physical* context, is often essential in distinguishing between two meanings of the same word. Take the word *foul*, for instance. If you are watching a baseball game, the word *foul* means one thing; if the game is basketball, it means something else. The word *cell* has one meaning in a biology laboratory and another in the city jail. Both kinds of context—verbal and physical— should be carefully noted, for both help you to discover the meaning of unfamiliar words.

● EXERCISE 4. Following are ten words. After each one are given two different physical contexts, labeled *a* and *b*. Arrange your paper with numbers 1a, 1b, 2a, 2b, etc., along the left side. After each of these numbers, write the meaning that the word in question will have in the physical context given.

EXAMPLE   1. organ   a. a church
                      b. an anatomy laboratory
            1a. *a musical instrument with large pipes*
            1b. *a body structure with a particular function*

1. *delta*	a. a Greek class b. a geography class	4. *carrier*	a. a health department b. a naval base
2. *bench*	a. a park b. a court	5. *switch*	a. a railway yard
3. *pipe*	a. plumbing b. smoking		b. a hair-dresser's

6. *coach*   a. a railway
                 station
             b. a gymnasium
7. *colony*   a. a history
                 class
             b. a bacteriol-
                 ogy labora-
                 tory
8. *secretary* a. a business
                 office

              b. a furniture
                 store
9. *bridge*   a. a dentist's
                 office
             b. a naval
                 vessel
10. *jacket* a. a metal-
                 worker's
                 shop
             b. a book shop

29c. Learn to find the meanings you want in the dictionary.

To build up your vocabulary systematically, do not rely entirely on context clues—as helpful as they are. Track down the word further in the dictionary.

Very few nonscientific words in English have a single meaning. Most have many meanings, often entirely different when the context is different. Therefore, the first step in finding the meaning of any new word is always to determine how it is being used when you read it or hear it for the first time in conversation.

To help you in this way, dictionaries often provide sample contexts. One dictionary, for example, lists twelve definitions of the word *bond* when it is used as a noun. The list begins with the most common use, "that which binds or holds together; a band; tie," and proceeds through more and more specialized contexts, for example, the meaning of *bond* in law, in finance, in insurance, in commerce, in building, etc., and ends with its very specialized meaning in chemistry. This arrangement of definitions allows you to find quickly the one that best suits the context of your word.

Some dictionaries may enter definitions in the order of frequency or importance. In this type the first meaning given will be the one considered the most common and the one given last will be considered the least common. A dictionary using historical order, for example, would give as the first definition of the word *forum* the notion of a Roman marketplace or other open public area and would list the idea of a public meeting much later. A dictionary that arranged its definitions in terms of contemporary importance would reverse this procedure.

● EXERCISE 5. Number your paper 1–10. The italicized words in the, following sentences all have a number of different meanings. Consult your dictionary to find the meaning that best fits the context of the word in the sentence. Then write the meaning after the proper number on your paper.

1. The pasture creek was fed by three tiny *affluents*.
2. Mr. Compton was a teacher of high *caliber*.
3. At the bottom of the *defile*, the river appeared like a silver thread.
4. The image on the screen *dissolved* from the housewife smiling at her sink to a panorama of giant cacti.
5. Pails and buckets are *galvanized*.
6. The cold-induced *inertia* of grasshoppers allows fishermen to catch them easily in the early morning.
7. The imprint of the huge scorpion was found in a *matrix* of Devonian sediments.
8. From his *disheveled* state, it was obvious that John had met with an accident.
9. At the bottom of the jar was a peculiar purple *precipitate*.
10. To defend his interests in the suit, Mr. Jones *retained* a young attorney.

Finding the Right Word

29d. Select the word that conveys the precise meaning and impression you want to give.

You cannot use the dictionary for very long before discovering that there are many words meaning approxi-

**29
c-d**

mately the same thing. The distinctions in meaning between synonyms, though sometimes very slight, are important and are carefully preserved by people who want their speech to be as lively and expressive as possible. Consider, for example, the multiple ways a person can *say* something. He can

utter	query	expostulate	hint	declare
whisper	question	vociferate	drawl	enunciate
grate	probe	insinuate	plead	state
lisp	asseverate	intimate	demand	respond
roar	aver	opine	threaten	announce
coo	argue	insist	proclaim	preach
reiterate	retort	descant	answer	perorate
recite	observe	comment	expatiate	deliver

As you can see, none of these verbs are interchangeable, but some are nearly so. Remember that a useful vocabulary is one that for every common word has a good stock of synonyms but preserves the differences between them.

● EXERCISE 6. Number your paper 1–10. For each sentence below, choose from the list the most appropriate synonym for the word *say*. Use a different synonym for every sentence, and change the tense of the verb to suit the context. Write the word next to the proper number on your paper.

1. Asked for the fifth time, Ted —— angrily that he had no more.
2. Endlessly, Mr. Bronson —— the rule until the class knew it by heart.
3. Reminded of his oath, the witness —— that he had heard nothing.
4. Quick-witted Marie —— instantly to the taunt by her brother.
5. The subject was complex and difficult; accordingly, Mr. Ives —— on it slowly and methodically.
6. Told that promptly on February 2 the woodchuck comes out of his burrow to calculate the length of his shadow, Mr.

Ranby, our biology teacher, removed his glasses and —— that there was more fancy than fact in that story.
7. Lucy was not bold enough to state her suspicions openly; she merely —— that the little boy had stolen the cookies.
8. The President —— that henceforward the day would be dedicated to the memory of the war dead.
9. The civil authorities —— that the rioting stop.
10. Unwilling at first to commit himself, Mr. Dixon —— that at a later date he would announce his intentions.

● EXERCISE 7. Write the letter for the synonym nearest in meaning to the words in the list at the left below.

1. *abut*	a. ram	b. adjoin	c. hint
2. *allay*	a. soothe	b. befriend	c. juggle
3. *anneal*	a. toughen	b. cancel	c. recover
4. *cajole*	a. heal	b. calculate	c. coax
5. *decimate*	a. operate	b. destroy	c. decide
6. *encumber*	a. burden	b. consume	c. undermine
7. *enervate*	a. soar	b. strengthen	c. weaken
8. *espouse*	a. marry	b. comb	c. respond
9. *fabricate*	a. butcher	b. make	c. descend
10. *furbish*	a. darken	b. sign	c. brighten
11. *gird*	a. plow	b. release	c. encircle
12. *imbibe*	a. bribe	b. sponsor	c. drink
13. *mollify*	a. reduce	b. soothe	c. repair
14. *ossify*	a. harden	b. classify	c. restore
15. *preclude*	a. prevent	b. pray	c. foreclose
16. *prevaricate*	a. anticipate	b. sicken	c. lie
17. *recant*	a. argue	b. disavow	c. republish
18. *ruminate*	a. meditate	b. enlarge	c. belittle
19. *simulate*	a. enliven	b. imitate	c. discourage
20. *vacillate*	a. anoint	b. inject	c. waver

PREFIXES AND ROOTS

Many words now part of the English language have been "borrowed" from another language. Word borrowing takes place when a foreign word comes to be used so often by speakers of another language that it becomes a part of their native language.

Many words now part of the English language have been borrowed from Latin. Latin has contributed more words to the English vocabulary than any other foreign language. Greek has also contributed a number. The different elements making up words borrowed from Latin are often quite clear at once to students of Latin, but students who have not studied Latin can, with a little study, learn some of these important word elements, for the same Latin word elements occur again and again in a multitude of English words. Once learned, they provide a key to the meaning of many unfamiliar words.

Short elements that come before the main part of a word are called *prefixes; circum-* and *trans-* are common prefixes. The main part of the word is called the *root; -port-* and *-fer-* are roots. The part which is added at the end of the main part of the word is the *suffix; -ion* and *-ence* are suffixes. *Transportation* and *circumference* are words formed from these elements.

29e. Learn some of the common Latin and Greek prefixes.

● EXERCISE 8. Using your dictionary, give the meaning of the prefix printed in bold-faced type. Then, again by referring to the dictionary, show how each of the prefixes is related to the meaning of the word.

EXAMPLE   *advent* = *ad* (*to*) + *vent* (*come*) = *arrive*

1. **ab**erration
2. **ad**here
3. **bi**annual
4. **circum**vent
5. **com**pile

Latin Prefixes

Learn the meaning of the following prefixes.

LATIN PREFIX	MEANING
contra–	against
de–	from
dis–	away, from, not
ex–	out of
in–	in, into, not
inter–	between, among
intra–	within
non–	not

● EXERCISE 9. Follow the directions in Exercise 8.

1. **contra**band
2. **dis**integrate
3. **ex**cavate
4. **in**carnate
5. **inter**pose
6. **intra**mural

LATIN PREFIX	MEANING
per–	through
post–	after
pre–	before
pro–	before
re–	back, again
retro–	back
semi–	half
sub–	under
super–	above
trans–	across

● EXERCISE 10. Using the dictionary, write the meaning of each word in the following list. Be prepared to give the meaning of each prefix and to explain how it is related to the meaning of the word.

1. perennial
2. posthumous
3. preempt
4. profane
5. revoke
6. retroactive
7. semiannual
8. subjugate
9. superhuman
10. translucent

29e

Greek Prefixes

The following Greek prefixes are found in many words in English as well as other languages. Learn them for the exercise that follows.

GREEK PREFIX	MEANING
anti–	against
em–, en–	in
hemi–	half
hyper–	over, above

● EXERCISE 11.   In a numbered list on your paper, write each prefix and, on the line below, each word. After each prefix, write its meaning. By referring to the dictionary, give a definition of each word.

1. antibiotic
2. hypercritical
3. embellish
4. encroach
5. hemisphere

● EXERCISE 12.   By referring to the dictionary, define the following words by showing the relationship of the Greek prefix to the meaning.

1. hypo–   (under) + tension =
2. para–   (beside) + phrase =
3. peri–   (around) + meter =
4. pro–   (before) + logue =
5. syn–   (together) + thesis =

Changed Prefixes

Sometimes, as the exercises have shown, English words use the original forms of Latin and Greek prefixes. But sometimes the original forms have undergone change. The word *abbreviate*, despite its present form, does not illustrate an original *ab–* prefix but instead an original *ad–* prefix. The *d* of this prefix changed to *b* because it was much easier to say *abbreviate* than *adbreviate*. This is why the word now has two *b*'s in it. This change took place for the sake of convenience—to make the word easier to pronounce. The change is called *assimilation* and can be seen in many other prefixes besides *ad*.

ad	*com*
ad + cumulate = accumulate	com + lect = collect
ad + cord = accord	com + cord = concord
ad + peal = appeal	com + rupt = corrupt
ad + tain = attain	com + exist = coexist

dis	*ex*
dis + fer = differ	ex + fect = effect
dis + ficult = difficult	ex + fort = effort
dis + gest = digest	ex + lect = elect
dis + lute = dilute	ex + rode = erode

sub	*in*
sub + ceed = succeed	in + legal = illegal
sub + fix = suffix	in + mortal = immortal
sub + port = support	in + regular = irregular
sub + pend = suspend	in + reparable = irreparable

As you can see, assimilation often disguises the original prefix. Despite this change, you can easily analyze words into their original components with the aid of any dictionary. It is a great aid to vocabulary building to do so.

● EXERCISE 13. Number your paper 1–10. Write opposite each number the following words in order. Then, in the second column, write the original form of the prefix. Use your dictionary to find this. In the third column write the root or base part of the word; this will be the remaining part of it.

EXAMPLE 1. *divert*   *dis–*   *vert*

1. access
2. allude
3. annex
4. appose
5. arraign

6. collapse
7. collide
8. confuse
9. corrode
10. elect

● Exercise 14. Follow directions for Exercise 13.

1. efface
2. egress
3. elude
4. immerse
5. impart

6. succumb
7. suppose
8. sustain
9. symbol
10. sympathy

● Exercise 15. Number your paper 1–10. Copy after each number the words that use the italicized syllable as a *prefix*. Do not copy the other words, in which the syllable is not a prefix. You may use a dictionary.

1. *ad–*   adamant, adder (snake), adjust, admire, advise
2. *bi–*   Biblical, bibliography, bilateral, bilingual, biplane
3. *com–*   coma, comedy, comet, commute, compose
4. *de–*   deacon, debtor, decimal, defect, decline
5. *dis–*   disappoint, discard, disciple, disease, dislocate
6. *para–* parachute, parade, paradise, paragraph, parasol
7. *per–*   perceive, percussion, perky, permeate, permit
8. *pre–*   preach, precious, precise, preface, pretzel
9. *re–*   rebound, recent, recite, reduce, regal
10. *sub–* subconscious, subject, subjugate, submerge, subscribe

Latin and Greek Roots

It isn't hard to tell what beginning elements of words are prefixes. The *un–* of *unclear*, the *mis–* of *mistreat*, and the *re–* of *return* are obviously prefixes. It is somewhat more difficult, however, to identify a root.

Some roots are called *free forms*. Free forms can appear with prefixes (*untrue, distrust, misspell*), but they can also appear by themselves (*true, trust, spell*).

Bound forms, on the other hand, can appear only with prefixes or suffixes. They cannot exist alone. We can have, for example, *conclude, transgress,* and *receive,* but we cannot have *clude, gress,* and *ceive.*

Free or bound, however, roots are easy to learn and, once learned, they allow us to understand the meanings of many different words.

● EXERCISE 16.   Number your paper 1–20, and make three main columns on the page: In the first, copy the following words in order. In the second, copy the prefix. In the third copy the base or root—the part remaining.

1. preclude	8. depend	15. interject
2. concur	9. restrict	16. subvert
3. propose	10. extend	17. transfer
4. support	11. submit	18. corrode
5. recede	12. supersede	19. retrogress
6. reflect	13. extract	20. transfuse
7. introduce	14. define	

29f. **Learn some of the common Latin and Greek roots.**

Learn the meaning of the following Latin roots in preparation for the exercise that follows.

LATIN ROOTS	MEANING
–dic–, –dict–	say, speak
–fac–, –fact–	do, make
–junct–	join
–pon–, –pos–	place, put
–scrib–, –script–	write
–spec–, –spic–	look, see
–tract–	draw, pull
–vert–, –vers–	turn
–voc–	call
–volv–	roll, turn

● EXERCISE 17.   Copy the words in bold-faced type onto your paper. Referring to the dictionary, underline the root of each word, write the meaning of each root, and give the meaning of the word as it is used in the paragraph.

The governor read the letter which the secretary handed him and began to dictate an answer in faultless **diction**. His **facile** delivery was not marked by any hesitation for thought as he explained his **position**. "At this critical **juncture** in the affairs

29f

of our state," he said, "we place confidence in the integrity of our **legislators**. We do not all **subscribe** to the same party policies, but we rely on one another's **perspicuity** to see the issues clearly. These **distractions** designed to **subvert** the public welfare are bound to fail, and in the face of the public outrage which has been **provoked,** we will do the duty that **devolves** upon us."

● EXERCISE 18. Learn the following Greek roots and their meanings. While studying these words, refer to a dictionary to see how the meanings of the words in the third column are found in the meanings of their roots.

GREEK ROOT	GENERAL MEANING	WORD
1. –anthrop–	man	anthropology
2. –chron–	time	chronometer
3. –gen–	birth	genealogy
4. –geo–	earth	geology
5. –hetero–	different	heterogeneous

Study the meaning of these Greek roots.

GREEK ROOT	MEANING
–bio–	life
–homo–	same
–hydr–	water
–log–	word, science
–mon–, –mono–	one
–morph–	form

● EXERCISE 19. Using the Greek roots above, define the following words by dividing each word into parts. Refer to a dictionary.

EXAMPLE   1. monogamy
        1. *mono (one)* + *gamy (marriage)* = *one marriage*

1. homogeneous
2. anthropomorphic
3. biology
4. monologue
5. metamorphosis

GREEK ROOT	MEANING
–neo–	new
–ortho–	straight
–pan–	all
–phon–	sound
–psych–	mind
–scop–	seeing
–tech–	skill
–tele–	far

● EXERCISE 20. Using the preceding lists of Greek roots, copy the elements in bold-faced type, and write their meanings in the words below. Then, by referring to the dictionary, write the meaning of the entire word.

EXAMPLE 1. live in a **demo**cracy
　　　　　1. *demo—people; democracy—rule of the people*

1. **anthrop**oid ape
2. **psych**osomatic ailment
3. a **hydr**aulic jack
4. an a**morph**ous substance
5. wearing a **mon**ocle
6. a beautiful **pan**orama
7. the science of **eugen**ics
8. **phon**etic symbols
9. a famous **geo**physicist
10. the **ortho**pedist operated
11. mental **tele**pathy
12. the **chron**ology of history
13. of wide **scop**e
14. the words are **hom**onyms
15. a **neo**phyte in a convent

● EXERCISE 21. Number your paper 1–10. Looking up the following words in the dictionary, select the appropriate word for each blank in the sentences below, and write it after the proper number. Be prepared in class to identify and explain the prefixes and roots or bases.

anagram	metabolism
epilogue	neolithic
epitome	orthodontist
hypodermic	philanthropist
lithograph	protozoan

1. A concluding section added to a literary work is called an ——.
2. The later Stone Age is referred to as the —— age.

3. A dentist who specializes in straightening and adjusting teeth is called an ——.
4. Many adults dislike the sight of a —— needle.
5. A microscopic, one-celled animal is called a ——.
6. A word formed from another by transposing the letters is called an ——.
7. A person who loves and does good for mankind is called a ——.
8. A picture made from a stone or a plate is called a ——.
9. The process of building up food into living matter is called ——.
10. A condensed account or summary is called an ——.

● EXERCISE 22.   Copy column A on your paper. Referring to your dictionary, write next to each word the letter of the best meaning from column B. Be prepared in class to identify prefixes and roots or bases in these words.

A	B
1. anarchy	a. the slaying of a king
2. anathema	b. a speech of praise
3. epitaph	c. a device for measuring
4. eulogy	d. a box for storing things
5. euthanasia	e. stopping and starting again
6. indictment	f. an implied comparison
7. intermittent	g. absence of a system of government
8. metaphor	h. a mass of stone
9. regicide	i. legal accusation by the grand jury
10. repository	j. painless killing
	k. a person or a thing accursed
	l. a short statement on a tombstone

● REVIEW EXERCISE.   Divide each of the following words into prefixes and roots, and explain how these parts make up the meaning of the word.

EXAMPLE   1. predict
1. *pre* (*before*) + *dict* (*say*) = *to say beforehand*

1. circumspect
2. retrospect
3. repose
4. aspect

5. subordinate
6. adjacent
7. controversial
8. conspicuous
9. bipartisan
10. diverge
11. transport
12. interpose
13. symbiosis
14. permeate
15. induce
16. recede
17. posthumous
18. parasite
19. homonym
20. periscope

WORD ORIGINS

29g. Learn the origins of words as an aid to remembering meaning.

In many cases knowing the origin and history of a new word will help you to remember it and use it well. The study of word origins may also provide some surprising information about words you have known for a long time.

Words with Interesting Histories

Many words have very interesting histories. Often our modern English words conceal within themselves references to romantic persons and places or to old, well-known stories. We all know the word *jersey*, for instance, for a pullover upper garment, but few of us know that this word comes from the name of the Island of Jersey in the channel between England and France. We all know the word *tantalize*, but few of us know that this word goes back to the Greek name *Tantalos*. Tantalos was a great evildoer who was punished in the afterlife by being placed in water that he could never drink because it always receded away from him and by having above him branches laden with fruit that always eluded his hungry grasp. Your dictionary is likely to give you short summaries of these histories.

EXERCISE 23. Each of the following words in italics is derived from the name of a mythological or actual person.

29g

Number 1–10 on your paper. Referring to your dictionary, give the meaning and origin of the words in italics below.

EXAMPLE   1. The outraged citizens resolved to *boycott* the store of the quarrelsome merchant.

   1. *boycott—refuse to buy—from Captain Boycott, the first man so treated*

1. The *chauvinistic* statesman made a warlike speech.
2. The winner said his *mentor* deserved more credit than he did.
3. The woman hammer-throwing champion was built like an *amazon*.
4. His *jovial* manner deserted him as he grew weary.
5. Rip Van Winkle's wife was a *termagant*.
6. The quiz contestant met his *nemesis*.
7. Only *herculean* strength could have accomplished the feat.
8. It is sometimes difficult for a slow person to get along with one of *mercurial* disposition.
9. Faced by a *titanic* task, the man had the inclination to give up.
10. The quick thinking of the policeman prevented *panic*.

Recently Borrowed Words

English is filled with borrowed words—in fact, there are in the English language many more words borrowed from such languages as French, Latin, and Greek than there are words from the original Anglo-Saxon or Old English phase of the English language in use between the fifth and eleventh centuries. Words given to illustrate Latin and Greek prefixes and bases or roots in the preceding pages will illustrate. Many of these originally borrowed words are now so thoroughly native and so completely familiar to us that it comes as a surprise to think that they ever were foreign words. But we have continued to borrow foreign words ever since early times, and we are still borrowing them. Sometimes we run across words borrowed rather recently, words that have been in the English language for so short a time that we still feel that they are foreign rather than

English. These words may give us problems in determining their meanings (as well as their forms, spellings, and pronunciations).

● EXERCISE 24. Refer to the dictionary to find the meaning of each foreign word or phrase in column A. Copy column A on your paper. After each item write the name of the language it comes from; then write the letter of the matching item in column B.

A	B
1. nom de plume	a. a dabbler in the arts
2. junta	b. a stroke of good luck
3. dilettante	c. noninterfering
4. bonanza	d. pen name
5. laissez-faire	e. a secret council

● EXERCISE 25. Consult your dictionary; write the meaning of the following words on your paper, and use them in a sentence.

EXAMPLE   *à la carte—with a stated price for each dish. Because he wanted a special combination of food, he ordered his meal à la carte.*

1. à la mode
2. entre nous
3. fait accompli
4. tour de force

● EXERCISE 26. Consult your dictionary; write the meaning of the following words and use them in a sentence.

1. bona fide
2. ex officio
3. gratis
4. terra firma

● EXERCISE 27. Look up each word in column A in your dictionary. Write after each number the letter of the item in column B that expresses the meaning of the word.

A	B
1. alma mater	a. sudden and decisive move
2. con amore	b. principal woman singer in opera

3. blitzkrieg c. slip in manners
4. denouement d. farewell
5. hoi polloi e. one's school or college
6. smörgåsbord f. outcome of a play or story
7. coup d'état g. the masses
8. prima donna h. a variety of side dishes
9. auf Wiedersehen i. with tenderness
10. faux pas j. violent offensive in war

WORD LIST

As a result of your study of this chapter, you will recognize many of the words in the following list. You will find that a great many contain familiar prefixes and roots. Make it a regular practice to learn new words from the list. Add them to the list in your notebook, giving the pronunciation, meaning, and derivation as you find them in the dictionary. Ten words a week will be as many as you can handle efficiently. After learning the words, use them as often as you can in your writing and speaking.

aberration	anagram	balmy
aborigines	analogy	bandy
abstemious	anneal	bauble
abut		bedlam
accredit	anthropology	beneficent
accrue	antipathy	bestride
acumen	apprehensive	botch
affable	apprise	
affianced	arbiter	boycott
affiliate	archaic	brigand
	aroma	brooch
affluent	artifice	brusque
alacrity	ascertain	buffoon
alienate	assiduous	cajole
allay		candor
alleviate	atrocious	cant
ambiguous	augury	caprice
amulet	axiom	carnage

cavalier
changeling
chastise
circumspect
clangor
cliché
coffer
colloquial
comely
commute

compatible
concession
condolence
conducive
conifer
consign
consolidate
contemporary
continence
credo

cursory
dearth
debase
decimate
decorum
defile
degrade
delectable
demagogue
disrupt

dissipate
distraction
diversion
dogmatic
dross
dulcet

effrontery
electorate
elite
emaciate

emetic
encumber
engender
enjoin
epicure
epitome
equilibrium
erratic
espouse
exacting

exhilaration
expedient
explicit
extricate
fabricate
facetious
farcical
fastidious
fiasco
figurative

flagrant
fraudulent
furbish
galvanize
garb
gauntlet
genealogy
gird
glib
gregarious

hackneyed

harbinger
heresy
hoax
holocaust
humanitarian
hypercritical
idyll
illicit
imbue

impassive
impeccable
imperceptible
impetuous
imposition
inadvertent
inalienable
inarticulate
inclement
incognito

incoherent
incongruous
indigent
indomitable
inertia
infallible
innate
innovation
inscrutable
instigate

interloper
intrepid
intrinsic
introvert
irksome
itinerary
jaunty

lampoon
lassitude
latitude

lexicon
lieu
longitude
loquacious
ludicrous
luxuriant
magnanimous
maladroit
matrix
maudlin

mendicant
mentor
mettle
mien
militant
misanthrope
miscreant
mollify
mosque
mull

mutable
mystic
nomenclature
nondescript
notoriety
obese
oblivious
odium
omniscient
ornate

orthography
ossify

ostracize
paean
palatable
pallor
panoply
paradox
paraphrase
parsimonious

patent
pecuniary
peremptory
periphery
personification
perspective
phalanx
phlegmatic
pillory
plaintiff

plait
polemic
posthumous
potation
potency
precept
preclude
precursor
predispose
prelude

prepossess
pretension
pretext
prevalent
prevaricate
probation
proboscis
prolific

promontory
propriety

prosaic
protracted
protuberant
provision
provocation
proximity
puerile
pulverize
purge
purloin

qualm
quibble
rampant
rankle
raucous
recant
recipient
recourse
recrimination
rejuvenate

remiss
remonstrate
reprehend
repress
requiem
resourceful
respiration
retainer
retribution
rift

rivulet
ruminate
sadistic
sagacious

satiate
scenario
scintillate
scruple
sedulous
senile

simulate
skeptical
sojourn
soliloquy
sordid
sporadic

steppe
stratagem
stringent
subjugate

subsidize
succulent
superfluous
supersede
symposium
synopsis
tacit
tentative

throes
transitory

translucent
ulterior
unremitting
usury
vacillate
venerate
vociferous
voluble
wreak
zephyr

PART EIGHT

Development
of English

CHAPTER 30

The History of English

Origins and Development of the Language

English is a member of one of the largest and most widespread language families in the world. It is related to nearly all of the languages of Europe and to a number of those of nearer Asia, including Persian and several of the chief languages of India. This circumstance is the result of a long sequence of historical events. In examining this history, we become conscious of the fact that language is a part of the culture of those who speak it and that, just as all societies are in a constant state of change, so the languages that they use are also constantly changing. We do not speak exactly like our fathers, and we speak even less like our grandfathers. With the passage of long periods of historical time, small differences become greater. One group of speakers influences another or even displaces it; groups break up and separate, until changes have become so great that speakers of what was originally one language can no longer understand one another. In this way, then, does it come about that from one language, spoken thousands of years ago, a far-spreading family of related languages has developed. The history of English properly begins with the story of this great family of which it is a member.

INDO-EUROPEAN

Four or five thousand years ago a seminomadic people wandered in tribes which even then were fairly widely spread over eastern Europe or western Asia. We surmise from their vocabulary that they herded flocks of sheep, kept horses and dogs, knew cold and snow; and from their subsequent history we guess that they were good fighters and good travelers. Probably at least as early as 2000 B.C., groups or tribes of this people began a series of migrations that were ultimately to spread the later forms of their language over half the globe. This language, as we reconstruct it from the records of its descendant languages, we call Proto (first or earliest) Indo-European. The large family of languages that descends from it we call the Indo-European family.

Early Branchings

The earliest of these tribes to split away from the parent group moved, doubtless in successive waves, over western Asia and Asia Minor eastward, ultimately to northern India by way of the Iranian plateau. Today, in some of the modern languages and in surviving examples of the ancient literatures of India and Persia, we may see the distinct yet closely related languages which developed from the dialects spoken by these people. A second early migration, beginning perhaps as early as 2000 B.C., moved southward or westward into Greece, the adjacent islands, and the coastal area of Asia Minor. Successive waves of invasion resulted in several varieties, or dialects, of the language, though modern Greek descends from only one of these, the dialect of Athens.

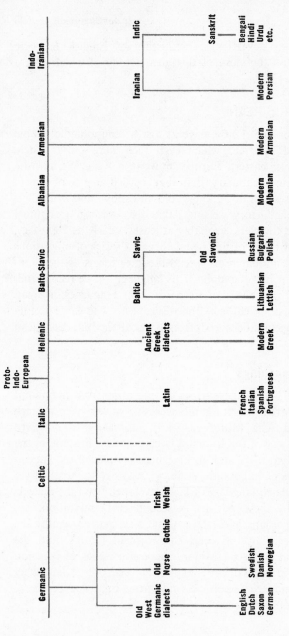

This chart shows the branches of the Indo-European family that have living modern descendant languages. In some instances, important ancient languages also appear. The two empty sub-branches under Celtic and Italic indicate ancient languages that have no important descendants.

The following table gives the words for <u>ten</u> and <u>three</u> in some important Indo-European languages. Notice the similarities. Where differences exist, notice that the variations tend to be consistent within a single branch. Thus, all Germanic languages have initial <u>t</u> where the others have <u>d</u> in the word for <u>ten</u>. This kind of resemblance is a mark of close relationship within a branch of the language family.

Germanic	English	*ten*	*three*
	Saxon	*tehan*	*thrie*
	Old Norse	*tiu*	*thrir*
	Swedish	*tio*	*tre*
	Danish	*ti*	*tre*
	Norwegian	*tie*	*tre*
	Gothic	*taihun*	*threis*
Italic	Spanish	diez	tres
	Italian	dieci	tre
	French	dix	trois
Slavic	Old Slavonic	desja	triye
	Russian	desat	tri
	Welsh	deg	tri
	Greek	deka	treis
	Sanskrit	dasa	trayas

Somewhat later, a migration westward carried into Italy a group of dialects, one of which was the ancestor of Latin. Centuries after this, as a result of the conquests of the Roman Empire, dialects of Latin were spread over much of Europe, and it is from these that the modern Romance languages, including French, Spanish, Italian, Portuguese, and Romanian, descend. Two other important language groups which migrated away from the Indo-European homeland are Celtic and Balto-Slavic. After a very great expansion over much of Europe and even into Asia Minor, the Celts were gradually conquered and their language largely displaced by dialects of Latin and Germanic. The most important surviving Celtic languages are Welsh, Breton, and Irish, with its Scottish dialect, Scots Gaelic. Balto-Slavic comprises two closely related groups including Lithuanian and Latvian and the Slavic languages of the Balkans from Bulgaria to Poland as well as the various dialects of Russian.

Germanic

In addition to several less well-known languages, one more group of major importance descends from Proto-Indo-European. This group is Germanic, one of whose most important members is English. In the first centuries of our era, the great expansion of Germanic peoples began, eastward into the Baltic territory, westward into what is now France, Spain, and England, southward to North Africa, and northward to the Scandinavian countries and on to Iceland. The modern Germanic languages include many, though of course not all, of the languages of these areas. Best known are German in its various forms, Dutch, Norwegian, Danish, and Swedish, as well as English.

The migration of Germanic tribes into England was the event that marked the beginning of English as a separate language. In the fifth century the Roman colony of Britain was a relatively peaceful and civilized community, the principal languages of which were one or more varieties of Celtic, though many important persons also spoke Latin. In the later fifth and the sixth centuries, there descended upon this island waves of Germanic invaders, coming by sea from the lands along the North Sea coast of modern Germany, Denmark, and the Low Countries. During more than a century of fighting, these relatively primitive and warlike tribes drove back the Britons until only a comparatively small part of their country was left to them, chiefly the western and northern mountainous areas of the island. With the displacement of the Celtic-speaking Britons, the language of the new country was henceforth the Germanic speech of the conquerors. This language and the new country which they had founded came relatively soon to be called *Englisc* and *Engla land*, or "land of the Angles," after the largest of the invading tribes.

● EXERCISE 1. Find in a dictionary or encyclopedia a detailed chart of the Indo-European family of languages (there is a good one in *Webster's Third New International Dictionary* at the entry "Indo-European languages"). With the help of the chart and the material of this chapter, plot the migration of the various IE languages on an outline map of Europe and Asia. Begin at a point somewhere in southeastern Europe or southern Russia and draw in the movements, first east and south to Iran and India, then west and south to Greece, etc. Be sure to include the Romance languages and, above all, the movement of peoples that resulted in the establishment of a Germanic language in England.

THE DEVELOPMENT OF ENGLISH

English was the first of all modern European languages to reach the status of a literary language. There are in existence documents containing written English from as early as the seventh century, and from the eighth century we have a considerable body of surviving literature. But, as may be imagined, very great changes have taken place in English in the 1300 years of its recorded existence. For the purpose of studying the history of these changes, we divide the language into three periods: Old English (or Anglo-Saxon) from the beginnings to about A.D. 1150, Middle English from 1150 to about 1450, and Modern English from 1450 to the present. The languages of each of these periods differ considerably in sounds of speech, in grammar, and in vocabulary, these being the three features by which languages are usually described.

Old English

During the very long Old English period, considerable change naturally took place in the language, clearly distinguishing it from the western Germanic dialects from which it originated. To the end of the period, however, it retained most of the features characteristic of an early Germanic language. From the point of view of language history, the most significant of these features were grammatical. Old English, like the other members of the Indo-European family, was an inflected language. This means that the relationship between the words of a sentence was usually shown by endings added to the roots of words. Thus each noun in Old English had a set of endings the presence of which might signal that it was subject, direct object, indirect object, a possessive, a singular, or a plural. Adjectives also and articles or demonstratives like *the* or *this* had complete sets of endings to assist in the process of showing relationship. This is to be contrasted with Modern English in which these relationships are shown almost entirely by word order and by otherwise almost meaningless signaling words like articles and prepositions. The contrast may be seen in the following sentence from the Old English poem *Beowulf*:

Thone sithfaet him snotere ceorlas lythwon logon.

Literally and word for word, this translates, "That journey him wise men not at all criticized." This translation, without the word order and other signaling devices of Modern English, is nearly meaningless. However, the inflectional devices of Old English make it perfectly clear. Among other indications, the ending *–ne* on *thone* marks the following noun as a direct object; the third word is marked by the ending *–m* as a dative, usually to be translated as "to him"; the ending *–as* on the fifth word marks a plural subject; and the last word is marked as a past tense plural verb by the form of the stem and the ending *–on*. Thus the meaning signaled by these devices is seen to be "the wise men criticized that journey to him not at all." Modern English makes these signals almost entirely without the aid of inflectional endings. The subject is signaled by position before the verb and by the presence of *the*. The verb, identified by its ending, is placed after the subject. The position of the noun *journey* (identified as a noun by the presence of *that*) immediately after the verb signals that it is a direct object. The sense of the old dative is signaled by the preposition *to* before *him*. The difference between the older inflectional system and the new is very great.

A second grammatical feature in which Old English resembles the other members of the Indo-European family is its possession of gender. In accordance with this system, the nouns of Old English are divided into three groups, or genders: masculine, feminine, and neuter. The adjectives and other modifying words each have three sets of endings, one for each gender. Each noun must be accompanied by a form of the adjective, demonstrative, article, or pronoun having an ending suited to the gender of the noun to which it refers. This feature adds greatly to the grammatical complexity of any language, for it means that each noun, wherever it occurs, must be properly classified and matched with the appropriate form of the adjective, article, or pronoun. We may see this system in modern European languages such as German, where *die Hand*, *der Fuss*, and *das Auge* are respectively marked as feminine, masculine, and neuter by the varying forms of the definite article, *die*, *der*, *das*. In Old English, too, these words appear as *seo hand*, *se fot*, and *thaet eage*—masculine, feminine, and neuter; but in Modern English, where this feature is almost entirely lost, all are what we may call common gender, and the article is invariable: *the hand*, *the foot*, and *the eye*.

● EXERCISE 2. Latin is one of the best-known languages with a fairly full set of inflections. In this respect it resembles Old English, as well as other early forms of Indo-European languages. In the following sentences *agricola* means "farmer" and *puella* means "girl." Identify the grammatical features which distinguish subject from direct object in the Latin. Do the same for the English translations.

Agricola puellam vocat.   [The farmer calls the girl.]
Agricolam puella vocat.   [The girl calls the farmer.]

● EXERCISE 3.   You now know something about the subject and object forms of this class of nouns. In addition to this, the grammatical gender system of Latin classifies *agricola* as masculine and *puella* as feminine. The adjective *bon-* meaning "good" has in this system a set of forms for use with masculine nouns and another for use with feminine: thus, for subject case *agricola bonus* but *puella bona*, and for object case *agricolam bonum* but *puellam bonam*.

Try writing the following sentences in Latin. Since Latin does not use articles in the way that English does, simply ignore the word *the* whenever it occurs.

The good boy [*puer*, masc.] calls.
The good queen [*regina*, fem.] calls.
The good boy calls the good queen.

● EXERCISE 4.   In the following Old English sentence *hund* "dog" is masculine and *wylf* "wolf" is feminine; *sliehth* means "kills." The remaining four words are forms of the demonstrative "the": *se* and *thone* are subject and object forms of the masculine, *seo* and *tha* are subject and object forms of the feminine. Explain how the inflectional system signals the meaning in the two sentences.

Se hund tha wylfe sliehth.
Thone hund seo wylf sliehth.

Like the grammar, the Old English vocabulary too was almost entirely Germanic, except for a relatively small number of words borrowed from Latin. This contrasts strikingly with Modern English, more than half of whose vocabulary consists of words borrowed from French, Latin, and other languages. Modern English is, in fact, remarkable for the ease with which it adopts words from other languages. Old English, in its resistance to this kind of borrowing, resembles more the other members of the modern Germanic family. Generally, the Germanic system of filling new needs in vocabulary is to form new words out of native materials, usually by compounding. Modern German, for example, has formed from common German elements the compound *Fernsprecher*, literally "far-speaker," in order to name the new instrument which English calls *telephone*. Modern English, however, instead of using native English word stock, has freely and quite typically borrowed word elements from Greek, *tele* "far" and *phone* "sound," to add one more to its stock of foreign loan words. Similarly, to give a name to a person who can speak in such a way as to disguise the nature and source of his voice or, as we say, "throw his voice," English borrows the very hard word *ventriloquist* from Latin, which forms it from the Latin words for "belly" and "speak." Norwegian, however, instead of borrowing the Latin word, translates it into native Norwegian elements, producing *buktaler* from Norwegian *buk* "belly" and *taler* "speaker." This, too, is characteristic of Germanic methods of word formation.

This, then, is the way of Old English. Sample Old English compounds are *laececraeft* "the science of medicine," from *laece* "physician" plus *craeft* "art, skill, or craft"; *tungolcraeftiga* "astronomer," from *tungol* "star" plus *craeftiga* "one skilled in a craft." Typical of the Germanic method of translating Latin words into native elements is the Old English word for the Trinity. Modern English, characteristically, borrows its word from the Latin *trinitas*, formed in Latin from *tres*, *tria* "three." Old English, however, like Norwegian in the example above, translates the Latin into English elements, producing *thri-nes*, from Old English _thri_ "three" plus _nes_, which is equal to Modern English −_ness_, meaning "state of being."

● EXERCISE 5. In the course of its history, English has acquired new words through two important processes: borrowing from other languages and formation from native elements. Look up the etymology of the following words in a dictionary that traces each element to its ultimate origin. Which words are formed of native elements and which are borrowed? Some of these words are similar in meaning to one or more of the others, though having different origins. Which are these?

advocate	eyeglass	lunatic	retain
canine	firebug	nostril	spokesman
dogtooth	foresee	pyromaniac	withhold
doomsday	loony	resist	word-hoard

Toward the end of the Old English period, there began to appear grammatical developments of the type that in later centuries greatly altered the nature of the language. These developments, however, were probably much hastened by the historical events of the late Old English and early Middle English periods.

These events began with the Norman Conquest. In the year 1066, the last king of the royal English line of Alfred the Great died. At his death there arose three powerful claimants for the English throne, though none of them had a really legitimate claim. By law, however, the English council of state was empowered to choose a successor, and they chose, naturally enough, the one of the three who already had the power of England pretty much in his grasp. This was Harold Godwinson, who had been the most powerful of the late king's officers. In the succeeding months Harold prepared for battle against his rivals, and in October he met and defeated the second claimant, Harald, king of Norway. Almost immediately after this battle, however, and before Harold could gather sufficient new troops, the third claimant, William, Duke of Normandy, landed in England with a great army. Near the town of Hastings on October 14, 1066, Harold met William and was defeated and killed. The throne of England thus passed to a line of foreign kings, a significant event in the development of the English language.

The Duchy of Normandy in the eleventh century was a large and powerful state occupying most of the lands along the French coast of the English Channel. The language of the Duchy was a variety of French. When William took the English throne, he took into his hands also the high offices of the land and gave them, together with many of the great estates of England, to his French-speaking followers. This process of replacing the native English governing classes with men whose native language was French continued until, in a relatively short time, an entirely new French-speaking ruling class was created.

For most of the first 150 years after the Conquest, we may safely say that French was the native, and often the only, language of most of the upper classes and that it was very probably spoken by many of the merchant classes as well. By 1200, however, the situation was changing, and during the succeeding century, while French continued to be spoken by great numbers of Englishmen, especially of the upper and educated classes, English was increasingly the common language of all. By the first years of the fourteenth century, French was almost everywhere in England a language to be learned only from schoolbooks, while English was again becoming the language of literature, of the law courts, of the schools, and of business.

Middle English

Despite this long interruption in the use of English by the governing classes, we must remember, however, that it always remained the language of the great majority of Englishmen. And during all this time the familiar processes of change continued to be at work upon the language: changes of pronunciation, of grammar, and above all of vocabulary. The dialects of the different parts of England, already different in Old English, continued to develop differently, each in its relative isolation. This, as we have seen already, is the natural way of languages, one which has always gone on and which always will go on so long as they are used by living and changing societies. Yet there has probably been no other equivalent period of time in the history of English when change has been so great and so rapid.

Probably the most important factor contributing to this extraordinary change was the contact—we might almost say conflict—of the two languages, English and French. We have seen that for a long time French was the language of the upper classes, of government and law, and of education. We have seen too that there was a long period in which the usage of these classes and these activities was in transition between French and English. When we see, therefore, that the Middle English vocabulary of these areas of discourse is almost entirely borrowed from French, it is not hard to guess what had happened. During the period of French dominance, English was not used at all in these areas, and, accordingly, the English vocabulary necessary to them was forgotten. Then, as English gradually began to reestablish itself, it became necessary, in the absence of English terms, either to invent new terms or to borrow from French. Since the classes occupied with these activities were obviously intimately familiar with the traditional French vocabulary of the areas, nothing could be more natural than for them to adapt the French terms to English.

French borrowings were, however, by no means concentrated in the political or educational area. Many, in fact, are among the most common words in the language: *city, close, chair, catch, chase, sure,* and many others. In addition, most of our terms of rank or social place are French. The vocabularies of religion and the church, of the arts and sciences, of military affairs, and especially of social life, clothes, manners, and food—all are heavily French. It is interesting to observe that in the latter category the division of the social classes of medieval England is reflected in the distribution of French and English vocabulary.

Words for the animals of the field, for example, are commonly of English origin, for English was of course the language of the countryman: the peasant, the herdsman, and the small farmer. Thus *cow, calf, sheep,* and *swine* are English. But when the meat of these animals is brought to the table as food, it becomes of interest to the upper classes as well, and hence it appears in both Middle and Modern English by French names: *beef, veal, mutton,* and *pork.*

● EXERCISE 6.   Look up the etymology of the following words in a good dictionary. What do they tell you about the history of the English language, the roles of English and French?

authority	herb	paper	sermon
bacon	herdsman	peasant	servant
baron	holy	pen	sir
beauty	hound	pity	song
boil	house	plow	speak
castle	jail	porch	stomach
constable	judge	prayer	story
court	manor	private	study
dinner	meal	poet	tale
earl	medicine	public	taste
feast	music	roast	tower
grammar	noun	saint	write
gruel	pain	sausage	wound

We have noted above that at the end of the Old English period there were already appearing certain grammatical developments that in the Middle English and Modern periods were to change completely the nature of English. One important cause of these developments was a feature that had appeared at a very early time in Germanic, before it had begun to separate into different languages. This was the fixing of a strong stress accent on the root, or main syllable, of each word. The result of this was, inevitably, the weakening of stress on the remaining syllables. We may see the operation of this weakening in Modern English words like *contract* (v.) and *contract* (n.), where the vowel in *con* is very markedly weaker when it is not under stress, as in the verb. Another, more striking, example may be seen in words like *police* and *Korea* or *career*, where the absence of stress on the first syllable sometimes results in complete loss of the vowel, as in the pronunciations "p'lice," "K'rea," and "c'reer." In late Old English this weakening of unstressed syllables was apparently continuing, and by the early Middle English period it had produced important changes in the grammar of English.

The grammatical endings of Old English were not stressed (since they were endings, they could not at the same time be root syllables). They were, most often, distinguished one from the other by differences of vowel. In early Middle English, as they became more weakly stressed and thus less clearly pronounced, the vowel differences which distinguished them gradually disappeared. For example, in Old English the nominative plural case of many nouns ended in *–as*, and the genitive (or possessive) singular ended in *–es*. In the line from *Beowulf* on page 610 above, we see an example of the plural subject in *ceorlas* or "men"; the genitive singular of this noun would be *ceorles* or "man's." By Middle English times the distinction between these endings had disappeared and both had become *–es*. This is of course still true in Modern English, where there is no distinction in sound between these forms of most nouns (e.g., *boys/boy's; churches/church's*).

This disappearance of the distinctions between the various grammatical forms of words was speeded by another force which very commonly operates in languages. This force is called analogy, and we may perhaps describe it as our desire to make new words behave according to whatever pattern is already most familiar to us. Thus a child, knowing that for more than one cat we say *cats*, and knowing also *roots, cans, pans, coats*, etc., reasons—quite unconsciously of course—that when we mean "more than one" we add *–s* to a word. Accordingly, when he uses the word *foot* or *man* he forms, by analogy, the plurals *foots* and *mans*. Though in these particular instances the child may be incorrect, this kind of logic is very important in languages generally. We may see it operating in English today as we fit new words, easily and without any conscious application of "rules," into our grammatical system. Thus when we create such new terms as *laundromat* or *motel* or when we borrow *sputnik* from Russian, there is never any problem about selecting a special plural form for the creations or any question of adopting the Russian plural *sputniki*. Instead, everyone quite naturally fits them all into the normal English pattern and simply adds *–s*. This is analogy at work in language.

In the rather complex grammar of Old English, there were several different classes of nouns, adjectives, and verbs. Some nouns formed the nominative plural by adding *–a* or *–e* to the stem, like *aex* "ax" and *wylf* "wolf," the plurals of which were *aexa* and *wylfa*. Some added *–u*, like *spere/speru* "spear"; some added *–n*, like *oxa/oxan* "ox," *blostma/blostman* "blossom"; some added *–ru*, like *cild/cildru* "child"; some changed the vowel of the stem, like *boc/bec* "book," *fot/fet* "foot," *toth/teth* "tooth," *cu/cy* "cow"; and some added nothing, like *sceap/sceap* "sheep," *hors/hors* "horse," *word/word* "word," etc. But the largest class of all was that which added *–as*, like *stan/stanas* "stone," *giest/giestas* "guest." We may see among these classes some words which in Modern English have kept their old nominative plural forms: *ox* still adds *–n* in the plural *oxen*, *foot* still becomes *feet*, *sheep* still adds nothing, and we may still see the added *–r* in *children*. But most nouns have changed classes to become like *stone* and *guest*. This is the result of analogy. The most common way to form plurals was by the addition of *–as*, which by Middle English times had become *–es*. Hence, more and more, people began forming the plurals of nouns by this most familiar means, whether or not the particular word had formed its plural in this way in the older language. The result is that by the end of Middle English times, a very small proportion of English nouns remained in the old special classes.

A similar development took place in the adjectives and verbs of Old English. Partly as a result of the reduction of unstressed syllables and partly as a result of analogy, the only surviving adjective ending in the Middle English period was a final *–e*, and even this completely disappeared by the end of the period. The verbs in Old English, as in Modern English, were divided into two large classes, strong verbs such as *singan* "sing" and weak verbs such as *fyllan* "fill." These were distinguished then, as now, principally by the method of forming the past tense and past participle. The strong verbs formed these by means of a vowel change (*sing, sang, sung*) and the weak by the addition of *–d* or *–t* (*fill, filled, filled*). In Old English the weak verbs were very much the more numerous, and the principal development in Middle English was the change of considerable numbers of strong verbs into weak. This again was the process of analogy, the more common pattern attracting to itself numbers of words originally belonging to the less common one. This development continues to the present time, with a number of verbs still in the process of moving from one class to the other. The past and past participle forms of *crow*, for example, may be the strong forms *crew, crown* or the weak form *crowed*. The past participle of *swell* may be either *swelled* or *swollen*, that of *shave* either *shaved* or *shaven*. These and many more verbs were strong in Old English but have become, or are in process of becoming, members of the larger and "regular" class.

● EXERCISE 7. The following verbs are, and in many cases have long been, in the process of shifting from one class to the other. In some, both the past tense and the past participle are shifting—or at least have developed double forms. In others, only the past participle has changed, and in some cases the double forms of the participle have developed different meanings, one for the verbal use and one for the adjective.

Look up these words in a good dictionary (i.e., one with full treatment of the principal parts). Determine exactly what development the past tense and past participle forms have undergone.

abide	awake	bid	bite	dig
forget	get	hang	shine	strike
chide	dive	heave	hew	hide
knit	light	mow	plead	sew
shear	show	speed	thrive	work

Modern English

As has already been suggested, the almost complete loss of grammatical endings in Middle and early Modern English had a very important effect on English grammar as a whole. We have seen earlier that Old English, like the other languages of the Indo-European family, showed the relationship between words of a sentence primarily by means of an elaborate set of inflectional endings. As these endings were lost, it was necessary for the language to develop other means of showing relationship between sentence parts such as adjective and noun, subject and verb, verb and object, etc. The means which developed was, of course, that of Modern English. More and more regularly, the subject began to be indicated by its place before the verb; nouns began to be identified less by their endings and more often by noun-marking or signaling words that preceded them, such as *the*, *a*, *some*, *his*, etc.; prepositions increased in number and began to take over more of the task of signaling relationships that formerly had been shown by the cases of nouns.

An additional result was the complete loss of grammatical gender. Gender had always depended on the endings of nouns and the masculine, feminine, and neuter forms of the accompanying adjectives and demonstratives. With the loss of these endings and the reduction of the demonstratives to a few invariable forms (*the*, *that*, *those*), it became impossible to distinguish between genders. Except for the relation between the form of the personal pronoun and the sex of the so-called antecedent, gender in English simply disappeared. (In connection with the last two paragraphs, the student should refer to the discussion of inflection and gender on pages 609–11.)

By the last of the Middle English period, then, the grammar of English was essentially that of Modern English. In the modern period there were some additional developments in the grammar of the verb, particularly in the verbal compounds such as the progressive tenses. Other minor changes took place also, such as the loss of the second person singular personal pronouns *thou*, *thy*, *thee*, *thine*, but the main grammatical developments were complete in Middle English.

A short quotation from the last quarter of the fourteenth century will illustrate how far the changes from Old English had gone. Except for the spelling and a few words that have changed somewhat in meaning, the passage might almost be Modern English. No really significant difference of grammar or word order is to be found.

Myda hadde, under his longe heres,
(Midas had, under his long hair,)

Growynge upon his heed two asses eres,
(Growing upon his head two ass's ears,)

The whiche vice he hydde, as he best myghte,
(Which deformity he hid, as best he might,)

Full subtilly from every mannes sighte.
(Most artfully from every man's sight.)

After the Middle English period the most important changes were in pronunciation. These were very sweeping in their effect on the language but were much too complex to explain here in any detail. The changes in pronunciation were so extensive that an oral reading of the foregoing passage in the pronunciation of Chaucer would be very difficult for us to understand, even though the vocabulary and grammar are relatively familiar. Some idea of the changes that took place in Modern English can perhaps be briefly suggested. In Middle English the *i* of *nice* or *vice* was an "ee" sound, like the modern vowel of *teeth*. The *e* of *meet* or *see* was in Middle English an "ay" sound, like the modern vowel of *late*. The *a* of *name* or *late* was in Middle English an "ah" sound, like the modern vowel of *father*. The *o* of *tooth* or *moon* was an "oh" sound, like the modern vowel of *coat*. Early in the Modern English period, extensive changes brought all of these and most of the other vowels of Middle English fairly close to the quality that they have at present.

As we might expect, however, vowel changes differed considerably in the different dialects of English. In some dialects, for example, *er* remained more or less as it had been in Middle English, eventually becoming the "urr" sound heard in the northern American English pronunciation of *servant*. In others, however, it changed to *ar*, as in Modern English *parsley*. In the course of time, as a more or less standard pronunciation developed, a mixture of dialects resulted in some of these words having *-ar* and some *-er*. Even in present times we still find words of this group that are pronounced differently in different parts of the English-speaking world. Most, like *far, carve, harbor, farm*, are consistently pronounced as *ar*. Many others have remained *er*, like *perfect, perch, sermon, verse, verdict*. At least one, *sergeant*, is spelled with *er* but always pronounced *ar*. But a considerable number are, or have until recently been, pronounced differently in different dialect areas: *learn, servant, serpent, virtue*, for example, were in the last century very commonly pronounced in many areas "larn," "sarvent," "sarpent," "vartue." The Modern English *varsity* survives as a shortened form of a similar pronunciation, "univarsity." In England the word *clerk* and the place names *Derby* and *Hertford* are always pronounced in the standard dialect as if they were "clark," "Darby," and "Hartford." The spellings of the names *Clark* and *Hartford* are representations of this pronunciation, just as the names *Carr* and *Kerr* are spelling representations of two dialect variants of the same personal name.

A great many other English words that differ in pronunciation from one dialect or region to another are traceable to the sound changes that took place in various dialects in the earlier centuries of the Modern English period. Some examples, with the variant or, in some cases, "non-standard" pronunciation respelled in quotation marks, are *deaf*/"deef"; *head*/"haid"; *either*/"eyether"; *home*/"hum"; *roof*/"ruf" (i.e., with a vowel like that of *foot*). Many of the strange-looking rhymes in older poetry also represent dialect variants of earlier stages through which the pronunciation of English has gone. Samuel Pepys (1633–1703) rhymed *root/foot/dispute;* Alexander Pope (1688–1744) rhymed *head/paid/shade;* Philip Freneau (1752–1832) rhymed *deaf/relief*. Pope, John Milton (1608–1674), and Robert Herrick (1591–1674) regularly rhymed *home/come;*

and rhymes of *home* with *from, some*, etc., were very common in the seventeenth and eighteenth centuries.

These variations in the pronunciation of both early and recent Modern English are, of course, part of the explanation for the inconsistency of English spelling. The very period during which these various changes were taking place in the dialects of English was also the time when English spelling was beginning to be fixed in something like its present form. Thus, in many instances, the modern spelling reflects a pronunciation that is no longer in ordinary use. A simple example is the curious fact that the vowels of *meat, great*, and *dead* are all spelled with *ea*, yet all are differently pronounced. In Middle English these belonged to a large class of words pronounced with an "eh" sound like the lengthened vowel of Modern English *there*. In early Modern English some dialects changed this to a sound like the vowel of Modern English *meat*. Others changed it to a vowel like that of *great*, while yet others modified the Middle English sound very slightly to the sound heard in Modern English *dead*. Thus these three words survive as representatives of each of these three developments.

The spelling and pronunciation of English may be seen, then, as a record of particular events in the history of our language. The other characteristic features of Modern English are, of course, also the product of the historical process. The virtual absence of grammatical inflections is the result of a gradual loss that has been going on for thousands of years. In their place has grown up a system of identifying noun, verb, adjective, and adverb, and of relating one word or word group to another, by means of more or less fixed word-order and by a set of function words like *the, of, may, if*, etc. The change that has taken place has often been referred to as grammatical simplification. It is very doubtful, however, if this term is entirely accurate.

It is obviously true that the Modern English inflectional

system is simpler than that of Old English. This is not the same thing as saying, however, that the total system of Modern English is simpler than one based on full grammatical inflection. We have only to consider a few of the many complexities of our system. The order of the various types of adverbs and adjectives in English, for example, is flexible, but only within very definite limitations. The order of the adjectives in "the little new red ranch-type house" and the adverbs in "slowly walks upstairs now" may be rearranged within limits, but we are not likely ever to see or hear such an order as "the ranch-type little red new house" or "upstairs walks slowly now." Or we may note the difficulties involved in the idiomatic use of verb-adverb combinations like *bring to* and *look up*. We may see, for example, that these two behave similarly in the sentences "the unconscious girl was hard to *bring to*" and "the information was hard to *look up*." And the elements of both can similarly be separated in "*bring* her *to*" and "*look* it *up*." But while we may say "*Look up* the information," we do not say "*Bring to* the girl." Or, again, we may note the complication of the differing orders of subject and verb in independent and subordinate clauses after words like *where*, *why*, *what*, etc. Unlike many languages, English reverses the order of subject and verb in an independent interrogative structure like "where *are you* going," but retains the regular subject-verb order in the subordinate construction "I don't know where *you are* going." Can we truly say that these patterns are simpler—easier to learn—than a system of grammatical endings would be? Probably not, and it may well be that they are actually harder. Whatever their relative difficulty, however, these and the other syntactical patterns of English are the system which the events of our language history have produced for us.

So far we have already considered *spelling, pronunciation,* and *grammar*. Another major feature of English that we have examined is its vocabulary. Here, too, special characteristics provide a record of the history of the language. One of the most prominent characteristics of our vocabulary is the great number·of words borrowed from other languages. As we have seen, many French words entered our language as a result of the Norman Conquest. Latin too, because of its great importance as the international language of learning, has been the source of much word-borrowing from the earliest times to the present. Contacts with other European languages have resulted in borrowings which very often show in themselves something of the nature of the contact between the nations. For example, some Spanish words have been borrowed as a result of commercial contacts between Spain and England (*apricot, brocade, embargo*), and others have come into American English through contacts in the Southwest of the United States (*corral, rodeo, alfalfa*). Italian words appear in English especially in the field of the arts (*stanza, violin, studio*) and, in the United States, in the names of a few foods (*pizza, ravioli*). German has contributed words in some of the sciences, the names of some foods, and a small miscellaneous group (*quartz, sauerkraut, delicatessen, hamburger, kindergarten, loafer*).

Contacts between the English-speaking peoples and nations beyond the borders of Europe have resulted in many other borrowings, especially in more recent times. As early as the Middle Ages, however, contacts with the great Arabic civilizations resulted in the importation into many of the languages of Europe of words for new things and new concepts in the field of knowledge (*cipher, algebra, sugar*). Later expansion in both the East and the West have brought new words to English from, among others, various African languages (*gumbo, voodoo, banjo, juke*), American Indian languages (*squash, hominy, moccasin, raccoon*), Australian languages (*kangaroo, boomerang*), and Indian languages (*punch, afghan, jungle, calico*).

We have now summarized, very briefly and incompletely,

something of the history of the pronunciation, vocabulary, and grammar of English. This summary should at the very least suggest one general observation. The English language, like all languages, is the product of an almost infinitely complex series of events, of the interaction of innumerable forces and influences. Modern English is likely to seem to a native speaker of another language enormously complex and exceedingly inconsistent. True enough, it is; so, indeed, are all languages. We may see, however, that much of the interest of language study comes from our recognition that within this apparent complexity there is much that can be ordered, rationalized, and explained. If we can know enough, each inconsistency and all the complexities become examples to us of the processes of language and the events of language change and language history.

● EXERCISE 8. Look up the etymology of the following words in a good dictionary. Arrange them in groups according to the language of origin. What do they tell you of the history of English?

stampede	zinc	cafeteria	frankfurter
yam	agenda	church	gorilla
manual	alibi	barbecue	balcony
bungalow	semester	animal	skirt
devil	extra	ouch	piano
opera	alcohol	pope	posse
propaganda	priest	zero	giraffe
camel	poodle	pump	dock
shanty	Santa Claus	they	veto
macaroni	tea	orange	clan
freight	umbrella	sandal	spaghetti
comedy	knife	scream	tattoo
alarm	syrup	black hand	cyclotron
atomic	take	wiener	boss
snoop	dumb	gingham	potato

● EXERCISE 9. Write a composition of about 500 words on the effect of historical forces on the English language.

As this is a very large subject, it will be best to limit your discussion to some particular feature of language, such as vocabulary, or to some particular period of time. Illustrate your more important points by using well-chosen examples drawn from this chapter, from the list of words in the foregoing exercise, or from your own reading or investigation.

Creative
Writing

Creative Writing

All writing is creative in the sense that any piece of writing is a creation; it is something that never existed before. However, the term "creative writing" has a special meaning. It usually means a more personal kind of writing than the kind normally required in school courses and in life after you graduate. It includes stories, personal essays, and poems. Creative writing is literary writing as distinguished from practical workaday writing. It is imaginative rather than factual. It attempts to interest the reader, to stir his feelings, to amuse and entertain him, rather than to inform or to explain.

Many of the skills of the creative writer, however, may be used to good advantage in any kind of writing. Some of these skills are explained in the following pages. Study them and practice them. They will enable you to add interest and color and life to all your writing; furthermore, creative writing is fun for both writer and reader.

DEVELOP THE HABIT OF CLOSE OBSERVATION

Because the writer of stories and personal essays is mainly concerned with describing the world around him and the people in it, he must learn to describe accurately whatever he sees. He must be a close observer of life.

In the following paragraph, Paul Horgan shares with us an experience he enjoyed when, as a small boy from the city, he lived for a few days on a farm. Alone he explored the meadow. Because he observed closely and remembered what he observed down to the smallest detail, he is able to convey to us the full flavor of his experience.

● EXERCISE 1. Read the paragraph; visualize the scene; prepare answers to the questions following the paragraph.

I was there a giant among grasses that rose to my waist. Long wide slopes lay up behind the white farmhouse and showed waves of white stars and snowflakes bent into shadow by the breezes—daisies, milkweed, Queen Anne's lace, poppies, with here and there goldenrod and wild cosmos in every color. When I slashed my way through this meadow with important strides, the soft stems of the wild flowers gave up a tickling fragrance, and the long grasses stung my bare legs with their wiry whips. I had to watch out for bees, and if I fell down I had to look along the tiny forest aisles of the plants and grasses at my very eyes to see if a garter snake might be watching me there on the damp brown earth which smelled like a cellar. Getting up, I went on to a real woods. It stood where the meadow became a low hill which dipped down to meet another hill making a wandering cleft where flowed a steep and narrow little creek.[1]

1. Explain "waves of white stars and snowflakes."
2. Besides the sense of sight, which of the other senses (sound, touch, taste, smell) does the author appeal to?
3. Point out a verb and an adjective that you think were particularly well chosen.
4. What comparisons does the author use to make the experience vivid?

● EXERCISE 2. Write a paragraph in imitation of Mr. Horgan's, in which you describe a simple childhood experience, perhaps an exploration of your own, and make clear to your reader what you saw and how you felt.

To sharpen your powers of observation, jot down in your notebook every day for a week, brief detailed descriptions of things you see, preferably ordinary, unimportant things you may not have observed closely before or indeed even noticed at all. Your descriptions need not be

[1] *Things As They Are* by Paul Horgan. Copyright © 1951, 1963, 1964 by Paul Horgan. Reprinted by permission of Virginia Rice.

written in sentence form. Think of them simply as the part of a sentence following "I saw. . . ." It is your ability to observe details, not the quality of their expression, that is important in these descriptions. The following examples, all written about things observed on the way to school, will make clear this kind of recording of observations.

1. water standing in the gutter, a film of oil reflecting in rainbow swirls
2. a workman—big stomach like a basketball above his belt—drinking coffee from a white cup held with both enormous hands
3. a metal garbage can, dented, leaning drunkenly by the curb, a greasy bag thrown on top like an afterthought, spilling bits of lettuce, dried bread, coffee grounds
4. the driver of a car that stopped below my window on the bus, grim, unshaven jaw holding a big black pipe, hairy elbow resting on the window frame
5. Jane, bent nearly double by the load of books in her arms, running for the bus, books slipping, long black hair waving up and down
6. a discarded beer can on the school lawn, its silver end reflecting in the sun, like a bright flashlight
7. a little whirlwind skittering across the parking lot, a funnel of leaves, papers, and dust

● EXERCISE 3.   Bring to class five observations from the week's recording in your notebook. Share them with your classmates. Evaluate one another's observations for their accuracy and the effectiveness of the details.

An example of the effective use of detailed observation is the following description of an old-fashioned oil lamp, the kind of table lamp found in most houses before the advent of gas and electric lighting. The style of this passage is "literary"; you should read slowly and attempt to see the lamp exactly as it is. The author supplies enough details. Prepare answers to the questions below the passage.

1. It is late in a summer night, in the room of a house set deep and solitary in the country; all in this house save myself are sleeping; I sit at a table, facing a partition wall; and I am looking at a lighted coal-oil lamp which stands on the table close to the wall, and just beyond the sleeping of my relaxed left hand; with my right hand I am from time to time writing, with a soft pencil, into a school-child's composition book; but just now, I am entirely focused on the lamp, and light.

2. It is of glass, light metal-colored gold, and cloth of heavy thread.

3. The glass was poured into a mold, I guess, that made the base and bowl, which are in one piece; the glass is thick and clean, with icy lights in it. The base is a simply fluted, hollow skirt; stands on the table; is solidified in a narrowing, a round inch of pure thick glass, then hollows again, a globe about half flattened, the globe-glass thick, too; and this holds oil, whose silver line I see, a little less than half down the globe, its level a very little—for the base is not quite true—tilted against the axis of the base.

4. This "oil" is not at all oleaginous,[1] but thin, brittle, rusty feeling, and sharp; taken and rubbed between forefinger and thumb, it so cleanses their grain that it sharpens their mutual touch to a new coin edge, and the odor is clean, cheerful, and humble, less alive by far than that of gasoline, even a shade watery; and a subtle sweating of this oil is on the upward surface of the globe, as if it stood through the glass, and as if the glass were a pitcher of cool water in a hot room. I do not understand nor try to deduce this, but I like it; I run my thumb upon it and smell of my thumb, and smooth away its streaked print on the glass; and I wipe my thumb and forefinger dry against my pants, and keep on looking.

5. . . . In this globe, like a thought, a dream, the future, slumbers the stout-weft strap of wick, and up

---

[1] oily

this wick is drawn the oil, toward heat; through a
tight, flat tube of tin, and through a little slotted
smile of golden tin, and there ends fledged with
flame, in the flue; the flame, a clean, fanged fan.[1]

1. Following the details given in the third paragraph of the description, draw in rough outline a picture of the lamp. Compare your picture with those of your classmates. What
   information that would be helpful did Agee omit?

2. From paragraph 3, select three or four descriptive details that
   were most helpful to you when you were drawing the lamp.

3. In paragraph 3 Agee appeals to the sense of sight. To what
   senses does he appeal in paragraph 4?

4. Is Agee's description of the lamp limited to the nature of the
   lamp and oil, or does it include his feelings about them?
   Explain.

5. Explain the meaning of the following pieces of description:

   paragraph 3 "solidified in a narrowing"
   paragraph 4 "it sharpens their mutual touch to a new coin
             edge"
             "as if the glass were a pitcher of cool water in a
             hot room"
   paragraph 5 "In this globe, like a thought, a dream, the
             future, slumbers the stout-weft strap of wick."

6. Find evidence in the selection to support the following statement: In his description of the lamp, Agee shows that he is a
   close observer.

● EXERCISE 4. Take any object that interests you, observe it closely, and write a detailed description of it. Make
your description so accurate that a reader could draw a
picture of the object. If you can, let the reader know your
feelings about the object, as Agee let you know his feelings
about the lamp. Your description will be easier to write
and more effective if you choose a small object like the
lamp, rather than a large object like a car or a plane or a

[1] Abridged from *Let Us Now Praise Famous Men* by James Agee
and Walker Evans. Reprinted by permission of Houghton Mifflin
Company.

building. You might write about a ball-point pen, a light fixture, a beat-up book bag, or a classmate's shoe.

IN DESCRIPTIVE WRITING, SELECT WORDS THAT APPEAL TO THE SENSES

Everything we experience, we experience through our senses. It is impossible to write a description of anything without appealing to at least one of the five senses: sight, hearing, smell, touch, and taste. The sense most commonly appealed to, of course, is the sense of sight. But because many experiences involve one or more of the other senses, too, the skillful writer is alert to notice how these other senses are affected by what he observes. He increases the effectiveness of his description by referring to as many senses as he can.

To appeal to the senses, a writer needs words that describe, or identify, the various sights, sounds, smells, tastes, feelings (touch) that he wishes his reader to experience.

● EXERCISE 5.   Copy on your paper the following list of words. After each word, write the sense to which it refers. Some may refer to two senses.

1. hot	6. salty	11. scraping	16. glassy
2. spicy	7. icy	12. bitter	17. glittering
3. sour	8. bright	13. acrid	18. thump
4. clang	9. roar	14. heavy	19. square
5. green	10. moist	15. smoky	20. burnt

Describing the sense of sound

Most of the words we use to describe sounds are words that suggest in themselves the sounds to which they refer. *Clang*, for example, suggests the sound of metal striking metal; *bong* suggests the sound of a large bell, while *tinkle* suggests the sound of a small bell. The use of words of this kind is called onomatopoeia, and the words are said to be onomatopoetic.

● EXERCISE 6. Supply an onomatopoetic, or sound-imitating word, for the blank in each item. Copy the entire item on your paper. You may, if you wish, qualify the words with adjectives; thus "the crash of thunder" might become the "ear-splitting crash of thunder."

1. the —— of pages being turned
2. the —— of footsteps in the corridor
3. the —— of the wind
4. the —— of wheels on gravel
5. the —— of water dripping
6. the —— of a fire
7. the —— of a piano
8. the —— of distant rifle fire
9. the —— of a door opening
10. the —— of a jet plane

Describing the senses of smell and taste

Since smell and taste are closely related, the same words may be used to describe both. For example, the word *pungent* may be used to describe both taste and smell. Similarly, the words *bitter*, *musty*, *sweet*, and *stale* may describe both sensations.

● EXERCISE 7. Supply an adjective you think appropriate for each blank.

1. the —— taste of coffee
2. the —— smell of strong cheese
3. the —— taste of pickles
4. the —— aroma of fresh bread
5. the —— smell of pizza

In the following paragraph, John Updike describes the smells he associated with the city of Reading, Pennsylvania, when he was a young boy. Discuss with your classmates the effectiveness of Updike's descriptions of smells.

> Yet to me Reading is the master of cities, the one at the center that all others echo. How rich it smelled! Kresge's swimming in milk chocolate and violet-

scented toilet water, Grant's barricaded with coco-
nut cookies, the vast velveted movie theaters dusted
with popcorn and a cold whiff of leather, the bake-
shops exhaling hearty brown drafts of molasses and
damp dough and crisp grease and hot sugar, the
beauty parlors with their gingery stink of singeing, the
bookstores glistening with fresh paper and bubbles of
hardened glue, the shoe-repair nooks blackened by
Kiwi wax and aromatic shavings, the public lavatory
with its emphatic veil of soap, the hushed, brick-red
side streets spiced with grit and the moist seeds of
maples and gingkos, the goblin stench of the trolley
car that made each return to Shillington a race with
nausea—Reading's smells were most of what my
boyhood knew of the Great World that was suspended, at a small but sufficient distance, beyond my
world.[1]

Describing the sense of touch, or feeling

The sense of touch applies to two kinds of feelings. One
kind is the sensation of actually touching a surface or being
touched by something. Such words as *smooth, rough, icy,*
and *slimy* describe the feeling of a surface when we touch
it or are touched by it.

In the following passage Lois Hudson recalls the sensations she experienced as a young girl on a North Dakota
farm when the temperature one winter night dropped to
50° below zero.

> I was well acquainted with the shock of stepping
> from the warm kitchen into a winter night. But none
> of the freezing memories of the past could prepare
> me for the burning air that night. It was like strong
> hot smoke in my nostrils, so that for one confused
> instant I thought I was going to suffocate with the
> cold that was so cold it was hot. I gasped for breath-

[1] From "The Dogwood Tree: A Boyhood," © Copyright 1962 by
Martin Levin. Reprinted from *Assorted Prose* by John Updike by
permission of Alfred A. Knopf, Inc.

able air, and my father said, "Don't do that! Breathe through your nose—your breath is warmer that way when it gets to your lungs."

We walked carefully down the hill to the barn; then I slithered down the steps, chopped in a snow-drift in front of the door, and slid it open. The barn was very old, but, always before, it had been warm with the heat of the animals kept in it all day long. But that night being inside didn't seem to make any difference. I still had the kind of ache in my temples and cheekbones that I always got when I took too big a mouthful of ice cream.[1]

The other kind of feeling is internal, a feeling like nausea or weakness or sensations of fear—a rapid heartbeat, breaking out of perspiration. The following passage describes how a boy felt after having been critically ill with a high fever that finally broke. The sensations are not those of touch as we usually think of touching something, but they are internal sensations closely related to the sense of feeling.

After fever my body and head felt light, like a piece of dew-damp vegetable. The illness had emptied me so completely, now I seemed bereft of substance. Being so long in that sunless, fever-spent room, I was filled with extraordinary translations.[2] I felt white and blood-drained, empty of organs, transparent to color and sound, while there passed through my flesh the lights of the window, the dust-changing air, the fire's bright hooks, and the smooth lapping tongues of the candle. Heat, reflections, whispers, shadows, played around me as though I were glass. I seemed to be bodiless, printed flat on the sheets, insubstantial as a net in water.[3]

[1] From "The Cold Wave" from *Reapers of the Dust* by Lois Phillips Hudson. Copyright © 1958 by Lois Phillips Hudson. Reprinted by permission of Atlantic-Little, Brown and Company.

[2] Mr. Lee means that he feels his body has been changed.

[3] From *The Edge of Day* by Laurie Lee. Copyright © 1959 by Laurie Lee. Reprinted by permission of William Morrow and Company, Inc.

● EXERCISE 8. Write an adjective or a phrase that describes the sensation of touching the following.

1. velvet
2. marble
3. silk
4. corduroy
5. denim

6. earthworm
7. fish
8. fur
9. baseball
10. tire

● EXERCISE 9. Write a paragraph (approximately 100 words) in which, by appealing to as many senses as you can, you convey your feelings at a time when you were under a strain, or the opposite—a time when you were feeling especially relaxed and happy. You could, like the author of the preceding description, tell how you felt when you were ill or were convalescing. You might describe your nervousness before an examination or a public performance, the sensation of fear or anger, the feeling of complete physical well-being or of complete laziness. You should make clear in the beginning exactly where you are and what the general circumstances are.

FILL YOUR WRITING WITH VIVID DETAILS

Most writing, no matter what kind it is, goes from the general to the particular. Whether you are writing a description or telling a story, you make general statements and then back them up with supporting details. Writing shorn of its details is dull and lifeless. Although it is important to give many details, quantity is never so important as quality. Through close observation, a skillful writer sees the details needed to convey a picture clearly.

In the following selection, which describes an observer's reaction as he sits on the sideline at a basketball game, the author supports his opening generalization with details. Which senses does he appeal to?

> Gayforth became bewildered by the confusing swiftness and wild intensity of the play. He heard

the constant thud of soft-shod feet striking the hard floor, the dull clang of the basket frame as the ball hooked itself down into the net, and the instant sharp yell that followed from the onlookers. Two men, colliding, fell at his very feet. He glimpsed the contortion of pain that flashed across the face of one; he saw the shine of the lights on their wet faces and shoulders, and caught the sharp odor from their hot, sweating bodies. The whole floor was a maze of moving legs and arms, a bewildering kaleidoscope of shifting pose, with the ball making long arcs across from man to man, or curving through the air toward the basket.[1]

In the following paragraph, Edmund G. Love recalls the barber to whom he and his brother went when they were children. Find two general statements about Joe Gage and point out the details that support the general statements.

I do not think that Joe Gage overcharged for his haircuts. A boy certainly got his money's worth. He was the first barber I ever knew who gave away lollypops to his customers. He also gave balloons, tops, kites, and baseballs. He entertained his customers as he cut their hair. He would stop in the middle of whatever he was doing and put on the boxing gloves and go a quick round with a boy. He would Indian-wrestle, play mumblety-peg, or teach a boy how to whittle. He would repair a coaster wagon or paint a name on a sled. He was a talented man in many ways. He was the best whistler who ever came to Flushing. He could imitate birds or whistle a song. He could sing. He could tell stories. Sometimes in the middle of a haircut he would get so engrossed in one of his own stories that he would draw up a stool and sit down. When my brother Walter stalked into his shop and asked for a shave, a shave was forth-

[1] From *Prose Specimens* by C. S. Duncan, E. L. Beck and W. L. Graves. D. C. Heath: Boston, 1913. Reprinted by permission of the publisher.

coming. Joe lathered Walter's face, used the back of
a comb to shave off the lather, applied a hot towel,
and finished off with a generous application of witch
hazel and lilac water.[1]

● EXERCISE 10.   Each of the following places has its own
atmosphere. Select one place—or, if you prefer, a place not
listed here—and write a one-paragraph (approximately 150
words) description conveying its atmosphere. Support your
general statements with as many appropriate details as you
can. Appeal to as many of the senses as possible. Let your
reader know your feelings in this place.

pizza parlor	library
greenhouse	schoolroom
automobile repair shop	zoo
city playground	restaurant
city street	indoor swimming pool

USE COMPARISONS TO MAKE YOUR WRITING CLEAR AND INTERESTING— SIMILES AND METAPHORS

The skillful writer gives full play to his natural tendency
to think in terms of comparison. In the models of good
writing in this chapter, we have seen many examples of
the use of comparisons. In Mr. Horgan's account of a
childhood exploration of a meadow, you noticed his use
of comparisons. He writes of "waves of white stars and
snowflakes" when he refers to the meadow flowers; on the
ground, looking through the meadow grass, he refers to
the "forest *aisles* of the plants and grasses." He says the
damp earth smelled "like a cellar."

In his description of a glass lamp, James Agee said its
base was a "fluted, hollow *skirt*," thus drawing a comparison
between the lamp base and a skirt. He says that the lamp
wick *slumbers* in the oil, comparing the wick to a live

[1] From p. 66 in *The Situation in Flushing* by Edmund G. Love
(Harper & Row, 1965). Reprinted by permission of the publisher.

thing asleep, and he describes the flame at the top of the wick as a "clean, fanged fan."

In his description of how he felt after a severe illness, Laurie Lee writes of a candle flame as "the smooth lapping *tongues* of the candle." You may remember that he used other comparisons when he wrote, "I seemed to be bodiless, *printed* flat on the sheets, *insubstantial as a net in water*."

Comparisons like those you have been reading are called figures of speech, and the language in which they are expressed is called figurative language. A figurative expression is the opposite of a literal expression. An expression is literal when it is completely factual. It is figurative when it is imaginative rather than factual, when it compares things that are not alike in reality but are alike in the writer's imagination. For example, a writer describing the sensations of a lookout in the bow of a ship at sea on a winter night might say, "The wind in his face was strong and cold." This would be literal, not figurative, description. On the other hand, he might say, "The wind cut his face like a knife." While there is really no similarity between wind and a knife, the comparison does make sense imaginatively. It is a figurative expression, a figure of speech.

Comparisons are common features of your speech and writing. Often you use them without thinking: "busy as a bee," "hard as a rock," "straight as an arrow." We speak of a person as "a good egg," and we talk about a "flood of words" and "death's door." Such everyday comparisons as these are to be avoided in writing because they are "tired" and commonplace. They have lost their effectiveness as description. But the ability to fashion fresh, original comparisons is a very important writing skill.

The two most common figures of speech are simile and metaphor. A simile is a comparison between things essentially unlike, expressed directly through the use of a comparing word such as *like* or *as:*

They slept *like* the dead all day.
The flame rose *like* a pointed flower.
He is as dangerous *as* dynamite.

A metaphor is a comparison between things essentially unlike, expressed without a comparing word such as *like* or *as*. The comparison is suggested, not directly stated:

Between precipitous walls flowed the swollen *stream* of rush-hour traffic.
The sun *hammered* at our defenseless heads.
The blooming orchard *was a pink cascade* on the hillside.

● EXERCISE 11. Identify each of the following as simile or metaphor by writing *S* or *M* after the proper number. If you find two figures of speech in one item, identify both. Be prepared to state what things are being compared and to evaluate the effectiveness of the figure of speech.

1. Buildings are waterfalls of stone. —Louis Ginsberg
2. The modern racehorse, inbred for speed, carrying the maximum amount of muscle on the minimum amount of bone structure, is as frail as a pastry shell. —Ernest Haveman
3. A tree of pain takes root in his jaw. —John Updike
4. The lifted hand [was] like a curved claw. —William Faulkner
5. Her face was deep-carved stone. —Maurice Walsh
6. Cleaving the city down the center, the cold waters of the Neva move silently and swiftly like a slab of smooth gray metal. —George Kennan
7. An island [Manhattan] uttered incandescent towers like frozen simultaneous hymns to trade. —Malcolm Cowley
8. He turned off on the gravel and we sprayed along with the rocks crunching and hopping up against the underside of the fender like grease in a skillet. —Robert Penn Warren

● EXERCISE 12. Using your imagination, complete the following similes in as fresh and original a way as you can. Take time to wait for your imagination. Don't write down the first comparison that comes to mind; it may be a well-known, worn-out expression.

1. Cars climbing the distant hill looked like . . .
2. He had a chin like . . .
3. Bright beach umbrellas like . . .
4. To press his hand was like . . .
5. Trees outlined against the sky like . . .
6. The heavy fog was like . . .
7. High above us a jet plane moved across the sky like . . .
8. The room was as quiet as . . .
9. The clouds were like . . .
10. She looked as happy as . . .

● EXERCISE 13. Write a three-paragraph composition (approximately 300 words) describing the experience of going to school in the morning or returning from school in the afternoon. Whether you walk to school or take a bus, your experience will certainly not be lacking in things and people to describe.

Show by your use of specific details that you have observed closely. As you describe your sensations, appeal occasionally to senses other than sight. Include at least three figures of speech: similes or metaphors. You will probably want to consult your notebook in which you have recorded your observations on your way to school. (See Exercise 3.)

Tab Key Index ▶

CORRECTION SYMBOLS

ms	error in manuscript form or neatness
cap	error in use of capital letters
p	error in punctuation
sp	error in spelling
frag	sentence fragment
ss	error in sentence structure
k	awkward sentence
nc	not clear
rs	run-on sentence
gr	error in grammar
w	error in word choice
¶	You should have begun a new paragraph here.
t	error in tense
∧	You have omitted something.

Index

653

K
L
M
N
O
P
Q
R

8
9
0
1
2
3
4
5